TOO GOOD TO BE TRUE

Too Good

JAMES TRAUB

THE OUTLANDISH
STORY OF WEDTECH

to Be True

DOUBLEDAY

NEW YORK LONDON TORONTO SYDNEY AUCKLAND

PUBLISHED BY DOUBLEDAY
a division of Bantam Doubleday Dell Publishing Group, Inc.
666 Fifth Avenue, New York, New York 10103

DOUBLEDAY and the portrayal of an anchor
with a dolphin are trademarks of Doubleday,
a division of Bantam Doubleday Dell
Publishing Group, Inc.

Library of Congress Cataloging-in-Publication Data

Traub, James.
  Too good to be true : the outlandish story of Wedtech
James Traub.—1st ed.
      p.   cm.
    1. Wedtech (Firm) 2. Defense contracts—United States—
Corrupt practices. 3. Government purchasing—United States—
Corrupt practices. I. Title.
HD9743.U8W4384   1990
364.1′323—dc20   90-30172
CIP

ISBN 0-385-26182-9
Copyright © 1990 by James Traub
Printed in the United States of America
July 1990
First Edition

To E.W.E.

CONTENTS

PROLOGUE

PROLOGUE

The Awful Truth

THERE IS A PHOTOGRAPH, now gathering dust in the files of the United States Attorney's office in Manhattan, of a man gesturing violently with both hands at the end of a long conference table that glitters with highlights from two splendid chandeliers overhead. The man, who has spectacles, thick hair, and big, unfashionable sideburns, is John Mariotta, chairman of the Welbilt Electronic Die Corporation. (The company changed its name to Wedtech in 1983.) Sitting next to Mariotta is Senator John Chafee of Rhode Island, whose arms are crossed and whose eyebrows are raised in what seems to be a look of faint incredulity. Farther on is Vice President George Bush, and beyond him Treasury Secretary Donald Regan, who is staring across the room in frank boredom. Next to Regan, Representative Barber Conable of New York is busy scribbling on a pad. On the other side of the room, his face bathed in light, is President Ronald Reagan. The President's chin is raised, and he is gazing at Mariotta with rapt attention. The frenetic Mr. Mariotta appears, in short, to have lost everyone in his audience save the President of the United States.

Mariotta did not altogether understand what he was doing in the White House Cabinet conference room that morning of January 19, 1982. He knew that the meeting had something to do with the President's urban enterprise zone initiative, which he thought was a good thing. The enterprise zone idea, as he understood it, was that you bring jobs instead of welfare to the ghetto. That was exactly what John Mariotta had done. An uneducated Hispanic, he had built up a defense-contracting firm that handled several million dollars' worth of work in the middle of the notoriously impoverished South Bronx.

Still, Mariotta was a bit confused. The meeting had been scheduled as part of the publicity campaign for upcoming hearings on enterprise zone legislation, but Mariotta thought that he had been invited to some kind of "think tank." He had learned that term only a few months earlier, when he was invited to speak at a symposium sponsored by a conservative group in Atlanta. Mariotta was unnerved by the grandeur of the Cabinet conference room and by the suavity and importance of the other guests.

When he first entered the conference room that morning, Mariotta found the others standing and chatting comfortably. Feeling alone and self-conscious, he sat down behind his name card. There was a yellow pad at his place, and this frightened him all the more. Mariotta did not know how to write, and he suffered agonies of anxiety lest others discover his illiteracy. There had been a yellow pad in Atlanta, too, but he had been accompanied to that meeting by a Welbilt employee who was, at least to John, an intellectual. Now he was alone. The President had not yet arrived, but when Vice President Bush walked in, the meeting began. As the others spoke of this and that, Mariotta took out his calculator, bent his head over his yellow pad, and started toting up figures.

Somebody, perhaps Mayor Vincent Cianci of Providence, Rhode Island, said that the tax breaks and deregulation promised by the enterprise zone legislation were scarcely going to cure inner-city poverty; that federal funding was needed as well. He sounded negative, as did the others. John Mariotta became more and more agitated. These people didn't think there was an answer, but he knew there was. Suddenly he broke into the conversation: "Can I say something?" As Mariotta, who seems not to have forgotten a second of this momentous episode, recalls, "Everybody looked at me, like saying, 'Oh my God, he talks.' " He then launched into a monologue that seemed to teeter on the edge of lunacy. Vincent Cianci remembers it as "extremely emotional, difficult to understand." "It was a little bizarre," says Stuart Butler, a scholar at the conservative Heritage Foundation who had championed the enterprise zone idea.

Mariotta spoke as if in a trance, but as these were words he was to recite many times over the years, he has no trouble recollecting them. His speech consumed at least a quarter of the hour-long meeting. "Gentlemen," he said, "this is a think tank, and let's us think positive. Only through positive thinking do we find a solution to a problem. I'm a New York Rican. For those people who don't know what a New York Rican is, it's an individual that cannot speak English and cannot speak Spanish. I'm in the Twilight Zone." Mariotta explained that Welbilt had fabricated components for the B-52, for the Sidewinder guided missile, and for other weapons systems, and had never had a part rejected. "And with what, gentlemen? People that you've described that they're only good for *welfare?* Blacks and Puerto Ricans. That's a cop-out. Gentlemen, I was speaking with a dope pusher"—and at that moment President Reagan walked in, and Mariotta froze. Everyone stood up and then sat down. Mariotta, who had remained seated, then jumped up. "Sit down, Mr. Mariotta," said the President in his mellow, soothing voice. "You were talking with the dope pusher . . ."

Even at the best of times Mariotta is an extremely nervous man who speaks in high-pitched gasps and squeaks, almost in sobs. Now, with the President listening, he returned, in what must have been a falsetto shriek, to his encounter with the drug pusher. "I says, 'Yeah, well, I don't like what you're doing with our people.' He says, 'Bug out, John! What I'm doing with our people is nothing worse than what this society is doing with our people. It's killing our people by giving them opium—opium of welfare! Hey, John, it kills a man in twenty or thirty years. I kill 'em in a year or two years. I get 'em out of their misery.' And I stood there *flabbergasted.* And he says, 'You better get your act together, John!' " And Mariotta turned to Ronald Reagan and said, in his gasping voice, "Mr. President, not only are you killing the people with opium of welfare, you're killing the taxpayer of this country by strapping a welfare on the backs of the taxpayer. Let me explain to you what Welbilt is doing."

Mariotta then referred to his pad and the numbers he had scribbled—the one form of writing at his command. He told the President that Professor Nathan Glazer of Harvard had personally told him that the government spent $25,000 to support an indigent family of four. Thus, a company that gave a thousand welfare recipients jobs would save the government $25 million while generating $100 million in new business. Ten such companies in the South Bronx would save or create over $1 billion. "Mr. President," Mariotta concluded, "spread this penicillin to a hundred cities, and you will save *one hundred billion dollars!*"

Mariotta panted to a halt, exhausted by his sermon. The meeting soon broke up, and the group moved to an adjacent room for lunch, where they were joined by others. Mariotta hoped to be seated next to Elizabeth Dole, head of the White House Office of Public Liaison, because Welbilt, despite its vaunted dedication to the free market, had been desperately pulling strings within the administration in the hope of landing a huge contract for which it was thoroughly unqualified. Instead, he was shepherded to a small table near a fireplace. Mariotta took this to be punishment for his outburst. Consumed by his own message, he had failed to notice what others had: the President's attentive and satisfied expression.

When the President of the United States was announced, he threaded his way across the room to the table of, to the seat next to, the New York Rican from the Twilight Zone. Mr. Reagan turned to Mariotta and with his crinkly smile and his velvet voice, said, "If we had more people who could motivate like yourself, we could put a handle on this situation." It was a blessing—from one evangelist to another. John Mariotta had become one of the presidential exemplars, the star of one of the vignettes Mr. Reagan could recite to prove to the Democrats and to the American people that some conviction of his own, however inchoate, was founded in fact. Two years later the President would affirm Wedtech's symbolic status by declaring John Mariotta "a hero for the eighties."

The President thus became the most illustrious of the many who were deceived by Wedtech. Only five years after that morning in the White House did the world learn what the President could not have known— that the company had succeeded not by heroic toil in the fields of free enterprise but by bribery and influence peddling; that John Mariotta and his friends had lied to the shareholders and stolen millions of dollars from the company. Everybody had been duped by the noble crusaders from the South Bronx. The lawyers hadn't known, nor had the bankers and the accountants; the politicians and government servants who had moved heaven and earth to help Wedtech mete out its penicillin hadn't a clue about the chicanery and the theft. Even the powerful men who were convicted of colluding in Wedtech's innumerable frauds, the congressmen and lobbyists and political appointees, insisted that the revelations had come as a shock to them. And they were not altogether wrong.

Nor were they, any of them, altogether right, either. The transactions that took place between Wedtech and its many helpers in the great world, transactions that elevated the company to a position of great wealth and prestige, were not so simple as they seemed, nor so tidy. John Mariotta and his colleagues were not quite as villainous as subsequent events made them seem, and the outsiders not as guiltless. The story of Wedtech may be a sort of morality play, but it's neither a satisfying nor a straightforward one. It has to do with deceit, of course, but also with self-delusion, that faculty which permits men to believe what is useful for them to believe.

John Mariotta's fervor that morning was not stagecraft. What he said about his company was true. It *was* a miracle. Almost everyone who visited the facilities in the catastrophic environment of the South Bronx came away glassy-eyed with faith. Here was the sparkling shop floor, and here the robotic machinery turning out sophisticated products for the Defense Department. The workers were Puerto Ricans and Asians and Russian émigrés, and amidst the devastation they worked long hours and took pride in their labor. John Mariotta, who built the company, believed in them, and so, to one degree or another, did the men who ran the firm with him; and they believed even as they stole and lied and bribed.

But John Mariotta also told a little story that he knew the President would like. He left out the parts that didn't fit, and polished it up with a moral that put a shine in a conservative's eye. John Mariotta believed his story—he *always* believed his stories, no matter how wrong—but he told it in such a way that the President would want to believe it, too. And the President did want to believe this tale, or fairy tale, of a little company shaking off the opium of welfare. The President believed many fairy tales, about weapons that would bring peace, and right-wing guerrillas who would bring democracy. They were useful stories, so he believed them. John Mariotta had given the President a little bit of magic to conjure with. And the President, in turn, blessed Mariotta's noble venture. In plain terms, they helped each other.

And that, in plain terms, is how Wedtech made its way in the world. Sometimes the quid pro quo was perfectly plain, with no mystification, but often it was not. Wedtech gave everyone a reason. "Nobody wanted to say no," as an official of the Small Business Administration, one of Wedtech's great benefactors, put it. And no one, or scarcely anyone, did say no. Wedtech made it in everyone's interest to say yes—through the projection of moral beauty, through political pressure, through stacks of cash stuffed in envelopes. The moral beauty gave the outsiders the justification for succumbing to the pressure and the money, and it gave even the insiders a pretext for breaking the law when it suited them.

There's nothing like a good cause to let you do what shouldn't be done. A good cause all but sanctifies self-aggrandizement.

Nobody ever said no. That was the moral that John Mariotta and his colleagues drew as they moved into ever more rarefied atmospheres. They were unworldly men, but they were very smart, even gifted; as they moved from one realm of power to another, they kept their eyes wide open. There was something in them of Candide, innocents abroad, registering with fresh eyes the passions and hungers behind the polished surfaces. "Innocents," perhaps, is a bit strong. But they set out to promote their little company, not to corrupt the world; once embarked on their crusade, they discovered that the world was willing to be corrupted. It wasn't a simple matter. There was no one coin with which all men could be paid. At the bottom there were those who could be had for a free lunch. Toward the top were the congressmen who took campaign contributions and the grave professionals who took stock. And at the very top were the exalted personages of the White House, who took nothing more tangible than Wedtech's vindication of the President's beliefs. But nobody said no.

Wedtech did not corrupt the world. "Nobody corrupts anybody," said Mario Moreno, one of the company's owners, at the Biaggi trial. "People corrupt themselves." Wedtech, often enough, simply acquiesced. The first politician of national repute the Wedtech boys ever met, New York Representative Mario Biaggi, showed up at the door one day, took the tour, praised their wonderful achievements, and offered to use his influence in exchange for a monthly retainer. That was an eye-opener. Even the men who make the laws are willing to be bought. You just have to know the appropriate form of tender—retainer, campaign contribution, consulting fees, stock. You give and you get. That, apparently, was the way of the world.

Perhaps the Wedtech boys were more like immigrants than innocents. (Two of them *were* immigrants.) They knew they wanted to get ahead, but they didn't know the rules. So they listened and learned; they adapted; they became what they beheld. They patterned both themselves and their company after their betters, the big successes. And the company became, in the process, a parody of contemporary business and political culture, a gaudy illustration of the worst features of modern life. In its later years, for example, Wedtech was completely obsessed with quarterly earnings, stock value, ingenious financial devices, and potential takeovers—just like the big companies.

But what Wedtech exemplified above all was an almost complete lack of moral consciousness. Nobody, or scarcely anybody, chastised John

Mariotta and his colleagues as they told their little lies or their big lies. Nobody was horrified. Nobody said right is right and wrong is wrong. There were always equivocations available to make wrong seem right. "These actions were being condoned by some highly respectable people," as Tony Guariglia, another of the company's core group of executives, put it. "Could it be wrong, what we were doing?"

So the story of Wedtech is a modern morality tale. But beyond all that, what is fascinating, even enthralling, in the tale of Wedtech is the erratic line of its progress, and the sheer improbability of the men who were nominally in control. While the members of the educated American middle class seem to have attained a strong family resemblance, Wedtech was run by men who were not educated, not American, or not middle class. They were, if not extraordinary, then very much out of the ordinary. And they operated their $100 million defense-contracting firm not from some bungalow community in Nassau County or from the flats of Texas, but from the apocalyptic precincts of the South Bronx. That these men, with a great deal of help from others, were able to perpetrate a massive fraud and escape detection for years, even long after the company went public, is testimony to ingenuity of a very high order.

The story of Wedtech is not only immensely complicated, but confusingly digressive, with far too many characters and incidents and venues to make for, say, a convincing Broadway drama. But it is not an incoherent story. The four or five men who directed the company's fortunes are the central characters, and Wedtech's history takes the classic narrative form of the rise and fall. For convenience' sake the Wedtech story may be divided into six phases, each with its characteristic crimes and follies and fantasies.

In the first phase, located almost entirely in the Bronx, Wedtech progressed from John Mariotta's dismal little sandbox to a concern performing several million dollars' worth of work a year for the Pentagon. Mariotta was joined, first, by Fred Neuberger, a crude though by no means uneducated Rumanian Jew who had literally walked his way out of the Holocaust as a teenager, and later by Mario Moreno, a Colombian who was as amiable and diplomatic as the other two were gruff and coarse. In these early years Wedtech lacked the power and the ingenuity to do anything spectacularly illegal and was perforce limited to the crimes typical of marginal companies trying to survive in a competitive world.

There followed, from 1981 to 1982, the first of the firm's two Washington interludes. The Reagan administration became its ally almost from the beginning, and Wedtech was able to use its influence in the White House to win a $28 million contract to build engines for the U.S. Army. This was the great coming-of-age event in the company's history.

The next phase came in 1983, when the company issued $30 million worth of stock to the public. The insiders, by selling off a portion of their holdings, became instantly rich, and their Washington lobbyists and consultants and retainers were able to share in the future they themselves were creating. The company then embarked on a series of financial frauds and embezzlements that over the years would become increasingly dazzling—and increasingly desperate. The master of these games was an accountant, Tony Guariglia, a brilliant numbers cruncher, if a fatal egoist, who would eventually control Wedtech, insofar as anyone did.

The fragile company of the early Reagan administration days was now a juggernaut. In its second Washington interlude, from the fall of 1983 to the spring of 1984, Wedtech, through a brilliant combination of bribery, threats, sweet talk, and political steamrolling, won a contract from the Navy even larger than the one it had extracted from the Army, and looked forward to stupendous wealth and prestige.

Now Wedtech was a big, respectable firm, and it began to seek the approbation of Wall Street. Since the insiders were stealing millions of dollars from the shareholders, the company resorted to spectacular lies to appease its investors—and the accountants, bankers, and lawyers, sometimes in the dark and sometimes, perhaps, not, signed off on them. There were early signs of trouble: in the fall of 1984 a congressional committee launched an investigation of the company that Wedtech barely succeeded in quashing. Moreno and Guariglia were supplanting the pioneers, Mariotta and Neuberger. In early 1986, after a violent struggle, Mariotta was fired.

Wedtech was no longer a minority-run firm nor a symbol of entrepreneurship. It was a middle-sized defense contractor trying to become very big. At the same time, the level of thievery was becoming self-destructive; the wheels started coming off the juggernaut in the middle of 1986. Wedtech had always lost money, but now Tony Guariglia had run out of tricks to disguise the truth. Meanwhile, federal investigators had caught on to a few—a very few—of Wedtech's crimes. Subpoenas arrived during the summer; the news stories began in the fall. In mid-December the company, then employing fourteen hundred people all over the Bronx, in Long Island, in Michigan, and in Israel, declared bankruptcy. Six weeks later all the core members save Mariotta agreed to plead guilty to some state and federal charges and to cooperate in the myriad prosecutions that were to come.

The wonderful thing about trials, aside from their inherent drama, is the sheer mass of information they bring to the surface—not only incriminating information but the incidental facts, the narratives and inadvertent revelations. By the time the Wedtech trials drew to an end, the entire life of the company had been exposed. In all, there were six federal trials, as of this writing, leading to the conviction of, among others, the former White House official Lyn Nofziger (though the conviction was reversed on appeal); Representatives Mario Biaggi and Robert Garcia; E. Robert Wallach, a close friend of former Attorney General Edwin Meese; and Stanley Simon, Bronx borough president. The transcripts of these trials ran to over forty thousand pages, in addition to the thousands of documents submitted into evidence.

This minuteness of exposure may make Wedtech unique in the annals of white-collar crime. Moreover, in their testimony the conspirators who cooperated with the government offered an amazingly intimate and ramified, if not always completely trustworthy, record of their own thoughts and stratagems.

For the purpose of this book, both Tony Guariglia and John Mariotta agreed to speak at length, though Mariotta abruptly ended the conversation long before it was finished, and refused to resume. Mario Moreno granted a two-hour interview. Over two hundred other people also submitted to lengthy interviews, including former company employees, current and former government officials, Wedtech's lawyers, friends and colleagues of the principal actors, aides of the Reagan Administration, including Ed Meese, congressional staffers, and, of course, prosecutors and investigators, the one group always eager to speak about events such as these.

From these sources, as well as from investigations by a congressional committee and an independent counsel, it has been possible to piece together a story so unlikely, so bizarre, that one feels comfortable in saying that we shall not see its like again.

PART ONE

The Early Years

ONE
ONE

The Little Company
That Could

JOHN MARIOTTA was a short, squat man with a disproportionately large head made larger still by a wavy crest of pomaded black hair. "Banana Head," Fred Neuberger used to call him, in one of his fonder locutions. He wore, at least until he underwent a sort of corporate make-over in the early eighties, thick black glasses, long sideburns, and short, wide ties. But nothing was so strange about John Mariotta as the manner and matter of his speech. He was extremely excitable, and he spoke in a wild stream of words, his voice getting higher and higher and thinner and thinner until he seemed almost to be choking.

During the years he ran Wedtech, Mariotta often said things so unaccountable that only the people who knew him well realized that he wasn't kidding. There was the time that a group of Japanese businessmen came to the factory and asked to see the miraculous coating technology of which Wedtech had boasted in its annual report. No ways no how, said John; it's a secret. The investors protested that they had come all the way from Japan to consider licensing the process. The investment would have represented a tremendous coup for Wedtech, which considered the revolutionary process the key to enormous future profits, but John was adamant.

"It seems that you don't trust us," said one of the group.

"Of course not," said John. "Don't you remember Pearl Harbor?"

John didn't trust the Japanese, the government, businessmen, and educated people generally. On the other hand, he believed in those around him with an almost childlike faith. John Mariotta sometimes seemed to be two distinct people—trusting and suspicious, ebullient and despondent, generous and vindictive. Mario Moreno concluded that John was a manic-depressive, and the abrupt swings of mood, the shifts from prophetic self-belief to despair and paranoia, make the amateur diagnosis plausible. On two occasions Mario was convinced that John would kill both of them and Fred Neuberger by driving into a building or another car.

In his epic fights with Fred, which had something of the comic grandeur of the graveyard scene in *Tom Jones,* John would pick up and throw anything that came to hand—chairs, books, writing pads, and once a wing-shaped piece of metal that embedded itself several inches in the office wainscoting. At those moments, which became more common over the years, John seemed to be in the grip of frenzy. Sometimes, with a look of hate in his eyes, he would scream at Mario, "You stupid motherfucker, you don't do any fucking thing in this company! You're fucking useless!" And Mario, a gentleman by temperament, would stand there and take it, a look of resignation fixed on his broad face.

John was also as generous and tenderhearted as a girl. When workers had to be laid off, John wept, and sometimes he rehired employees fired by others in the company. Tom Mullan, one of Wedtech's small cadre of managers, recalls John handing him a $6000 check after Mullan had been fired over John's objections. "He says, 'Don't tell anybody about this; it's a personal check.' " Much of the rank and file genuinely revered him. "The guys were superloyal to John," says the Reverend Hermes Caraballo, whose Glad Tidings Church supplied a good part of the Wedtech work force. "We're taught to be loyal to the man who is good to us. John would call at three in the morning to finish a project, and they'd be there."

Whether it was pity, self-pity, fury, or hope, John was utterly at the mercy of his raging emotions. He believed with passionate certainty things that were utterly false—things about others, things about himself. He was incapable of self-reflection. He was highly intelligent, even gifted, but he was incurably irrational.

John was from the streets, and he never pretended otherwise. He was born in Spanish Harlem in 1929 and moved with his family to the Bronx when he was seven or eight. The well-adjusted kids in the neighborhoods where he grew up joined gangs and got high. John, the class dummy, the kid with marbles in his mouth, kept to himself and fiddled with mechanical things. "I had a chemistry set," he recalls, in a story he must have told a hundred times, for John developed the habit of turning his life into legend. "I wanted to be a chemist. I built—how you say?—a tube-set radio. We used to walk down the street, me and my cousin Mario, and we'd have his sister play records, and we were transmitted around the area." John remembers figuring out how fluorescent light worked, and putting a homemade bomb under a trolley car on V-J Day, and building a simple jet engine from plans he ordered from *Popular Science.* "I used to go to the junkyards on my bicycle and bring it back home. Mom was always mad, me bringing junk into the house and taking it apart, just to see what made it tick."

John's parents had emigrated from Puerto Rico around 1920. His father was a cabinetmaker, but even before leaving Puerto Rico he had run out of jobs and taught himself tool-and-die work instead. John Mariotta, Sr., was a beautiful dreamer and a violent drunk—"like Dr. Jekyll and Mr. Hyde," says the son. When he went on a bender, which he did practically every payday, John and his mother would ride back and forth on the subway until it was safe to return to the apartment, which John Senior sometimes reduced to matchsticks before passing out.

Yet the father, like the son, could be a different man altogether. In the little machine shop he kept in the apartment, the elder Mariotta tried to make a perpetual-motion machine, using magnets. Even in his working life he was an artisan of fantasy, fabricating the sort of mechanical animation displays now seen in Christmas windows. He made displays for the 1939–1940 World's Fair, and took the boy behind the scenery to show him how the magic worked. It was an age when mechanical contrivances still seemed marvelous.

John managed to graduate from junior high school with only the haziest idea of how to read and write, though it took him until he was about sixteen to get even that far. He went on to high school, for which he was so obviously unsuited that he was packed off to vocational school. This was the first school that ever agreed with John, but he says that he spent so much time at home protecting his mother that he was finally booted out of the one institution that had a shot at educating him.

John began working his way through the hundreds of little machine shops that then dotted the Bronx. In the years after the war, before the working class moved out and the junkies moved in, before the abandonment and the fires, the South Bronx, where John Mariotta lived and worked, was a beehive of entrepreneurship. It was not then the hopeless place it is now, and there were plenty of opportunities for a young man with energy and mechanical skill. John went from shop to shop, learning the tool-and-die business. His gifted but hapless father set up Mariotta Mechanical Display but could never seem to get any orders, and when John was drafted in 1951 the business collapsed. When he was discharged two years later John worked in another succession of machine shops, and again tried to start up a business with his father. This one failed, too, and in 1957 the alcoholic and diabetic father died of what John calls the Asiatic flu. Eight months later John's younger brother died, and John was shattered. Being alone in the world only intensified his sense of failure.

It was then, when he felt he could sink no lower, that John began to prove he had that almost inhuman tenacity with which great entrepreneurs—and great failures—are endowed. He found a job at yet another tool-and-die outfit, but he refused to close his own tiny business. On Saturdays he made the rounds of the little factories in the Bronx, asking for work. When one door was slammed in his face, he went to the next, and in time he got a few customers. John was still so green that when one of his clients asked him to dinner, he made up some excuse, because he had never been in a proper restaurant and had no idea how to behave.

In the early sixties John opened yet another tool-and-die factory, out on Long Island, and failed once again. He moved back to the Bronx, where one of his old customers, Irving Lonstein, who manufactured baby carriages, caught up with him. John improvised a new piece of equipment to improve the heat sealing on Lonstein's carriage frames. Lonstein had been trying to persuade John to work for him; now he took him in as a partner.

A tool-and-die man is an inventor of the most practical type, a man who composes elaborate abstractions with greasy hands. He stands at the front end of the production chain, forming the machines and the tools that make the ultimate product. It's not too fanciful to say that the tool-and-die maker speaks the language of the machine. And just as some inarticulate men are blessed with a beautiful singing voice, so John Mariotta had the gift of fluency with machines. What was hopelessly complicated to other men was perfectly clear to him. At one of the "dog and pony shows" put on by the company to attract investors, the projector John was to use had been wired for European voltage. He asked one of the potential financiers for a knife, pried the machine open, fiddled inside, and converted it to American current. Then he announced that he was ready to begin. "Don't bother," the investor said. "We'll buy."

When he talks about the machine shop, John Mariotta is not only grandiloquent and fervid, as he is on all topics, but strangely compelling as well. His voice catches on certain words, he runs out of breath, and he seems almost to swoon with passion and anguish. "We are the individuals responsible for making the pen that you hold, the paper that you have, the seat that you sit on, the machines that made the fabric, the machines that made the carpenter to use a more effective *tool.* We are the individuals that have to *create* something that does not *exist.* Everything that you find in this world, you go to the shelf and pick it up. But a tool maker *cannot* go to the shelf and pick it up. He has to *create* the tool. You have to, in your mind, look and *see* how a tool functions. The *idea* is there, but it requires you to go through trials and errors to make the final product." It requires, that is, logic, patience, and creativity.

With his new partnership John Mariotta had moved up in the world, but not very far. And when Lonstein decided to sell his baby carriage business, the new partnership lost its principal customer. In 1965 the two men moved the machine shop operation to 148th Street in the South Bronx, and, at Lonstein's inspiration, rechristened it the Welbilt Electronic Die Corporation. John was shopping around for customers once again. Although, as always, he worked like a beast, he was unable to land any contract larger than $30,000. Lonstein was in semiretirement; by 1970, after an accident in which several of his fingers were crushed in a press, he decided to stay in Florida and leave the whole mess to his indefatigable young partner. But while John could run the shop floor, he knew he would have to find someone else to organize the business.

John had recently picked up some work from a sheet-metal company called Fleetwood, where he had dealt with one of the two owners, Fred Neuberger. As dismal as was Welbilt's condition, Fleetwood was in still more dire straits. The company was barely surviving, and Fred's partner was ready to sell out. With Lonstein gone, John needed another one of those smart Jewish businessmen. John had come to think of the Jews as a race of intellectuals, and Fred Neuberger was the most intellectual man he had ever met. He spoke foreign languages; he had graduate degrees; he was at a level that John felt he could barely comprehend. And so these two failures became partners.

Fred Neuberger had one characteristic in common with John Mariotta: he was a survivor. Life had been far more cruel to Fred than even to John, and Fred, correspondingly, was a far harder man. He was born in Rumania in 1927. His father was a man of substance, a lawyer and a judge. Fred was a sickly but bright boy; his personal life, and the life of his family and his community, came to an end when fascism began to engulf the country in 1939. The family fled to the capital, Bucharest, which was engulfed in violence the following year, when the local fascist brigade, the Iron Guard, took to the streets to unseat the ruling party. The work of exterminating the Jews began in earnest.

While out on the streets trying to earn some money for his parents, who were hiding in the homes of friends, Fred was seized by the Iron Guard and taken to a rail depot, where he and hundreds of other Jews were loaded onto a cattle car to be taken to a concentration camp. A boy as sickly as Fred would have faced almost certain death in the camps even before being sent to the gas chamber. Yet frail as he was, the boy was able to slip between the locked and chained doors of the car and somehow return home without being apprehended.

The ultimate Nazi horror had not yet arrived. The International Red Cross was still permitted to aid groups of young Jews to travel to Palestine. This time Fred boarded a train to save his life. The train, however, stopped a few hours after leaving Bucharest, and the passengers were ordered to walk—down the length of the Balkans, across Turkey, through what is now Syria and Lebanon. It is scarcely possible to imagine the sheer terror that these children must have felt as they trudged, without money or food, across an endless and utterly forbidding landscape.

"I remember the voyage as though it was yesterday," Fred Neuberger wrote to his sentencing judge. "I was fourteen years old when I left Europe. Walking at night, hiding by day, eating raw potatoes off the field. We were always afraid of German patrols, or of being denounced by local farmers. It was like a long nightmare from which you did not wake up; it lasted four weeks."

By the time he arrived in Palestine, the boy may already have concluded that he could rely only on himself. Rather than go to a kibbutz, he found work on his own, moving, as John Mariotta would a few years later, from machine shop to machine shop. He found work in one shop that made and repaired weapons for the Jewish underground. By this time some Jewish freedom fighters were conducting a campaign of terror to force the British out of Palestine. Fred had never had the chance to avenge himself against the Nazis who destroyed his life and presumably murdered his parents and nearly everyone he had ever known. He joined the Irgun, the terrorist force run by Menachem Begin, among others. In later years he would tell John, almost with awe, how he had handed a booby-trapped package to a British soldier and watched as the explosion ripped him apart. He had been especially struck by how dust seemed to fly off the man's body.

In the late 1940s, Fred left Israel for the United States. Once in New York, he began working at odd jobs during the day while pursuing a degree in mechanical engineering at New York University at night. Over the next several years he worked himself up to the position of foreman in a precision metal company. In 1954 he and a partner, Murray Brown, founded Fleetwood Metals. The company made sheet-metal parts for manufacturers of electronics goods. When the electronics business changed in the early sixties, Fleetwood was left behind. A company that had once had eighty-five employees shrank to nothing. Then in June 1970, Fred joined up with John Mariotta.

As a working couple the two men fell somewhere between Felix and Oscar of *The Odd Couple* and Martha and George of *Who's Afraid of Virginia Woolf?* John saw limitless possibilities everywhere; Fred saw dangers. John was impassioned; Fred was steely-eyed. John was generous; Fred was tight. Both men had fought their way through disasters; they were fearless and, at bottom, angry. Neither would ever forgive the world for his suffering. Rather than temper one another's ferocity, each had the effect of corroding the other's already tenuous inhibitions.

No argument was too small to tip over into "body language," as John describes his donnybrooks with Fred. There was the yellow-pad-throwing fight, back in the mid-1970s, when Fred had picked up a $2500 check the company desperately needed and used it for a monthly mortgage payment. There was the chair-throwing fight that took place about five years later. There was the time one of them poured a cup of hot coffee over the other's head, prompting the wet one to throw a punch. The fights had their verbal accompaniment. Fred would shout, "You dumb fucking Puerto Rican!" and John would make his high-pitched inarticulate noises and occasionally scream something about Israel. Blood was drawn, but nobody ever got hurt. It was more like savage slapstick than outright warfare—more like Abbott and Costello than George and Martha. And when they had exhausted each other, they would head into Spanish Harlem for lunch.

Fred never really lost his temper in the way that John did. He had seen too much to get excited about anything. He was beyond attachment, and, middle-aged and short and pudgy and myopic as he was, Fred Neuberger was beyond fear—or perhaps he had disciplined himself never to show fear. One day when John raced his Lincoln up off the road and on to the sidewalk, and Mario cried out in horror, Fred sat in the back as calmly as the Buddha. He seemed contemptuous of death, as he was contemptuous of nearly everything.

Fred kept his cynicism out front, like the big cigar he always had stuck in his mouth. He had no intention of forgiving the world for the horrors it had visited on him and on his family. When John would rave about how Wedtech was going to transform society, Fred would clamp down hard on his cigar and say, "The hell with society! They killed six million of my people and nobody said a word." They, whoever they were, were all Nazis in Fred's mind. The only cause he believed in was Israel, which had rescued him from the storm that was the world.

Fred lived for pleasure. John worshiped his own wife, Jenny, who in turn, protected him with the vigilance and solicitude of a mother. Fred, though married, was an alley cat. It was as if he felt he was living on borrowed time, that the Nazis might return at any moment. Sex was one of the few things Fred was willing to take seriously. Come four-thirty in the afternoon, he would get up and leave, no matter what was happening. *"Von via, von putz,"* John used to say to him, a phrase he translates as "By the dick it shall lead you." Fred's success with women amazed everybody. He was short; he wore the world's cheapest-looking rug over his thinning hair; he fouled the air with his stogies; he was unsentimental to a fault. But he always had a girl. Fred was living proof that charm is overrated. There was something masterful about Fred, a sense of superiority that took the form of disdain. He seemed immune from the consequences of his own recklessness. He was exceptionally intelligent, even cultivated. And beyond all that, Fred was the sort of old-fashioned roué for whom no diamond was too big and no fur too fine.

Part of Fred's enjoyment of sexual conquest may have been the pleasure he took in courting danger. John remembers sitting with him at a honky-tonk bar near Tinker Air Force Base in Oklahoma when an attractive woman walked in. "No sooner that she comes and sits at the bar, Fred is sitting at the bar. And I says, 'I'm getting out,' because Freddy yelled out before she came in, they were dancing the hustle, and Fred says, 'Hey, you people don't know how to dance the hustle!' " It takes a fair amount of moxie for a short, middle-aged Jewish refugee from Rumania to make that claim in a bar in the middle of Okie country.

Fred had a wife, Helen, whom he spoke of as the most beautiful woman he had ever known. Whether because of Fred's philandering or for some other reason, Helen was an extremely troubled woman and a drug addict. Sometimes she would show up at the 164th Street plant "wigged out of her mind," as John recalls. In 1975 Helen took Fred's .45 caliber automatic with her into the bath and fatally shot herself. A police investigation found powder burns on Fred's hand, but not on Helen's. Fred explained that he had pried the gun from Helen's hand as she lay in the bath, and that her own hand had then fallen into the bath. In the absence of any further information, or any apparent murder motive—Helen did not have a large insurance policy—the death was ruled a suicide. In later years Fred would recall Helen's death with a depth of feeling he accorded to very little else.

When the construction of Lincoln Hospital forced John and Fred in 1971 to move the company from 148th Street to new digs at 164th Street and Washington Avenue, the company found itself in the middle of Fort Apache—"between the dope pusher and the car thief," says John, in one of his ritual formulations. Fortunately for historians of Wedtech (as, for the sake of convenience, we shall refer to it from here on), though unfortunately for the South Bronx, the neighborhood has changed very little in the intervening years, and you can still see the vacant lots with tiny piles of shattered brick, as if whole buildings had been atomized; stripped cars beached in yards and along the curbs; structures entombed in walls of cinder block where doorways once were; and men, idle men, lounging with an almost tropical languor.

These days, actually, the South Bronx fairly hums—or at least murmurs—with possibility, and only a few blocks down Washington Avenue a moderate-income housing project is scheduled to fill a vacant lot. In 1971, though, the South Bronx was widely considered a dead organism; the fact that Wedtech rose amidst its ashes was to become an indispensable element of the corporate mythos. After the riots of the 1960s had focused the nation's attention on the inner city, the South Bronx swiftly became the symbol of the misery, the rage, and the despair of the ghetto.

Long before President Jimmy Carter, and later the candidate Ronald Reagan, dropped by Charlotte Street in 1977 to describe its dismal wreckage in partisan terms, Robert Kennedy, in the summer of 1967, flew directly from Senate hearings on urban unemployment to the South Bronx. Great Society money, and Great Society rhetoric, poured into the South Bronx, but neither had much effect. In 1970 Ramon Velez, a political leader who had capitalized on the emerging poverty industry, called on President Nixon to declare the South Bronx a disaster area. Journalists began to make pilgrimages, and they told the country of a city that resembled London after the blitz. "The South Bronx," declared Stewart Alsop in *Newsweek*, "is visibly dying, as though of some loathsome, lethal disease."

Exactly what this disease was remains a matter of dispute to this day. Alsop, a conservative, blamed the poverty programs of the Great Society for fostering a passive, dependent mentality among the poor—much the same argument with which John Mariotta would delight President Ronald Reagan ten years later. Liberals, on the other hand, blamed the collapse of the public school system, the lack of resources for development, and the rapacity of landlords, who burned down buildings to collect insurance rather than make costly repairs. In fact, though all of these factors may have contributed to the illness, the South Bronx, like many of America's inner-city ghettos, seems to have been flattened by the loss of low-level employment, above all in manufacturing, after World War II, at precisely the moment when unskilled laborers were pouring in.

The South Bronx, however, had it worse than other such areas. Most of the roughly twenty thousand Puerto Ricans who left the island each year in the 1950s arrived in Spanish Harlem, and moved from there to the Mott Haven and Hunts Point sections of the Bronx, where rents were cheaper. The islanders came with little education and few skills. With jobs scarce, a large fraction of the young men in the South Bronx began turning to heroin. Middle-class and working-class families fled, though their destination was often no farther than the huge Co-op City complex in the northern Bronx, completed in 1968. By the time John Mariotta and Fred Neuberger moved to 164th Street, the entire area was rapidly turning into an encampment of junkies.

And now the fires began. Landlords burned out tenants to collect insurance, tenants burned themselves out to collect emergency relocation assistance, and junkies torched buildings so that they could strip out and sell the copper piping and the fixtures. First one building would go, then its neighbor, then the whole block. The South Bronx began to look less like wartime London than wartime Dresden. In one three-hour span in the mid-1970s, forty fires were set, eighteen of them classified as major, in a seventy-block area. People gathered to witness the annihilation of their own neighborhoods. Vendors sold grilled meat and taco sauce to spectators in lounge chairs. "For them," said the author of a 1975 article in *New Times*, "the apocalypse has arrived."

Amid the apocalypse, John Mariotta, Fred Neuberger, and about half a dozen of their employees were toiling away on tiny contracts for Western Bed Products, Eaton Manufacturers, and the baby carriage industry. It was proving almost impossible to get work or capital or help of any kind from the larger world, which looked on the South Bronx as the ninth circle of hell. Fred went to a friend, an attorney named Max Delson, an old lefty who recognized a good cause when he saw one and tried to scare up some loans for this faint ray of hope in the awful darkness. But when the banks heard "South Bronx," they fled. Delson's associate, Raja Pillai, says that he tried to interest wealthy Indians in the company, but even they were appalled by the combination of the poverty and the bizarre manner of the principals.

In 1975 John and Fred, still making do with nickel-and-dime work from their traditional customers, stumbled into defense contracting. As John remembers it; Fred had an appointment with an eye doctor, and along the way stopped at the nearby offices of the Defense Contract Administration Service, which at that time kept the plans for available contracts on file for the public. A notorious skinflint, Fred was always looking for jobs nobody else wanted on the grounds that Wedtech could build at a lower cost than anyone else. The job that he brought back from DCAS, a filter assembly for helicopter engines, was the perfect example. "He brings in a bid to me," recalls John, "and says, 'You think we can do this?' And I say, 'I cannot even read the blueprint.' 'Well, if you cannot read the blueprint, we'll get the contract, because nobody will be able to quote on it.' " The blueprint was so illegible that John had to use his imagination to complete lines and markings that had disappeared from the page. Nobody else bid on the filter assembly except the previous contractor, who was unwilling to do it as cheaply as the Army wanted. That is how Wedtech found itself in the defense business.

TWO

Marvelous Minority Land and Mario

AT ROUGHLY THE SAME TIME that John and Fred learned of the filter assembly contract, they heard of a federal program designed to help people like themselves. Federal agencies, like the Pentagon, that contracted out work to private companies set aside some of the contracts for minority-run businesses. And all you had to do to qualify was to get on the approved list of minority firms kept by the Small Business Administration. Once you were on the list, you could get not only contracts but loans, grants, technical assistance, and so on.

There was only one problem. When he received the application for membership in the SBA's set-aside program, Fred discovered that a firm couldn't qualify unless majority ownership was vested in a member of a certified minority group. Fred and John had split the ownership fifty-fifty. All Fred needed to do was yield to his partner a little piece of the company, not very valuable at the time. But Fred was not the type to give back what he had. Instead, he lied, writing on the SBA form that John owned two thirds of the company, and he, one third. John, Fred would later testify, approved of the imposture. (John testified that Fred had voluntarily yielded up a portion of his own stock, for an unrelated reason, at just this time.)

It was not, at least by the debased standards of the set-aside program, much of a lie. The program had been improvised by President Lyndon Johnson immediately after the race riots in the summer of 1968, and was fully developed by President Richard Nixon in the hope of creating a class of "black capitalists." The program, also known as 8(a), after the statutory authority that led to its creation, had never been thought out by the White House, or even considered by the Congress. With no real purpose other than mollifying angry minorities, the set-aside system had turned into a kind of welfare program for a few politically savvy entrepreneurs. Many of them were not members of minorities. A North Carolina conglomerate called the Dunn Group received $16 million in contracts in the early seventies. The Dunn Group was allegedly controlled by a seventy-three-year-old black man named Henry Ferguson. Actually, Ferguson was a farmhand working for one of the white men who ran the conglomerate, an illiterate who signed his name to SBA documents with an X. "For a lucky, mainly non-disadvantaged few," a congressional report concluded in 1978, "the 8(a) program is a gravy train of impressive proportions."

Fred's lie was not, then, a very big lie, but it was the first lie, and as such it deserves memorialization, like Babe Ruth's first home run. It set the pattern, on several counts, for Wedtech's frauds. First of all, Fred proposed, and John disposed. Only rarely over the years would John Mariotta initiate his company's crimes, and as time went on there would be many schemes that he scarcely understood. But though John later insisted in court that he had lived in a bubble of innocence while his colleagues constructed their sinister devices, in fact he allowed nothing to happen without his permission, at least until he began losing his grip on the company in 1985.

Wedtech's initial crime was easy and thoughtless. It involved no moral reflection, agonized or otherwise. Fred was a man with very little respect for the law, and none at all for moral convention; lying to the government held no horrors for him. John had struggled all his life against what seemed to him implacable forces, and he was scarcely about to pull up short because of some government regulation. He would do whatever was good for the company. Neither man had set out to deceive the U.S. government, but when circumstances made deception seem necessary, or even merely expedient, they didn't hesitate to resort to it. Like so many of Wedtech's crimes, this one was committed opportunistically.

In time Wedtech was to become the gorilla of the 8(a) program, the most powerful manipulator the system had ever known. Now, though, it was an infant concern willing to try anything to get some work. The application went through, and it wasn't long before the 8(a) designation began to raise Wedtech from the mire in which it had been struggling for the previous decade. For over a year John and Fred had been hoping to land a contract to build bell cranks, which are boomerang-shaped devices that regulate the air intake of the combustion chamber of a jet engine.

John had devoted much of his life during these years to proving to the Air Force that he could build this relatively simple device, and, mechanical Michelangelo that he was, he had constructed and discarded hundreds of bell cranks until he had it just right. It was, all by itself, a heroic story of rejection and acceptance and rejection again, but finally the Air Force had certified Wedtech's competence to build the part. This was one of the great achievements of John's life. With the help of a consultant, the Air Force was persuaded to set aside the bell crank for an 8(a) firm. Wedtech was the only 8(a) firm formally qualified to manufacture the part, and thus it won the contract. The contract was worth only $115,000 in 1976, but with renewed orders, the firm ultimately received over $2.5 million from the Air Force.

Wedtech was beginning to experience that most exhilarating of feelings, growth. The tiny factory space on 164th Street, which measured all of three thousand square feet, would no longer do. In early 1976 John and Fred approached Bankers Trust about a $250,000 loan in order to move around the corner to 1049 Washington Avenue, which was four times the size of their current home. The paperwork, apparently, was beyond even Fred's profound knowledge of business affairs, and the bank suggested that John take a course for fledgling minority entrepreneurs given by an organization called the Urban Business Assistance Corporation. It was here that John met Mario Moreno, without whom Wedtech would never have amounted to much more than a decent, marginal little manufacturing concern in the middle of the wilderness.

Mario Moreno was every bit as remarkable, in his way, as John or Fred. He too had struggled, but the impression he gave was one of effortlessness. He had a Latin grace, an innate sense of tact, that made him pleasing in a way that John or Fred could never be. He had the flattering habit of paying genuine attention. Mario was a soft man. His voice was light, his manner courtly and reflective, and he had the round face of a Latin American peasant. Yet he had, as well, something of the peasant's capacity for endurance, stubbornness, and silent stoicism.

Mario had grown up in the provincial Colombian capital of Cali, the eldest child in a family of eight. His father was the principal of an elementary school, and Mario had always taken learning and education to be paramount virtues. He went to night school at the United States consulate in Cali in order to learn English, and worked as a messenger at a branch of Citibank and as a guide for American tourists. It is not difficult to imagine Mario as an earnest Third World boy with a becoming manner, sharp-eyed, precocious, determined to make it out of his little backwater come hell or high water.

And in 1961, at the age of nineteen, Mario did just that. He boarded a plane for New York with $300 that he had borrowed and the name of a hotel in Brooklyn. The day after arriving at the hotel he took the subway to Manhattan and got off where everyone else was getting off. It happened to be Wall Street. He bought a newspaper and started looking for a job. His English was never good enough, but finally the boy found a job as a night messenger at Bache & Company. He worked on his English by memorizing editorials in *The Wall Street Journal,* a habit that may account for his later broad-minded interpretation of the rules of free enterprise. Within three months, in any case, Mario had passed the high school equivalency exam, and he enrolled as a freshman at Pace College.

And now Mario demonstrated that he had that willingness to work twice as hard as everyone around him which makes for the immigrant success story. He was still working at night, and, as he recalls, "I had to work overtime, many nights, from seven to eight or nine o'clock in the morning. So my classes started at ten. And I used to sleep between classes in the toilet. On weekends I was exhausted completely." He would come home on Saturday afternoon and sleep until Monday morning. "I went that way for five years. I was very, very motivated."

As soon as he had his bachelor's degree, with a major in accounting, Mario enrolled in the graduate business program at New York University. He also brought over his parents, his brothers, and his sisters. By the early 1970s, when John Mariotta and Fred Neuberger were flailing around to keep their heads above water, Mario, working at a succession of shipping firms, was learning at first hand how companies are run. By the mid-1970s he was moving up the ladder at a firm called American Export Lines. But for all his unappeasable hunger for success, Mario was also taking postgraduate classes and contemplating a doctorate in economics and sociology. Perhaps, he thought, he would then return to Colombia and run for office (a choice that might have led to an early grave rather than a jail cell). Mario was ambitious, but without the anger of John or Fred. He was not ruthless, and he was eager to dedicate himself to worthwhile projects.

Mario was also thinking about starting his own business, so when an NYU professor told him about a new institute being established to help minority entrepreneurs, he agreed to give some of his time as a scantily paid consultant and then as a teacher. Mario found that he loved teaching. He also found that his marriage of thirteen years was unraveling. He and his wife and son had moved to New Jersey, but he was now scarcely ever home.

John was the same refractory student he had always been. But in 1976, after he met Mario, a Hispanic with a graduate degree in business, John was like a college boy who takes a class just so that he can put the moves on the teacher. Eagerly he brought his problems to this articulate scholar. And Mario set to work. He and three other business school students, all of them volunteers, spent five months on John's application for the loan from Bankers Trust. They worked over the documents for the bell crank contract. Wedtech got the loan and the contract.

John spent the next year and a half in Mario's class, wooing the teacher for all he was worth. He kept taking Mario out for drinks and asking him to come to work at Wedtech. "We have too many of you MBAs down here on Wall Street," John would say, "and not enough in the South Bronx." But Mario was moving ahead at work, and he wasn't ready to take the risk. When American Export was sold, however, Mario quit. He was living with his girlfriend, Caridad Vasquez. He and Conchita, as her friends called her, had a catering business, and ran dances on Saturday nights. It was not what Mario had gotten his MBA for. Every time John took him up to the South Bronx, Mario felt the tug of his idealism: the little factory amid the rubble had the makings of a miracle. Mario was a believer—and he needed the work. In May 1978, he agreed to come to work at Wedtech three days a week for $150 a day.

In its new growth phase, John needed not only more advice, but more hands. He needed skilled machinists; unfortunately, there were no machinists in the South Bronx. John, who personally hired every new employee until around 1983, took it on himself to invent what he could not find. "You have to take into consideration," he says, "my two competitors were welfare and jail. That's why I says when I got a live one that wants to work, I says *yes*. I didn't care whether the individual could read or write or *anything*, because I can't write. Am I going to ask them to be able to write?" Given the labor source he was drawing from, illiteracy was the least of his problems; a drug history was a good deal more common than a job history. A number of workers used to break things all the time, and John realized after a while that they were hoping to be fired in order to collect unemployment insurance. Others refused to work overtime for fear of topping out at the ceiling for welfare benefits.

There were the guys who invited John out for a fight, and the loonies, and the substance abusers. "I remember one time at 164th Street in the summer," John recalls, "and Freddy and I were talking outside, and all of a sudden we hear something going 'Dunk! Dunk! Dunk!' " They assumed that some kind of construction must be going on. "When I walk inside I see this individual, wigged out of his *mind,* hitting an iron beam with his hand, practicing *karate,* and he doesn't feel a thing, because he's all doped up."

Since few of the men had any skills, John hired on the basis of attitude. "If he see you present yourself good," recalls Sherman Billingy, "he give you a chance." Billingy was eighteen years old and working the late-night shift at a McDonald's in the spring of 1978 when he picked up an early Sunday paper and saw an ad in the classified section for a machine shop assistant. When he telephoned Wedtech, John told him, in his high-pitched squeal, to come on over. Billingy had gone to trade school in aviation and knew something about machines, so John, after giving him a tour, told him he had a job as assistant for quality control. And Billingy, like practically everyone else from those early days, stayed at the company to the bitter end.

For the uneducated, unskilled men who came to Wedtech, many of whom had never held a steady job in their lives, John Mariotta was coach, cheerleader, and role model. On Saturday mornings he would make the rounds of his workers who had poured their paychecks down their throats the night before, and pound on the door until someone woke up. "I'm going to give you two more hours to get in there," he'd shout. "Come in late, but come on in." Over the years he developed a system in which he would pay 75 percent of the costs of any form of education or training. "I didn't care if the individual was learning something related to me, or related to anything else, because it only makes that individual that much better."

In short, John was precisely the evangelical business leader celebrated in management books like Thomas Peters' *Search for Excellence.* Uncorrupted by the formalism of business school, he was a natural entrepreneur. He led by example, he respected his employees, he taught patiently, and he created, against all odds, a true *esprit de corps.*

THREE

THREE

There's a Congressman at the Door

MARIO BIAGGI was Wedtech's first politician. Like all the subsequent ones, he did not play hard to get. It was Biaggi, in fact, who initiated the courtship. A friend of Fred's had spoken of the company to a friend of Biaggi's, and then Biaggi had read a laudatory newspaper article about the company. That was enough. In January 1978 the congressman's office called Wedtech to say that he would like to pay a visit. Fred was unimpressed and assumed that it was just the usual shakedown, but John was thrilled. Congressmen, like intellectuals, were somewhere up in the stars for John; he believed that the world was given to them, and they could do great things.

John and Fred took Representative Biaggi on a tour of the little plant on Washington Avenue, and Biaggi couldn't find enough good things to say about the company and its owners. Several days later he invited them to pay a visit to his law offices in lower Manhattan. At this time it was not illegal for a congressman to draw income from a law firm, though in the post-Watergate atmosphere it was less common than earlier. Biaggi's

firm, it's true, was not making either the congressman or his two partners, Bernard Ehrlich and John Lang, very rich. The firm had perhaps
half a dozen associates, and no very large clients. Only such a firm could
have looked on Wedtech as a significant potential client.

There was no pretense about the purpose of the Wedtech visit. John
and Fred were not even constituents; Biaggi represented the northern
rather than the southern portion of the Bronx. Biaggi wanted to do
business. He told John and Fred that his firm was willing to represent
Wedtech. Until then, it had never occurred to either of them that they
needed a law firm enough to keep one on a retainer. They ran a tiny
company, and they had never had any legal problems. But Biaggi made it
clear that he wasn't talking about paperwork; he was talking about influence. Wedtech was doing business with the government, and he and one
of his partners, Bernie Ehrlich, knew the right people in City Hall and in
Washington.

It was just what Fred had expected: a politician with his hand out. Fred
wanted to bid contracts and make products. What Biaggi was selling, he
had no interest in buying. John, however, dreamed of a Wedtech far
greater than the humble factory he was then operating, and he thought
that a man like Mario Biaggi might help get it there. He turned to Mario,
who would soon join the company. Nobody got ahead in government
contract without political clout, Mario explained; that was how the system worked. In April 1978, Wedtech agreed to pay Biaggi's law firm
$20,000 a year, a considerable sum in those days.

Mario Biaggi was, in a way, a successful version of John and Fred. Born to
a poor immigrant family in East Harlem in 1917, Biaggi had made his
way in life through sheer diligence and an unmistakable will to power.
After six years as a mailman he had succeeded in landing a job on the
police force. He turned out to be a fearless officer; in twenty-three years
he had been wounded ten times and received twenty-eight citations,
including the Medal of Honor for Valor, the highest decoration available
on the force.

By the early 1960s Biaggi had gone about as far as his uniform was
likely to take him. He had suffered an injury to his leg in one of his heroic
exploits, and his days of active service were coming to an end. A big,
vigorous man, and an extremely handsome one, he had graying hair that
set off the flushed complexion often associated with a hot temper. He
had moved up in the Italian-American hierarchy of the police force, and
he seemed a natural for public life. First, however, Biaggi went to law
school. Though he had never gone to college, and therefore needed

special dispensation to enroll, Biaggi worked his way through NYU Law School, graduating in 1963. Only three years later he ran for Congress in the largely Italian northern Bronx, and won handily. Had he not been convicted in federal court twice in two years, the seat could have been his for life.

Biaggi's partner, Bernard Ehrlich, born in Bermuda, had also grown up poor, on New York's Lower East Side. After serving with the Special Forces in South Korea, Ehrlich had returned to New York and hung out a shingle as an attorney. Like Biaggi, he had very little interest in or even aptitude for the practice of law; he was a fixer rather than a lawyer, a man who buttered up or dressed down government officials for a living. Once he formed the firm with Biaggi, in 1967, Ehrlich found his influence coming from his well-known association with the congressman. But Ehrlich was also something of a government official himself. He had kept up his military ties by joining the New York National Guard and rising through its ranks. When he began working with Wedtech, Ehrlich was a colonel, and he made sure that everyone knew it.

Bernie Ehrlich was a man who enjoyed projecting authority. Everywhere he went he bore himself as an officer, standing ramrod straight and using military jargon, delivered in clipped cadences. His voice, however, tended toward a quack, and despite his square head and close-cropped hair, his jowls, soft chin, and small, round eyes lent him an air of irresolution. Ehrlich was that ancient staple of comic literature, the *miles gloriosus,* or swaggering soldier. A former associate at Biaggi & Ehrlich recalls that on the day before Guard exercises Ehrlich would appear in the office in his fatigues, carrying a camouflage pen. It was not unheard of for Ehrlich to swagger through the lower orders of the city bureaucracy in his combat outfit, intimidating the junior paper pushers and making the less impressionable roll their eyes.

Biaggi, Ehrlich & Lang, later Biaggi & Ehrlich, attracted clients solely because of the connections and power of its senior partner, like a great many law firms in New York or Washington or wherever government work is transacted. Most legal work is carried out far from courtrooms, or even boardrooms; what matters is whom you know, not what you know. Mario Biaggi was a man with many friends in New York, though, unlike the pedigreed clubmen of Wall Street and Park Avenue, most of his friends were regular guys, "ethnic" types like himself. The firm's clients were a fairly humble lot, and much of its work came from the city's uniformed unions, whose members had prepaid legal services. It was Ehrlich who did almost all of the client work, which usually called for breaking bread with this or that city official. If actual legal work had to be done, Ehrlich would turn to one of the associates, most of whom had been hired because of their political connections.

Biaggi, unlike Ehrlich, was a forceful, even frightening, man: but his writ did not run quite so far as it seemed. Too much the old-fashioned ward heeler to make a heavy mark on policy in Washington, he moved in a circle that did not extend much farther than the New York delegation and his fellow Italians. "He was," says Bernard Ehrlich, "a congressman more for getting your Social Security, getting your mom into a nursing home, anything for cops, anything with a focus on Italian or Irish issues. Beyond that, forget it. He was a lonely guy in Washington."

Though lost in the marble halls of Congress, Biaggi was a well-known figure in New York, and it was there that he saw his political future. In 1972, with Ehrlich now acting as an adviser as well as law partner, Biaggi ran for mayor. The decision turned out to be a ruinous one, for his past caught up with him. Biaggi had grown up in an era when a politician expected to make a good dollar from the favors he doled out—"honest graft," as the Tammany Hall worthy George Washington Plunkitt had called the system. Biaggi had been regularly availing himself of this form of extortion, but it was only when he announced his candidacy that his habits became known to the public.

In January 1973, *The Daily News* asked Biaggi whether he had refused to answer questions before a 1971 federal grand jury. He had been asked, among other things, whether he had taken money in exchange for introducing in Congress over two hundred private immigration bills, whose purpose is to give special consideration to specific immigrants; whether he had arranged a no-show job for his daughter Jacqueline at the Yonkers Raceway; and whether his friend Generoso Pope, the owner of *The National Enquirer,* had paid the salary of any of his congressional staffers. Biaggi flatly denied to the paper that he had taken the Fifth Amendment.

But the story wouldn't go away. Three months later the *News* and *The New York Times* reported that Biaggi had taken the Fifth numerous times. Biaggi denounced the stories as "a complete hoax" and accused the papers of "moral cowardice." But the stories kept coming, and in early May Biaggi conceded that they were true. The transcript of his grand jury testimony revealed that he had invoked the privilege against self-incrimination sixteen times.

None of the questions at which Biaggi balked led to an indictment or a publicized investigation, so Biaggi's role remained mysterious. He might have saved the day by expressing contrition for having lied about his testimony and for having vilified the press. But now Biaggi was betrayed by the same characteristic that had brought him so far: an unwavering belief in himself, an angry certainty that whatever he did was right. Nobody was going to stand in judgment of Mario Biaggi. At a press conference soon after the news broke, Biaggi was described in *The New Yorker* as sweating and stuttering and storming with fury, choking the microphone and "half lunging at reporters whose attitudes he resented." Biaggi's New York political career was over, and he retreated to the haven of his congressional district.

No-show jobs and influence peddling were little more than the ancient prerogatives of the big-city politician. But a far graver and more frightening allegation shadowed Biaggi, never to be resolved, as he stalked off the stage of mayoral politics. The charge involved the 1959 incident in which he had won his Police Medal of Honor, as well as his enduring tabloid title, "Hero Cop." According to the story Biaggi told his colleagues, he was driving in the Bronx in a friend's Cadillac when he was pulled over at gunpoint. As he circled the block in accord with his assailant's orders, Biaggi worked his gun loose and fired over his shoulder, killing the man, a twenty-three-year-old hood named Andrew Porcu. It was an incredible story; indeed, suspiciously incredible. But the ensuing police investigation proved inconclusive.

A number of circumstances pointed to a very different narrative. The Cadillac belonged to a suspected gangster, Anthony Trinca. Biaggi had invested $3000 in Anthony Trinca and Associates, and his wife was listed on company records as the vice president. Porcu had allegedly been driven to the scene by an ex-con, James Forella, whose car was found abandoned nearby with several guns in the trunk. It looked like anything but a bungled stickup. A former Bronx assistant district attorney says that Mario Merola, the Bronx DA who had reopened the investigation when new evidence surfaced in 1973—that fateful year—was convinced that Biaggi's story was a cover, though his sources disappeared when the press learned of the renewed investigation.

Not until the Wedtech trial would Biaggi be publicly accused, rather than privately suspected, of trafficking with gangsters.

In the months after Wedtech placed his firm on retainer, Biaggi signed his name to several letters seeking help for Wedtech in winning Defense Department contracts and purchasing new headquarters in the Bronx. The letters were sent out on congressional letterhead, and did not identify Biaggi as Wedtech's lawyer—a serious breach of congressional ethics. But in January 1979, the Ethics in Government Act became law, and it placed sharp limits on the amount that a federal legislator could receive in outside income. The flow of letters from Biaggi on Wedtech's behalf stopped after 1978, even though the letters represented him as a concerned congressman rather than a paid lawyer. On September 1, 1979, Ehrlich bought Biaggi out of the partnership for $320,000, to be paid in annual installments over the next decade.

The firm, however, continued to be called Biaggi & Ehrlich, and as far as Wedtech was concerned, Biaggi remained its protector, its *padrone.* Fred would have nothing to do either with Biaggi or Ehrlich, and John was too busy down on the shop floor, so the job of liaison fell to Mario, who found that he had a natural aptitude for getting along with powerful men. A subtle man, Mario had a gift for intrigue, for the back channel, for saying little and implying much. He became one of those anonymous men who glide down the long corridors of the congressional office buildings, accomplishing nameless deeds.

Mario often flew down to Washington with Ehrlich, with whom he became the best of friends. The two would always stop in at Biaggi's office before proceeding elsewhere. Biaggi, in turn, was careful to protect his investment. He insisted on receiving regular briefings from Mario on the state of the company, generally when he flew up to New York on Friday evenings. The congressman would arrive at the law office downtown, and Mario would obediently pay court.

By the fall of 1979 Wedtech was really humming. The company had been able to exploit its status as one of the relatively few proven manufacturers of military equipment in the 8(a) program to land a series of contracts, including additional parts for jet engines and a job building fin assemblies for the Navy's Sidewinder missile. And then, toward the end of the year, it had been selected for a $4 million contract to build refrigeration kits to cool the engine of the Army's M-113 armored personnel carrier. The contract carried an option for another $4 million the following year, and for who knew what other opportunities in the huge M-113 retrofit program.

Every year for the past three Wedtech had done about $1.5 million worth of business. Suddenly it would be doubling, tripling in size. Maybe it wasn't General Motors yet, but neither was it just John, Fred, and Ceil Lewis, factotum and sometime bookkeeper, rattling around the office by themselves. Now there were sixty employees, including the small work force at Fleetwood, and soon there would be a great many more.

Wedtech was succeeding not because of bribery or political influence —not yet—but because of the skills of the men who ran the show. Everyone who came to know Fred and John realized that they were a perfect team. The one picked up where the other left off. John could look at a part and immediately recognize which machine he would need to grind a curve or how to stamp out a die to manufacture a new component. And

Fred could read a blueprint the way John could read a piece of metal. Fred was responsible for ordering what Wedtech didn't make itself, and it only took a glance at the blueprint for Fred to recognize what was needed.

There was something of Methuselah about Fred: he seemed to have been around forever. He had the sexual drive of a seventeen-year-old, and he kept dirty magazines scattered around his office, but his round, lined face and his thinning hair showed his fifty-two years, and more. Fred knew all the angles, and then some. There wasn't anyone in the metal-cutting business that Fred hadn't hoisted a few with or cut a quiet little deal with. When something was needed, Fred would summon to his office the head of purchasing, Mario Gonzalez, and bark, "Call up my friend Jack and tell him we need these forgings and when he says that'll be $4.85 apiece, you tell him it's for Fred, and Fred says he wants 'em for $4.50." And he would get them for $4.50.

As the company grew it began to acquire an international flavor. John had always believed, for some reason, that Indians were good at quality control, so Wedtech had long had an Asian contingent. Then came the Russians. One day in 1977 or 1978—John is vague on dates—Dima Guner, a Russian émigré who spoke no English, had walked in the door. John, the last man to hold linguistic limitations against a potential employee, had hired him as a draftsman, to keep proper records of his hurried sketches. The two got along just fine, communicating by hand signals and drawings. Guner brought in his wife, Lyuba, who had a degree in physics, to run Wedtech's production. It was the beginning of a boom. For many Russians arriving in New York with a university degree and no English, Wedtech was the dreamed-of employer, though scarcely in the dreamed-of locale.

The Hispanics had begun to form a separate community within the company. John did a lot of his hiring through the local Protestant churches, and employed a number of ministers. One of them, Mario Rosado, established a Pentecostal cell on the shop floor. A room was set aside as an impromptu chapel for the Holy Rollers, as John called them. Rosado and his disciples would gather at lunchtime and sing and chant and shout God's praises, to the unending embarrassment or irritation of Wedtech's non-Christian or secular employees. John himself had too direct and personal a relationship with God to subscribe to any particular set of teachings—he believed in all of them—but he was very proud of the chapel. Fred thought it was downright idiotic, but to John it signified Wedtech's higher calling.

Rosado, though, was a perennial source of agitation in the company.

Every Friday he would make the rounds of the shop-level employees, collecting a tithe for his good works and handing it over to an associate, who was known to offer loans at 25 percent. To noninitiates Rosado's collection seemed a good deal like a shakedown, especially when he firmly asked that they ante up as well. Sherman Billingy, for one, told Rosado to get lost. One day Billingy went into the stamping room, where Rosado worked, to look at parts for quality control. As he went behind the huge stamping machine, Billingy recalls, Rosado hit a foot pedal, and the stamp came crashing down. Billingy barely whisked his hand away in time to keep it from being pulverized. A big man, Billingy rushed at Rosado with the specific intent of killing him, but was restrained by a co-worker.

John could never even be talked to on the subject of Rosado; in any case, the preacher seemed to him vastly preferable to the thugs who ran the union Wedtech had recently accepted. Local 875 of the Teamsters had represented the employees of Fleetwood since the late 1950s, and in 1977 Fred persuaded John to let them organize the shop floor at Wedtech. Fred considered paying off politicians offensive, but paying off corrupt union officials was more or less the state of nature, at least in his patch of the ecosystem. It was one of those straightforward transactions Fred appreciated: you make a generous gift to the gentlemen who run the local, and the workers are instructed to keep their complaints to themselves. At Christmastime in 1977, Fred handed over a gift of $1000 or $2000 cash—he can't remember which—to Richard Stolfi, secretary-treasurer of 875. By 1980 the Christmas gift had reached $10,000.

Outsiders were now beginning to visit the ravaged precincts of Washington Avenue. Project managers from the big contractors drove up to Fort Apache, men who were accustomed to looking over plants out in the leafy suburbs or in quaint little Southern towns. They were white men accustomed to working with other white men, and they were easily put off. John ascribes much that went wrong to racism, and there is no doubt that Wedtech lost a good deal of business over the years because it was a minority firm run out of the barrio. John knew that Wedtech had two strikes against it the moment these men drove over the bridge and into the Bronx.

What he lacked in formal education John made up in street smarts. For his skeptical white men John developed a confidence trick inspired, he says, by a scene in *The Sting.* "When I used to get someone who was coming from Ford Motors or RCA or Sunoco, I did not used to have enough fellas. You have to take into consideration that a buyer is always scared of giving you a job. And here they are, coming into the South

Bronx, all bombed out. They look at this place and they say, 'Oh my God, are we going to put our work into this place?' So what I used to do, I used to go around the corner, get the fellas at the grocery drinking beer, and I had the coat jackets with the company's name on the back, and I would grab them, and I would set up the machines to take a cut on the lathe."

John would instruct his human props to move a piece of metal back and forth to make a cut, or to run something on the grinder to produce impressive sparks. He told one of his men to run the presses up and down for additional noise-and-motion effect. John himself would leave blueprints strewn across work tables. He figured that the corporate types sent up for The Tour wouldn't know the difference between real and show. And by the end of the visit the emissaries were wondering, says John, whether Wedtech wasn't too fully booked to fit in another job. It was one of the company's more picturesque acts of deception.

FOUR

FOUR

Near-Death Experience: I

JOHN WAS a reckless chief executive if ever there was one. Fear, anger, and faith goaded him on—a fear of collapsing into nothing, like his father and brother; an abiding bitterness at the world that had made him suffer; a sense of calling that was almost a feeling of divine selection. His destiny and that of Wedtech were one and the same. He was obsessed with making the company big, so big that it could never be pulled down. In his millennial mood he would proclaim that Wedtech was on its way to becoming the General Motors of the South Bronx. Since he had never had a company larger than himself and a partner, John simply did not understand that you could grow your way to bankruptcy. He never thought about whether the books were balanced or whether the company was turning a profit. And, at least in these early days, he was willing to do without money. In 1978 he and Fred were paying themselves $20,800 apiece.

Fred was far more prudent than John, but even his caution could be dangerous. Fred was basically a cheapskate, and when he bid on a job, which was his specialty, he would submit a figure low enough to ensure that Wedtech would win, but also so low as to preclude any profits. Mario Moreno had now taken over the books from Ceil, but he had little influence over Fred and John. Between the tightness of the one and the ambition of the other, Wedtech was always running out of money. And even by the time the company had sixty or seventy employees, little had changed since John first began attending Mario's classes on the basics of small business. There was simply nobody around who had the vaguest idea how to run a middle-sized company. "It was totally the most disorganized place I've ever seen," says an employee from that time. "It was total insanity." Wedtech lurched from loan to loan.

In 1978 the firm received a loan of $550,000 for working capital from Citibank, guaranteed by the SBA. And then the SBA came through with the half million dollars in business development funds to go with the cooling-kit contract for the M-113. But it wasn't nearly enough. Wedtech was bursting the seams of 1049 Washington Avenue, and needed cash to pay for a much larger building that John and Fred had found at 595 Gerard Avenue, only about a dozen blocks south of Yankee Stadium. But commercial banks, without a government guarantee, weren't about to get near a military contractor in the South Bronx.

In late 1979 Mario started preparing the paperwork to apply for a $2 million loan, plus a $2 million loan guarantee, from the Economic Development Administration, a branch of the Commerce Department. For the first of many, many times, Wedtech had spent itself into virtual bankruptcy. By January 1980, the company was waiting every day for word from the EDA's regional office in Philadelphia. The fact is that Wedtech's request was exorbitant. The EDA rarely gave a loan and a guarantee to the same company, especially one that was scarcely on a sound financial footing to start with; if Wedtech wound up scanting either payment, the agency would have to foot the bill. The Philadelphia loan officer, Jack Geraghty, said it would be weeks or even months before the loan could be made final.

In a high passion John raced down to Philadelphia with Bernie Ehrlich in the big white Lincoln Town Car that John considered his good-luck car. Luck, however, was not on his side. When they arrived, it turned out that John hadn't thought to make an appointment, and there was nobody in the office to see them. The two men repaired glumly to Bookbinder's, the famous seafood restaurant, figuring that they might as well enjoy a last good meal before the company sank from sight.

But in fact this was only the first stage, the ritual low point, in a pattern Wedtech was to repeat again and again. The company's existence was so precarious, and its method of doing business so self-destructive, that the Grim Reaper seemed to pay a visit almost annually. The scythe would drop, and then, at the very last moment, something would be interposed —some plausible lie, some raw display of political power. The shadow would be lifted, and the company would race off to its next near-fatal encounter. It was a nervy existence, and it was just as well that none of the insiders, with the possible exception of Mario, was made of very sensitive material.

Since the previous summer, John and Mario had been talking to their local congressman, Robert Garcia, about their problem with the EDA. Garcia had been elected for the first time in 1978, after representing the South Bronx for twelve years in the New York State Assembly and Senate. Garcia had grown up in the Pentecostal churches in the South Bronx, where his father had been a preacher. In New York's Hispanic neighborhoods, churches, whether Catholic or Pentecostal, are the binding institutions of the community, and they had formed Garcia's base of support. The preachers liked him, the congregations liked him; he was the rare politician for whom scarcely anyone seemed to have a bad word. Before going into politics he had worked as an engineer, and between one thing and another he had made a name for himself as an honest, hardworking, completely aboveboard person.

By the time Garcia decided to run for Congress, Wedtech was one of the larger businesses in the South Bronx. He had visited the company in the course of the campaign, and John, Fred, and Mario, eager to get on the good side of their local representative, had each donated $1000 to the election effort. Garcia quickly made a point of inviting John and Mario to his fund raisers, and the Wedtech boys, enjoying their new prestige, made a point of attending. In 1979 Mario had made a $3000 contribution to Garcia's campaign fund, Conchita chipped in $1500, and Ceil Lewis wrote out a check for $500.

Bobby Garcia was a naturally obliging man, pleased to be able to do a favor for a friend. By 1979, Wedtech was clearly a friend. Mario and John had talked over the loan problem not only with the congressman but with his administrative aide, Lou Benza, who had contacts in the EDA's Philadelphia office. Soon after John's pointless round trip to the EDA office, with the company's cash flow dwindling to nothing and the federal bureaucrats still taking their sweet time, John and Mario went down to Citibank's midtown office for one last attempt to thrash out the issue with the bank and the EDA. Garcia agreed to send Benza along, and Benza proceeded to save Wedtech's neck. He arrived at the meeting and announced, "I'm not leaving until we've got this problem solved." The

EDA must have been impressed with the congressman's concern, because an understanding was worked out before Benza left. At the end of February, Wedtech received an EDA loan of $2,040,000, and a 90 percent guarantee for a loan from Citibank of $2,171,000.

But Wedtech couldn't keep up with its expenses. The 130,000-square-foot building at the corner of 150th Street and Gerard Avenue, with its two vast floors for fabrication, its dozens of offices built around a courtyard, its strange conning tower sitting up on top, was costing a fortune. John hired dozens of new employees to work on the cooling-kit contract, and he bought the latest computer-controlled equipment with the abandon of the poor cousin who suddenly comes into the family fortune. By the fall of 1980 the $4 million, incredibly, was gone. The Army would not start paying for the M-113 parts until it had received shipments. Mario could see disaster looming—until a new employee in the accounts department, Jonah Paolercio, made a startling observation.

Paolercio discovered that when he had inadvertently submitted to the Pentagon's auditor, the Defense Contract Audit Agency, invoices for work that had not, in fact, yet been done, Wedtech was reimbursed without a peep. In the normal course of things military contractors receive what are called progress payments only after they do the work; Wedtech was being paid *before* doing the work. Paolercio suggested to Mario that the DCAA's somnolence might be Wedtech's opportunity. It wouldn't be stealing, of course, since Wedtech would be reimbursed for the work in any case; it would just amount to borrowing the government's money without interest, and without letting the government know. Anyway, it was just a temporary expedient until Wedtech regained its balance.

With such plausible arguments did Mario try to persuade himself, and then John and Fred, to do something that was obviously illegal. Mario had already become a party to the lies told before his arrival. He had filled out SBA forms restating the two-thirds–one-third stock arrangement, which he knew to be false. But he had not yet initiated a crime. Until this moment Mario had lived an essentially blameless life. He was a businessman with a graduate degree, an immigrant who had struggled hard not only to succeed but to succeed in an honorable way. Unlike John and Fred, Mario had no personal stake in Wedtech; he was only a consultant, and for all he knew he might soon be back in the corporate world. But Mario had signed on to John's crusade. He too was a believer, and he saw the cause vanishing before his eyes. "At that time," says Mario, "we had only about two hundred jobs. And if we didn't do that, all those people could go home."

Mario was torn. He had neither the blind self-belief of John nor the profound indifference of Fred. He was a man with a conscience. But he was also, like John and Fred, an outsider determined to get in, a passionate and energetic man intent on succeeding. "Whenever there is a wall," as he puts it, "if I have to do it I will go through the wall." This was Mario's first wall. He sat down with Paolercio to suggest the fraud to John and Fred. It was a Friday, payday, late in the year, and a heavy snow was falling. Mario had barely slept in days. The company, he said, would go bankrupt unless something drastic was done. Fred accepted the need to cheat right away, but John resisted. At a second meeting soon afterward Mario explained to John once again that they were all teetering on the edge. This time John understood that there was no choice, and he instructed Mario and Paolercio to go ahead.

Of course there *was* a choice: the company could have gone bust. Most small businesses do go bust: they face a capital squeeze, they flail around, and the creditors move in. The marketplace is a Darwinian world. But when the inexorable laws of the market closed in on John, Fred, and Mario, they agreed to circumvent the laws. They were survivors, and if they had to cheat to survive, they would.

The fraud was simplicity itself. Paolercio would take an invoice from a supplier of, say, machinery or sheet metal, make a copy, white out all the information save the company name, and write in a new date and new dollar amounts for nonexistent expenses to Wedtech. The company would then mix the concocted bills with real ones and receive reimbursement for both from the Army. Wedtech's total revenue still couldn't exceed the amount called for in the contract, but it now benefited from what was essentially overdraft privileges. Moreover, with interest rates then running as high as 18 percent, Wedtech was making a fortune playing the float. And the DCAA auditors noticed nothing. "I couldn't believe how stupid they were," says a Wedtech bookkeeper. When the auditors, Samuel Barkan and Joshua Purec, started demanding original invoices rather than Xeroxed copies, Paolercio ran off fresh pieces of letterhead.

The temporary expedient became a fixed feature of Wedtech's accounting, saving the company from its continual brushes with bankruptcy. Before the fraud was detected, in 1983, the company had submitted as much as $6 million in bogus invoices. John claims to have known nothing of the fraud, but it was he who signed nearly all of the bogus invoices. The bookkeeper quoted above insists, "He was fully aware of the fact that we were getting money ahead of time." When this man left the company John thanked him by saying, "You helped me rob a bank."

PART TWO

PART TWO

Washington
Interlude: I

FIVE

The Cause
That Needs Assistance

BY THE SPRING of 1981 Wedtech had lasted much longer, and grown far larger, than anyone who knew John Mariotta ever would have imagined. It had so mastered the process of obtaining and performing metal-fabrication jobs for the military that its future as a stable and profitable, if modest, minority contractor seemed almost guaranteed—if it didn't spend itself into oblivion. Of course the company was defrauding the Defense Department and the Small Business Administration, and had recently begun taking kickbacks from suppliers; but in the ordinary course of events there was no reason that these rather conventional deceptions would come to light. And then a gentleman with big, limpid eyes beneath sprouting eyebrows, a small man with a small voice, gentle manner, and a yellow rose for a boutonnière—in short, E. Robert Wallach—flew to New York to alter forever the path of this little firm in the South Bronx.

Wallach had arrived on a mission of mercy, though he and the Wedtech principals had decidedly different ideas about the nature of his benefactions. An old friend of Wallach's, a private investigator named Hal Lipset, who had gained notoriety with the Watergate committee, told him that he had been hired by a tiny defense-contracting firm in the South Bronx to look into the past of an Army official who had been obstructing its bid for a big contract. Lipset had suggested that the firm might do better by speaking to Wallach, a lawyer in San Francisco. Wallach's best friend was Edwin Meese, III, counselor and close friend of the new President of the United States, Ronald Reagan.

Wallach heard about the South Bronx and the minorities and the crusading spirit, and decided to go to New York to offer his wisdom, his legal talents, and perhaps the good offices of the man he would always elliptically refer to as "my friend." Wedtech heard about Ed Meese, and decided that everybody should climb into the good-luck Lincoln to pick up Wallach at his hotel. What followed was a blinding moment of fusion, as fantasy, guile, political reach, and large quantities of money combined to produce an irresistible force.

Bob Wallach, like John Mariotta, like Ronald Reagan, was a man with a dream. John Mariotta dreamed of rearing up a General Motors in the South Bronx; Bob Wallach, who lived on a far more ethereal plane, dreamed of raising monuments of virtue, himself primary among them. He was a strange case, Bob Wallach. For all that he had made millions of dollars as one of San Francisco's leading personal injury lawyers, for all that his political ambition had led him to run for the U.S. Senate, he seemed to breathe the pure air of a convent girl. On the wall of his office he had proudly framed a piece of doggerel he had penned for the Star and Crescent Society at Los Angeles High School in 1952:

> I live for those who love me
> For those who know me true
> For the heaven that waits above me
> And awaits my spirit too
> For the cause that needs assistance
> And the wrong that needs resistance
> And the future in the distance
> And the good that I can do.

Wallach's history, like Wedtech's, was an inspiring tale of triumph over adversity. He was born in Brooklyn in 1934, and raised in the final surge of the Jewish working class into middle-class respectability and assimilation. But rather than the cozy, if often clangorous, upbringing experienced by such children, Wallach found himself uprooted at the age of seven, when his parents divorced. Wallach, his mother, and his grandfather boarded a train and crossed the country to Los Angeles. There, Wallach's mother kept the family together by working in a factory, and young Bob became what was probably one of the few Jewish boys to make pocket money by mowing the lawns of black families. "Every school I went to," Wallach recalls, "I was the only Jewish kid." Wallach also remembers being a very serious and unhappy boy, sharply grained with the moral passion and class pride of his grandfather, a labor organizer who preached Workmen's Circle socialism yet remained an Orthodox Jew.

As a young man Wallach was always running for something, and always as the reform candidate. At the University of Southern California, where he was granted a debate scholarship, Wallach ran for sophomore class president against the starting pitcher on the varsity, and when he won he got his class to sponsor a boys' club in the black ghetto of East Los Angeles. He went on to Boalt Law School at Berkeley, planning on making his grandfather proud by becoming a politically committed labor lawyer. He got through Boalt by working at a cannery, where he refused to take the "white boy jobs" and insisted instead on the most onerous tasks. He was thrilled to find that the poor blacks he worked with readily accepted him.

In his third year at law school Wallach was asked to join the intercollegiate moot court team with a good-natured classmate two years his senior, Ed Meese. Thus began a friendship between two utterly unlike men that was to withstand every change in circumstance but finally destroy them both. Ed Meese was everything that Wallach, unsure of his place, was not. Meese seemed to be not so much rooted in his life as anchored. The family was a fixture in Oakland, where Meese's father was the county treasurer, a position of genuine political power. The Meeses had spent over a hundred years in the tight, self-regarding society of the Bay Area without becoming even remotely aristocratic, possibly because they lived in Oakland rather than in San Francisco.

In the Meeses Bob Wallach saw the kind of family life he had only dreamed of. "It was an absolute *Life with Father* image of a middle-class American family," says Wallach. "Gentle, Christian people, nice, modest home, completely satisfied with life as a routine, completely invested with their children. It's terribly seductive. I used to love going to their home. Ed and I were writing briefs down in the basement, his mother would come down with the sandwiches. It was right out of Andy Hardy. It was the kind of home I had never experienced."

Young Ed Meese, big and doughy and genial, full of the innate good cheer of California in the 1950s, was in training to be a third-generation public servant. He had gone off to Yale to study public administration before returning home for law school. He had interrupted his professional education by signing up for a two-year stretch of active duty in the National Guard, where he had been assigned to an intelligence unit. Meese had loved the military, with its discipline and clear definition and elaborate organization, and down in the basement he used to spend hours showing Wallach the intelligence charts from his reserve unit. Meese was already married, already preparing for his career. He was considered able rather than bright. Wallach was the smart one; Meese was the solid one. It may have been Wallach's agitation, his yearning for a higher sense of purpose, that Meese found so refreshingly different from his own insular world.

The two men, predictably, embarked on very different careers. Rejected by San Francisco's leading labor law firm, Wallach went instead into personal injury law, which at the time was something like going into shady tax shelters after failing to get into rabbinical school. In fact, Wallach had stumbled on a line of work for which he was supremely suited. His air of sweet understanding endeared him to juries. "Bob's trademark is physical closeness," says a former associate, Gerald Stearns. "The hands on the biceps, something in this low voice with a kind of knowing nod. He would make you feel that your problem was important." Wallach's manner, together with his intelligence and the oratorical skills he had sharpened in competitive debating, made him one of the two or three leading personal injury lawyers in San Francisco.

But he remained eager to make his mark in the public world. He was still running for things, looking for wrongs that needed righting in the small world of the San Francisco bar. There he became known as a tireless networker, making friends and placating enemies. In 1974 Wallach ran yet another insurgency campaign, this one for president of the staid and starched Bar Association of San Francisco. Miraculously, he won, and soon turned his liberal politics into a series of crusades.

A little taste of greatness may have been enough to intoxicate him. In 1976 Wallach announced for the Democratic nomination to the U.S. Senate, despite having no background in politics and no base of support. It was the first time he had done something that struck others as betraying a lack of self-awareness or evincing an overweening egotism. Wallach ran on a platform of gay rights legislation, the decriminalization of marijuana, and opposition to nuclear power. Having attracted very little attention from the press or the public, he dropped out one month before the primaries. The following year he ran for the board of governors of the California State Bar, and lost that, too. The Bob Wallach crusade seemed to have outreached itself.

While the sixties gathered force and Wallach was becoming a classic liberal and Jewish lawyer, San Francisco activist, his friend Ed Meese, a Republican of glandular convictions, was earning a spot on the starting team of the forces of reaction. As an assistant in the notoriously conservative Alameda County District Attorney's office, Meese distinguished himself by arresting hundreds of protestors in the Berkeley Free Speech Movement and swiftly and efficiently moving them through the arraignment process. It was the kind of organizational achievement of which Meese was especially proud, and it brought him to the attention of higher powers.

In 1967 Governor Ronald Reagan made Meese his legal affairs adviser, promoting him the following year to the key position of executive secretary. In this post Meese became a greater object of hatred by students and the left than even Reagan himself. He was the governor's man at Berkeley when the police fired on students in People's Park and killed a spectator standing atop a building. He led an unsuccessful but relentless drive to extirpate California Rural Legal Assistance, a legal services organization. And he spearheaded Reagan's effort to appoint avowedly conservative judges, an effort he would undertake again a decade later.

Wallach and Meese's fifties-style friendship weathered not only the political upheaval of the sixties but the cultural reformation of the seventies. While Meese was conducting a life of perfect Lutheran rectitude, Wallach, following a marital separation, learned all the new steps. "The butterfly came out of the cocoon," says Gerald Stearns. Wallach developed a new set of eccentricities, including the yellow rose in the buttonhole and the constant companionship of a beautiful Saluki dog named Sally, that were to mark him as a dandy or a slightly off-key hipster. He continued to write his name in small letters, a habit he had picked up from a high school teacher and, oddly enough, had never dropped. These were strange affectations for so serious a man. In his desperation to be noticed, Wallach came very close to making a fool of himself.

And yet despite his bachelor life and the Senate campaign, Wallach remained a fast friend of Meese's. Once the two had lived down the street from each other in Oakland and looked after each other's children; now Wallach traveled down to Sacramento as often as he could and made a point of telling friends that he was "going to see Ed." The balance of the friendship may have begun to tip. Wallach was accumulating wealth and honors, but "the future in the distance," in his redundant phrase, remained maddeningly distant. Meese, who had always seemed content where he was and had never showed much ambition, apparently had hitched his humble wagon to a shooting star, in the person of Ronald Reagan. The old B-movie star who combined the convictions of Barry Goldwater with the TV host's emollient air of geniality had narrowly lost out to Gerald Ford for the 1976 Republican presidential nomination but was the odds-on favorite for 1980.

In 1979 Reagan's campaign manager, John Sears, had tried to get the ineffectual and slow-moving Meese fired as chief of staff, but loyalty carried the day, as it always did with Reagan. Meese stayed, and Sears was fired. Reagan, of course, was elected, and Meese expected to move into the White House as chief of staff. Some of the new men who had come to surround the President, however, recognized that Meese was no more suited to play the role of adroit, all-seeing courtier than he was to conduct brain surgery. The President's new campaign manager, James Baker III, essentially made himself chief of staff, and Meese was placed several heartbeats farther from the Oval Office as the President's counselor. Nevertheless, along with Baker and Michael Deaver, Meese was a part of the President's famed troika, and Baker could do nothing about the fact that Meese remained the First Friend.

In late 1979 or early 1980 Wedtech learned that the Army had made a contract available through the 8(a) program that would dwarf anything the company had ever before undertaken. The job was to take over from Chrysler the building of a six-horsepower engine, known as the military standard engine, designed to power portable field generators. Chrysler had completed its final production run in 1977, and late the following year the Army, concluding that it needed another batch of engines to tide it over before switching to a new prototype, placed the contract in the 8(a) program. There were no engine-making companies in the 8(a) portfolio, but the Army was eager to prove that it was taking seriously the obligation to help develop minority business. The Army turned to the Latin American Manufacturers Association, a Hispanic lobbying group, to find it a qualified company. LAMA's president, Jose Aceves, proposed his own company, Hartec, for the job, but when a preliminary survey disclosed that Hartec had neither a facility nor even employees, the Army told Aceves to take a walk. Aceves, who had mentioned the contract to John, offered to solve his problem by taking on Wedtech as a subcontractor.

By this time the Army had thoroughly repented of its decision to set aside the engine contract in the first place. Dr. Thomas Keenan, chief of procurement at the Troop Support and Aviation Materiel Readiness

Command in St. Louis (known with typical military logic and euphony as TSARCOM), was eager to go competitive with the contract, but his hands were tied. Several months earlier the SBA had included the engine contract in its "pilot program," a set-aside within the set-aside that allowed it, and not the contracting agency, to designate the appropriate 8(a) firm. The SBA thus had a lock on the contract. A survey of Wedtech only increased TSARCOM's doubts, but there was nothing for it: on October 3 the command dutifully sent the SBA the contract specs and a bid solicitation.

In early November, just before the presidential election, John, Fred, Mario, and Colonel Ehrlich, the in-house military expert, flew out to St. Louis for a precontract conference. It was not an altogether amicable session. Ehrlich tried to make soldier-to-soldier small talk about the idiosyncrasies of the engine, which he knew from experience—how tough it was to start up in cold weather, how you had to turn the thing off to refuel it. John hopped around and carried on in his high-pitched, breathless voice about his spear carriers in the South Bronx. Fred blew smoke in Keenan's face while he waved his big cigar. It's unlikely that Keenan had ever met anyone like John or Fred, and he was not amused. He made it clear that he felt he was being railroaded by the SBA, and that he considered Wedtech a dubious candidate for the engine contract.

The Wedtech boys trooped home in disarray. They *deserved* that contract. Hadn't the SBA given them its seal of approval? John knew he could build those engines, the same way he knew he could build the H-bomb if somebody gave him a clear set of specs. But it was a white man's Army, as John knew all too well from the racist gibes he endured during his stretch as a soldier. He and the others concluded that the Army was going through a charade. Keenan, especially, was toying with them; hated them, in fact. From the time of this first meeting, the Wedtech principals fastened with the obsessiveness of true paranoia on Dr. Keenan. He was in league with the big contractors; he was in league with competing minority firms. He was an out-and-out racist.

Maybe Keenan *was* a racist. Maybe he was by nature indisposed toward any contractor located in the South Bronx and run by a Hispanic and a Jew. The Army, after all, remains a highly conservative institution. Minority contractors who deal with the Pentagon typically complain of contemptuous treatment. Yet Keenan was not the problem. The other officers of TSARCOM took a dim view of Wedtech's bid. The Hartec experience had begun the process; the Wedtech visit only confirmed the low expectations. And these encounters, in turn, exacerbated the inherent problem of the entire 8(a) program, which compelled contracting agencies, above all the military, to consider policy goals completely alien to their own sense of mission.

The military had always bridled at the 8(a) program, though the Army less than the other branches. Over the years the services had accommodated themselves to the program by handing out contracts for food services and the like. But the engine contract was a manufacturing job of almost unprecedented dimensions. And to this extent, at least, Wedtech may have been right: the military was not inclined to entrust a substantial manufacturing job to a largely untested minority firm in the South Bronx. An element of racism may very well have been involved, but Wedtech's problem was almost certainly institutional rather than personal. And it was also, as it always would be, of its own making.

Wedtech's darkest suspicions were confirmed soon after the executives returned from St. Louis, when the command established a fair market price of $1485 per engine, or $19 million for the entire contract. Fifteen hundred dollars seems like a lot of money for a little engine, but John and Fred considered the price outrageously low. TSARCOM price analysts had reached the figure by multiplying Chrysler's costs by a suitable inflation factor. In fact, a seasoned engine manufacturer might have had no trouble completing the contract at $1485 per engine, or perhaps a little more, but Wedtech, starting from scratch, would have to spend millions on new equipment, facilities, training, and so on. In other words, it might have been a fair contract had Wedtech been qualified to perform it in the first place. But the Army was not obliged to take an 8(a) contractor's particular disabilities into account when drawing up a price.

And now John and Fred made a critical decision. They could have walked away. They could have concluded that they were in over their heads, which they were. But they were not to be denied. The company was always spurred by a sense of injured merit, a faith that the justice of its cause vindicated all ambition. Wedtech lived from enemy to enemy. And in Dr. Keenan the company had a genuine enemy, for good reason or for ill. Wedtech would fight a political battle with political weapons. So after the executives returned from St. Louis, John and Mario accompanied Ehrlich to the law offices in lower Manhattan. They told Biaggi that something had to be done about Keenan. Biaggi, who after six terms in Congress was a man with very little influence in Washington, said that he would talk to his friend Joe Addabbo.

Joseph Addabbo was the congressman Mario Biaggi would never be. A fellow Italian from Queens, Addabbo had been in office since 1961 and had become a respected force in Congress. He was the chairman of the Small Business Committee, and that was how he made sure he was addressed: Chairman. His writ ran far not only in the SBA but in the Pentagon, for he sat on the defense subcommittee of the Appropriations Committee. Before he died, in April 1986, he became one of Wedtech's great benefactors, and Wedtech acknowledged his many kindnesses with the coin of the Capitol realm, which is to say, campaign contributions. For now, however, Addabbo simply set up a meeting for John, Mario, and Bernie Ehrlich with an aide on the Small Business Committee.

TSARCOM had insisted from the outset that the 8(a) company selected by the SBA work with a large contractor of the Army's own choosing. The one and only firm that had been willing to take on this foster-parent role was the Avco Corporation, a big engine and aerospace firm. Through late 1980 and early 1981 Avco worked on a bid for the engine contract. The labor was to be done in collaboration with Wedtech, but apparently no one at Wedtech so much as saw Avco's figures until they arrived in St. Louis on February 27, 1981. The Wedtech people blanched when they saw Avco's bid. At TSARCOM, the bid provoked "hysterical laughter," as a pricing specialist later told a congressional committee. Avco and Wedtech had bid $99 million for a contract the Army estimated at $19 million. Two and a half weeks later TSARCOM asked the Secretary of the Army to remove the engine contract from the set-aside program.

This was the final indignity. Wedtech was now convinced that Avco was hoping to discredit its minority partner in order to win the contract itself, and that it was doing so in collusion with Dr. Keenan. The Avco bid was, in fact, utterly implausible, though it's likelier that the company was trying to slip out of its own obligation rather than to supplant Wedtech. But as far as Wedtech was concerned, the gauntlet had been thrown down. Biaggi hadn't been enough; Addabbo hadn't been enough. Wedtech would have to go for the groin. In early April David Epstein, a p.r. man who wrote speeches for John and carted him around to events, called the private investigator Hal Lipset to ask him to check out the evil Dr. Keenan. Lipset, in turn, suggested Wallach. It was thus that E. Robert Wallach found himself rattling through the slums in the lucky Lincoln, squeezed between, as he recalls, "two Hispanic guys and this little rough-cut Jew."

The car pulled up at 595 Gerard, in the same neighborhood where forty years earlier Wallach had gone to visit his uncle, and he followed his tatterdemalion escort through a set of rundown offices to "one of the most unbelievable sights I had ever seen." What he saw was like a story, as if one of the mechanical displays John Mariotta's father had created had suddenly sprung, Disney-like, to life. In a gleaming industrial space in the middle of the ghetto dozens of Spanish-speaking men were purposefully working metal on the most advanced robotic machines. Wallach was introduced around, and noticed that all the men called John Mariotta by his first name. The only pictures on the walls were of Christ, and in a room off a corridor was an interdenominational chapel. Upstairs, in the research and development area, Wallach heard men in white lab coats conversing in what sounded to his ears like the Yiddish of his childhood. These were, of course, the Russian Jews who seemed to be emigrating from Moscow directly to the South Bronx. Wallach, a man naturally prone to moral transports, experienced the transport of all time. "It was," he reflects, "like my whole life."

After The Tour, John, Fred, and Mario stood around nervously while they tried to think of a restaurant that a wealthy lawyer with White House connections would consider adequate to his dignity. Of course, they had it all wrong. It was Bob Wallach who wanted to be accepted by them, not the other way around. Wallach asked them to please take him wherever they normally ate. Brightening considerably, the group drove off to a joint in Spanish Harlem, El Deportivo, where they spent hours schmoozing about their lives—John's gifted, self-destructive father; Fred's glorious past as an Israeli terrorist; Mario's childhood in Colombia.

Wallach spoke of his beloved grandfather, who had fled the tsar's draft and escaped to America so that, he, Bob Wallach, could be there in the South Bronx at this charmed moment, living for those who loved him, or would love him, when he used his influence to rescue them from persecution. "This is great!" he remembers saying. "I'm going to take this to Ed." And the wheels of destiny, inaudible to the four men, commenced to grind.

SIX

SIX

Ed

ED MEESE was a big, galumphing man with a firm handshake and a hearty, Rotarian manner. He had ginger-colored hair and bags under his eyes, and when he tried to be stern he seemed only gruff, like a fondly remembered high school gym coach. Indeed, it was easy to picture him standing with a whistle around his neck while the fiery young revolutionaries of the new Reagan order dribbled up and down the court. Everyone in the White House liked Ed. It seemed incredible that to the larger world he was becoming known as "Mr. Conservative," the zealous ideologue who held the fort against "pragmatists" like Jim Baker, the chief of staff. Meese wasn't a conservative or a pragmatist; he was a loyalist. "He believed," says a former Meese aide, "in whatever Ronald Reagan believed in. The President used him. The President found someone who was guileless and who would have walked into a buzz saw for him. When all the President's kids were going bananas on the campaign, who got to handle them? Uncle Ed."

Meese was not, of course, agnostic on the basic conservative principles. He had made a name for himself jailing protestors, trying to "reform" legal services for the poor, and laying down doctrinal tests for the judiciary. He opposed affirmative action and didn't see the point of government bodies like the Environmental Protection Agency. But he didn't seem so much to believe these things as to take their truth for granted. He had none of the hardness of the true believer. Like the President himself, he was a soft man with hard beliefs.

It was true that the President used Meese, as powerful men always use loyalists. But it wasn't a simple relationship. Meese was, in a way, the President's tether to reality. Ronald Reagan lived on the plane of magic. He and his wife, after all, had been movie stars, or rather movie personalities, during the golden age of Hollywood, when publicists constructed fictitious personalities for the stars to inhabit, and a nation of fans was invited to adore this beautiful, backbiting family. Reagan, to an unusual degree, became one of his own fans. He believed in magic, in the persistence of the homey old images—the picket fence, the harmonious small town—and the noble sentiments. He had the capacity to give himself fully to almost any belief he chose. In *Reagan's America*, Garry Wills points out that over the years Reagan came to describe as literally true the war record invented for him by the studios. The President believed and induced belief.

Ed Meese lived on the plane of the actual. Not only was he not a dreamer, he was not gripped by the quasi-religious, or explicitly religious, vision of social transformation that moved so many of the men who had been swept into office with the President. Meese was a government man, and he understood the issues in secular terms. For fifteen years he had been with Ronald Reagan almost continually, murmuring, explaining, mapping things out. He was the honest broker, "the President's *consigliere*," as Michael Uhlmann, a member of the domestic policy staff that served under Meese, thought of him. "The number of occasions when the President would turn to Meese and say, 'What do you think, Ed?' was just extraordinary," says Uhlmann.

Practically everyone who ventured into the White House was struck by the intuitive rapport of the two men, at least on matters of policy. At moments of uncertainty the President would sometimes look to Meese, who would nod or shake his head as the moment demanded. The combination of Reagan's serene indifference to detail, and his unshakable faith in his old friend, meant that in many ways Meese took on the ordinary business of being President—making policy—while Reagan smiled against heartwarming backdrops, preached the virtues of capitalism, and swapped jokes with Frank Sinatra.

Meese really was amazingly powerful. After being blocked from the job of chief of staff, he had gained control over the entire policy-making apparatus by insisting that virtually the entire government—the domestic policy staff, the Cabinet, even the National Security Adviser—report to him. He stood at the head of the government. And yet Meese cast such an immense shadow that it was easy to lose sight of what a small man he was. He was an ordinary man with no special gifts. "I don't know what this guy had going for him," says a man who worked closely with Meese during his tenure as Attorney General. "I look on him as a guy who was a long-term friend of Ronald Reagan's who somehow worked his way up so that he could get good jobs in this administration."

Unlike Reagan, Meese worked very hard. And yet there was something slack about him, something misty and indistinct. He shared the President's complacency and self-satisfaction. In the fierce tumble of ambition and ideological contention at the White House, Meese always seemed able to lumber along, steady as an elephant. Michele Davis, an aide to Lyn Nofziger, another member of the Reagan inner circle, remembers a poker game with Nofziger, the Meeses, and a few friends early in the first term. The man who coordinated all domestic and all foreign policy for the President, she discovered, had spent the previous night laboriously drawing up a crib sheet to explain to his wife, Ursula, the difference between three of a kind and a full house.

That was Ed Meese—passionate about the trivial, blind to the world around him. "There's something missing in the makeup of the person," says the former Justice Department colleague. It's hard to describe what that thing was, perhaps because it was so elementary, so much a part of the makeup of the ordinary person. "A lack of judgment," the former associate ventures; "a lack of prudence." At times he would express opinions that were nothing short of the troglodytic—"You don't have many suspects who are innocent of a crime," or a Supreme Court decision "lacks the character of law"—and then look baffled when everyone jumped down his throat. Maybe what Meese lacked was self-awareness. He had, like his boss, an ingenuous belief in himself, a certainty that he was in the right. And he felt the same way about any of his friends, whether it was Ronald Reagan or E. Robert Wallach.

The election of Ronald Reagan had opened up thrilling vistas to Bob Wallach, who was a liberal Democrat of very pure pedigree. It was clearly time for a change. He was about to split from his law partner and was ready to offer himself to the nation. Going to Washington might entail financial hardship, he told Meese in a memo written the day after the inauguration, "but not something I would not set aside, as have untold thousands before me, to serve in a public capacity, for country, and for self . . . I am your friend, and would not interpret as an abuse of friendship any request you felt appropriate to make."

Wallach sent along lists of friends and acquaintances who he felt were likewise committed to the nation's future, as well as ruminations on subjects dear to his heart, including "the AWAK," his rendition of the AWACS aircraft; legal services for the poor; personal health; and the need to guard against liberals more concerned with hurting the administration than helping the nation. Gleams of pure self-aggrandizement sometimes show through the moral drapery, as when Wallach asks his friend to meet with the American Jewish leader Howard Squadron, if only because "it would assist my own standing in the Jewish community."

Among the dozens of pages of musings with which Wallach was burdening Meese's already groaning desk were his first comments about a wonderful little company in the South Bronx. Wallach grasped from the outset that Wedtech could be the perfect Reagan administration poster child. He knew that Reagan had what amounted to a theological faith in the miraculous powers of capitalism. Reagan promised to liberate the marketplace from the "disincentives" of tax and regulation. To poverty, the answer was not more welfare, which he considered another word for socialism, but more free enterprise. In the course of the campaign, Reagan had latched on to an idea advanced by Representative Jack Kemp of New York, who had suggested that ghettos be declared "urban enterprise zones," ready for the benefits of economic activity. The idea that tax cuts and deregulation, by themselves, could cure inner-city poverty may seem simplistic, but it was precisely the sort of solution that appealed to Reagan.

The Wedtech memos, as Wallach stressed at his trial, were but a slim portion of the voluminous and one-sided correspondence he directed to the counselor to the President. Meese's staff threw out many of the memos before Meese saw them, an obstacle Wallach tried to circumvent by sending copies to Meese's home in Virginia. Meese himself says that he "read many of them," skimming those which contained information he had already discussed with Wallach. Were there any particular insights of Wallach's that shaped his thinking on an issue? "This was part of the sum total of information that was factored in," says Meese. Can he recall any single observation, of all that he read and skimmed and kicked around, which stood out from the sum total? Mr. Meese says that he cannot.

The fact is that Wallach was sending memos into oblivion. Ever since his Army Reserve days Meese believed that he had a special gift for organization and administration. It quickly became clear that he was pathetically self-deluded. "Imagine if you will," says a former aide, "a man who has carved out a role for himself as deputy President of the United States who has every Cabinet head reporting through the Office of Cabinet Affairs to him directly. To do a lesser job, Cabinet agencies employ thousands of people. Meese thought he would have a lot of time to think about these issues. He didn't understand that he was being strapped to a Saturn V rocket, and it was being ignited, and on Inauguration Day that rocket was heading to the moon. [And you wanted to say], 'Ed, *wake up!* We are in a cyclone of paper.' And he just fell from that, and kept on bumping all the way to the bottom."

By the time Bob Wallach started sending his friend memos about Wedtech, documents were being piled into vast stacks, never to be seen again. After a time Meese would claim to have read the papers, and they would be shifted from one pile to another. The same thing would happen to proposals. Every morning at seven, Meese, who worked with the stolid routine of a beast of burden, would hold a staff meeting. There the staff would raise the day's list of what were called "action items." There were separate categories for issues that had to be decided that day, soon, or in the future. After a few months a new category had to be invented—the "frozen action item"—for matters of pressing importance that no one was ever going to get to. Frozen action items were filed away and never retrieved. As David Stockman put it in his memoir, *The Triumph of Politics,* Meese had "entombed himself beneath a pyramid of paper and disorganization."

Bob Wallach, however, was undaunted. On the very day of his visit to Wedtech, he sent off a letter to his new friends suggesting they assemble a brochure, including an assertion of their "free enterprise commitment," as well as photographs of employees with pictures of Christ at their work stand. The eager beavers at Wedtech quickly assembled Wallach's p.r. package, and by mid-May Wallach had given it to Meese. He had also sent to Meese, and to Meese's office, the first of dozens and dozens of letters, memos, documents, and messages on the subject of Wedtech.

Wallach's Wedtech memos were of several kinds. Some were like newsletters, designed merely to keep Meese posted on the daily status of one of Wallach's many pet causes. Others asked for direct intervention, though, at least at first, the writer pretended to a degree of timidity. In his very first memo, written on May 11, 1981, Wallach explained that

Wedtech had asked nothing more than that the Army audit its recent $38 million bid for the engine contract. "Perhaps," he wrote, "a direct interview with Secretary [of the Army John O.] Marsh or the intervention of Secretary Weinberger might be all that is necessary to accomplish the task." It was a modest request. Wallach was asking Meese, who was then overseeing the most drastic reappraisal of domestic policy since the advent of the Great Society, to persuade Secretary of Defense Caspar Weinberger, who was then overseeing the greatest peacetime buildup in the history of the American military, to intervene on behalf of a microscopically small contractor embroiled in a dispute with the Army.

At around this time Fred Fielding, the White House counsel, was circulating through the White House a directive that stated, "In recent years, the public has become increasingly sensitive to the allegations of improper influence in the awarding of government contracts. Obviously, no member of the White House staff should contact any procurement officer about a contract in which he has a personal financial interest or in which a relative, friend, or a business associate has a financial interest."

Meese says that he thinks that he was "vaguely aware" of the Fielding memo. But Meese says he didn't think that Wallach was actually asking *him* to contact Caspar Weinberger or Jack Marsh. "If I thought about it at all," says Meese, "I thought that this was a contact that he would make or someone else would make on behalf of the company. I don't think that I took any of these as actions I should take. I didn't intervene and my recollection is he didn't ask me to."

In fact Meese instructed his chief aide, Edward Thomas, to look into Wallach's complaints. Thomas delegated the task to Craig Fuller, the director of Cabinet Affairs. In a notation that affords a clear idea of what Meese's staff thought of the boss's friend, Thomas wrote, "Bob Wallach, even though he uses low[er] case [letters], is an extremely close friend of Ed Meese." And at the end of May, Fuller sent the request one rung lower on the ladder of delegation by instructing his assistant, T. Kenneth Cribb, to find out from the SBA what was going on.

What was going on was that the Army, with increasing stridency, was asking the SBA to remove the engine contract from the pilot program, thus restoring control over it to the Army. The Army was starting to run out of engines and was keen to open the contract for competitive bidding. But the 8(a) bureaucracy was not about to relinquish a $20 million contract without a fight. The SBA supported Wedtech's request for an audit to prove that the company would, indeed, need $38 million to undertake the job. But the Army insisted that Wedtech's needs were irrelevant. As a Pentagon official wrote to one of the congressmen Wedtech had rounded up to argue on its behalf, "Such an audit may substantiate the validity of the proposed costs but would not validate the likely costs under normal competitive conditions."

Mario and John were now hearing from their friends at the New York regional office of the SBA that the Army was out to dump Wedtech. Wallach was their only hope, and they turned to him frequently with a running narrative of their plight, their strategy, their dark suspicions. Wallach, in turn, relayed this material, in raw form, to his friend. Often he would dictate these messages in idle moments between meetings, on the plane, or at home, and apparently he would simply keep talking until he ran out of gas. In an epic, six-page memo dictated in early July, for example, Wallach dilated, at numbing length, on Wedtech's case against the Army's $19 million figure, as well as on its case against what he called, without further explanation, the "10 percent stipulation." He assumed that Meese would remember what he had written in previous memos, and what they had evidently discussed in person.

What is even more amazing about this and so many other letters of Wallach's is that he would repeat, at length and with no attempt at verification, Wedtech's often paranoid accusations against its every adversary. "While I have not been able to confirm this call for obvious reasons," he wrote, "the Welbilt people advised me that the same Houston man [an apparent competitor whose name Wallach couldn't remember] has in the past had on hand the precise number of spare parts which the St. Louis office of the U.S. Army has indicated it needed . . . Other than coincidence the repetition of this event, described as three or four times, could only be explained by advance knowledge of the amount of the request for spare parts." How could Ed Meese have read such passages without questioning his friend's rationality?

With every note Wallach included his modest calls for action. Someone should "advise" the Army to delay its decision; someone should "contact Frank Cardenas," by which Wallach meant the SBA administrator, Michael Cardenas. (Wallach never checked names or spellings.) It might be time for a meeting with Marsh or Weinberger. Wallach would then relate these fanciful proposals to John and Mario as if they were being seriously considered at that very moment in the highest councils of government.

Certainly Wedtech was not being ignored; the job of tracking the company had simply been bucked down to Ken Cribb. Cribb knew that the Wedtech matter involved a very close friend of Meese's, but, he says, he dealt with it as "just something that came across my desk." He had several conversations with Robert Turnbull, assistant to Michael Cardenas of the SBA, in which Turnbull explained that the Army was pushing and the SBA resisting.

Meese, strapped though he was to a Saturn rocket, was not about to let Wedtech vanish in the press of business. Four days later he wrote a note to himself reflecting a conversation with Cribb: "Ken Cribb will stay on top of situation." This did not, as Meese points out, count as contacting a "procurement officer," in the words of the Fielding memo. Meese says that he was not interfering in the process. "My whole purpose," he says, "was to make sure that there was communication between the different departments when they felt they were being ill-treated."

Of course communication from the office of the counselor is not quite the same thing as communication from a concerned citizen, or even from a congressman. When a messenger from the Olympian peaks of the White House lands on some backwater agency like the SBA, his curious questions instantly take on the form of admonitions. No political appointee at the agency level, like Robert Turnbull, is likely to have trouble recognizing signs of White House interest. Moreover, while SBA officials were accustomed to being strong-armed by local officials, even by congressmen, about specific contractors, White House interest was virtually unheard of. Thus it seems extremely likely that Cribb's modest display of curiosity had the effect of stiffening the SBA's spine.

Certainly Wallach felt that he recognized the source of the agency's stubbornness, throughout the summer, in the face of a hostile Army. On August 10 Wallach visited Meese and afterward spoke by phone to David Epstein, at that time his principal contact at Wedtech. In a memo to John, Fred, and Mario, Epstein quoted Wallach as saying "that there's no question but that [Meese's] intervention has produced such good results as have occurred," and that "bob's friend will not 'surface' on the matter but will otherwise 'pursue' it."

SEVEN

The Cause
That Repays Assistance

THE COMPANY that existed in Bob Wallach's imagination was not, even then, quite the same as the one that crawled through the grime of the South Bronx. Wallach knew nothing of the progress payment fraud or the deceit about ownership or the payoffs to the Teamsters. Indeed, just as Wallach was urging the White House to enlist in the Wedtech crusade, Richard Stolfi of Local 875 was telling Fred that the $10,000 Christmas present wouldn't cut it anymore; he wanted a monthly take. Stolfi was one of those unsentimental types who had no place in Wallach's idealized view of Wedtech. The union leader had looked around at the buzzing new headquarters at 595 Gerard and realized that Wedtech's ability to pay was markedly higher than it had been. Fred agreed to pay $3000 a month to Stolfi and Frank Casalino, the number two man in the local. John didn't like it, but Fred had been paying off union officials since the current crop was in junior high school. It was just a fact of life.

Anyway, it was the price of success. By the summer of 1981, Wedtech was a thriving and self-confident concern. Net revenues in 1980 had amounted to $5.6 million, triple those of the year before. In 1981 revenues would reach almost $10 million. Down in the bowels of 595 Gerard a growing labor force was working on the $4 million options on the cooling kits, in addition to parts for the M-60 tank and jet engines, the bell cranks, and items for a number of other contracts from the early days. The company also won its first sizable competitive contract, to build suspension assemblies for the M-113. The suspension-kit contract was serious money—$7,195,000.

The last contract was stunning proof that Wedtech was a professional outfit that could stand on its own two feet. Or maybe it wasn't. For the last year John, Fred, and Mario had been assiduously courting one of the contract officers involved with the M-113 program, Gordon Osgood. When the company first sought the cooling kit, in late 1979, Osgood had been sent out from the Army's procurement office in Warren, Michigan, to look over the company. Often enough he happened to be around the plant at mealtime, and, according to testimony from Fred and Mario, he proved amenable to being taken out to some of the tony locales they had begun to frequent, such as Windows on the World, atop the World Trade Center. Osgood had seen fit to tell the Army that Wedtech was fully qualified to build the cooling kits.

In the course of one of their meals, Mario testified, Osgood mentioned that he had hired a patent lawyer to help with several patents he had developed for a company he ran on the side. He let drop the lawyer's name; he left John and Mario with a copy of the lawyer's bill. The two were as yet largely unfamiliar with the protocol of bribery, but this was explicit enough. There were a few more bills, totaling, Mario stated, "under $10,000." Each time he received a bill Mario discreetly sent off a check to the lawyer.

Starting in January, according to a federal indictment filed against Osgood, Wedtech began sending checks to the Army officer's company, Multi-Mac, generally $3000 to $4000 a month. Osgood, it is alleged, responded with favorable surveys every time Wedtech applied for another piece of the M-113. The armored personnel carrier was the most common vehicle in the Army, and the retrofit program had a potential value of hundreds of millions of dollars. Osgood's most valuable service, according to Mario, was persuading his superiors in 1981 or early 1982 to place the options on the suspension assembly into the 8(a) program. There it would be—and indeed was—safely Wedtech's forever. Osgood was a meal ticket worth tens of millions of dollars.

He was also an educational experience. Osgood was Wedtech's first military man, the first crack in the implacable old-boy network that handed out the goodies in the Pentagon. John had always believed that the whole world was dead set against him, and he harbored a special grudge against the Grummans and the Sikorskys and all the other giant contractors who seemed to be conspiring to keep little Wedtech in its place. John's bitterness had infected the entire company. Bernie Ehrlich, the military man, corroborated John's fears, and Bob Wallach, the worldly lawyer, swallowed them without a murmur. Wedtech would never get into that inner circle by itself, John thought; that's why you needed a barracuda like Osgood to tear off a chunk of something good. Osgood—or Addabbo or Wallach or LAMA—was the only way to right the balance.

And the fact is that John was right. There may no marketplace in the free world quite so corrupted by logrolling, backscratching, and outright collusion as the one in which the U.S. government purchases military products. The allegations of favoritism that the Wedtech boys were making, and that Bob Wallach was forwarding to the White House, may have been the merest of rationalizations, but what they would not have been is shocking. The Pentagon procurement system is a competitive process in which, according to a 1981 government study, 6 percent of the dollars are awarded after competitive bids. The other 94 percent, which comes to over $150 billion, is handed out after a political competition in which rival contractors struggle for advantage.

The Boeings and the Sikorskys didn't sit around waiting for the results of fly-offs. They made friends, in Congress and the Pentagon, and they rewarded them handsomely. John, and even more, Mario, had begun to glimpse this process during their forays to Washington. Here was Representative Addabbo, a liberal Democrat who made fine speeches about the need to cut military spending, raking in tens of thousands of dollars at campaign time from Long Island contractors whose interests he defended in the Pentagon. The really big defense firms gave congressmen weekends at hunting lodges and free vacations to "inspect" military hardware all over the country. Wedtech didn't have a hunting lodge, and couldn't very well offer an all-expenses-paid round trip to the South Bronx; all it could offer was campaign contributions.

But what was even worse was that John, Fred, and Mario were not members of the club. They were, after all, two Hispanics and a Rumanian Jew whose military background consisted of a stint peeling potatoes in South Korea and service in the anti-British terrorist underground. They were outsiders, and they always would be. The big contractors, the ones with the hunting lodges and the women, were like giant veterans' associations, stocked with ex-military types fresh from jobs with the Pentagon. And the revolving door made the whole system go. The revolving door was indeed the accurate metaphor for the system. High-ranking Pentagon officials, or even low-ranking accountants, were fully expected to retire and quadruple their salary by working for one of the big contractors whose interests they had, only a short time before, been subordinating to those of the public. And in the struggle for the soul of that colonel running the procurement, who was going to beat out the colonel's old comrade-in-arms?

"Defense Boondoggle Systems" was the title that Air Force official and Pentagon critic A. Ernest Fitzgerald gave the procurement market. It was a system based on co-option. If you had enough money, you could buy all the co-option you needed. As Wedtech was bidding for the engine contract, to take only one example, Hughes Aircraft was winning a contract to build the Maverick missile for the Air Force. Hughes then hired two hundred former high-ranking Air Force officers and civilians to work on the Maverick missile contract it had just won. Two weeks after the Air Force's director of testing retired, in August 1982, Hughes announced that it had hired him, too.

Thus the lesson of Gordon Osgood: you could buy your way into the system. You could get in by the back door. Just as you could find a congressman to take your money and do your bidding, so you could find a military man. In buying Osgood, Wedtech was only imitating its betters, though in its typically unrefined manner. Everyone in the defense business knew that you got ahead by playing the game. Wedtech had to be resourceful enough to invent a game of its own.

But Wedtech didn't have any friends in the Army who could help with the engine contract, so it needed friends who could lock the intransigent Dr. Thomas Keenan in the old half-nelson. Those kinds of friends lived in Washington. Mario Biaggi's name meant nothing to the Army, and in any case he wasn't willing to stick his neck out in public. Joe Addabbo, on the other hand, meant a very great deal to the Pentagon. Over the years the Wedtech executives and their wives would give over $20,000 to Addabbo's re-election campaigns, and on Election Day Mario would even hire fleets of cars to ferry volunteers across the district.

Bernie Ehrlich came up with a more indirect approach to the Chairman. Ehrlich's superior in the National Guard was Vito Castellano, an ancient buddy of Addabbo's. Castellano, who had a desk and a phone in the congressman's office, considered his access a key resource in the consultancy deals he had with a number of defense contractors. In 1979 Ehrlich had asked John and Fred for money with which to compensate

Castellano and was given $3000 in cash. Castellano, in turn, made sure that the Wedtech boys had Addabbo's ear whenever they needed it.

Friends and relatives of powerful politicians could always count on a check from Wedtech, however tenuous the relationship. At roughly the same time that the company was enlisting Wallach in the holy crusade, David Epstein was getting in contact with Dicky Dyer, a fellow member of the Harvard class of 1939. In his home state of New Jersey, Dyer claims, "I'm literally known as Mr. Republican"; he concedes, however, that his appeal to Wedtech was based on a distant relationship to George Bush, which he was not modest about advertising. "I'm the older brother of the kid sister who married the older brother of George Bush's wife," as Dyer puts it. Dyer had caused Bush aides occasional heartburn over the years by allegedly making free with this slender tie.

In May, Dyer became a part-time consultant to Wedtech, at a rate he recalls as $250 a week. He had the prudence not to contact the White House on Wedtech's behalf, but later in the summer he used his Mr. Republican credentials to persuade two New Jersey Republican representatives, Christopher Smith and James Courter, to write to Army Secretary John O. Marsh, Jr., on Wedtech's behalf.

Throughout the spring and summer Wedtech bombarded Marsh and other top civilians in the Army with letters and telephone calls from supporters on Capitol Hill, most of whom, like Smith and Courter, did not even have Wedtech employees as constituents. Representative Manuel Lujan of New Mexico was happy to write a letter on behalf of his fellow Hispanics. Representative William Dickinson of Alabama, a member of the Armed Services Committee, wrote another letter. And so did Representative Addabbo and Wedtech's most powerful new friend, the recently elected New York senator, Alfonse D'Amato.

Over the years Senator D'Amato would become Wedtech's most dogged and most visible ally on Capitol Hill. He never tired of badgering civil servants on the company's behalf, and he never thought to hand off the work, as Mario Biaggi did, to someone else. D'Amato was a hyperactive, pop-eyed man in aviator glasses who loved to shout into telephones and bang on desks and slap backs and cut deals. He liked badgering the government on behalf of a constituent; that, as he understood it, was what political representation was all about. He was like a shameless operator in a David Mamet play, save that he was a U.S. senator. He was everybody's idea of a New Yorker.

D'Amato may have been the last true machine politician in the Senate, though he hailed from a very unorthodox machine. Political machines, such as Tammany Hall or the Pendergast gang in Kansas City or Mayor

Richard Daley's disciplined army in Chicago, have traditionally been Democratic and largely Irish; they took root in large, older cities. Al D'Amato learned his politics in probably the nation's only Italian Republican suburban machine, the Nassau County organization run by the county executive, Joseph Margiotta.

The Margiotta organization was a reincarnation of Tammany Hall without the Thanksgiving turkeys delivered to widows and orphans. It was a middle-class machine in a middle-class community. County employees were expected to kick back 1 percent of their income to the party. Promotions depended on party loyalty, and patronage was freely dispensed to friends and family. Firms that wanted to do business with the county government were expected to pay off political leaders. One of the recipients was Margiotta himself, D'Amato's mentor, who was eventually convicted and sent to jail for his role in the shakedown. The grand jury that indicted Margiotta concluded that the scheme would not have worked without the knowledge and involvement of D'Amato, then supervisor of the town of Hempstead. D'Amato was not indicted, and there was no indication that he himself had taken money.

For a long time, this was to be the story of D'Amato's career, lived at the edge of an endless series of investigations that never engulfed him. After a completely unexpected victory over a weak field in the 1980 Senate race, D'Amato proceeded to a career in the nation's highest deliberative body, swapping favors, cutting deals, and playing the angles like a crapshooter. He thought nothing of calling up a Cabinet secretary to make sure that a friend received a coveted job. He let the White House know that his vote on crucial issues would have to be purchased with favors—not personal favors, but political ones, normally involving funds for New York State. No favor, no vote: it was a standing threat that earned D'Amato the nickname "Senator Shakedown."

D'Amato was New York's fiercest advocate, but exactly who in the state received his favors depended on who gave them. He used his position as chairman of the Senate banking subcommittee on securities to obstruct or temper legislation opposed by investment banks, including efforts to limit the use of junk bonds in corporate takeovers. He blocked efforts by commercial banks to expand into the securities field. And the brokerage houses, in turn, gave D'Amato over $500,000 for his re-election effort, according to a count made by *The Wall Street Journal*. The firm of Drexel Burnham alone gave over $70,000, much of it at a fund raiser requested by D'Amato himself. Another portion came days after he watered down his own antitakeover legislation. The timing, he said, was "absolutely coincidental."

What makes D'Amato so unusual is his candor about the barter system, and the brutal directness of the exchange; anyone, it seems, can have his vote for a price. Yet even though D'Amato's style comes from the Nassau County machine, his is only the most blatant expression of a general phenomenon. As Brooks Jackson wrote in *Honest Graft: Big Money and the American Political Process,* "The system of money-based elections and lobbying rewards those who cater to well-funded interests." Democrats every bit as much as Republicans have discovered that a congressional seat can be a lifetime posting, since political action committees for every conceivable interest stand ready to contribute thousands of dollars to the campaign fund—as long as the congressman makes the right vote. Once upon a time lobbyists slipped envelopes into congressmen's pockets in the secrecy of the cloakroom. Now they do their purchasing in full view of the public by way of campaign contributions.

D'Amato appears to have understood instinctively what Mario Biaggi, Robert Garcia, and Joseph Margiotta did not: if you don't take it for your personal use, you're not corrupt. D'Amato has used his power to enrich his brother's law firm, to employ his father, to bring a swimming pool funded by the Department of Housing and Urban Development to the middle-class, all-white suburb where he was born and raised, and to swing projects toward his cronies. All that comes under the heading of old-fashioned machine politics. But when he goes back to Long Island, he stays with his parents. It is his political station, not his economic station, that he yearns to improve. And he has thus far remained unscathed, despite his continual proximity to wrongdoing.

It was Mario Biaggi who first delivered Senator D'Amato for Wedtech. Back in 1980 Biaggi had been among the most prominent conscripts of Democrats for D'Amato, a group of conservative Democrats hostile to D'Amato's opponent, Elizabeth Holtzman, a liberal. A Biaggi aide ran the organization. Bernie Ehrlich had even had the foresight to do some volunteer work for the campaign, in exchange for which D'Amato appointed Ehrlich his "military adviser," a title that added a few stripes to Ehrlich's beloved decorations without entailing much serious work. He also made Ehrlich's daughter his assistant press secretary.

More important, Mario Biaggi could call on his senatorial friend and fellow Italian any time he wanted. Almost as soon as D'Amato had assumed office, Ehrlich complained to his chief aide, Michael Hathaway, about Wedtech's treatment at the hands of Avco, and Hathaway relayed Ehrlich's complaint to an SBA official. Then in early April, with Wedtech marshaling its forces to agitate for an audit of its bid, John, Mario, and

Colonel Ehrlich flew down to Washington and convened in Biaggi's office. Biaggi heard them out, and then, for the first of many times, called Senator D'Amato to say that he was sending the Wedtech boys across the Hill to his office.

The meeting that ensued was typical of those which were to come. The three walked over to D'Amato's office, met briefly with the senator, and were then turned over to Hathaway. The Wedtech officials aired their grievances about Dr. Keenan and Avco and the rest of the enemies' list. Soon after the meeting, D'Amato called Army Secretary Marsh to express his concern; Hathaway called lower-level Army officials. On April 16 D'Amato put his signature to a lengthy letter, written by Hathaway and Ehrlich, rehashing Wedtech's sorry treatment and throwing in a pointed, if irrelevant, comment about "President Reagan's views for the vital role of small business in our economic recovery."

That was the great thing about Alfonse D'Amato—he wasn't reluctant to throw his considerable weight around. He wanted to be in the loop, and Wedtech kept him there. Hathaway never seemed altogether thrilled to hear from Ehrlich, but Ehrlich kept in touch with him anyway, and sent him copies of Wedtech's letters to officials in the Army and the SBA. And in August, with everyone getting more and more desperate for an audit, and Ken Cribb from Ed Meese's office barely holding the fort, John, Mario, and Bernie Ehrlich paid a return visit to the senator to plead for more help. D'Amato came through again by calling officials in the Army and the SBA—presumably Secretary Marsh and Administrator Michael Cardenas—as well as his fellow members of the Wedtech congressional bloc.

By the summer of 1981, with Mario hopping back and forth on the shuttle with Bernie Ehrlich in tow, moving between the SBA and the Army and Capitol Hill, Wedtech was making its influence felt. The SBA was a staunch ally, and the Army was momentarily halted. But it still wasn't enough. The Army had to be turned around on the audit, and pressure from Wedtech's congressional front, and from Ed Meese's office, hadn't yet done the job. In fact, the Army was backpedaling, but no one knew that. Wedtech needed strength from another quarter. At the decisive moment, it arrived.

Wedtech was always willing to pay its friends to go that extra step beyond nonpartisan help. Since the previous year the company had not only been paying for its membership in LAMA, the lobbying organization, but supplementing the meager income of its president, Stephen Denlinger, with small and irregular payments. Denlinger, who had succeeded Jose Aceves, had introduced Wedtech to his organization's chairman, Ferdinand de Baca, and to its "special adviser," Philip Sanchez, both of them prominent Republicans. By early 1981 Wedtech was paying stipends to all three of them, effectively converting LAMA into a private, undisclosed, lobbying group.

Soon after the election, de Baca had formed the Hispanic Coalition for Economic Recovery, an organization that supported the President's proposed economic package. The group had taken out a quarter-page ad in *The Washington Post*, extolling the President's program, and Denlinger had prevailed on Wedtech to pay for it. In March, Philip Sanchez started making contacts with the White House Office of Political Affairs on Wedtech's behalf, citing the company's support for the administration and lauding John Mariotta as a made-in-heaven photo opportunity for the President. Nothing came of Sanchez's suggestion for another year, but Denlinger and de Baca were also working to convince White House officials that Wedtech could be an important ally.

Their first triumph was persuading an official in another White House body, the Office of Public Liaison, to sign a letter, written by Denlinger, to Secretary Marsh, extolling Wedtech as a paragon of minority enterprise. But Denlinger eventually wound up seeking help from the same source as Sanchez had: the Office of Political Affairs, and the pudgy, ill-kempt political mechanic of whom the office was a personal extension, Lyn Nofziger.

Lyn Nofziger was the first Reagan disciple. He predated even Ed Meese. A former reporter with the Copley newspaper chain, Nofziger had earned his stripes in the Goldwater campaign before joining Ronald Reagan's staff, in early 1965, as Reagan prepared to run for governor of California. In manner Nofziger remained the old-fashioned newspaper hack—a friendly slob who drank and smoked and swore, a gimlet-eyed character who knew the price of everything, if not necessarily the value of anything. Like a lot of reporters, he loved politics as a form of combat rather than as a symposium in public policy. "He was a Richard Nixon conservative," says Ed Rollins, another Republican politico of long standing. "Lyn's loyalties were to Reagan first, conservative Republicans second, and the conservative movement third."

Lyn Nofziger was one of the few who never strayed far from the fold, though he had never been easy to live with. He was fired from Reagan's staff in 1968, then joined the Nixon White House the following year as assistant for congressional relations. The year after that he was made deputy chairman of the Republican National Committee and was sent back to California in 1972 to make sure that Nixon carried the state. This act of exile had the fortuitous effect of sparing Nofziger any involvement in the Watergate break-in and cover-up, though in 1973 a memo surfaced in which Nofziger suggested that the newscaster Chet Huntley be threatened with economic harm unless he temper his critical comments on Nixon.

Unlike Meese, unlike many of the Reagan followers who professed to despise government, Nofziger was genuinely bored and disgusted by the business of governing, and after Nixon's victory he remained in California and opened a public relations firm. But Nofziger also had no aptitude for business, and he returned to Reagan when the governor began training his sights on the White House in 1975. The following year he became the first executive director of Reagan's exploratory campaign committee, Citizens for the Republic, thus making him, in effect, the first paid member of the Reagan presidential campaign.

In those days Reagan was still a lonely voice in the wilderness of the right, a crank with a motley following of Liberty Lobbyists and millennialists and kooks from the edge of the edge. Mainstream Republicans laughed him off when they weren't casting nervous glances over their shoulder at the Huns gathering at his side. He was a crusader rather than a candidate, and only the true believers stood with him. It was a faith that both Reagan and his followers, who were pleased to call themselves Reaganauts, were to carry with them into the White House. It was a faith whose highest virtue was loyalty to the cause; above all, loyalty to the man who embodied the cause.

Loyalty was the one thing Lyn Nofziger did believe in. After years with the paranoid Nixon, Nofziger had developed the instincts of a chamberlain in the court of the Borgias. There was something almost gleefully vindictive about his manner. Among members of the press he was known for handing out seats on the campaign plane as gifts for positive coverage, and for shielding the candidate from serious or impromptu questioning. Six weeks before the election he was quoted as telling a roomful of campaign workers, "I see certain people here who were for Ford, certain who were for George Bush, and other people I don't like. This is the way I feel: I'll love you until November 4, and then I'll be out to get you."

Like Meese, Nofziger had almost become an extension of the President. Where Meese was the librarian of Reagan's ideas, Nofziger was the archivist of his campaigns. He knew every pledge that Reagan had ever made, every Republican lady who had stuffed envelopes, every city official who had discreetly made sure that the campaign rally went off without a hitch. "He was also," says Rollins, "the hater of the group—and I

mean that in a positive way. He was the guy who remembered who
screwed who, who didn't want to be a delegate in 'seventy-six. He was the
scorekeeper. Lyn was someone who believed, if blacks came out in support, you took care of your blacks. You don't take care of NAACP blacks
or Jimmy Carter's blacks. You took care of the ones who supported you.''

After the 1980 election, when every right-winger on the continent was
converging on Washington to join the millennium, Nofziger prepared to
go back home to California. For him, the fun part was over. But James
Baker, the new chief of staff, shrewdly recognized that he could use
Nofziger to protect himself from "movement conservatives," who had
already begun to prate that Baker was a mole from the camp of the
moderates. Nofziger, on the other hand, was the much-loved Yogi Bear
of the right. Baker asked Nofziger to stay on in Washington as the
scorekeeper, or, rather, as Saint Peter at the pearly gates of Reaganism.
Nofziger would decide who among those thousands of aspirants deserved a place in the firmament of the administration, and where. With
the fossil record of Reaganism at his fingertips, Nofziger would ensure
that no loyalist was overlooked and no Johnny-come-lately unduly rewarded.

Every administration, of course, has its scorekeeper. Richard Nixon
had Charles Colson; even post-Watergate good shepherd Jimmy Carter
had Hamilton Jordan keeping watch over the flock. Every administration
has a vast personnel apparatus as well. But never, at least in recent
memory, had there been an office in the White House officially dedicated
to the distribution of patronage and spoils. One can well imagine Richard Nixon organizing an Office of Political Affairs, and then trying to
keep it secret. But candor about partisanship was part of the new atmosphere Reagan had created. The Jimmy Carter era of Christian humility
was over; America didn't want its leaders to get too schoolmarmish about
the uses of power.

Nofziger relished his reputation as a brutal infighter and political
mechanic. He was the street fighter in the midst of Nancy's china and the
President's opulent soirées, the flash of the Nixon knife in the Reagan
parade. Nofziger was proud of his association with Nixon, and he had
even installed the new office in the suite of rooms in the Old Executive
Office Building to which Richard Nixon had retreated in the final days of
his presidency. Intellectually, Nofziger was a know-nothing; but he fit in
perfectly with the ideologues whose transcendent certainty of their own
rightness made them view politics as a struggle between truth and false-
hood. Revolutions have need of men like Nofziger.

The Office of Political Affairs quickly became the jam-packed ante-oom of the Reagan administration. The White House aide Michael Deaver referred to it as "the Star Wars Bar." "Everybody who had ever been one of those wild-eyed Reaganauts for so long," says Michele Davis —who was put in charge of "political clearances"—"that was the office they felt they could get a clear shot out of." Loyalists milled around with their résumés, dropped by to use the phones, commandeered corners of the few available desks. And Nofziger was the switchboard. Every day Cabinet officers would call up and Nofziger would thumb through his files in search of the deserving candidate. The fundamental decisions were made by the troika—Meese, Baker, Deaver—but what became known as "the Nofziger hold" guaranteed the scorekeeper a forty-eight-hour period to contemplate a nominee and run the name past the clerics of the right.

Nofziger enjoyed a watered-down version of the power one associates with the director of the secret police. He knew everything about everyone, and literally hundreds of middle-level officials in the Reagan administration were personally beholden to him. He had his own informants, known as "the Nofziger network," composed largely of the executive assistant types who normally serve Cabinet-level officials directly, and know more about what goes on in their agency than the boss does. Every month or so the loyalists would be called into the home office for a debriefing; that was how Nofziger kept score and ensured that the agency heads did not become "captives" of "official Washington." Nofziger couldn't get the Cabinet head fired, much less arrested for ideological deviation, but he could encourage his contacts. This appears to be precisely what happened at the SBA, where network member Robert Turnbull, the man whom Kenneth Cribb had contacted, would turn against two different administrators in order to advance the White House interests.

When Stephen Denlinger of LAMA succeeded in making contact with the Office of Political Affairs, he was turned over, as a figure of very little account, to the liaison with "ethnic groups," Pier Talenti. A wealthy businessman, Talenti had volunteered his services, and was enjoying the modest taste of power that came with his title and his desk and his proximity to real heavyweights. An Italian, he was the closest thing the office had to an "ethnic," so he was asked to handle minority groups and other such chaff. Around the office he was known as "the Dorkmaster." He was a little bit of a nuisance and a little bit of a joke, but nobody told him to stop what he was doing.

Denlinger spoke to Talenti in July, and implored him to go to Wedtech to see for himself what a splendid beneficiary of administration largesse it would be. On August 17, with the SBA still sitting on the Army's request to yield up the engine contract, and with the pilot program scheduled to expire in six weeks, Talenti became yet another visitor to the Wedtech dream factory. He was moved; he was impressed; he was energized.

Talenti returned to Washington ready to flex his muscles. Ed Rollins, then Nofziger's deputy, recalls Talenti mentioning Wedtech "a couple of times," but does not remember Talenti asking him for permission to act on the company's behalf. Soon after returning, Talenti phoned the Army general counsel, Delbert Spurlock, one of the few blacks to have supported Reagan since the dark ages of 1976, to press for an audit. Then he did something much more dramatic than anyone from Meese's office had. On August 28 Talenti convened a meeting in his office with three Army officials and told them that Wedtech deserved a chance.

Robert Stohlman, a deputy assistant secretary in the Army's procurement office, later testified that the Talenti meeting turned the Army around. His office had resisted the Congress, had resisted the SBA, but it wasn't prepared to stand up to the White House. Stohlman had been ready to release a competitive solicitation for the engine contract as soon as the SBA relaxed its grip, but now he and his superior agreed to grant Wedtech its wish. On September 15, an Army official formally notified the SBA that the Army would conduct an audit and would overlook the expiration of the pilot program.

It was a small concession but a fatal one. Once the Army conceded that Wedtech's $38 million bid merited serious discussion, the company had only to split the difference between itself and TSARCOM. When a pair of technicians from the St. Louis procurement office visited the Bronx, they found that Wedtech had neither the equipment nor even the building with which to undertake the engine contract, though they conceded that, given enough time, Wedtech could finish the job. An audit team found itself frustrated by Wedtech's lack of detailed pricing or budget information, and concluded that $6 million of its $39 million bid could not be justified. What the auditors apparently meant was that even Wedtech could build the engines for $33 million. But that wasn't how Wedtech saw it. As far as John, Fred, and Mario were concerned, the Army had just conceded that $33 million, not $19 million, was the fair market price. All they had to do now was force the bastards in St. Louis to face the truth.

Over the next several months Wedtech's consultants laid siege to official Washington in an all-out effort to have Keenan fired or overruled. The Army, however, was still giving ground by inches, and Keenan stayed put. What was more important, though, was that Wedtech had succeeded in blending its own ambitions into the political objectives of the White House. It was a cause worth adopting. In late October, Philip Sanchez had finally obtained the meeting with Lyn Nofziger he had been seeking almost since the outset of the administration. Talenti could start the ball rolling, but only Nofziger could get it somewhere. The two men spoke of Hispanic initiatives generally and Wedtech specifically. Sanchez mentioned the interest shown earlier by the Office of Public Liaison. And this time, he penetrated Nofziger's consciousness deeply enough so that Nofziger sent a note to Elizabeth Dole, director of Public Liaison, referring to his chat with Sanchez, and suggesting they work together on "the South Bronx idea."

Nofziger would not have needed much prompting on Wedtech's symbolic significance. Here, after all, were poor people in the inner city who wanted to make it on their own, just as the President said they should and could. Here were minorities who believed in the system. Better still, they were Hispanics. An emerging Republican doctrine had it that, while blacks had become slaves of the welfare state, and thus virtual wards of the Democratic Party, Hispanics had the sort of entrepreneurial values and conservative personal morals typical of new immigrant groups. They were natural Republicans, if only they knew it, and they were rapidly becoming key voting blocs in Texas, Florida, and California. It was Nofziger's job to make precisely this sort of calculation.

Perhaps most important of all, Wedtech was in the South Bronx, the symbolic battleground for the competing orthodoxies of Republicans and Democrats. In 1977, when President Carter had visited bombed-out Charlotte Street, he had promised to reverse the neighborhood's decline, but his program had vanished into a bureaucratic thicket. Before Ronald Reagan the candidate had made a point of visiting the same block, on August 5, 1980, he had spoken to a meeting of the National Urban League and for the first time endorsed Jack Kemp's urban enterprise zone. Once in the South Bronx he had ridiculed President Carter and insisted that tax incentives to the private sector, rather than federally funded housing programs and jobs programs and training programs, would lift the ghetto from its plight. A crowd had gathered across the street to chant "You ain't going to do nothing," and "Go back to California." Reagan got himself into a shouting match and fled in confusion. It was a bad scene. But the President had made a pledge, and it was also Lyn Nofziger's job never to forget a presidential promise.

EIGHT

EICHL

An Anatomy of Influence

BY THE FALL of 1981, when the White House was discovering Wedtech's value as an ideological marketing tool, Mario Moreno began to feel exploited. It was he who had saved the company by proposing the bookkeeping fraud, and he never quite got over the fear that it would be exposed. He was now coordinating the company's expanding Washington contacts. He had helped to make Wedtech a $10 million company, yet he himself remained a consultant; he had raised his fee from $150 a day to $250 a day. In August, Mario told John and Fred that he wanted a full-time salary and some ownership of the company. They agreed. Mario would receive a salary of $80,000 a year, and Conchita would get $35,000 for a no-show job at the security firm they had started, Bronx Boro Security. Mario and Conchita could finally afford to stop giving the Saturday night dances. More important, John and Fred awarded Mario a 9 percent ownership of the company. John and Fred, in turn, reduced their ownership to 45.5 percent each. The change in ownership was not, of course, disclosed to the SBA.

Mario was now earning more money than John or Fred, whose joint income was limited by a clause in the Economic Development Administration loan to a total of $90,000. John bitterly resented the limit; he felt that he deserved a lot more. Fred, too, felt that Wedtech was making everybody rich but himself. It was time to find a way to take some more money out of the company. Over the past several years the two had gotten around the EDA covenant by siphoning off small sums from the company. They had established a clandestine account, FHJ Associates, operated by Ceil Lewis. The initials stood for Fred, Helen (Fred's wife), and John. They had paid themselves only a few thousand dollars a year apiece out of FHJ, most of it in the form of kickbacks from the firm that purchased Wedtech's scrap metal. The firm would overcharge, Wedtech would pay the whole amount, and the surplus would be kicked back. In Fred's mind kickbacks from suppliers occupied the same position in the universe as bribes to union leaders: they were just part of the order of things. Life was a deal. You did what you had to and what you could.

Now, however, John and Fred decided to open up the spigots. For years Fred had worked with a supplier named Henry Zeisel, who operated an equipment business out of New Jersey with his brother, Murray. In the late summer of '81, according to testimony by both Fred and Mario, Fred called up his old friend and asked him to pay a visit to the South Bronx. When Zeisel arrived, he and the three principals piled into the lucky Lincoln, and they drove around the Grand Concourse, the major thoroughfare near 595 Gerard. They stopped not far from the Bronx County Courthouse. Fred, with his habitual bluntness, told Zeisel that they wanted to take some money out of the company and would make it worth his while if he would submit inflated invoices for his equipment, then kick back the difference. Zeisel agreed. Over the previous eight months, according to the company's bank records, $500 had been deposited in the FHJ account. In the four months following the conversation with Zeisel, the numbers added up to $362,958.88.

Zeisel, according to testimony, was to become one of the great sources of Wedtech's secret wealth. He was also indicted for hiring a professional arsonist to torch a building. He was acquitted of the arson charge, then indicted once again; this time he was convicted of conspiring to drive down the prices of equipment sold at auction and of pocketing part of the proceeds of a private resale.

John and Fred now had money for the first time in their lives, and they both began spending it. They ate in expensive restaurants, stayed at fine hotels when they traveled, and indulged themselves as they had always wanted to. Fred took his honeys on cruises. John, who had felt so much shame and bitterness in his life, craved respectability; he used the money to build himself a house in Scarsdale. In fact, the house was in the neighboring, middle-class suburb of Yonkers, but John always said Scarsdale. It was a big ranch house on a quiet street. There was a pool in the back and a sunken living room and thick wall-to-wall carpeting and an air of neatness that bordered on the sterile. It wasn't so much a house as an idea of how to live.

All the hugger-mugger, the fugitive transfer of assets, the doctored papers, was taking place backstage; out in front, under the lights, Wedtech was performing its miracle play. In the letters sent from the LAMAsery to many of the leading figures in the administration, from Senator D'Amato to the SBA, from Representative Addabbo to the Army, and from Bob Wallach to Ed Meese, all in the first weeks of the new year, the imagery was always the same—little Wedtech, the defense contractor with the heart of gold, was being bullied by the Pentagon.

The symbolic high point of the Wedtech vision came on that blazing moment on the morning of January 19, 1982, when Ronald Reagan smiled on John Mariotta and said, "You were talking with the dope pusher . . ." Reagan's benediction had absolutely no practical effect on Wedtech's fortunes. Ed Meese was there, but was not moved to further action. John finally found Elizabeth Dole and handed her a letter restating Wedtech's case, but this too led to nothing in particular. The Army was not moved to surrender. But you couldn't visit the company without learning of the presidential laying-on of hands. A miracle had happened, and it lent further reassurance to the Wedtech visionaries that the company was destined for great things.

In the visible world, however, nothing changed for Wedtech. At a meeting a few days before John's sermon, the Army had made it clear that, audit or no audit, it wasn't going to budge. The previous month a TSARCOM pricing specialist had raised the fair market price from $19 million to $23.7 million in order to account for a year's worth of inflation, and perhaps also to counter charges of intransigence; but that was it. Only if Wedtech came down, or if the Small Business Administration made up the difference, would the Army award the contract. But that, said Administrator Michael Cardenas and Deputy Administrator Donald Templeman, was out of the question. The next day an Army official formally asked the SBA to close the gap or withdraw the contract from set-aside.

It was to be Lyn Nofziger, finally, who saved Wedtech's hide—but Nofziger would do it for money, not for his President. Nofziger was not a man for institutions: he hated memos and bureaucratic pettifogging, and the million little rules that make everyone in Washington count to ten and breathe deeply before taking a step. When he was told that he could bring only a few people over for a White House tour, he'd bring six. He refused to wear his White House pass. That was what people found refreshing about Nofziger. At the same time, he felt that he had lost the loyalty war to the cosmopolitan James Baker. Traditional Republicans were getting jobs while diehards pouted in the wings. As early as the fall Nofziger started to talk to friends about what he might do on the outside. Politics was the only thing he knew, except perhaps journalism.

But Nofziger had never made a nickel—like many of the worker bees of Reaganism, he believed in money but had no talent for business—and he was getting older, and his wife was ill. He was planning to hit the lecture circuit, where, as the first man out of the new administration, he could attain instant wealth by stringing together some anecdotes and a few off-color jokes into something vaguely resembling a speech. And then he was approached by a colleague from the 1980 campaign, a California media consultant named Mark Bragg. What Bragg proposed, essentially, was that Nofziger do what he was already doing, only less of it. Bragg would open a "public relations"—which is to say, lobbying—office, hire staff, find clients, and do all the dirty work; Nofziger would lend his mighty name and make a phone call or two to one of his good friends in the administration when the client needed a hand. He wouldn't have to know anything about public relations, of course, or the law or even the policy issues that might concern his clients. All he needed was his Rolodex. And he would make a fortune.

The only obstacle was the Ethics in Government Act, which had been passed in the post-Watergate atmosphere of 1978. At that already distant moment, when President Carter had been offering a return to civic virtue after years of Nixonian darkness, the act had been passed in the vain hope of slowing the revolving door through which White House officials passed to lucrative careers by using their influence and access on behalf of private clients. President Carter had, of course, been sent into igno-minious exile, and the atmosphere he had hoped to create had dissi-pated. When he became a private citizen Jimmy Carter built housing for the poor, but that was Jimmy Carter. In the Reagan era no stigma was attached to the pursuit of wealth. The revolving door was a fact of life, and Lyn Nofziger was the first high-ranking official of the new regime to enjoy its efficiency.

But Nofziger knew that he had to tread carefully because of the ethics law. Toward the end of 1981 Nofziger and an attorney, Martin Artiano, paid a visit to Fred Fielding, the White House legal counsel. Nofziger asked whether he was allowed to consider job offers before leaving the White House, and Fielding explained that he could not. That seemed to be all Nofziger wanted to know, but Fielding recalls giving him a copy of the memo for departing White House officials, which included an explanation of the Ethics in Government Act.

The act forbade office holders from entertaining job offers, so Nofziger kept Bragg at arm's length for the next few months. "He was very, very careful when he was leaving," says Ed Rollins. "He sort of got that side of it right." In January, Nofziger announced that he was leaving to form Nofziger & Bragg. The firm would bill at a rate of $400 an hour, as much as anyone in town; but, then, Nofziger had the most powerful friends in town. Over the years the firm would charge its corporate clients as much as $20,000 a month and $800 a day in expenses, often for only a few letters or phone calls. Senator Daniel Patrick Moynihan of New York would refer to these payments, in a committee hearing, as "a bloody outrage." But the clients were satisfied.

In mid-February, Stephen Denlinger of LAMA met with Bragg, and the two agreed that Nofziger & Bragg would take on LAMA as a client, though Wedtech would pay the bills. The retainer would come to $5000 a month. In exchange Bragg promised access to Nofziger's successor, Ed Rollins, and to Ed Meese and others. That was what it was all about: money for access. The retainer agreement was signed on March 8, 1982.

Before contacting Nofziger and Bragg, Denlinger had written a nine-page letter to the Army general counsel, Delbert Spurlock, setting out Wedtech's position on the pricing of the engine contract. Spurlock had responded by restating the Army's rationale for the $24 million figure. Denlinger had then written a six-page response to Spurlock's response. Both men were arguing the merits, and doing so with care and judgment. It was precisely the sort of exchange that consultants are theoretically supposed to have with government officials. Of course it was getting Wedtech nowhere, because as far as the Army was concerned, Wedtech had no business building those engines.

But that was where Nofziger & Bragg came in. Mark Bragg knew better than to write long memos to Delbert Spurlock. Instead, he met with Spurlock and told him that this was something the administration wanted. That was how Bragg almost always put his case, as if he and Lyn Nofziger had been hired by the White House rather than by their client. Nofziger was so close to Ed Meese and the White House crowd that officials at the distant edges of the universe had every reason to assume it was true. And Delbert Spurlock was a receptive audience. Because he was one of Reagan's blacks, Nofziger had seen to it that he got a good job. Spurlock, in turn, had made himself accessible to the Office of Political Affairs. Over the next several months Bragg would speak to Spurlock by phone three or four times, and meet with him on two occasions in the offices of Nofziger & Bragg.

But Mark Bragg was only a glorified advance man. He could hector, he could bullyrag, but whatever he did, his firepower was borrowed. At the end of March, Nofziger himself was trundled into battle like a giant artillery piece. First, Spurlock was summoned to the Office of Political Affairs, where Talenti told him that Nofziger would be calling Army Secretary Marsh to "indicate the presence of White House interest in contracting in the South Bronx where Welbilt is located." Nofziger phoned, as promised, later that day, just before Marsh was to meet with Army officials yet again over the engine contract. Marsh, however, was unmoved, and the Army decided to call on the SBA once again to remove the contract from 8(a).

It was now obvious that the White House itself would have to be engaged. On April 5, Nofziger met with his ancient friend and fellow traveler Ed Meese, and in the course of hashing over things generally made a point of reminding him of Wedtech's plight. Meese couldn't have needed much reminding, since in a note to Denlinger written six weeks earlier he had reassuringly written, "This Administration is very familiar with Welbilt." On April 8 Nofziger wrote Meese a memo about the company's problems with the Army which indicates the level at which he played. "I am sure," he noted, that Secretary Marsh "would listen carefully to [Defense Under Secretary Frank] Carlucci or Weinberger or Meese or even Reagan." After hitting the ritual note about satisfying the President's campaign pledge, Nofziger concluded, "Ed, I really think it would be a blunder not to award that contract to Welbilt. The symbolism either way is very great here."

What is noteworthy about this brief message was that its author, while acting as a paid shill, was able to speak to one of the most powerful men in the White House as one official to another. That, of course, is why his services were worth $400 an hour. Indeed, several months later the administration would call Nofziger out of retirement to help line up the loyalists for the controversial tax "reform" forced on it by moderate Republicans. His ex officio status allowed him to blur the distinction between the administration's projects and his own. Lyn Nofziger's interest became "the White House interest."

But Lyn Nofziger wasn't in government any longer, so he was walking on very thin ice. The Ethics in Government Act, which Fred Fielding had made a point of handing Nofziger a few months earlier, expressly barred officials from dealing with their former agencies—the White House, in this case—on matters of importance to the administration for a year after retirement. The April 8, 1982, letter, a jury would find many years later, violated the act. (The conviction was to be overturned on appeal.) What's more, Nofziger was inviting Meese to ignore Fielding's directive of the previous year, prohibiting officials from helping friends through the procurement process. Fortunately, Nofziger had found in Ed Meese a man incapable of recognizing a wrong as long as it was committed by one of his friends or by himself. Fielding's memo suggested that anyone receiving such a request for intervention must first refer it to Fielding's own office. Other White House officials had done, and would do, just that when asked to give Wedtech a boost. Meese simply referred the matter to his staff.

The previous November, Meese had acquired a new chief of staff, Jim Jenkins, a former Navy engineer who was trying, with very little success, to apply his sense of military discipline to the mass of paper that was the counselor's office. Among other things, Jenkins had told Meese that if Bob Wallach were to continue trotting in and out of Meese's office, without prior appointments, for his interminable discussions of the state of the world, Jenkins could not be responsible for his schedule. Meese, who apparently had never stopped to think that Wallach was absorbing hours of his time, was visibly irked, but agreed to tell Wallach to call before coming.

Jenkins received Nofziger's note and obtained Meese's blessing to pursue the matter. Jenkins says that he had no idea that the Army had a legitimate grievance against the company, that Meese's office had helped Wedtech the year before, or that Bob Wallach had anything to do with the company—this despite the fact that Meese had given Jenkins a Wallach memo on Wedtech several months earlier. Jenkins thus seems to have approached the vast tangle of the engine contract with a reality all of his own, clear and simple and completely wrong.

On April 16 Jenkins sent a note to the Cabinet Affairs officer, Craig Fuller, stating that Nofziger had asked Meese to work on the Army for Wedtech. After suggesting several courses of action, Jenkins wrote, "Quite possibly, we should do nothing at all. Do you have existing guidance on this kind of thing?" Fuller, a consummate insider viewed with some suspicion by the Reaganauts, was well aware of the Fielding policy and believed in playing by the rules. He returned the Jenkins note the next day with a message in the corner: "I strongly recommend no

White House action be taken." Jenkins himself wrote his comment underneath: "Too late." And he plowed ahead.

"I was willing to stay out," says Jenkins, "but when I found that this was not a selection process, that all they wanted was to put together a financial package, then it was no longer anything I thought Craig Fuller would care about." A certain mistiness obscures the tale at this point. Jenkins had presumably learned this version of events from Bragg, but the Nofziger letter gave the clear impression that the Army was trying to opt out of the "selection process." Jenkins might have called the Army, but didn't. He saw Spurlock regularly, but apparently Spurlock never explained to him how things stood. The political calculus, Jenkins says, meant nothing to him. Nofziger, however, was an old friend, and he was eager to help. Nofziger & Bragg, he took it, represented LAMA, not Wedtech; Bragg had given him that impression. And so, plodding through the fog of ignorance and half truth and forgetfulness, Jim Jenkins hauled Wedtech up to the top of the hill.

The Army was now backing and filling. After it decided at the end of March to call on the SBA to surrender the contract, nothing happened. The Army was confirming its decision without acting on it. Two weeks later, at the same time that Jim Jenkins was writing to Craig Fuller, it was agreed to notify LAMA, the SBA, and the various interested members of Congress that the Army would have the engine contract released for competitive bidding. Assistant Secretary of the Army Dr. J. Raymond Sculley instructed his staff to wait for a week in order to give the politicians a chance to let off some steam, and then issue a request for proposals. That would have been the point of no return. And again, nothing happened. St. Louis was instructed to hold off. On the bottom of a May 3 memorandum detailing the critical shortage of engines for electric generator sets, Under Secretary of the Army James Ambrose wrote, "I thought this was settled. What happened?" And two weeks later an officer from Dr. Sculley's office responded, "Mr. Spurlock continues to place a hold on the competitive solicitation." Spurlock has denied that he did any such thing, but apparently Jenkins or Bragg had won him over.

Meanwhile, Wedtech's crew of sappers had been working on the SBA. Back in February, Administrator Michael Cardenas had been fired from the SBA after less than a year in office, an embarrassing admission by the administration that its sole high-ranking Hispanic couldn't cut it. "To say that he was hopelessly incompetent is to give him a compliment," says Tom Trimboli, formerly the chief investigator for the House Small Business Committee. The new administrator, James Sanders, was an insurance man from Southern California, which presumably meant that he understood the problems of small and minority business, and an old friend of the White House deputy chief of staff, Michael Deaver, which may not have hurt.

On April 22 Jenkins sent a letter to Sanders: "Ed Meese has asked me to look into the Welbilt problem . . . which has been too long on the back burner." Jenkins asked to have either Sanders or a subordinate come to the West Wing to brief him on the SBA's views. Sanders recognized a summons when he heard one, and decided to go himself. "It was," says Sanders, "the only time in my four years that the White House took an interest in anything at the SBA," with the exception of the time the administration tried to abolish it.

During the first week in May, Wedtech bore in on Sanders. On Monday, May 3, he accepted an invitation to lunch at Nofziger & Bragg. Sanders recalls it as a benign occasion. "There was never anything that Nofziger or Bragg did that was untoward. It was only 'Boy, I sure hope that thing can get put together, because it sure would be an important feather in the cap of the administration.' " Similarly, when he went to see Jenkins that Friday, Sanders recalls, Meese's aide simply "confirmed that the President was very desirous of doing something in the South Bronx, and this seemed like the ideal candidate." The following Monday Bragg brought in Denlinger, who had tried and failed to reach Sanders earlier to discuss the engine contract.

A few of the career people at the SBA, including Donald Templeman, the deputy administrator, took umbrage at the pressure. But Sanders was a political appointee, he was new to the job, and as he saw it the White House was asking him to help out a deserving member of the 8(a) portfolio in the South Bronx. In short order Wedtech had a new advocate at the very top of an agency critical to its prosperity. Sanders never left Wedtech's corner. Without him, the company would almost certainly have crashed long before it did.

And now the congressional stalwarts rose once again. At the end of April Bernie Ehrlich, who liked to hang around Senator D'Amato's office playing "military adviser," told D'Amato's aide, Mike Hathaway, that Wedtech was close to putting together the financing. The SBA would close some of the gap, as would additional funds from HUD. If the senator could call the White House and say that the company had the funding lined up, and if the White House could tell the Army to stop fooling around . . . Senator D'Amato called up Jenkins and told him, apparently, just that. Everything was coming together.

Perhaps the one source of institutionalized neutrality in the highly politicized Reagan White House was the office of the legal counsel. Fred Fielding was not a Reaganaut; he was a long-time Washingtonian fully imbued with the local sense of caution. When the equally careful Craig Fuller saw a copy of Jenkins' April 22 letter and realized that his advice had been disregarded, he forwarded a copy to Fielding with the note "How advisable is this?" Fielding recalls receiving the Jenkins letter and thinking "it was a lousy idea." An aide, H. P. Goldfield, sent a note back to Fuller, saying flatly that "the White House should not get involved," and advising Jenkins not to call a meeting of the various government agencies as he had planned. Fuller appears to have relayed the message to Jenkins; but in the contest between the rules of governance and the rules of politics, governance never had a chance. Jenkins called his meeting.

Wedtech had effectively succeeded in blurring the normal definition of "the rules." The company advanced, and the White House, for its own reasons, eagerly accepted, a formulation in which the rules meant the intransigence of self-serving bureaucracies like the armed forces, while "politics" referred to the sphere in which policy concerns, such as increasing employment in the South Bronx, could be recognized and promoted. This is called "bringing your agenda in line with the White House agenda." Thus, when Jim Jenkins convened a meeting of all the parties to the engine contract on May 19, he felt that he was going to advance the White House interests *and* champion a cause that needed assistance. He was going to knock heads for the public good.

The meeting, which was held in the White House basement, lasted only about half an hour, but it represented the greatest triumph to date of Wedtech's political power. The gathering resembled one of those scenes at the end of a bedroom farce when everybody finally appears onstage at once, all conflicts are resolved, and a happy ending is plucked from disaster. The role of the embittered but powerless guardians of the old order was played by the U.S. Army. Jenkins sat at one end of a long conference table; John and Mario sat at the other end, with Bragg nearby; and along the sides were Denlinger, Sculley, Spurlock, Templeman, and representatives from HUD and the Economic Development Administration. Jenkins says that he was surprised Bragg wanted to come; it was only then that he realized that the consultants represented Wedtech, not LAMA.

Jenkins opened the meeting by saying that the administration wanted to do what it could to help the South Bronx, that the Army agreed that Wedtech could build the engines, and there didn't seem to be any reason that the parties in the room couldn't work out the problem of financing.

Spurlock, Mario later testified, seemed to be taking Jenkins' admonitions in stride, but Dr. Sculley was grinding his teeth. "He looked as if he had been dragged in there like a little dog on a leash." Sculley complained about Wedtech's price. Mario then waved a sheaf of paper and said that Wedtech had brought its figure down by $5 million.

Jenkins decided that now was the time to knock heads. He cut the discussion off by saying, he testified, "that I was not going to stand for any bullshit." Nor would he "stand for any foot dragging or fogging up the issue . . . I wanted them to know that besides my knowing that I would be able to tell immediately if they were pulling this stunt, I wanted them to know that I wouldn't stand for it and that I would be talking to them directly, or their bosses about it, if I ran into evidence of such foot dragging." In the case of the intransigent Dr. Sculley, a political appointee, that meant Secretary Marsh, a good friend of Ed Meese's. Sculley would have had no reason to think that Jenkins was bluffing.

The Army now had no choice but to accept a financial package if Wedtech could put one together. It was the corner the Army had painted itself into when it had agreed to an audit the previous summer. HUD was willing to kick in some money, as was New York State, but only the SBA could make up most of the difference. Wedtech had been seeking from the SBA as much as $10 million in business development expenses (BDE). It was an insanely high figure, larger than the entire business development budget for the New York region. Earlier in the year, Donald Templeman had written to an Army official, "For us to make a multimillion-dollar grant to a single firm would, we believe, raise questions about our management of the 8(a) program as a whole." And then, in the course of the White House meeting, Templeman reported that the SBA was considering an offer of $3 million in BDE, as well as $2 million in advance payments, which would act as an interest-free loan.

Sanders is unrepentant about his decision—for it was his decision—to give the money to Wedtech, though it was several orders of magnitude larger than any such package the SBA had ever put together. "I'm not sure I wouldn't do the same thing today," he says, citing the large amount of BDE money that had to be spent before the end of the fiscal year. Templeman, however, has never denied that the agency simply bent before political pressure. Like the Army, he felt that Wedtech was the wrong company for the engine contract in the first place, and he scarcely saw the point of shoveling all the 8(a) program's eggs into one very rickety basket. At the Nofziger trial he was asked whether the specter of White House involvement had made the SBA agree to "do things that you otherwise would not have done." It had, he said. "I think we would not have gone along with the contract had it not been for Mr. Jenkins' interest."

After May 19 the SBA moved in whatever direction the White House joy stick indicated. On June 15, Jenkins, acting at Bragg's behest, telephoned Templeman to ask why the agency had not yet formally committed itself to the $5 million contribution. Templeman, who understood that resistance was pointless, hastily drew up a letter of commitment, which was signed by Sanders and sent off three days later. The letter stated that the SBA was "in receipt of" Wedtech's request for the $3 million grant and $2 million loan, and that, subject to certain conditions, the funds would be released. Unfortunately, the SBA was in receipt of no such thing, since Wedtech had never submitted a request for the money. It was one of those technicalities which had been overlooked in the headlong rush to do whatever had to be done. When the SBA discovered its mistake, Wedtech was asked to draw up the formal request, which it sent to the New York regional office ten days after the SBA had approved it. Sanders told a congressional hearing that he was "disappointed" at the sequence of events.

The Army continued to hope that the negotiations would collapse, but cooperation became inescapable. In mid-June Dr. Sculley, after further prodding from Senator D'Amato, notified Wedtech and the SBA that the Army would be willing to raise its fair market price as long as it could be assured of the additional financing discussed in the meeting. And after the SBA accepted a new Wedtech financing plan in early August, Sculley instructed TSARCOM to make "all possible efforts" to wrap up negotiations before the extension of the pilot program expired on September 30.

Everything could have come unraveled once again, since a sequence of audits disclosed that Wedtech's cost estimates were unrealistic, and that the engine contract stood a fair chance of bankrupting the firm. But by now the Army had stopped resisting. With what must have been a collective shrug of disgust, the Army raised its fair market price an additional $4 million, taking into account still more inflation, new contract specs, and some of Denlinger's heretofore ignored arguments about Chrysler. And that ended the stalemate. On September 13, 1982, Wedtech accepted the Army's offer of $27.7 million, and thereby ushered in a new era of staggering growth and suicidal ambition.

The President of the United States came very close to solemnizing Wedtech's smashing victory over the massed forces of the U.S. Army. On August 31 Bob Wallach, who in recent months had been limiting his memo output to exegeses of the administration's problems ("James

Watt's rhetoric imperilled and obscured his conduct and his goals. Secretary Haig's adamancy has lent fuel to a pacifist sentiment dormant in Europe since the 1950s . . ."), dashed off a jovial note to Jim Jenkins. Some time earlier, Wallach noted, "Ed and I spoke about a possible major media event, at Welbilt, including the President as a major show of commitment to the South Bronx, Urban Zones, minority contracts, self-help getting off welfare, free enterprise, and a legitimate list of worthwhile values which this company represents." Jenkins obviously took this advice to heart, since Jenkins wrote a note to Bragg, saying "I have suggested to Dole *(urged)* that the President go to the South Bronx, award the Certificate of Excellence *and* the Army contract." The Certificate of Excellence was an award the Pentagon was giving Wedtech for the quality of its work on the M-113, a stamp of approval of which John Mariotta felt even more proud than of the Presidential pat.

The award of the certificate and of the contract came and went without the President, but in late October Wedtech tried again. John had fired David Epstein, who had been in charge of refining his feverish incantations into coherent English, and whoever took over the job was more faithful than Epstein had been to John's speaking style. "It has been a joint venture between our silent partner God and the Ronald Reagans of our society. Only through the caring and assistance of those who are in positions to lend a helping hand can this miracle continue to manifest itself. If this penicillin could be injected into all our infested areas . . ."

Whether it was because of the penicillin or the deification of the President, a stop at Wedtech was actually placed on President Reagan's schedule. One of the dozens of new employees Wedtech was hiring to gear up for the engine contract, Tom Mullan, recalls coming up to 595 Gerard for an interview with Mariotta one Friday and finding Secret Service men climbing all over the property, installing telephones and cable. Everyone at Wedtech was braced for the visit. And then John received a call saying that at the last minute the President had been compelled to stay in Washington.

In early October Jim Jenkins sent his boss a note attached to a LAMA publication announcing Wedtech's receipt of the engine contract. Jenkins wanted to make sure that credit was going where it was due. "EM," he wrote, "though you cannot tell from reading any of this, your personal 'go-ahead' to me saved this project."

Meese says that the note was hyperbolic, and in speaking to the independent counsel he stated that he did not remember issuing a "go-ahead." Indeed, he did not really remember anything at all. For a man who lived on the plane of actuality, a man who served as unofficial deputy President, it was strange to note the fog in which he seemed to live, as if his mind were incapable of catching hold of anything solid. It was his boss, after all, who was supposed to have such difficulty with solid things. Could Meese himself have been equally misty?

The independent counsel could not, in the end, grant Meese his full portion of dither. As the counsel's report stated, "In view of (1) Mr. Meese's close personal relationships with Mr. Wallach and Mr. Nofziger; (2) the intense interest of those two individuals in Welbilt; (3) the written and oral communications from them to Mr. Meese; (4) Mr. Jenkins' various efforts on Welbilt's behalf; and (5) Mr. Jenkins' testimony that he discussed the matters with Mr. Meese, the independent counsel has concluded that Mr. Meese was aware of and sanctioned the actions of his staff in assisting Welbilt in the matters described above." This comment, says a member of the independent counsel's staff, should be taken as a way of saying that Meese is lying.

PART THREE

PART THREE

Going Public

NINE

NINE

Beautiful Dreamers

WEDTECH was now swelling to incredible proportions, like one of those tiny pellets that expand into a dinosaur when you drop it in water. After almost doubling its business to $10 million in 1981, the company had doubled once again, to $20 million, in 1982. And this wasn't even counting the engine contract. Wedtech had won a great plum for itself when it got the job to make parts for the armored personnel carrier. In April, while the Army was fending off the onslaught over the engine contract, it was also routinely agreeing to the SBA's decision to give the company a $13 million contract to manufacture more cooling kits. And in September, just as the smoke had finally cleared on the engines, Wedtech received another set-aside, this one for the suspension assemblies. This was the job that Gordon Osgood had allegedly maneuvered into the 8(a) program. The suspension kits were worth another $8.4 million.

The big headquarters building at 595 Gerard was frantic with activity. Downstairs, on the two lower floors, work was going on in three shifts, twenty-four hours a day. Upstairs, the growing management staff was spreading out among the offices on all four sides of the building's central courtyard. There was always a security guard in the foyer at the front entrance, for there were plenty of crazies and junkies in the neighborhood, and somebody, if not everybody, could be counted to work until the middle of the night. The main floor was up a flight of stairs. Beyond the reception area, on the left, was the coffee room where the employees could sit, and where Ceil Lewis often came with a cake or cookies. Then came Ceil's office, which was always locked, since all the FHJ money came through the safe in her office. Along the corridor were administrative offices, and then, in the big sunny room at the corner, the engineering staff, which kept up a nonstop gabble of Russian.

Along the back wall was the big computer room, with its NO SMOKING sign, and then, to the right again, a series of labs and small production rooms. Mario had a small office at the corner. Along the corridor that faced Gerard Avenue was the big conference room, with its long table and leather chairs. John and Fred were starting to smarten the place up. John had built himself a huge office, maybe twenty-five by eighteen feet, with a desk the size of an aircraft carrier and a big blue leather armchair. His office had a Xerox machine, a bar, thick carpeting, and dimmer switches for the lights. Picture windows looked out on the tiled courtyard.

Between John's and Fred's offices was a tiled bathroom with a shower and elegant faucets. Fred's office was not quite as large as John's, and his desk was normally obscured by papers, boxes of unopened cigars, and girlie magazines. Paintings that he'd bought leaned against the walls. The place was a pigsty, but that was how Fred liked it.

With the award of the engine contract, life at Wedtech took on a thrilling sense of possibility that must have differed very little from what the piratical band of wonks at Apple Computer, fired by a charismatic boss, felt when it fashioned the first Macintosh. The company was gearing up to do the impossible, which is probably the most electrifying thing a company can do.

It *was* impossible. In order to build the engine, Wedtech needed everything, including a manufacturing facility. The company had bought an abandoned dry-cleaning plant a few blocks down Gerard Avenue in which, it claimed, it would soon be bolting together six-horsepower engines. It's hard to believe that the Army could have taken Wedtech seriously. Tom Mullan, who quickly became production manager for the new contract, goggled the first time he was shown the new digs. "It was an old loft-type building that was protected by guard dogs that lived in there," he recalls. "You didn't dare go in there with those animals. There was debris all over the place. The clothes hanger–type equipment was there. There was no way in hell we could use that at the time."

In fact, the new plant proved beyond redemption, and Wedtech ultimately manufactured the engines at 595 Gerard and at another building it hastily leased several blocks away. Even in this building, on Bruckner Avenue, a leaky roof had made the upper floor uninhabitable, and 260 panes were missing from the windows. Not until the spring would this building be functional. Wedtech also had scarcely any engineers, scientists, or even skilled technicians. Mullan started making the rounds of aeronautics schools and local military contractors, including the infamous Avco. Since Wedtech lacked the ability to make the sophisticated dies needed to stamp out the parts for the engines, Mullan had to go to Germany to get them made. They started arriving the following summer, at approximately the time Wedtech had promised the Army it would complete the first few engines.

A whole new cadre of managers started to arrive. Mihai Soiman, a professor of thermodynamics from Rumania who arrived in the United States, speaking virtually no English, in 1982, was hired in May 1983 after ten hours of interviews, most of them with John. Soiman was to be the head of testing and, in effect, the chief scientist. He had come from a country numbed by decades of inertia, and within months after arriving in the land of the free and the home of the brave was invited to step aboard a rocket to the stars. It was an émigré's fantasy, and it practically blew his mind.

"It was impossible," he says, "to come from no engine background to build engines in the south of the Bronx. The idea was a crazy one. You need forty years of experience to build an engine. You need the technology. You need the pool of skilled labor. The idea was so exciting to me. They said, 'We have to have the first article in six months.' I told them it was impossible. They said, 'This is the building. Do you want to try?' I said, 'Why not?' "

Over the next year or so Soiman, Mullan, and other members of the new managerial class conjured up from nothing an engine division that ultimately delivered to the Army thousands of military-standard engines —extremely late but flawless. It was, in many ways, a noble experience. "What I found outstanding and I would say moving at Wedtech," Soiman recalls, "was that it was a Tower of Babel. There was the Anglo-Saxon group. There was the Hispanic group. There were blacks. Later, there were Russian engineers. And there were Indians in quality assurance. I cannot recall any conflict all this time."

• • • •

But of everything at Wedtech that was noble, marvelous, and inconceivable, there was nothing to compare with the coating technology. That John Mariotta, with his delusions of grandeur, should have stumbled across this alchemical process and its mysterious inventor, Dr. Eduard Pinkhasov, seems proof that the gods have a sense of humor, and an extremely cruel one at that.

Dr. Pinkhasov had joined Wedtech as an ordinary tool-and-die man in 1980. Fred claimed to have met him when he climbed into a cab Pinkhasov was driving, though John says that Wedtech's mad scientist had heard about the company on the Russian grapevine. As John recalls, Pinkhasov, then working on the shop floor, came to see him one day. Unfortunately, Pinkhasov's English was a good deal worse than John's. "He comes in," says John, "and says, 'I'd like to talk to you in regard to the coatings.' I says, 'The coatings? I don't make coats.' "

Flummoxed by this rejoinder, Pinkhasov went off and fetched an interpreter, who explained to John that the man had been a scientist in the Soviet Union, and had worked on a process that could bond metals even to such porous substances as paper or cloth. If John would agree, this assembly-line worker would perfect the technology right here at Wedtech and earn the company countless millions. A more rational businessman would have thanked Pinkhasov for his interest and instructed him to pursue his hobby on his own time. But John Mariotta was a believer in the miraculous. He agreed to give Pinkhasov a room and the help of some machinists in building the two-foot-square chamber in which, Pinkhasov explained, he would deposit a millimeter-thick layer of an ultra-hard metal on practically any material John could dream up.

The incredible thing about it was that Pinkhasov's alchemy actually worked. After several months of tinkering with his arc-vapor-deposition chamber, Pinkhasov began to coat paper and plastic and, more important, the inside of pipes and the outside of drill bits, with alloys like titanium nitride. He could give soft things the properties of hard things, and prevent hard things from losing their hardness. And he could do this in a little box in a factory in the South Bronx. Pinkhasov's coating process had absolutely nothing to do with anything else Wedtech did, but it carried the force of magic. When Bob Wallach was shown Pinkhasov's sample room that fateful April morning, he was floored, and neither he nor John ever quite picked himself up.

The Pinkhasov legend was born when, at some point in 1981, an FBI agent came to the South Bronx and was brought to John's office. He said that he wanted to see Pinkhasov. John, baffled, put him in the conference room with the scientist, who had always been rather evasive about his background. After the agent had satisfied himself, he returned to John's office and said, "Do you have any idea who that man is?"

"He's a tool-and-die maker," said John.

"Dr. Eduard Pinkhasov," said the agent, "was one of the most famous physicists in Russia." Apparently the federal authorities had lost track of him and, once they had confirmed his presence in the South Bronx, as far as anyone knows, exited from his life.

Now even Fred took Pinkhasov seriously. In the fall of 1981 he and John had agreed to make the scientist director of research and to pay him $80,000 a year, the same salary Mario was receiving. He seemed worth that, and more. The process that Pinkhasov had presumably brought with him from a state laboratory in the Soviet Union was unique, and it enjoyed one critical advantage over competing methods: it did not require heat. His was not, for example, the only technology that could extend the life of a drill bit by coating it with a tough alloy. But no one else could deposit that same alloy on a piece of sponge, since the sponge, known as the substrate, would be destroyed in the heating process required to make the alloy bond to it.

In effect, Pinkhasov could, and unfortunately did, coat anything with anything. In his legendary sample room a visitor can still see such early creations as a bug coated with the gold-colored alloy titanium nitrite, and a coated square of toilet paper and a coated polystyrene coffee cup.

Pinkhasov seemed to have uncovered the equivalent of the vulcanization of rubber, if not the philosopher's stone, and it wasn't only John and Wallach who considered him the most lucrative scientific property since Thomas Edison. The technical people who later came to Wedtech believed that the coating process could bring Wedtech literally hundreds of millions of dollars, if only Pinkhasov could learn to perfect it. Among the uses seriously contemplated for the coating technology were the development of lightweight batteries consisting of nickel-coated sponge, currency coated with a conductive material to foil counterfeiters, engines coated with an alloy to counteract metal fatigue, military uniforms coated with fire retardant for tank crews.

The list was endless and not in the least fantastic. There appears to be no reason, at least technically, that any of these or thousands of other applications could not work or may not be made practicable in the future, ensuring infinite wealth to Dr. Pinkhasov, who continues to hold the patent. Schoolchildren of another generation may be taught to speak his name reverentially. Unfortunately, the coating process never made a nickel, or even a nickel-coated penny, for Wedtech. John poured millions of dollars of the company's precious capital, and immeasurable quantities of his energy and his dreams, into what turned out to be a dry hole.

Pinkhasov was a man consumed by paranoia. Perhaps this was because, as John maintains, his father had been sent to Siberia for some nameless offense. Certainly Pinkhasov's secretiveness was of truly Russian dimensions, the secretiveness of a man dreading the sound of the official boot on his stairway. The very preciousness of his treasure made his mistrust manic. Pinkhasov would hire no colleagues but fellow Russians. He spoke only in Russian, except when he had to communicate with an outsider. He wrote his notes and instructions in Russian, and refused to translate them for his employers. He installed locks on every door, and handed out few keys. He turned away visitors who came to witness the process, including key employees and fellow scientists eager to verify his amazing findings.

In John Mariotta, Pinkhasov had an employer scarcely less paranoid than himself. John proudly recalls his ingenuity in instructing Pinkhasov to commit his discovery to paper and send it to himself by registered mail before venturing out to see a patent attorney. Patent attorneys stealing patents? "Don't be so naïve," says John triumphantly. "Look at Mr. Diesel." To John, who thought of much of the larger world as engaged in a conspiracy against himself, the coating process was as vulnerable to rapine as the golden fleece. If Pinkhasov wouldn't let scientists see the process, John was just as adamant toward investors. "They says, 'Mr. Mariotta, we're pouring in $30 million into this thing.' I says, 'I got news for you. I've got five *billion* into this thing here. I don't need your Tom, Dick, and Harry to set up this thing, how you say, across the street.'"

No two men ever frustrated their own ends more efficiently than did John Mariotta and Dr. Eduard Pinkhasov. John was fascinated by the process. He pored over technical journals, tearing out articles and circulating them through interoffice mail. Reading wasn't easy for him, but he obviously understood what he was looking at. He was desperate to make the technology work. Yet it never did, because it was neither consistent enough nor fast enough for commercial application. Dr. Pinkhasov, recapitulating the most ruinous aspects of Soviet science by shutting off his findings from all outside scrutiny, almost ensured that his process would remain a laboratory curiosity instead of becoming a critical component of industrial technology. His lavish establishment was, Mihai Soiman finally concluded, "a Jules Verne creation." And John refused to let anyone tear him away from his mad-scientist routine.

By the fall of 1982 John and the good doctor felt ready to dazzle potential clients with their findings. The two men, accompanied by Bob Wallach, went to the headquarters of AMF to give a demonstration to the technical people. Pinkhasov spread out on the table his gold-plated sponge and his gold-plated toilet paper and the dollar bill and all the other amazing proofs of his genius. And then, as he went to do something or other to demonstrate the process, he knocked over a beaker of liquid and spilled it all over the table. End of experiment. Still, the AMF people had been encouraging. They had hinted at a contract worth hundreds of millions to coat the inside of pipes. It was probably only a vague expression of interest, but John knew that it was destiny. The coating technology, for John, was like a cult. As Mihai Soiman puts it, "He lost the reality."

TEN

Near-Death Experience: II

I^T WAS SUCCESS, not failure, that always did the most damage to Wedtech. A few strategic failures might have compelled it to make a modest and profitable living cutting up metal into parts for the M-113 and jet engines and so on. But Wedtech kept getting buried by its successes. Not only did the company get into the habit of winning contracts it couldn't afford to execute, but immediately after every triumph the fifth column formed a line at the teller's window. In 1981, for example, Mario paid $44,500 in monthly checks to Gordon Osgood's firm, Multi-Mac. But by September 1982, with the suspension contract safely tucked in the set-aside program, Mario had already doled out another $64,300, or over $7000 a month.

It was also apparently in the fall of 1982—the exact timing is not clear —that Nofziger & Bragg upped its monthly retainer from $5000 to $10,000. The lobbyists took credit—not without reason—for the engine contract, and they may have felt that it was time to stop treating Wedtech as an underprivileged minority. Henceforth Wedtech paid $5000 to the lobbying firm and an equal sum to a company called U.S. Trading Corporation, which Nofziger and Bragg controlled.

Back in early 1981, Richard Stolfi and Frank Casalino of the Teamsters had grudgingly settled for $3000 a month. But over the summer, when it had become clear that Wedtech was moving up in the world, Stolfi summoned John and Fred to his office in Queens and said that he too wanted to move up. He and Casalino had kept the workers in line, and it was time, he said, to raise the exaction to $5000 a month. John was furious, and even Fred was nettled, but they both knew that the union was better not trifled with, and they capitulated.

Mario Biaggi had had the same thought as Stolfi at the same time. Over the years Biaggi had succeeded in getting John to raise the firm's retainer from $20,000 to $40,000 to $55,000, and it was Biaggi himself who often harassed John about making the monthly payments. Ehrlich, who was the formal recipient, was too intimidated by John's tantrums to do so. But toward the end of 1981, when Mario told Ehrlich about the contract he had signed to become an owner of Wedtech, Biaggi and Ehrlich realized that they had set their sights too low. Ehrlich made out an agreement for Biaggi & Ehrlich just like Mario's. John said he would give the law firm a piece of the company, but nothing was ever signed.

By the summer, however, it was clear that Wedtech was going to be awarded the $27.7 million engine contract, thus making a piece of the company look like a very desirable thing to own. And Biaggi & Ehrlich was more influential than ever. In August, Bernie Ehrlich had been promoted from colonel to brigadier general, thus making him the commander of the 14th Street armory in Manhattan, and the second highest ranking National Guard officer in the state. His swagger, and his sense of power, increased accordingly. It had not, however, increased so far as to embolden Ehrlich to go *mano a mano* with John Mariotta. And so it was Mario Biaggi who requested a meeting with the chairman and chief executive officer.

As Biaggi and John sat around the pool behind John's home in Scarsdale, the congressman said that it was time to formalize the promise of ownership. John agreed, and Biaggi said they should all get together and talk numbers. John told Mario about the meeting, and the three men agreed to meet at Joe Nina's, a restaurant in the Bronx. Fred refused to attend. He considered Biaggi a parasite and a nuisance; he had told the representative to his face that he reminded him of the cop who puts his arm on the local bookie. The dinner began inauspiciously. Biaggi immediately understood the meaning of Fred's absence and said, "Where's that cheap bastard Jew?" Mario offered tactful excuses, which Biaggi brushed aside. Biaggi was mad, and that was never a pretty sight, for the congressman was prone to operatic fits of temper.

He came right to the point. "Bernie," he said truthfully, "has spent a lot of time with you on this engine contract. We already have notification that you are going to get the contract, and you are going to get the contract because of us." That part, of course, wasn't true. Biaggi said he wanted a piece of the company and 5 percent of every contract he and Ehrlich helped land. That, Mario explained, was impossible, since profit margins on government contracts were limited to 10 percent as a matter of law. But by the end of the evening the three had agreed that Biaggi and Ehrlich would get 5 percent of Wedtech, and a commission on any subcontracts they could arrange, since subcontractors were not governed by profit restrictions. Mario had already learned enough of Washington to realize that Wedtech's future lay in the hands of Nofziger & Bragg, and of Bob Wallach, not those of Mario Biaggi and Bernie Ehrlich. But Biaggi, like Richard Stolfi, was the wrong man to offend. It was better simply to acquiesce.

And so by the middle of September, when the engine contract was made final, Wedtech had a great many expensive obligations and very little revenue. Things had gotten so bad that Mario had gone to John and said that they would have to lay off fifty workers to save the company. John had raged and remonstrated and finally broken down and wept. He had never, even in the worst of times, had had to lay off the workers he had so lovingly culled from the ghetto. Every week after the firing John brought baskets of food to the employees and their families, and gave them small loans to get by. John says that he funded these acts of kindness himself, because he knew that Fred would never agree to such a waste of company funds.

The company was now living on advances from suppliers who would have lost a fortune had Wedtech gone under, and on its overdraft allowance from the friendly bankers at the New York National Bank. The bank had been formed in February of that year when Bankers Trust had joined a long line of other institutions in pulling out of the South Bronx. The manager of the branch, Serafin Mariel, had started up the new bank with a number of other black and Hispanic businessmen and officials, including the outgoing SBA regional director, Ivan Irizarry. Irizarry had been a good friend to Wedtech; now Wedtech's principals repaid the favor by purchasing what eventually amounted to $250,000 worth of shares in the bank, or 7 percent of the outstanding total. Like major shareholders in local banks everywhere, the Wedtech executives enjoyed privileges that ordinary depositors did not, such as nearly limitless overdraft privileges. In New York National, Wedtech had a bank of its own.

But by September the company had problems that an overdraft allowance wouldn't help. Every Friday was an adventure, and at times the company would write payroll checks with nothing in the bank, and then John, Fred, and Mario would spend the weekend scaring up enough cash to cover the checks. Mariel had already granted the firm a $150,000 loan. And then at the end of the month, according to court testimony, John and Mario met with Irizarry and Mariel to explain how dire their situation was. Unfortunately, said Mariel, bank regulations prohibited him from extending another loan to the firm, but, he said, "there is a person who I think would be willing to consider a request for financing. The only problem is that the interest will be very high, and the amount will have to be given in cash." The other problem is that the lender would want to be repaid in three months. Who, John and Mario wanted to know, was this loan shark? There's no need for you to know, said Mariel.

So the spiral of crime added another loop, and a dizzying one. It wasn't planned; nothing was ever planned. Things just happened. Every time John, Fred, and Mario looked up from their frantic labors, the choice seemed to be the same: bankruptcy or that giddy spiral which led one knew not where. It was nobody's fault but their own that they were always facing these life or death choices, but there they were. They had to choose, and survivors and strivers like these three men always knew the choice: life, at any cost. As with the progress payment fraud, back in 1980, Mario laid out the choice that was no choice, John hesitated, and Fred, with his fatalistic readiness for the devil's bargain, told John that they had to do it.

After another meeting with Irizarry, the three principals came to the bank's office around noon on a Friday. Irizarry was already there, but the group had to wait several hours, in an agony of anticipation, until Mariel arrived with a briefcase. At that point, Mario testified, "he told Fred, John, Ivan, and myself to go inside his office. The office was open at the top. It didn't have an individual ceiling. So we went there. He closed the door. He opened the briefcase and the bills were neatly packed there in I believe fifty- and hundred-dollar bills, and Fred Neuberger uttered an expression, 'Wow.' It apparently had been the first time he had seen so much money in a single briefcase." A satchel of cash was one of the few sights the world had to offer that could move Fred to an expression of awe.

Since the bank's counting machine was broken, Mariel and Irizarry tallied up the stacks of money by hand, coming up with $485,000 and a

$15,000 bank check made out to cash. Federal rules require banks to report any cash deposit of $10,000 or more, and Mariel and Irizarry said that they didn't want the money deposited in their bank. The group decided to place the money with another friendly banker, Alice Kennedy, who managed the United Nations branch of the European American Bank.

The counting finished, Mario recalled, "Mr. Mariel told the guard at the bank to accompany us, and we went and took John Mariotta's car. And we were turning over there at the corner of the bank when a police officer stopped us. And we were very scared. He just told us that we went through some white lines where cars were not supposed to turn around, around that area. But he didn't say anything more . . .

"Fred Neuberger told me that we didn't want the security guard to know what was happening. So . . . I started to talk to Fred in French so that the guard couldn't understand anything, neither John. And for a period of time, going under the Bruckner Boulevard, I told Fred that probably it would be better to go back and give this money because this was really a very dangerous situation. If we were not able to pay the money later on, we probably could be very easily executed. So for a period of time, maybe five or six minutes, we hesitated and there was a point where we almost went back, but then we decided that the company will collapse before next week and we decided to go ahead with the transaction . . .

"We went to the European American Bank at the United Nations Plaza and we went to the door and then the security guard opened [it was after hours], and we ask him to call Mrs. Kennedy, who was the branch manager there. And she came and she told the guard too that it was all right for us to go inside the bank, and she took us to a room at the back."

When the group explained that the briefcase they were carrying contained $485,000 in cash, Kennedy did not blanch. Fred's brother-in-law, a diamond dealer who dealt with large sums of cash, had joined them at the bank. Kennedy said, according to Mario, that the brother-in-law could deposit as much as $80,000 without attracting undue attention, but the remainder would have to be deposited in increments of less than $10,000. She offered them a safe deposit box for the weekend.

John, Fred, and Mario now set out to launder the cash as fast as they could. Over the next few days they had friends and relatives make out checks to Wedtech in amounts under $10,000 and in exchange doled out stacks of cash from the hoard in the safe deposit box. They thereby embroiled dozens of acquaintances and loved ones in their misdeeds, though none of them was indicted for complicity in the scheme. In under a week the three had converted the entire stash into checks.

Five hundred thousand dollars was a lot of cash, but it was not a lot of money, at least not for a $20 million company. Wedtech was now gearing up for the engine contract. With his usual heedlessness, John had gone on a shopping spree for the advanced robotic machinery that he adored, and that no one at Wedtech knew how to operate. In 1982 and 1983 together John would spend $10 million on machinery and equipment. He also started hiring not only machinists and die makers but managers, like Tom Mullan. Fred was ordering material from suppliers. The $3 million in business development funds from the SBA was not enough, and in any case it could not be used to cover general expenses.

There were still more claims on Wedtech's money. Bob Wallach was no longer content with merely psychic returns from Wedtech; his moral energy had been diverted from the grease-stained cause in the ghetto. Wedtech's knight errant had contracted a raging case of the Washington disease, though in his own peculiar form. In May he had rented an apartment in Georgetown—to be near Ed, as he told everyone. He had presented himself, like a new ambassador, at the courts of the local princes. He had called on Robert Strauss and Clark Clifford and Max Kampelman and Leonard Garment, the sagacious and leonine figures who transcended their party affiliations to constitute a sort of fixed arbiter class. He made sure each one knew about his friendship with the others—and, of course, with Ed—and he would invite them all, and anyone else on whom he had the most slender of claims, to his Christmas Eve parties at the carefully selected power restaurants. He was sensitive and soulful and grave, like a visitor from another planet eager to learn the ways of Earth. "There was something Chagall-like about him," recalls Leonard Garment, "a first impression of a floating quality, a mixture of the real and the not-real."

Wedtech was still the cause that needed assistance, but it was to assist him as well. It was something to conjure with in chats with his new friends, and, more important, it was a source of income to underwrite his new career as self-appointed insider and granter of access to the President's counselor. Wallach, like Biaggi, and with slightly more justification, had taken credit for the engine contract, and he had been telling Mario and John that he was ready to end his amateur status with the firm. He would devote serious time to the company, as its "legal and policy adviser."

In December, Wallach submitted a draft retainer agreement calling for a payment of $10,000 a month, plus a $50,000 lump sum payment, plus 1 percent of the future revenues from the coating process, plus 5 percent of any investment capital he raised to help finance the nascent technology—a characteristically audacious detail. The agreement was never signed, but John, who believed every word Wallach spoke and held him in awe, agreed to the monthly payment. At just that moment Wedtech was not in a position to make good on the arrangement, but John promised that they would start paying as soon as they could.

Yet they could no more pay Bob Wallach than they could pay their mysterious loan shark. In early January, John and Mario, in a state of near terror, returned to Mariel to beg for a rollover of the loan. The following day Mariel reported that their private banker would grant one, and only one, three-month extension, for which he would charge an additional $150,000.

Came April, and no miracle had occurred. There would be no progress payments until there were engines, but finished engines were another year away. And there was, as yet, no new financing, either. Mario called on Serafin Mariel once again, pleading for another stay of execution, for so he literally thought of it. Mariel said that he would speak to "the individual" again.

Mario, in a state of high agitation, called Mariel later in the day. "And he told us," Mario testified, "to go and see him personally in a church he was building, a Jehovah's Witness church that he was building with other people in the South Bronx, and apparently he was a member of that church. And John Mariotta and myself went to talk to him . . . The church was under construction. He came outside the church and told us that this individual—that it was impossible to get an extension, and that he was very worried . . .

"On the way back to the company I said, 'John, I am really very worried. These people may be very dangerous individuals and we don't know what may happen to us at this point.' Next day—General Ehrlich used to come a lot to the company—next day he came to my office at one of the corners of the building and I told him, 'General.' He told me, 'You look worried, Mario.' I said, 'Yes, I am very worried, because we have a very bad situation here.' And he told me, 'What is happening?' And I described to him what had taken place in the previous months regarding that loan. And he told me, 'Simone, if it is Simone, my partner knows him very well. Let me see if he can do something for you there.' "

Simone: it was a name on a business card they had found inside the briefcase of money, whether placed there by accident or on purpose, they didn't know. Fred knew the name. Pat Simone was a real estate developer in the Bronx and the owner of the gigantic Hunts Point Auto

Wrecking company. It was not the sort of professional background that soothed the anxieties of the debtors, though perhaps it was just prejudice. As Simone's lawyer, John Tartaglia, insists, "When you have an Italian man who is a good businessman who's in such a business and he's wealthy, the first word out of anybody's mouth is, 'He's got to be connected, he's got to be in the Mafia.' "

Certainly the thought occurred to the boys from Wedtech. Since they first learned of the man as the source of a suitcase full of cash, and in ensuing years, or so they claim, they found him amenable to a broad range of criminal acts, they perhaps may be excused for drawing that inference. Simone has in fact never been publicly identified as a Mafioso, and authorities in the Bronx describe him as an independent operator, not a "made member" of one of the five New York Mafia families.

Ehrlich was not wrong in thinking that Biaggi might have an in with this local potentate. Biaggi knew everybody who mattered in the Bronx, especially the Italians. In a sworn deposition, Biaggi volunteered that he had known Simone "less than ten years," that on occasion they had lunch together, that sometimes they spoke of Wedtech, and particularly of the money it had borrowed from New York National and was failing to repay. He was not specifically asked about the alleged cash loan.

Ehrlich, Mario testified, instructed him to raise the matter of the loan with Biaggi at a fund raiser at the Marina Del Ray in the Bronx. "When we went to enter the reception hall over there," Mario stated, "General Ehrlich started to ask where is Congressman Biaggi. He had not arrived. But just like one minute later he arrived at the reception. There was an individual carrying a tuxedo next to him . . . Congressman Biaggi told General Ehrlich that he had to change in one of the bathrooms over there. And the congressman told me, 'Come in, inside with me.' So we went together to the bathroom and he changed from his regular clothes to his tuxedo while I was explaining the whole situation with the loan to him and what we needed to do." Biaggi promised to speak to Simone and see whether he could arrange for a reprieve.

Ehrlich called several days later to say that Simone had agreed to another extension, and that Ehrlich would sit down with Tartaglia to work out a deal. Ehrlich then reported that Tartaglia had had the nerve to ask that he and Biaggi personally guarantee the loan. That was a nonstarter, and John and Mario then sat down with Tartaglia to make him an offer that he wouldn't want to refuse. Wedtech had already decided that it was going to be offering shares to the public, and Mario suggested that "we could generate some kind of transaction that the payment would really be due the day after the company went public . . .

and that perhaps they would be making additional funds out of the public money." In short, Wedtech offered to pay Simone out of the proceeds of the public offering, and also to sell him some shares on the cheap. Tartaglia accepted.

ELEVEN

Indecent Exposure

OWING TO ITS ROLE as poster child for the Reagan administration's free enterprise program, Wedtech had gained access to the highest realms of political power. John and Mario, in their very separate ways, had learned how to manipulate Washington; they had learned, in any case, that it was manipulable. But neither of them nor Fred had penetrated the professional caste that seemed to run the corporate world centered in Manhattan, the caste made up of bankers and lawyers and auditors, with their advanced degrees and their daunting logic and their private clubs and their aura of omniscience and rectitude.

So far Wedtech had selected its professionals from the teeming masses of the trades. Its bankers were vice presidents on the retail side, its auditors were local, and its law firm was, well, Biaggi & Ehrlich. Not until the very end of 1982 had Wedtech grown large enough to be propelled into the higher reaches of the professional order. And only then did John and Mario and Fred discover that the barons of the corporate domain were every bit as manipulable as the lords of Washington.

In the summer of 1982, Bank Leumi had informed Wedtech that it would not make a sizable loan unless the firm replaced its local auditor with a nationally recognized one and received fresh audits of the previous years, as well as of the current one. Larry Shorten, a former commercial banker and financial consultant whom Wedtech had hired on a part-time basis to work on bank loans, was assigned to find the company a suitably reputable auditor. He came up with the firm of Main Hurdman, a partnership formed from the merger, several years earlier, of Hurdman & Cranston with Main LaFrance.

The audit began in the fall. By December 1982, after he had worked his way back from 1981 and then to 1980, the head of the audit team, Anthony Guariglia, had discovered something exceedingly strange about Wedtech's books. When he added up all the invoices submitted to the Pentagon so that Wedtech could receive progress payments, he reached a figure $6 million larger than the actual expenses reflected in the company's accounts payable balance. He and his audit team then took all of the invoices and sorted them out, by supplier, on the big table in the conference room next to John's office. The pattern jumped out at them immediately. All of the computer-printed invoices from each supplier were reflected in accounts payable; none of the typewritten ones were. The typewritten invoices were obvious forgeries. Guariglia was stupefied. Defense firms were his specialty, and he had seen fraud before. But never in his career had he seen fraud of this magnitude. What he had found, of course, was the progress payment fraud that Wedtech had been perpetrating nonstop for the last three years.

The progress payment fraud was discovered on a Saturday. On Monday morning, Tony Guariglia went to Allen Ackerman, head of accounting standards at Main Hurdman and a senior figure. Ackerman was every bit as shocked as Guariglia. After taking up the matter with Main Hurdman's general counsel, and debating the matter at length, Ackerman ordered the audit team to disengage. On the following Saturday morning Guariglia went out to 595 Gerard with Richard Bluestine, the supervisor of the audit team, and they told John and Fred and Mario that they were leaving. They literally packed up their big black cases of work papers and walked out the door.

It was a devastating blow for Wedtech. It was bad enough that they had already run through the $500,000 cash from Simone; now they weren't going to have an audit, which meant that Bank Leumi wouldn't extend their financing. And if they were forced to disclose the progress payment fraud, the Army might cancel the engine contracts. John went crazy. John could never believe that he was responsible for wrongdoing of any kind.

He launched into one of his tirades, this one directed at Mario. Mario was an idiot, Mario was a dumb fucking moron, Mario had told them that nobody would ever catch on and now they knew. John had simply assumed that Mario's graduate business degree meant that in matters of finance he was the equal of any man. Mario protested mildly—the fraud, after all, had been a desperate expedient at a desperate time—but John rolled right over him.

It was at this critical moment that the three keen students of moral pragmatism who ran Wedtech discovered—or so Mario and Fred allege —that a partner in a major accounting firm could prove every bit as malleable as a congressman. John and Fred had already spoken to Richard Bluestine of Wedtech's limitless prospects, and of the central role that could be played by a person with real financial expertise. Bluestine had listened. And when disaster struck, he was willing to play an ambiguous role.

Later on the Saturday of Main Hurdman's withdrawal, according to Mario, Bluestine sat in on a meeting at 595 Gerard with the insiders and their lawyer, Bernie Ehrlich. Bluestine explained that the only way the company could restore itself to Main Hurdman's graces was to accept full responsibility for its frauds, blame the entire affair on the chief financial officer—Mario Moreno—and promise to remove him from his position of responsibility. He would then argue the company's case to his superiors. He authored a sort of drama of confession whereby Wedtech could expiate its sins and emerge new.

The assignment of Bluestine to the Wedtech audit was one of those fortuitous events that sustained the company in its hour of need. Destiny sometimes seemed to escort Wedtech through the world with a lantern, looking for yet another dishonest man. Richard Bluestine wore a pinky ring and a gold bracelet and an expression, judging from photographs, that bordered on a smirk. He was a man with his eye out for the main chance. As a young accountant at Touche Ross, Bluestine had worked as a volunteer in John Lindsay's successful 1969 campaign to be re-elected mayor of New York and had managed to wheedle a piece of the accounting work for the city's receipt of federal funds for the Model Cities program. Several years later he landed a job at Hurdman & Cranston by bringing this business with him.

Bluestine did not have the reputation either for mathematical acuity or for unremitting fidelity to the facts often associated with accountants. Even a good friend and long-time colleague at Main Hurdman, Don Rose, agrees that "wheeler-dealer" would be an apt description of the man. Another former colleague, Donald Stewart, describes him as "kind of sleazy. Everything was a deal. You always got the impression that when he told you stuff he wasn't telling you 100 percent of what the truth was, and there was some angle there." Few of his associates at Main Hurdman were surprised to learn that Bluestine had gone off to join a hot new firm. "Dick was a product of his environment," says another former colleague, Campbell Corfe. "He was caught up in a particular milieu—make a fast buck and do it whichever way you can. That to me was New York in the eighties."

Bluestine's theater piece went precisely as planned. At a meeting in Main Hurdman's midtown office, John and Fred offered up their partner as a sacrifice. It was Mario, they said, who had concocted the scheme, though in fact almost every progress payment had been signed by John, and the others had been signed by Fred. But Ackerman, perhaps impressed by Bluestine's acquiescence, accepted the explanation. He agreed to resume work for the company as long as Wedtech fully informed the relevant government agencies of its fraud, underwent the rigors of a much more extensive audit, and removed Mario Moreno from his position. Wedtech would live.

But it was all just theater. Mario remained vice president, though Larry Shorten was technically given responsibility over the books. More important, the disclosure was a sham. As the company's lawyer, Bernie Ehrlich was charged with the responsibility of fully informing the government. He told his friend Peter Neglia, New York regional director of the SBA, who had already proved his benevolence by unilaterally extending Wedtech's membership in the 8(a) program, that the company had some problems with progress payments and that Defense Department auditors were looking into the matter. Neglia said it was no business of his: if the Defense Department didn't object to the situation, neither would he.

And in a way Neglia was right. The progress payment fraud had been perpetrated on the Defense Contract Audit Agency, not on the SBA. It was to the DCAA that Ehrlich ought to have gone. But the auditors from the DCAA, Samuel Barkan and Joshua Purec, had long known about the fraud, or so Fred and Mario have said. Fred had offered Barkan a job when his retirement came up at the end of 1983. Indeed, it was obvious to Tony Guariglia that the DCAA auditors knew about the fraud, since they were working next door to the Main Hurdman team. He recalls Barkan walking into the conference room and asking to borrow additional account analysis pads. "I ran out of paper listing all those invoices," he said. Guariglia also recalls Barkan coming by, smoking his pipe, and casually asking, "Did they steal anything else today?"

Wedtech's entire disclosure of this multimillion-dollar fraud was Ehrlich's casual conversation with Neglia. The reassurance it offered to Main Hurdman, after the accountants had discovered what was in fact a felony, consisted of a letter, dated February 25, 1983, and signed by a Biaggi & Ehrlich associate, Paul Barnard, in which a reference to the progress payments was sandwiched between two other, unrelated matters: "Mr. Ehrlich has discussed the matter extensively with the SBA and the matter has been resolved." The SBA, the letter stated, was satisfied that Wedtech had inventory on hand whose value was greater than the amount the company now owed the Defense Department, so the company could, in theory, deliver products without reimbursement until it had made the DCAA whole.

Meanwhile, Wedtech was nailing down Richard Bluestine's loyalty. In January, as the audit team was returning to work, John took a trip to Japan, hoping to conclude a $2 million deal involving the coating process. He asked Bluestine, whom John considered the acme of business sophistication, to accompany him. The coating deal didn't work out, Bluestine or no, but apparently another deal did. Soon after they returned, John told his colleagues that he had completed the co-option of their chief auditor. They were driving down from the Bronx for one of their innumerable lunches together, at a Japanese restaurant on Columbus Avenue in Manhattan, when John, according to Mario's testimony, said that he had offered Bluestine a piece of the company if he would help them cover up the accounting fraud. Fine, Bluestine had said; give me 9 percent—fully as large as Mario's share. John, incredibly, had agreed.

Fred shouted that John had lost his mind, that he would give away the whole company if he weren't restrained—which was true—and John responded by shouting back, stepping on the gas, and driving down Manhattan as if bent on suicide. He screeched to a halt in front of the restaurant, dropped off Fred and Mario, and then suddenly clambered back into the Lincoln and gunned off down the avenue by himself. Anyway, it was a done deal, and Fred told Mario that they might as well enjoy their lunch.

Bluestine quickly made good his offer. "From December, when we discovered the progress payment," recalls Guariglia, "to the time he went to Japan, it was 'Look at every single piece of paper.' When he came back from Japan, it was, like, 'Aren't you guys done yet? Wrap this audit and let's get out of here.' " The auditors speculated among themselves about how much Wedtech had spent to purchase their boss's change of heart.

But Guariglia and his team were now conducting a full fraud audit, and they had to be painstaking. Mario and his bookkeeping staff had kept amazingly slipshod accounts, even for a small firm, and none of the numbers added up. It was a bottomless pit, and the Main Hurdman auditors were in it up to their eyebrows, logging hundreds of hours in the conference room at 595 Gerard. Then their spade struck something solid again. As he went through what was called the cash disbursements journal, Guariglia found checks coming in from suppliers, and then going out in the same amount to an account called FHJ Associates, for which there was no record. The checks totaled about $400,000.

Once again the auditors confronted the principals, and again the principals 'fessed up. Fred bluntly explained that he and John had siphoned the money off from the company in order to circumvent the salary restriction included in their EDA loan. John admitted that he had used the money to buy his house in Scarsdale. Since Wedtech was still a private company, the men were only stealing from themselves, though they were doing so in order to violate the terms of a loan agreement. Guariglia reported his discovery to Ackerman, and included it in his work papers. He also found, and reported, some illegal corporate political contributions and apparently fraudulent travel and entertainment expenses.

"Here we go again," Guariglia told his crew. This time, he thought, they would pack up and never return. But he was wrong. Bluestine recommended that the entire amount be accounted as a loan to Fred, who would then write out a promissory note to be satisfied with the proceeds of his stock sale when the company went public. Ackerman, according to Guariglia, was not upset by the revelation, despite Wedtech's assurance that nothing else was amiss. Struggling entrepreneurs, he pointed out, pay themselves out of the company till all the time. Of course in this case company officials had defrauded the EDA. But the EDA loan would soon be replaced by a commercial loan, and the restrictive covenant would no longer be in force. So Main Hurdman waved once again as the Wedtech train went roaring by.

Why? Why didn't Main Hurdman disengage once and for all? In part, it seems, because Richard Bluestine's word carried the day, and Bluestine's colleagues had no inkling that his word, as the Wedtech insiders allege, had been purchased. Bluestine may not have been a model of probity, but he was, after all, a partner. And Main Hurdman clearly had an incentive to retain a client that was about to go public, a client with tremendous growth potential. The audit had already been vastly more extensive, and thus more profitable, than had been expected. True, the Wedtech audit was not a black-and-white case. What ever is? The company had defrauded the government, but it had disclosed its fraud, even if it had done so to the wrong branch of government. The principals had siphoned hundreds of thousands of dollars from the company, again lying to the government, but it was their money to steal. The books were such a mess that it was hard to tell error from deceit. In short, everything they had done could be construed as acceptable.

So it was. At the end of April, after a grueling stretch of six months on the job, the auditors from Main Hurdman gave Wedtech a clean bill of health.

As lucky as Wedtech was in having stumbled on Richard Bluestine, the company was vastly more fortunate in having come in contact with Tony Guariglia. The thirty-one-year-old accountant was a young man of genuinely exceptional talent. "He was a real smart guy," recalls Donald Stewart of Main Hurdman, "a nice guy, very respected. The senior partners all said that he was one of the great stars we've got here." Stewart was struck by the contrast between the earnest Guariglia and the reptilian Bluestine. "Dick," he recalls, "was sort of a wise-guy, New York Jewish type of personality, where Tony was an Italian who grew up in Brooklyn and went to Catholic school." Like a lot of graduates of parochial school, Tony Guariglia was an extremely disciplined young man.

Tony had grown up in Bensonhurst, a heavily Italian section of Brooklyn where young men perform acts of violence in the hope of being noticed by the mob. Bensonhurst is part of the minor league system of the Mafia, and many of Tony's friends signed on. He was not, himself, a violent man, and he came from a solid working-class home. Tony's parents both worked in Manhattan's garment center, his father as a pattern maker, his mother as a machine operator. Tony did, in fact, go to a Catholic school, though after he finished junior high school his parents moved out to Long Island.

Tony went through high school as an indifferent student, enrolled on a part-time basis at nearby Adelphi University, and studied accounting for no other reason than that his older brother was making a success of himself in the field. After a year he quit, joined the Army Reserve, and when he returned to school after six months was inculcated with enough military discipline to apply his considerable intelligence to his studies. His grades shot up, though he was working forty hours a week in a factory at the same time, and he won a scholarship to pursue his master's degree in accounting. In his graduate year he interned with Touche Ross, and he joined the firm when he finished school in 1973. A straight arrow in the making, Tony got married on his graduation day.

Tony was a star at Touche Ross, but, discouraged by the immensity of the firm, he quit in 1975 to join Hurdman & Cranston, a small but elite firm. Here, too, he maneuvered on to the fast track, rising from senior accountant to supervisor to manager in four years. The young man with the square glasses and the wide, almost rubbery face and eager manner was the embodiment of an accountant's virtues. He had a genius for numbers, a ruthlessly logical mind, a working-class appetite for dogged labor, and a deep need to get things right. He even had the accountant's personality—narrowly focused, uncomfortable with the abstract or ambiguous, prone to denominate everything in dollars and numbers. He spoke coolly and rationally, though with his Brooklyn lisp he turned *r*'s into *w*'s, and he was wont to say things like "Fuhgedaboudid!"

As the Wedtech audit was winding down, Tony had learned from Fred that a small investment firm where Fred had friends, D. H. Blair & Company, planned on offering 60 percent of Wedtech's stock to the public for $4.5 million. Tony knew that he was dealing with unsophisticated men, but this was ridiculous. He marched into John's office and informed him, with the confidence of youth, that the company was worth $100 million, and suggested they sell 25 percent for $25 million. John's reaction could have been predicted. "He called me a moron," recalls Tony, "and he called me a typical accountant, and he threw me out of the office."

But Tony was sure that he was right, and he received permission from Mario and Fred to bring in an executive from Moseley Hallgarten, the bank that handled Tony's stock portfolio, for a presentation. Early in May, in an office at Main Hurdman, Larry Shorten made the company pitch to Peter Richard from the bank. Intrigued, Richard paid a visit to Wedtech and toured the coating laboratory as well as the manufacturing facility. The banker saw what the accountant had seen: enormous potential growth through a growing defense-contracting business and a breakthrough technology. The Wedtech officials had no idea what they were sitting on. On May 5, Moseley Hallgarten presented Wedtech with a letter of intent to underwrite a public offering. The letter valued the company at $100 million.

Tony had been right. Tony understood. John was thunderstruck, and concluded that Tony Guariglia was a genius, not a moron. Fred and Mario were equally impressed. This earnest and self-assured young man with the scallop of hair over his forehead and the light bouncing off his glasses was the missing piece in the Wedtech puzzle. In the new world into which it was swiftly moving, the company needed someone who spoke the recondite language of numbers. And it was obvious that in the realm of numbers, Tony had the gift of fluency that John had with

John's moment of glory. On January 19, 1982, Wedtech's guiding
spirit preached the free enterprise gospel to President Reagan.
(*The National Archives*)

Wedtech chairman John Mariotta poses with vice president Fred Neuberger in 1979, when their company was a little machine shop with grandiose dreams. (*John Sotomayor/NYT Pictures*)

Between the dope pusher and the thief. The factory at 1049 Washington Avenue lay in the dismal reaches of the South Bronx. (*Elizabeth Easton*)

In 1980 John, Fred, and Mario moved to a larger and more tranquil home at 595 Gerard Avenue, in the shadow of Yankee Stadium. (*Elizabeth Easton*)

Mario Moreno, Wedtech's master politician (left), with Bronx Borough President Stanley Simon, beaming from the throne in the office of Yankees' owner George Steinbrenner.

Representative Mario Biaggi, his arm around Fred Neuberger, was Wedtech's first political friend and ultimately its best paid.

In the spring of 1981, E. Robert Wallach stumbled on to Wedtech, and he recruited to the cause his friend Ed Meese, counselor to the President. (*Neshan Naltchayan*)

In the spring of 1982, Lyn Nofziger, the administration's chief political operative, became Wedtech's man in Washington. (*NYT Pictures*)

Supplying parts for the Army's M-113 personnel carrier was Wedtech's first big job. The company allegedly paid over $500,000 to an Army officer so that it could keep the contract. (*Official U.S. Army Photograph*)

In September 1982, SBA Administrator James Sanders (center) visited the company his agency had selected for a $27.7 million contract to build engines for the Army. (*Edward Hausner/NYT Pictures*)

The 1983 stock offering suddenly made Wedtech a $100 million company. After years of struggle, John and Fred were worth over $20 million each. (*Copyright 1990 Scott Barrow Inc.*)

The auditors Richard Bluestine (left) and Tony Guariglia (right) took jobs at Wedtech; the treasurer, Alfred Rivera, became a corporate director. Guariglia devised the company's most audacious frauds. Bluestine was fired after six months. (*Copyright 1990 by Scott Barrow Inc.*)

Bob Wallach found the company an impressive new lawyer, Howard Squadron (left), a highly respected attorney and a prominent American Jewish leader, shown here with client Rupert Murdoch. (*Richard Sandler*)

Representative Robert Garcia, from the South Bronx, demanded $4000 a month to help the home-town boys. (*Sara Krulwich/NYT Pictures*)

MR. GARCIA

machines and Fred had with blueprints and Mario had with the affairs of men. Wedtech now had the wherewithal to buy men like Tony. They had, after all, already bought Bluestine.

On the Sunday morning following Moseley Hallgarten's commitment, Tony was asked to come to a meeting in the conference room at 595 Gerard. That was typical of life at Wedtech: it was nothing to come to work on a Sunday morning. Tony was excited by the atmosphere, by the sense of camaraderie he had felt during his months poring over the books. He knew that Wedtech had cheated the government, but he also knew that the company had mended its way sufficiently to satisfy his superiors. If the money was there, he was ready to jump. Over the years he had been offered jobs by other grateful clients, most of them much bigger than Wedtech, but he had turned them down. His future at Main Hurdman looked extremely bright. He expected to make partner that fall, doubling his salary to $125,000. But Wedtech was about to go public, and that could mean money of a very big order.

John came right to the point: they wanted to make him a vice president and they were willing to offer stock. Tony then did a little conjuring trick for the boys. He talked about his prospects at Main Hurdman, whipped out his calculator, and toted up his expected lifetime earnings—*bip bip bip*, as Tony liked to say. The number, he announced, came out to $3 million. He would therefore need 3 percent of the company to compensate for forgone earnings. It was an opening gambit, of course, and after some discussion John offered 1.5 percent of the company and an $80,000 salary. "It's a deal," said Tony, and that was that. He was a hard young man, Tony Guariglia, but that was exactly what Wedtech needed.

As it moved toward the great moment of its public offering, Wedtech was acquiring a retinue, and a nicely panoplied one at that. First there was the elite accounting firm, and then the bankers, suited and booted. And then, just as the bankers were signing on, came the most glittering acquisition of all, the Fifth Avenue law firm of Squadron, Ellenoff, Plesent & Lehrer. For this classy association Bob Wallach deserved full credit.

Wallach wanted to fit Wedtech into his new career as self-appointed eminence and gatekeeper to the mighty. He wanted Wedtech, in short, to start employing the people he was trying to befriend, and thereby bring everyone together into a charmed circle of virtue, power, and wealth. One of the people he was especially eager to bring into the charmed circle was Howard Squadron, a major figure in the American Jewish community and one of the founders of a medium-sized law firm whose clients included the Australian media conglomorator Rupert Murdoch. Squadron was a New York version of the sages of Washington, which is to say that he was someone Bob Wallach wanted to be. He was the sort of man who could tell you that he'd had to postpone a trip to Paris because Menachem Begin had asked him to fly over to Israel to give him some advice—a man who mattered, and who was not bashful about saying so. In the nonstop wrestling match over the unofficial position of prime minister of the American Jews, Squadron, who had served as chairman of the American Jewish Congress and of the Conference of Presidents of Major American Jewish Organizations, was a perennial contender.

The two men had first met in 1981, when Wallach was trying to help Ed Meese and the Reagan administration mollify the American Jewish community over the proposed sale of AWACS surveillance planes to Saudi Arabia. The following year, Wallach says, their friendship deepened when he introduced Squadron to Meese. As an open partisan of Walter Mondale, Squadron had lost his welcome at the White House; Wallach says that he gave Squadron the precious gift of access, as he did for others in his quiet role as conduit between the White House and the American Jewish community. Squadron says that Wallach played this role only in his own mind, and it was he who provided Wallach access by introducing him to Leonard Garment and Max Kampelman.

Wallach felt that Howard Squadron was the lawyer for Wedtech's future, and he told the insiders that it was time for a change. Wallach could be shockingly blunt for a man who prided himself on sensitivity; in April he told Bernard Ehrlich, point-blank, "The company has outgrown you." Biaggi & Ehrlich could scarcely afford to be outgrown by Wedtech, since the company had become its principal client. But Ehrlich, for all his martial bluster, was a man who understood very well who could be barked at and who could only be muttered at. When Wallach gave him the back of his hand, Ehrlich only purpled, and muttered something about the long years of busting his butt and going into his own pocket for expenses. Biaggi, who resented Wallach and who was hoping to line up legal work for his friends, was not nearly so timid. The congressman called up Mario and launched into a tirade in which he called Wallach a "Jew bastard," among other epithets. But it was no use. Biaggi & Ehrlich would remain, but neither they nor their friends would be corporate counsel.

Squadron himself agreed to take on Wedtech as a client, and he reached an agreement with the firm for a retainer of $10,000 a month to be applied against hourly billings. Squadron says that he was somewhat nonplussed by Wallach's manner. When Wallach called him to his Washington office in early May 1983 to celebrate the agreement, the San Francisco lawyer laid out strawberries and champagne in the middle of a working day. Squadron's reaction was: the man lacks substance. But even if the company's adviser was a trifle unearthly, it was obvious that Wedtech was a client with tremendous potential.

As soon as the retainer agreement was signed, a group of lawyers from Squadron Ellenoff's corporate department began traveling up to 595 Gerard to prepare the registration statement that goes out to the public to announce a stock offering, and to exercise "due diligence" to ensure the accuracy of that information. The mingling of these two unlike communities produced a strong culture shock. "I used to have this notion of them being like Pigpen in *Peanuts* because of this shroud or enveloping mass," says Jeffrey Rubin, a Squadron Ellenoff associate who worked closely with Wedtech. "Or they were like Sam and Eric in *Lord of the Flies*. John, Fred, and Mario traveled as a unit. They seemed to be Siamese triplets. And when they would come here they would bivouac for hours." The Wedtech boys spent a lot of time in Manhattan, but never kept an office there. They often showed up at Squadron Ellenoff's front door and invaded a conference room, where they would sprawl like campers taking shelter from the rain. Rubin found himself thoroughly charmed by their lack of pretense and by their habit of turning everything into a bizarre narrative. He was a convert.

The law firm's principal contact at Wedtech, then and later, was Tony Guariglia. Tony was not colorful. There was a coolness and neutrality to his character that was an immense relief after the Abbott and Costello act of John and Fred. And he fairly radiated professional integrity. "When we were working on registration statements," recalls Rubin, "when we were working on SEC disclosure documents, and we would need to deal with an issue, he worried about that issue, that it would be done properly. He would come in here and spend fourteen, fifteen hours a day going through the documents in a very conscientious manner. Tony was a person who made clear to me that he knew the difference between right and wrong. In my relationship with him, he would consistently indicate that it should be done the right way."

The late spring of 1983 was a feverish time at Wedtech. Machinists at 595 Gerard were tooling up to build the engines, supplies were arriving in vast crates from vendors as far away as Germany, Italy, and Israel, and steel was finally being cut in the refurbished factory at 112 Bruckner Avenue. Upstairs at 595 Gerard, and in their offices in Manhattan, the bankers and the lawyers, and the lawyers for the bankers—the firm of Shearman & Sterling—were poring over Wedtech's books in order to prepare the registration statement. The offering had been scheduled for August, and the volume of work to be done was staggering. Management was allotting stock to the company's consultants and retainers. John was working all night on the engines, Tony was working all night on the registration, and Mario, as always, was doing a hundred things at once— scaring up new contracts, hacking away at a political problem involving the EDA loan, keeping all the friends and retainers happy.

Mario, in fact, almost killed himself from overwork. One day in the office he started hyperventilating and then blacked out. He was taken to the hospital, where he fainted again and again. He was unable to breathe, and Mario Biaggi's personal doctor, who had come to his bedside, was unable to figure out what was wrong. Mario says that he fainted forty times over two days before doctors realized that he had whooping cough, and that congestion was preventing oxygen from reaching his brain. He spent much of the summer recuperating at home.

Meanwhile, Squadron Ellenoff, like Main Hurdman before it, was finding that certain things about its rough-and-tumble new client were significantly out of plumb. According to the company's own stock ledger, John Mariotta did not own two thirds of Wedtech, as the company had been telling the SBA, but only 45 percent. The ledger was, in fact, a thicket, with shares transferred among Fred, John, and Irving Lonstein, the baby carriage manufacturer who had been John's partner in the 1960s. Many transactions were unrecorded. But from the records, and from what John and Fred explained, the lawyers understood—incorrectly, of course— that the ownership had gone from 66–34 to 45–45–9 when Mario had joined in August 1981.

Arthur Siskind, the Squadron Ellenoff partner who headed up the Wedtech account from the beginning, says that he took this to be not an act of fraud, but the kind of sloppy bookkeeping he had grown accustomed to finding in small firms preparing to go public. Yet even the partial truth that he had glimpsed meant that Wedtech had been defrauding the government for the past two years. Had the company admitted to the SBA that John owned less than 50 percent, it would have been booted out of the 8(a) program. Rubin says that he understood from the company's Washington counsel, Tim Sullivan, that Mario also qualified as an 8(a) minority even though he had not been formally certified. Sullivan, who had represented the company before the SBA since the mid-1970s, says that he never told Rubin any such thing, and it probably wasn't true in any case. And even if it were true, Wedtech had hidden the fact from the SBA.

The law firm was learning more than it may have liked to know. Tony says that he and Richard Bluestine visited Siskind in his office to explain the progress payment fraud. They described both the magnitude and the method of the fraud. Siskind, however, says that the explanation was sketchy at best. He understood that there were "irregularities" in the invoices Wedtech had sent to the Pentagon auditors, and that the company had been reimbursed for work it had not yet completed. No one, Siskind recalls, spoke of forgery or fraud, though it's not clear why Tony or Bluestine would have concealed from the corporate lawyers what the auditors already knew, especially since the auditors had pronounced themselves satisfied.

Corporations are obliged to disclose to the public any matter that may be "material" to an investment decision. Among such matters is the integrity of management, including, of course, acts of fraud. Wedtech had defrauded not one but three government agencies, and the fraud perpetrated on the DCAA was an extraordinarily gross one. Management should have disclosed the progress payment fraud, if not the others (which were not disclosed even to the relevant agencies). But it hadn't. And since Squadron Ellenoff considered the progress payment issue a minor transgression from Wedtech's past, an error that had been disclosed to the satisfaction of the government and the company's own auditors, the law firm pursued the matter no further, and did not insist on disclosure to the public.

The question thus arises once again: Did the lawyers, like the accountants, overlook what they wished to overlook? A shareholder's suit names Squadron Ellenoff as one of the "knowledgeable parties" in a conspiracy to cover up the progress payment fraud. Was there a conspiracy? Was there knowledge? Main Hurdman had full knowledge of the fraud, though the auditors may have been misled as to the extent of disclosure to the relevant government agencies. They hadn't pressed the issue; the Biaggi & Ehrlich letter had been satisfaction enough. And Squadron Ellenoff, in turn, had relied on Main Hurdman. The lawyers knew that Wedtech had done something wrong, though it's uncertain how fully they understood that wrong. They chose to rely on Main Hurdman, as Main Hurdman relied on Biaggi & Ehrlich. And so both sets of reputable professionals whom the public depended on for accurate information about Wedtech depended, in turn, on the word of a third-rate law firm with intimate and long-standing ties to the client.

It is all quite ambiguous, of course. What is obvious in retrospect, as Squadron Ellenoff partner Ira Lee Sorkin points out, was scarcely clear at the time. Now it's black and white; then it was gray. It was a matter of judgment, of interpretation. On a baseball field the foul lines determine what is in or out of bounds; in modern professional life, where the rules are complex and their application to specific situations far from self-evident, the lines are fuzzy. Their position depends on interpretation, and it is the professional himself who interprets them—at least until a court intervenes.

A skilled professional, whether lawyer, banker, or accountant, knows how to move in that gray area without ever crossing into the black; he knows how to accomplish what his client wants without breaking the rules. Sometimes the professional must perform some fairly strange mental operations to stay within the gray. He may have to place himself in a state of mind—ambivalence, uncertainty, dependence on the assurances of others—whereby his actions can be construed to have been inside the foul lines. It is, after all, a question of interpretation.

The unworldly lads from Wedtech, who understood little of the complexities of the law, may have misinterpreted the willingness of their high-priced legal and financial help to close the door on the company's spotted past. They concluded from the experience that there was always a way of doing what they wanted to do. There was always a way of satisfying their ambition. Sophisticated people, they learned, didn't break the rules; they bent them out of shape.

TWELVE

One Point Five Million Shares in the American Dream

SOME OF WEDTECH'S FRIENDS, as well as envious competitors in the 8(a) program, found it baffling that the company was going public at all. Tim Sullivan, the Washington lawyer, who was now with the firm of Dykema Gossett, tended to follow events in the South Bronx with a certain puzzled amusement. He recalls that when he first heard the news, "I probably wrote it off to wild dreams, if not wet ones. I always think of a public company as a company that really has it together, and these guys were not what you would consider a crack Harvard Business School management team. You don't manage by crisis, and that always seemed to be the operative theme there." Sullivan had met the new whiz kids, Larry Shorten and Tony Guariglia, and had not been impressed. Shorten, he says, struck him as "a guy who when you've finished your finance meeting would try to sell you a clock from inside his coat," and "Guariglia just seemed like a cold, calculating executive."

Not only was Wedtech run like an antic sitcom; the company was also completely untested. It had blossomed in the artificial environment of the minority set-aside program, and had never shown that it could fend for itself. Wedtech was an exotic plant from the government hothouse. It was hard to believe that Wall Street could take a hard look at this frail growth and declare it investment-grade. How could all these insanely overpaid bankers and money men have fallen for Wedtech? The answer is: You had to be there.

The spring of 1983 was one of the truly propitious moments in human history for a little defense-contracting firm with a patented coating technology to have offered shares to the public. It was a moment, not to put too fine a point on it, when chopped liver could have gone public. The country had been in a recession since September 1981. Unemployment had reached 10.8 percent, a postwar high. President Reagan's bold program of tax cuts had put money in the hands of the rich without stimulating the economy. The budget deficit, and the entire budget process, had spun out of control. A $200 billion deficit seemed a possibility. A former Federal Reserve member, Andrew Brimmer, warned of a new depression. Political professionals suggested that the President could forget about running for re-election if the economy didn't come around.

And then the economy did just that. "The long-awaited recovery is finally beginning," *Business Week* announced at the end of January. The Fed loosened the money supply, interest rates dropped, housing starts and car purchases increased. Oil prices dropped, and the Dow Jones index, which had been rising since the previous August, shot to record heights. Investment capital, which had been dammed up, now cascaded into all the major exchanges, especially in the form of new issues of stock by existing public corporations and initial public offerings by emerging firms. Only one firm had gone public on the New York Stock Exchange during the two previous years. In 1983 there were fourteen. On the NASDAQ exchange, which caters to smaller firms, the figure went from 333 in 1981 to 110 in 1982 and to a record 637 in 1983.

And it was the year of high tech. No one knew quite what the term meant, but the belief that high-tech firms would lead America out of its industrial decline had gained an almost universal acceptance. Not only every state, but virtually every county, had established an economic development agency designed to encourage the growth of high-tech firms. Market capital was scouring the landscape for embryonic computer and electronics and medical technology firms. A brochure for a new $1 billion high-tech mutual fund established by Merrill Lynch feverishly proclaimed that "we have reached a pivotal moment in the history of science and technology," meaning that technical breakthroughs were being turned into profitable companies with unprecedented speed. By the spring of 1983 high-tech stocks were selling at an average multiple of nineteen times earnings. In February a firm called Information Resources issued stock at $23 a share; by the end of the week the stock was selling at $41, a hundred times the previous year's earnings.

Wedtech was thus in the perfect position to have its shortcomings overlooked. It was a new issue, it was a high-growth firm, and, despite the fact that it was quartered in the South Bronx and cut up metal for a living, it was called high tech. Potential investors could be shown the brilliant Dr. Pinkhasov and his white-coated assistants tinkering in the arc vapor deposition chamber. The Japanese were interested. Of course the Japanese hadn't laid out a penny, and neither had anyone else who had looked closely at the process. But the possibilities were fantastic, and Wall Street was buying possibilities.

Nevertheless, some people at Moseley Hallgarten were reluctant to overlook Wedtech's shortcomings. Stanley Cohen, a senior vice president with the firm, though in financial planning rather than corporate finance, says, "I raised the question: How was the company going to survive once it goes public?" since at that time it would have to leave the SBA set-aside program. The answer, he was told, was that Wedtech would keep many of its key contracts after leaving the program—which was true—and that the company was already competitive—which, of course, was Wedtech propaganda. Cohen says that he had a low opinion of set-aside contractors in general, and he didn't see the value of the coating technology. He was destined to play the role of Cassandra.

"Wedtech and a few others," says Cohen, "were a bonanza for the brokers at Moseley." As senior underwriter, Moseley had the right to sell as much as half the projected 1.5 million shares, representing a potential fortune in commissions for the brokers. Brokers are always on the lookout for a hot new stock to tout to their customers, and Wedtech seemed as hot as they come. Cohen says that he might have taken down 10,000 shares or more for his own customers, but he declined to take any.

Until Moseley had committed itself to underwrite an offering, a share of Wedtech had been a thing of purely abstract value. Suddenly it was a unit of currency, and a very valuable one. The bankers felt that Wedtech shares could be offered for as much as $18, based on an overall value for the company of almost $100 million. It was not hard to grasp what this meant: 1 percent of Wedtech was worth $1 million. That simple fact put everything else—salary, bonuses, retainers, even theft—in the shade. Wedtech was no longer just a gallant little company turning out defense products against all odds; it was the Big Rock Candy Mountain, and everyone wanted a piece.

Throughout May and into June, John and Fred allotted pieces of the rock like royalty opening up the imperial treasury. They made a perfect pair. John was not only naturally generous but loved the sight of his betters prostrated by greed, and believed that he could control people by dangling before them the prospect of wealth; Fred could scarcely bear to give anything to anyone.

Kindness, of course, began at home. Over the years John and Fred had been compelled, by the terms of the EDA loan, to content themselves with salaries suitable to junior vice presidents at an insurance company, though they had supplemented their meager incomes through their various kickback schemes. Now they were going to make themselves stupendously, unimaginably rich. Even after giving away portions of the company to others, and selling another portion to the public, each man would be left with $25 million worth of Wedtech stock.

Mario's 9 percent ownership under the old scheme translated into 345,000 shares, worth well over $5 million. Another 153,000 shares were reserved for "additional senior management personnel" to be hired in the future. This was the amount allegedly promised to Bluestine, who had agreed to remain with Main Hurdman until after the offering was completed. Tony's 1.5 percent came to 67,000 shares, and John and Fred agreed to give Larry Shorten an equal number.

Bob Wallach, who had opposed the public offering and had spent recent months trying to persuade his many good friends with bottomless pockets to invest in the company instead, bowed to the inevitable and accepted 1 percent of the company, or 45,000 shares—not as payment, as he would explain later, but as a chance to "share in the American Dream." Lyn Nofziger and Mark Bragg, together, received an equal number, as did the firm of Squadron Ellenoff. John even decided to give his staunch friend Ceil Lewis, keeper of accounts, almost 12,000 shares of stock.

The previous fall John and Mario, though not Fred, had caved in to pressure from Representative Biaggi and agreed to award 5 percent of the company to the congressman and General Ehrlich. In the middle of May, when it was clear that 5 percent of Wedtech was worth a great deal of money, Biaggi came calling at 595 Gerard to make sure that no one had forgotten the promise. Biaggi knew that he had to get Fred's approval, and Fred had never bothered to conceal his contempt for politicians generally and Biaggi specifically. The meeting was held in John's office, and Fred started the ball rolling by saying that he considered 5 percent an outrageous sum, unless John cared to pay both Biaggi and Ehrlich out of his own pocket. Biaggi repeated the speech he had made the previous fall about the invaluable help he and Ehrlich had rendered in recent years, though as Wedtech had grown in power, the two men had become less and less useful. And he added a pointed threat: just as he had raised Wedtech to its present height, so he could destroy it.

Fred did not react well to threats, and he continued to talk about the company's need for capital. John, on the edge of panic, asked Fred to take a little walk with him into the next room, which happened to be the narrow bathroom with the shower and the elegant fixtures. The two men conducted a highly audible argument: John kept telling Fred that he couldn't go back on his word, and that the company couldn't afford to make an enemy of Biaggi. Fred finally threw in the towel—perhaps literally—and went back to tell Biaggi that he had won his 5 percent.

Tony had sat through the meeting in a state of reverence. He had just joined this upstart firm in the South Bronx, and here was the most powerful and famous Italian politician he knew of dropping by to talk about his role in the firm. "I remember," he says, "going home and telling my wife, 'I met Mario Biaggi tonight. I sat in a meeting with Mario Biaggi. I shook hands, he listened to what I had to say. And I was impressed. I was impressed with myself, and I was impressed with these people I was becoming a part of." Tony had no idea that Biaggi was committing extortion or violating income limits set by the Ethics in Government Act. He just thought that he was seeing how the world really worked.

Now that Biaggi had his $1.8 million worth of stock, he had to find a way of surreptitiously conveying it to himself. He had taken great care to disguise his involvement with Wedtech, neither contacting government officials directly on behalf of the company, nor even, to the surprise of his colleagues, attending the press conference announcing the award of the engine contract. Receipt of the funds ran counter to the Ethics in Government Act, and his entire relationship with Wedtech could be construed as a violation of the bribery stature, which prohibits the acceptance by public officials of "anything of value . . . in return for . . . being influenced in the performance of any official act."

At a meeting after his sit-down with Wedtech, according to testimony offered by Biaggi's accountant, Irwin Wolf, Biaggi asked what he could do to keep the stock. "The question arose," Wolf testified, "can it be put in the name of the law partnership and still have the congressman have some control or ownership of the stock?" This had been the original plan, but Wolf explained that Biaggi could exercise no control over stock given to a partnership of which he was no longer a member. The problem, says Wolf, was discussed "back and forth across the table" by Mario Biaggi, his son Richard, also a lawyer, Ehrlich, Wolf, and Biaggi's attorney, Louis Ruggiero—four lawyers and an accountant, all of whom must have understood that they were talking about circumventing or breaking the law. Finally, Wolf testified, the group decided that "the stock would have to be registered in the name of Richard, because there didn't seem to be any alternative." The other half of the stock would go to Bernard Ehrlich. Richard Biaggi had no relationship with Wedtech, but he had joined Biaggi & Ehrlich the year before. His own role in this decision seems to have consisted of little more than acquiescing to his strong-willed father. There was no question but that Richard was only the stand-in or nominee. In July, Wolf sent Ehrlich a letter in which he suggested a meeting to explain the tax effect of the receipt of stock on Ehrlich and Mario Biaggi.

In late May or early June, Tony explained to Arthur Siskind and Jeffrey Rubin that the biggest chunk of Wedtech stock would not be going, as planned, to the law firm of Biaggi & Ehrlich, but to Richard Biaggi and Bernard Ehrlich. Jeffrey Rubin knew that Ehrlich had hung with Wedtech through all the bad times, and Tony explained that the huge stock gift was a reward for services rendered. But "I didn't know [Richard Biaggi] from a hole in the wall," Rubin recalls. It seemed more than passing strange that one of the largest blocks of shares was going to someone with no known connection to the firm. Still, that was Wedtech's business. "Clients do things that you don't ask questions about," says Ira Sorkin, a Squadron Ellenoff lawyer. "How Biaggi and Ehrlich chose to whack up the stock is up to them."

Anyway, the lawyers had grown accustomed to Wedtech's doing all sorts of unaccountable things, especially with its stock. Soon after their engagement started, Tony had come to Arthur Siskind to say that Wedtech would be giving 40,000 shares to an offshore company called Bellinguer NV in exchange for a short-term loan of $500,000. The stock would serve, in effect, as collateral, and would be returned when the loan was repaid after the public offering.

What Siskind didn't know is that he was seeing the tail end of the cash-in-a-briefcase transaction from the previous fall. Bellinguer was a company set up by John Tartaglia for Pat Simone. The loan it made to Wedtech was, in fact, an ingenious sham. Once it received the money, Wedtech would write checks against it to the very same friends and family members who had laundered the original payment, thus "repaying" them for the "loans" they had made to Wedtech in the fall. The intermediaries were not, of course, permitted to keep the proceeds. After cashing the checks, they returned the money to Wedtech, which forked it back to Simone. Bellinguer was thus left with 40,000 shares of Wedtech stock, which it had purchased at 12.5, and which it would resell immediately after the closing at 16—a profit of $130,000, minus the underwriter's commission.

What troubled Siskind about the transaction was that Tartaglia had refused to reveal the owner of Bellinguer. Siskind says that he knew that Tartaglia represented Simone, but that, notwithstanding the popular prejudice against Italians who run gigantic auto-wrecking concerns in the Bronx, he had no reason to be concerned that Simone might be the ultimate owner. In fact, Rubin conceded in testimony that he understood that Simone was prepared to guarantee the transaction, and that "we were concerned that the company might be a criminal company." Squadron Ellenoff advised Wedtech that the company ought not sell the shares to Bellinguer, though the owners could accomplish the same end by selling their own stock. Rubin was asked whether this meant that Wedtech "did indirectly what you didn't want to do directly," and admitted that it did, though later in testimony he said that the two transactions weren't really the same. The effect, in any case, was that Squadron Ellenoff, along with the bankers' lawyers, Shearman & Sterling, was able to satisfy its due diligence obligation, since the firm was not constrained to disclose the details of a private stock sale, as it would have been with a corporate sale.

THIRTEEN

THIRTEEN

Near-Death Experience: III

EVEN AS WEDTECH was offering itself to Wall Street as the $100 million miracle of the week, the company was skating along the edge of bankruptcy. No other company, it seemed, could live as dangerously as Wedtech and still survive. Every time it failed by the rules of the marketplace, it had recourse to the political system, which is to say that Wedtech had become much like other defense contractors—or like many big firms that know who butters their bread—but more so. Wedtech had grown addicted to the opium of influence, and it was an addiction that would prove incurable, because it made life very much easier. Influence allowed Wedtech to fail its way upward.

The only thing standing between Wedtech and bankruptcy by this time was, Mario alleges, the good offices of Gordon Osgood. Over the years Osgood had allowed Wedtech to box up whatever parts it had finished on the M-113 cooling and suspension kits and send the crates down to the Red River Arsenal in Alabama. Osgood made sure that Wedtech's progress payments would be released before the rest of the parts had been sent, a practice known as "short shipping." Now, in early 1983, Osgood allegedly prodded the Defense Contract Audit Agency into accelerating the schedule of payments, thus providing upfront money, just as the progress payment fraud had done. And Wedtech's payments to Osgood's company, Multi-Mac, kept coming, $3000 or $4000 a month, with sometimes an extra check added in the middle of the month.

Bank Leumi was still holding off on the new line of credit. Wedtech owed the Economic Development Administration most of the $2 million from the 1980 loan, and Citibank most of the $2,170,000 loan that the EDA had guaranteed. Bank Leumi flatly refused to extend credit to Wedtech unless the EDA agreed to subordinate its interest on the 1980 loan and loan guarantee—to give the bank, that is, first shot at Wedtech's assets should the company become unable to pay. But the EDA was not about to take second position to a commercial bank, so it looked as if the company would collapse before it could make the public offering. It was like the engine contract all over again. If Wedtech didn't get the EDA to do what it was not inclined to do, and do it fast, it was curtains.

As of late May 1983, the scoring on the EDA subordination stood as follows. Larry Shorten had persuaded Bank Leumi to provide a $3.5 million line of credit and to assume the $2.2 million remaining on the Citibank loan, if the EDA would agree to subordination. But the principal officials in the EDA's Philadelphia branch had been unsympathetic to Wedtech's case. Bernie Ehrlich was leaning on the office, but to no avail.

Representative Biaggi may have seen Wedtech's dilemma magnified through the lens of his new financial interest in the company. Fred had just capitulated on the stock question, and Wedtech's survival was suddenly worth almost $2 million to the legislator. For the first time he visited Senator D'Amato himself to discuss one of Wedtech's problems instead of sending over Mario and General Ehrlich. He also invited the senator to one of his fund raisers for the express purpose, Mario testified, of intimidating an EDA official who was seated at the Wedtech table. At the end of the evening D'Amato was brought over to meet the official, who explained the EDA's position. The senator frowned and announced that he would see what he could do. Later he did place several calls to the EDA administrator to complain about Wedtech's treatment.

But Wedtech was getting nowhere. Ehrlich, Biaggi, and Biaggi's aide, Lou Benza, were supposed to roll over the middle-level bureaucrats in the Philadelphia office, but it was they who were getting rolled. On May 27 the regional administrator wrote that subordination would be possible only if Wedtech made up its delinquent payments and improved its cash flow projection. In any case, it would take time, which Wedtech didn't have. More important, the regional office decided to get out of the political storm; the matter was kicked upstairs, to the office of the EDA administrator, Carlos Campbell.

Biaggi and Ehrlich had failed to get the problem solved locally, where they had influence. John had never had a very high opinion of Ehrlich, and his esteem for Biaggi had faded as the congressman was overshadowed by more prominent figures. Now he decided that Fred had been right the whole time, and he stomped around the office denouncing the two, especially Ehrlich. But this was not 1980, and Wedtech now had the resources to deal on a national level. Biaggi and Ehrlich were supplanted by Bob Wallach and Mark Bragg. Wallach, like Mario Biaggi, had a serious economic stake in Wedtech's future. Mario had made it clear that the company could start paying Wallach's monthly retainer once it received the revenue from the stock sale, so Wallach picked up Wedtech's fallen standard and rushed into battle.

On May 20 he called Meese's aide Jim Jenkins, who had proved to be Wedtech's champion in the battle over the engine contract. Jenkins considered Wallach a nuisance, but he heard him out and then suggested that Wallach deliver a copy of the original 1980 loan agreement. From his years as a private consultant, Jenkins knew that the EDA didn't take a secondary position on loans. Wallach, though, was a consultant, not a clerk, and he wasn't about to waste his time with legalese and red tape. Instead of doing the paperwork, he sent Jenkins one of his Wallach-grams, detailing Wedtech's desperate situation and including the usual unsubstantiated and false rumor about what was going on behind the scenes. Jenkins sat on it.

On June 1, Wallach called again. The next day, he called again. On the sixth day he went to Jenkins' office and said that Wedtech was desperate. He called again on June 8 and yet again on June 9. Wallach was turning from a nuisance into a virulent pest. At some point in the midst of this blur of unannounced visits and unreturned phone calls, Wallach, sitting in Jenkins' office, virtually demanded that the aide call the Commerce Department and get Secretary Malcolm Baldridge to go over the head of Carlos Campbell, whom Wallach described as a sworn enemy, and agree to the subordination. Jenkins said that he would do no such thing. At this point, Jenkins recalls, "Wallach said, 'I'll go see Ed.' I said, 'We really shouldn't get Ed mixed up in this. Let EDA figure out what they have to do and do what they have to do.' Anyway, he said he would go down and see Ed. And I said to myself, I didn't feel comfortable with him relaying my thoughts. I better go myself. So I went with him."

Wallach literally walked down the hall, with Jim Jenkins trailing behind him, and, as he was accustomed to doing, strode straight into Ed Meese's office. He recounted the entire story to Meese, and complained of Jenkins' insistence that Meese keep his distance. Meese, according to Jenkins, then said, "That's good advice," the conversation turned elsewhere, and Jenkins felt it was safe to leave yet another Wallach gabfest. If Jenkins can be taken at his word, this scene would certainly rate as a rare victory for good government, but it does not seem to have been a lasting one.

Jenkins never did anything about Wallach's importunities except report them to the Cabinet Affairs secretary, Craig Fuller, and ask Fuller whether the White House could contact the Commerce Department to speed along the loan. Fuller sent a memo on the subject to the office of the White House counselor, Fred Fielding. Here, as on a different planet, the restraints governing White House activity were considered self-evident, as they had been the year before. "We should not, of course, attempt to persuade EDA concerning the merits of Welbilt's application . . ." wrote an associate counsel, John G. Roberts, Jr. "The action could easily be misinterpreted by Commerce and EDA, and misperceived by others, as White House pressure on the merits of the loan or the merits of the expedition request." One cannot but admire the writer's exquisite tact.

While Bob Wallach was hitting the panic buttons, Mark Bragg was putting the arm on Carlos Campbell. Though a loyal Republican and a friend of Nofziger's, Campbell was not a man who could be counted on to snap to attention when the partisan colors were waved in his face. He was one of the highest-ranking blacks in the administration; he was also, he says, a former spook with the Defense Intelligence Agency. Like Jim Sanders at the SBA, he had been given an agency that conservatives had long considered an impediment to the functioning of the free market, a clanking machine in the Great Society works.

The EDA's job was to provide loans to companies willing to invest in depressed areas, and was considered, even by some liberals who wanted to keep it in business, a tool in the hands of politicians trying to take care of constituents. Forcefully recovering loans was considered draconian. "Before my watch," says Campbell, a man not shy about listing his accomplishments, "the loan process was, a dollar down, and run you down." The delinquency rate had reached 42 percent. Campbell was instructed by David Stockman, budget director, to start collecting those loans while the Reagan troops abolished his agency. Campbell proceeded to chase deadbeats while turning down $80 million worth of

loans approved by his regional directors and making innumerable enemies in Congress.

Bragg made his first call to Campbell on May 23, as Wallach was
starting to besiege Jenkins. Campbell was used to hearing from congressmen and their aides; this was the first time he had heard of a loan
recipient with a lobbyist. Bragg used a very different approach from
Wallach's, though it was not a great deal more winning. "He was not
really what you would call courteous and mild-mannered," Campbell
recalls. "Mark tried to initially impress you. He said, 'Do you know who I
am?'" The aptly named Bragg proceeded to talk not only about his
partner, but about one of his children, who was dating one of the children of Helen Robbins, a powerhouse in the Commerce Department
who served as Secretary Baldridge's chief of staff. Bragg spoke of "the
White House interest" in a manner that hinted at undisclosed depths of
power. The hint implied a threat. "The way it came off," recalls
Campbell's deputy, C. Dale Randall, "was like we were not following
orders."

Campbell was willing to take that risk, and he made it clear to Bragg
that he had not determined the merits of the case. Both Campbell and
Randall felt that Wedtech was so busy marshaling support that it hadn't
bothered to furnish the documents that might have convinced them.
John and Mario and Bob Wallach and Bernie Ehrlich just took it for
granted that Campbell was yet another hostile bureaucrat susceptible to
nothing save brute force. Maybe he was, but nobody thought to suppose
otherwise.

With Wedtech expecting to go bankrupt any day, and Wallach playing
his friendship with Meese for all it was worth, Bragg turned up the heat.
He had Helen Robbins call Campbell several times. SBA Administrator
Jim Sanders, who had nothing to do with the transaction and had never
even spoken to Campbell before, also called. Even an old friend and
fellow black, the White House personnel officer E. Pendleton James,
called to talk about Wedtech, says Campbell, who insists that he refused
to return the call. Senator D'Amato called. Campbell began to feel as if
someone was beating on his head.

At the end of June, Campbell went on a ten-day government trip to
South Africa. Negotiations between the regional office, the bank, Wedtech, and Squadron Ellenoff had been proceeding in the meanwhile, so
several days after Campbell returned, on July 14, the Philadelphia office
recommended to headquarters that the loan be subordinated, given
certain conditions regarding repayment. As soon as he heard the news,
Bragg called Campbell once again. He assumed that Campbell was ready

to sign the agreement instantly, but he was not. Bragg was furious, and he dropped his few remaining shreds of civility. "He had no control," recalls Campbell. "He was yelling, he was shouting, he was threatening with obscenities. He wanted me to *do,* just do. He wanted me to sign something. He did not want me to have any kind of review of documents." Campbell tried to explain, and Bragg told him that he would have his head. Campbell told him to cool off, or perhaps worse.

There now ensued probably the most outlandish sequence of events in Wedtech's entire influence-peddling history. When Bragg told Wallach that Campbell was putting up a stone wall, Wallach, in what was now a permanent swivet, called the Bronx, where a birthday party for Fred was under way, and told Mario to leave the building, get in a taxi, and take the next shuttle to Washington. They would have to do something, though it wasn't clear what. Since Mario didn't have time to go home and get a change of clothes, Tony gave him $500 in cash, and off he went.

Once Mario arrived in Washington, Wallach, with his typical air of amateur spycraft, said that arrangements had been made "to get into the White House," and instructed him to appear in Lafayette Park, across from the White House, at 5:30 the next morning. Mario, who hadn't had time to shave or brush his teeth, met Wallach in the predawn darkness and then settled down on a park bench while Wallach disappeared into the White House, where, he said, "his friend" would be holding a "national security" meeting. Several hours later Wallach emerged to say that he had pulled Meese aside during a break in the meeting. "Wallach told me," Mario testified, "that his friend had called Secretary Baldridge at his house and that he was taking a shower at that time, and that his friend had requested that the secretary sign the subordination because he could overrule Carlos Campbell . . . Then he continued and he said that Secretary Baldridge himself would not sign the subordination agreement because it was too hot politically," but that he would try to get one of Baldridge's assistant secretaries to do so.

It is safe to say that this telephone call, if it was actually made, could easily be misinterpreted by Commerce and the EDA, and misperceived by others, as White House pressure for the loan. The situation is almost too bizarre to contemplate. The counselor to the President ducks out of a meeting with the National Security Adviser and other officials—or any meeting, for that matter—to telephone a Cabinet secretary at 6:00 A.M.—or any time, for that matter—to ask him to overrule one of his assistant secretaries on a matter governed by department regulations. All this to please a friend who works as a consultant to a small government contractor. Has the majesty of government ever bowed quite so low before

Rotarian chumminess? This was the same Ed Meese who had allegedly told Wallach only a month earlier that he would not intervene in the EDA matter. At the time, of course, he had Jim Jenkins around for support. He just couldn't say no. As Ursula Meese used to say of her husband, if he were a woman he would have gotten pregnant a hundred times over.

Baldridge died in 1987, and his widow has said that she does not specifically remember the call. Meese does not recall it either, but, then, Meese has been unable to recall almost any specific act he performed on behalf of Wedtech or Wallach. His calendar lists a 7:15 breakfast with Wallach, and he does remember discussing the EDA loan with his friend. Another note shows that Baldridge did call Meese later that day in response to a call from the counselor. The note includes the phrase, in Meese's handwriting, "Welbilt, Peo. coming in 18 July—want to do it!"

One of the signatures of Wallach's lobbying activity is that it caused an enormous amount of fuss and stir without necessarily leading to anything. It seems clear that Meese did, in fact, call Baldridge. That Baldridge then contacted his own officials is less certain. Helen Robbins did speak to the office of the Commerce Department's general counsel to ask that it look into the matter, though she has said she did so at the request of Mark Bragg, not of the secretary.

She may very well have been trying to find someone else to sign the subordination agreement in lieu of Campbell. Bragg instructed Mario to stay on his park bench like a bum in a business suit, and when Mario called in every hour Bragg kept him updated on the effort to find a signatory, or even to fill the vacant spot of under secretary in order to get the document signed—a proposal that sounds suspiciously like Bragg braggadocio. In any event, the effort failed. Campbell had scheduled a meeting in the EDA conference room for July 19. He would have to be bludgeoned, or converted, then.

Campbell says that he was converted; Mario says that he was bludgeoned. The July 19 meeting was attended by Commerce Department and EDA officials, including C. Dale Randall; Howard Squadron, Mario Moreno, and John Mariotta; and, to Campbell's surprise, Lyn Nofziger and Mark Bragg. Campbell didn't see why lobbyists should be attending the meeting, but, then, Bragg had gotten himself to the 1982 meeting in the White House basement over the engine contract. Mario insists that Campbell spoke against Wedtech until Nofziger asked him to step out for a moment. Fifteen minutes later, Mario says, Campbell returned a new man. Campbell insists that there was no such huddle, and both Randall and Squadron agree.

When he came to the meeting, Campbell says, "my position was that I didn't have a position." He wanted to be convinced. And, he says, Howard Squadron proceeded to convince him. Squadron argued that if the EDA's objective was to get its money back, the most sensible course was to accept the subordinate position in order to ensure that Wedtech received the interim financing that would permit the public offering to go forward. The stock, Squadron said, was virtually presold, so the EDA could feel confident that Wedtech would have no trouble repaying the 1980 loan from the proceeds of the offering.

Campbell had been hounded unmercifully by lobbyists and government officials, and he was eager to get the entire matter over with. No one had to tell him that Lyn Nofziger was the wrong man for a public official to disappoint. Campbell's position in many ways seems analogous to that of Dr. J. Raymond Sculley, the Army assistant secretary who thought awarding the engine contract to Wedtech was a bad idea and bristled because of the pressure he was subjected to, but eventually gave way rather than put himself in front of a speeding freight train. Very few government officials are eager to cross the line that separates integrity from martyrdom.

And yet, for all that, Squadron's argument was irrefutable, and it's not hard to imagine Campbell feeling relieved that he had good reason to do what expedience dictated he do. Wedtech, like any debtor teetering on the edge of bankruptcy, had its lender over a barrel. If the company failed, the EDA would be left with a fraction of the original loan.

Campbell, who believes that his later firing was a consequence of his intransigence over the Wedtech loan, views the entire exercise as a waste of energy. He insists that "the political influence hurt them. It took a situation that could have been resolved within two, three weeks and stretched it out over three or four months." It's a nice irony: Wedtech had become so addicted to the opium of influence that it declined to make a legitimate case for itself even when one was available.

FOURTEEN

FOURTEEN

The End of the Rainbow

EVEN BEFORE Carlos Campbell had been made to see the light, Wedtech was well into the process of discarding its old rags and donning the finery of a publicly held corporation. On June 17 a proper board meeting was convened for the first time. In the past John and Fred, and later Mario, had simply agreed to do something, and then done it. Now the three met in Squadron Ellenoff's twenty-third-floor conference room, along with Tony and Larry Shorten, Arthur Siskind, and a Squadron Ellenoff associate, Randi Zeller. The pattern was set for future board meetings, which were also held in the offices of Squadron Ellenoff: John would preside, and ramble and rumble about this and that, and read and reread documents, and demand to have things explained to him; and then Randi Zeller would redact the minutes into boardroom English. Thus: "Mr. Mariotta stated that the first order of business was the election of Directors. He noted that the Board of Directors had amended the By-Laws of the Corporation in 1979 . . ."

The board was ratified as consisting of John, Fred, and Mario. All of the loans, mortgages, investments, and business of the past several years were ratified, as were the scrambled jottings in the stock book. The distribution of shares to Richard Biaggi, Bernard Ehrlich, Tony, Larry Shorten, and the others, was approved. Arrangements were made for two new bridge loans, of $1 million and $500,000, desperately needed to keep the company alive until the EDA came through. And the company changed its name from Welbilt to Wedtech. When it had registered with the SEC, the company received a trademark complaint from the Welbilt Stove Company, and everyone had agreed on the name Wedtech.

On July 1, 1983, with the company still laying bridge loans end to end, it issued to the SEC the registration statement and prospectus over which its auditors, lawyers, and bankers had toiled for so many months. It was a cautious document, as such documents must be, warning that "investors should be aware" that the company "has shown substantial growth only in recent years." But what growth! From $1,515,000 in 1978 to $5,624,000 in 1980 to $20,492,000 in 1982 to $8,838,000 in the first four months of 1983. Investors were warned likewise that, in regard to the coating technology, the company "has no prior production or marketing experience." But what prospects! "The Company is currently testing applications," the prospectus stated, in the fields of computer cabinets, circuit boards, metallic pipes, fiber optics, ceramics, and turbine blades.

The registration statement and prospectus made up sixty pages of fine print, bland and businesslike, and like all such documents it gave an impression of unimpeachable factuality. Yet every lie the insiders had told, and every fraud they had committed, was enshrined in these pages. "During 1981," the authors droned under the heading "Certain Transactions," "the Company loaned Mr. Neuberger $185,000." That was FHJ. "On May 13, 1983, Messrs. Mariotta, Neuberger, and Moreno sold 18,200 shares, 18,200 shares, and 3,600 shares of Common Stock, respectively, to John Tartaglia," and on and on. That was the resolution of cash-in-the-briefcase. And then there were the 153,000 shares reserved for "additional senior management personnel." Even the profit-and-loss figures bore invisible fingerprints. Wedtech's net income for 1982 was listed at $3,134,000, its first significant profit and presumably a sign of growing stability. But $3 million of that amount was the SBA's business development funds. Tony says that he had wanted to list the grant under "additional paid-in capital" rather than profit, but was overridden by Allen Ackerman of Main Hurdman.

The Wedtech prospectus proved, if proof was needed, that you can't believe everything you read. But it may have also proved that people will believe what they wish to believe, even experts who get paid huge sums of money to separate fact from fiction. When the prospectus had been distributed, and the EDA problem finally settled, John and Fred and Tony and Larry Shorten began making the rounds of investors, accompanied by the bankers from Moseley Hallgarten. They put on a little show, as corporate managers are expected to do on these road shows, only theirs was a sort of opera buffa with numbers. And it worked.

Vincent Di Preta, head of marketing at Moseley, kept the group company most of the time. It was a unique experience. The first time he brought in the owners to meet a group of money managers in New York, Di Preta recalls, "the only thing that came to my mind—and I started perspiring profusely—was the movie *The Producers,* where they try to put on the worst Broadway show, and it turns out to be funny. John Mariotta got up and said, 'I'm the president of Wedtech, and I'm a New York Rican, and a New York Rican is a fella that can't speak English or Spanish.' And he said, 'A lot of people didn't think that us machete swingers and spear chuckers could really do it.' I just sat there, and my mouth was wide open. I couldn't believe what I was hearing. Everyone started laughing."

And then Fred talked about squeezing through the slats of the cattle car taking him to his death, and walking to Israel and emigrating to America and meeting John Mariotta. He told the story about finding Dr. Pinkhasov, and a few other stories, too. At the presentation in Los Angeles all the investors wanted to know if the headquarters was near the infamous Fort Apache, and were disappointed to learn that it was down the street from Yankee Stadium. Fred, however, reassured them that there was a prison only a few hundred yards away.

And, as with Dr. Pinkhasov's alchemy, the amazing thing about this presentation was that it worked. The bankers liked Wedtech's kookiness. "It's a refreshing change for a lot of the portfolio people who are used to the Harvard MBA types coming in to talk the numbers," says Di Preta. And perhaps, though they would be loath to admit it, even money men like to have something to believe in. Of course the men from First Fidelity and Dreyfus and so on didn't tell their clients to buy Wedtech because it was exotic, or because it would increase their self-esteem, but being colorful and virtuous didn't hurt.

Being connected didn't hurt either. The prospectus had baldly stated that Wedtech would have to leave the 8(a) program as a consequence of the offering, since John would no longer control a majority of the stock. (This expectation may have made the ownership fraud seem a matter of history.) In 1982, the company stated, 61 percent of its revenues were derived from contracts awarded under the 8(a) program; that fraction would grow swiftly as the engine contract took effect. How, then, did Wedtech propose to survive in the competitive atmosphere? Or, given the reality of defense contracting, who was in the company's corner? The money men wanted to know whether this Richard Biaggi was related to Mario Biaggi. Of course, Tony would reassure them, it's Mario Biaggi's stock; he's our guru. And then Tony and the others would talk about Bob Wallach and Nofziger & Bragg and all the other heavies in their corner. "They used to say, 'Terrific,'" Tony recalls. "'Circle me for 50,000 shares.'"

And so, between one thing and another, Wedtech and its underwriter found that selling 1.5 million shares was a snap. On August 25 the shares were formally offered to the public on the NASDAQ exchange. By September 2 they had been sold and the offering was closed. It was a wonderful, beautiful day, the culmination of months and years of hard work, the stamp of success, for John and Fred, on a lifetime of toil and of resistance to every sort of obstacle that destiny can throw across a man's path. Each of them had sold $2.7 million worth of their shares—a little piece, really—to the public, and they were suddenly richer than they had ever dreamed.

"I want a new car," John announced. They were returning uptown from a celebratory luncheon with the Moseley people down in Wall Street. John had always been a one-car man, just as he had been a one-woman man. He had driven the lucky Lincoln until it wore out; then he had bought a Cadillac, which he had given away to Mario Rosado, the Pentecostal minister who worked at Wedtech; then he had bought yet another white Lincoln Town Car. Now, however, John was made of money, and he wanted something new. He walked into the Mercedes dealership on Park Avenue and 56th Street. Several minutes later he walked out, spitting mad. He had thought that the slights and humiliations had come to an end, but he was still a dumb Puerto Rican in the eyes of the world, or so it seemed. The salesman had looked at him, with his tinted glasses and high crown of hair and piping voice, as if he wanted to hot-wire a car instead of buy one.

"I've changed my mind," said John. Oh, really?, asked the others. You want a BMW? No, said John, "we're *all* going to get a car." He was going to get the man's attention. So everybody—John, Fred, Mario, Tony, Larry Shorten—trooped into the Mercedes showroom and began mooning over the beautiful big cats couched inside. And the salesman, who had had quite enough, sharply asked John, "Do you want to buy a car or not?" And John raised his stumpy figure to its greatest height and said,

"No, I *don't* want a buy a car. I want to buy *six.*" And that is precisely what John did, though he was persuaded to lease the cars rather than buy them. He leased one Mercedes for each of them, and another for Blue-stine, for whom it would serve as a welcoming gift. It was a great moment in the history of Wedtech and in the history of John Mariotta.

FIFTEEN

FIFTEEN

Promises to Keep, Pockets to Fill

FOR MONTHS NOW Wedtech had lived hand to mouth, or loan to loan, but by September 2, 1983, investors had bought $30 million worth of stock. The company was fantastically rich—for a moment. For the first time, though scarcely the last, the insiders would watch mountains of capital slide through their fingers like so much sand. There were all those people to pay off. The first $6 million went to John, Fred, and Mario for their stock. The EDA had to be made whole—that was almost $4 million —and so did the vendors, many of whom had been supplying goods on credit, and the lawyers and the bankers and the bankers' lawyers and the auditors. The offering alone had cost $1 million. The bridge loans had to be paid off—another $1.4 million. And then there were the company's friends and relations.

Bob Wallach started pressing his case before the money even arrived. Wallach had waited patiently since the previous fall, when he had presented his retainer agreement. In mid-August he had called Mario, who was grounded at home by his whooping cough attack, and asked for the

$200,000 he thought Mario had agreed to. But Tony told Mario that the money just wasn't going to be there; they had all made too many promises. Mario came back to Wallach and asked him to accept $100,000. Wallach couldn't believe that the company didn't have the wherewithal to give him what he deserved after two years of working absolutely gratis, and he told Mario that he felt cheated. But he needed the money, and he settled with Mario for $125,000.

Mario also said that Tony wanted Wallach to ascribe the payment to supposed work on the public offering rather than to his influence peddling, which was what Wedtech was paying him for, or for his sage counsel, which Wallach believed he was offering. Tony had explained that any cost associated with the raising of funds could be accounted for as an expense of doing business, and thus would not be deducted from gross income. Accountants try to "expense" everything, but are usually restrained by, if nothing else, timidity. Tony, however, was not a timid man: he expensed everything. It seemed no great matter, in any case, and on September 7 Wallach sent Tony a brief note stating that "my fee for consultation relative to the registration and public offering is $125,000."

Everybody was now hewing mighty chips from the Big Rock Candy Mountain. The day after the stock sale John Tartaglia arrived at 595 Gerard, along with Pat Simone and his son Joseph, neither of whom the Wedtech people had ever met. They had come to trade in their 40,000 shares for $640,000, minus a commission of $48,000—the principal on their loan. The interest, they reminded the debtors, was expected soon. Two weeks after that, on September 6, Richard Bluestine signed on as senior vice president, the title he had insisted on, at $125,000 a year, which exceeded anyone else's salary at the time. He would receive, as of October 1, not only the 153,000 shares of stock but a corporate guarantee for a $900,000 loan to offset his tax liability.

The fact that all of the shares reserved for "additional senior management personnel" had been reserved for one man, and that that man reached an understanding with the company only two weeks after the offering, *and* that that man was Richard Bluestine, on whose assurances Main Hurdman had depended at moments of grave doubt, might have been expected to set off some alarms. The Squadron Ellenoff attorneys admit that they were surprised. Still, you can't tell a client what to do with its money. No alarms appear to have sounded, even at Main Hurdman.

The parade continued later in September, when Richard Stolfi of Local 875 called to remind Fred of a promise made earlier in the year. When Stolfi had learned, that spring, of the planned offering, he had suddenly become the hard-nosed union boss he had never been, informing Fred that he would ask for an increase of $3.00 an hour for his men over each of the next three years, five days' leave with pay for the death of any relative, a vastly expanded corporate contribution to the pension plan, and more. Fred knew the drill, but he also knew he had to play along. He told Stolfi that Wedtech would never knuckle under to such extortionate terms, Stolfi dropped by to iron out the differences, and, after a little haggling, the two men agreed on a $25,000 cash payment in exchange for the usual exploitation of the workers. In mid-September Fred had gathered up the cash from John and Mario, added his own contribution, and paid Stolfi the $25,000 plus several months' worth of the regular $5000 bribe.

Nor were the new executives ignored. On September 8, John called Tony and Larry Shorten into his office. "We've put a lot of cash in our pockets," John said, "and you guys deserve something for yourselves." John wanted to give each of them a $50,000 gift from himself, Fred, and Mario, but Fred, being Fred, said he wanted to make it a loan instead. So John handed each of them a check for $50,000, and Tony and Larry each wrote out three promissory notes, in the 45–45–9 proportion that had governed ownership and the spoils of the FHJ account.

John, Fred, and Mario had just, in fact, put an absolutely unbelievable amount of cash in their pockets. John and Fred had sold into the market 182,000 shares each, and on that wonderful day of August 25 received checks for $2.7 million; Mario had sold 36,000 shares and received $540,000. None of them had grown up in split-level Colonials in leafy suburbs; they had never had anything, and now they had practically everything.

Two years earlier they had taken Bob Wallach to El Deportivo when he asked them where they ate; then Wallach had introduced them to the places where he liked to be seen. Now they could be seen at those places, too. The Wedtech roustabouts made a habit of driving down from the South Bronx to dine in La Côte Basque or at the Plaza Athenée. There, after so many years of neglect and scorn, they could be welcomed with servile smiles by maîtres d's. There was nothing that the toffs at the next table could buy that their money couldn't buy just as well. And they were willing to spend more of it.

John was willing to spend anything to get people's attention and keep it. He fell in love with the River Café, a restaurant with huge windows that look out over lower Manhattan and the East River from the edge of Brooklyn, and he ate there frequently. When he arrived at the restaurant, John would hand the maître d' hundreds of dollars and tell him to get a table. He may have been the only customer who could dine at the River

Café without a reservation; even if every place was taken, the waiters would scurry to set up a table in any available space. John enjoyed the scurrying. He seemed not to carry bills in denominations under $100. John's generosity was impulsive and loud; he gave legendary tips; and he gave them with the nonchalance of a Saudi prince.

But John handed most of the money, at least the legal money, over to Jenny, who controlled all domestic details of the household. Jenny was a conservative investor, and put the funds into bank certificates. The couple did use half a million dollars to purchase a condo in the luxurious Condado Bay development in Puerto Rico. It was, to use one of Tony's favorite words, "gawgeous"—wall-to-wall marble, picture windows looking out over the bay. It was also, to use another of Tony's locutions, "yuge," an entire floor measuring maybe five thousand square feet. Over the next year John and Jenny filled the apartment with expensive Oriental furniture and gewgaws. John liked the idea of returning to Puerto Rico, which his parents had left fifty years earlier, as a big shot, and he and Jenny spent almost all of their vacation time in the condo.

John also gave away tens of thousands of dollars, especially the stolen money that came through the FHJ account. He gave to churches and synagogues and Hispanic groups and practically anyone who knocked on his door. John gave money away, and asked nothing in return. It was a form of grandiosity, certainly, but it was also a form of moral therapy. When Ceil Lewis, who kept John's bank records, would ask about his impulsive and almost heedless philanthropy, John would say that he was trying to wash dirty money. None of the others made a similar effort at absolution.

The only person Fred was willing to share money with was his girlfriend of the moment—Shoshana, Alicia, Theresa, known collectively as "the bimbettes." The bimbettes did well by Fred, for he kept them well supplied with furs, jewelry, cruises, hotel suites, and so on. Fred also bought himself a condo at Jackson Hole in Wyoming and a town house in London, and he invested in businesses in England and in Israel. Fred probably could have used a Jenny Mariotta to keep his hand out of his wallet, because the following spring Fred announced to an amazed Tony that he had run through the entire pile. He was broke. Tony arranged a $1 million loan from Bank Leumi to tide Fred over.

In the middle of September, as the money was going out in every direction, the insiders found a way to bring some home. The company was expanding, outgrowing 595 Gerard and the smaller facilities it had picked up over the years. Pat Simone, who confided to Tony that he owned $30 million worth of real estate in the Bronx and Westchester, had a structure under lease from New York State that he thought Wedtech might be able to use. Known as the Rodolitz Building, it was a massive, hangarlike affair, 201,000 square feet, a good 60 feet in height, looming up over the Harlem River at the eastern end of 149th Street. The building had been abandoned and was in an advanced state of dilapidation. There were no services, and a trench had been gouged in the middle of the floor.

After viewing this hulk, Simone and the Wedtech group concluded that it would take roughly $3 million to heave it into shape. It was a vastly larger construction job than Wedtech had ever undertaken. The project was discussed at several meetings by Wedtech executives and Simone at the latter's ominous headquarters at his Hunts Point Auto Wrecking Company, a mile or so north of the Rodolitz Building. At a third meeting, attended only by John and Tony from Wedtech, Simone, according to Tony, said that everyone could make a fortune if Wedtech agreed to let him run the construction work. Simone said that he would hire compliant contractors, pad the costs, and kick back the excess to himself and Wedtech. ("Simone denies that categorically," says Tartaglia, "and I know of no such agreement.")

In the ensuing negotiations, which were enormously complicated by Simone's refusal to use the telephone, Tony served as the conduit between Wedtech and the auto-wrecking king. Somehow, through the most circuitous and unlikely of paths, life had deposited Tony at the doorstep of the kind of mobster worshiped back in Bensonhurst. Simone and his son both carried guns on their hips; Tartaglia, who described himself as Simone's nephew (he denies having said so), kept his strapped to an ankle. Simone's other son had been killed a few years earlier in a holdup in Hunts Point, and it seemed to Tony that this fearsome figure was coming to look on him as a surrogate son. The feeling, says Tony, was not mutual, though success and toughness were two things he admired a great deal.

Even the atmosphere of Hunts Point, which was to become a familiar part of Wedtech's world, was forbidding. The neighborhood lies on the eastern edge of the Bronx, across the borough from Wedtech headquarters, and is principally known for the immense wholesale food market that dominates its waterfront side. A few blocks back, however, Hunts Point is the auto-wrecking capital of the Northeast, a place where cars go to die, and where stolen cars go to be dismembered. Pat Simone's home was a raw, brutal cementscape, a place of low buildings and immense pieces of equipment and stacks of shattered cars and big, grinding trucks. Giant forklifts wheeled across the streets with big hunks of car in their grasp. Prostitutes lolled behind wrecking establishments, flagging down the truckers.

And Pat Simone was the king of the auto wreckers. In Hunts Point proper he owed Parts Land USA and one other wrecking facility, and he owned a company called Imperial Bag and Paper. But his headquarters was located at the northern edge of the neighborhood, along the Sheridan Expressway. It was a world of its own, separated from the highway and the world beyond it by a yellow fence several hundred feet long on which HUNTS POINT AUTO WRECKERS was written in huge letters. Behind the fence at one side lay a vast automotive hecatomb, a storehouse of thousands of chopped-up car parts. Simone's office was behind the other side.

It was a scene out of *film noir*. At the edge of the mountain of glistening metal a private army of armed men prowled ceaselessly, on guard for intruders. Some of them were said to be retired city policeman. And at the head of this detachment was a large black man who kept a shotgun strapped to his back. This myrmidon was known as Curly, because of the tight corn rows in which he wore his hair. It all might have seemed faintly ridiculous if it hadn't been terrifyingly real.

By the time Tony's shuttle diplomacy had finished, Simone, according to Tony, had exacted 20 percent of the kickback for himself, 5 percent for the subcontractors, and 1 percent for a compliant bank to launder the cash. The other three-quarters went to the six men who would now run the affairs of Wedtech. This was crime in its purest form. Wedtech's survival was not at stake, nor was the cause endangered. The harum-scarum boys from the South Bronx were cutting a deal with a gangster in order to steal for themselves the money they had raised from the public. Fred and John, it's true, had been taking kickbacks from suppliers for years. Fred seemed to consider a 5 percent rake-off part of the order of nature. But this was different, and not only in magnitude. Wedtech was now operating under the scrutiny of shareholders and bankers and lawyers. It was a big, powerful company with hundreds of employees and a presence in Washington. Yet it was still driven by primal appetites.

"We're going to go to jail someday," Tony remembers telling Larry Shorten. Both men, Tony says, thought about leaving during the early fall, just as Mario had thought about leaving a few years earlier. They felt the vise closing, but they couldn't, or wouldn't, move. "I think we were convinced that we were going to make this fortune," says Tony. "We just knew we were going to hit the big time."

Tony had learned the professional's respect for the rules, and he had never played with the rules before. Now he found that a penumbra of lies seemed to be dimming all his clear, cool truths, that he had fatally compromised the integrity of the numbers, which was the only integrity he knew. The foundation was slipping; the numbers, it seemed, were only a game. But wasn't that the game everybody played? "I was influenced not only by John, Fred, and Mario," says Tony, "but by the fact that these actions were being condoned by some highly respectable people."

It wasn't just Mario Biaggi; it was Main Hurdman and Squadron Ellenoff and even the White House. He had heard Bob Wallach say, in a speech, that the only companies anyone talked about in the Reagan administration were Chrysler, which was then being sustained by emergency assistance from the government, and Wedtech. "It was like, my God, look at these people I'm with. I'm with people that are running the United States of America. These people are doing it. What are we doing wrong? And it was like a snowball: it just started rolling and rolling." It was a rationalization rather than an excuse, but rationalization was all Tony needed.

It *was* like a snowball—the rationalizations, the cover-up, and the greed. There could never be enough money. John, especially, seemed unappeasable. Wealth was to be the only thing to right the balance, to muffle the outrage from years of suffering and, he felt, ill-treatment. At a meeting in Richard Bluestine's office soon after Bluestine arrived in early October, John complained that the company was every bit as good as General Motors, but they were paid as if they were nobodies. He should be earning $300,000 or $400,000, he said, not $100,000. Tony pointed out that now that Wedtech was a public company they had to be careful not to upset the shareholders. "Fuck the shareholders!" yelled John. "This is my company and I'll take what I want to take."

John shouted at Tony a little longer and then pointed to his pocket and said that it was time to put some money in *la bolsa,* his pocket. Nobody disagreed about the goal. The problem was the means. John, Fred, and Mario wanted to restart FHJ, which had been shut down since Main Hurdman found it back in February. They had paid the union out of their own cash, and Fred was obliged to repay his $185,000 "loan." FHJ could be used to generate some quick cash. The newcomers were concerned that Main Hurdman would be looking for any activity in the FHJ account, but Fred said that his friends at the Banco Popular had opened the account without any identification number, and would destroy it the moment anyone came snooping around. John and Fred, in any case, had the last word, and FHJ was reopened. John and Fred would each receive a quarter of the proceeds, and the others would each get an eighth.

Soon after, Mario held a discussion with Wedtech's old friend Henry Zeisel. Mario suggested that Zeisel sell Wedtech used equipment but bill the company as if it were new. Zeisel, Mario testified, agreed, and about $190,000, enough for Fred's loan, came flowing into FHJ Associates. Between Zeisel and other sources, Wedtech was also able to repay the $300,000 interest on the Simone loan, and to make further payments to the union. Not until the following year would the FHJ spigots really open up and bathe them all in gold.

PART FOUR

PART FOUR

Washington
Interlude: II

SIXTEEN

SIXTEEN

A Bridge Too Far

WEDTECH'S GREATEST MOMENT was approaching. Over the final months of 1983 and the first months of the next year, the principals, above all Mario and Tony, would twist together two schemes of bribery and influence peddling into an elegant double helix. The company would defraud the SBA in order to win, corruptly, a contract from the United States Navy. The sheer ambition of the swindle is breathtaking to contemplate.

In early October, Stephen Denlinger from LAMA sent over a memo about a huge Navy contract to build pontoon causeways. Most of the work would be relatively simple, the kind of metal cutting and welding that an 8(a) manufacturer could perform, though the pontoons were not currently intended to be a set-aside project. A sane company in Wedtech's position, however, would not have gotten near the pontoon program. Wedtech was still months away from turning out its first engine, and it had only recently leased, from Pat Simone, the additional space it would need to assemble the thirteen thousand engines. It had taken years for the company to master the far simpler M-113 work. Another big contract could scarcely fail to carry Wedtech straight down to the bottom like a lead weight. Fred, as usual, told John that he was out of his mind, and this time he was right.

But Wedtech had become the impossible force. And it wasn't only John who felt that way; Mario did, too. Mario had been building up his arsenal of influence bit by bit; now he was ready to throw the whole thing into the breach. "My honest impression at that time," says Tim Sullivan, the company's Washington counsel, "was that these guys now viewed themselves as magicians, and it was just another rabbit they could pull out of a hat. Everyone was getting on the Wedtech bandwagon; it was difficult to oppose it. I don't think they were willing to *accept* anyone opposing them." Mario, like John, had become addicted to success: anything he could have, he would have.

But Wedtech couldn't even hope to get the pontoon contract, because it was just about to be exiled from the 8(a) program. In October 1980, Congress made one of its occasional futile stabs at reforming the program by requiring the SBA to "graduate" member firms after seven years; firms already camped in 8(a) seven or more years at the time the law was passed would have one more year in which to put their affairs in order. Seven years should have been plenty of time for students in set-aside university to ready themselves for the outside world, especially since the reforms instituted two years earlier, which had eliminated such refinements as the "sponsorship" system, under which black figureheads fronted for white concerns, had also focused the program on business development. The program was explicitly intended to create independence. Their period of nonage concluded, firms were to be packed off, duly prepared, to the competitive world.

Apparently, the reforms didn't quite take. The 1980 law triggered a spree of special pleading in which hundreds of firms explained, through their lawyers, why they needed more time under the federal canopy—if possible, a lot more time. The vast majority of the five thousand or so participants in the program had had neither the initiative to find government contracts for themselves nor the influence to induce SBA bureaucrats to locate contracts for them. Others, however, prospering in an environment devoid of natural predators, had grown as huge as old carp in a pond.

By February 1982, when Jim Sanders of the SBA invited representatives of the twenty-one largest clients to meet him for a chat in a Washington hotel room, and then told them they would be cast out into the cold, cruel world in six months, these veterans had logged an average of ten years apiece in 8(a) and all together had received $750 million in noncompetitive government contracts. Few of the firms had any significant experience in competitive bidding, and few of them would survive once they were out on their own. A 1988 study by the General Accounting Office found that of the 976 firms that had been graduated, which is to say, ejected, from 8(a), scarcely any had prospered in the outside world. Even by the time of Wedtech's public offering, it was clear that the business development incentive had been a total failure. A 1983 study by the SBA's own inspector general had recommended eliminating business development expenses altogether, on the grounds that the member firms weren't competent to use them nor the 8(a) staff to administer them.

Back in 1982 Wedtech hadn't fallen beneath Sanders' axe—perhaps the company wasn't big enough or old enough—but by the following year it had made itself perhaps the single likeliest candidate for expulsion in the entire "portfolio," in the mock-business terminology used within the SBA. Having joined in 1975, the company was now technically a postgraduate. In April 1982 it had received an eighteen-month extension; that was to expire in October.

By raising $30 million from the investing public, Wedtech had proved that it was not suffering from restricted access to capital, which formed one of the principal criteria of "economic disadvantage." The minority owner, John Mariotta, had just become an immensely wealthy man, having sold his stock for $2.7 million; the market value of his remaining shares was $25 million. And on top of everything else, John had surrendered his controlling interest in the company, as the prospectus had mentioned. He now owned 26.7 percent of Wedtech. The company was thus disqualified from the program on three separate grounds.

Wedtech's bravura performance in remaining within the gilded confines of the set-aside program, despite the program's regulations and its entire logic, would have been inconceivable without the help of Peter Neglia. Tall, handsome, spruce, and amiable, Neglia was a political hack of almost ancient lineage. His grandfather had been a U.S. marshal and his father, Joe, a Republican operative in Brooklyn who had held down a succession of painless jobs on various federal commissions. When Ronald Reagan was elected President, the New York State Republican Party chairman, George Clark, an old family friend, wrote to Lyn Nofziger suggesting Peter for the job of SBA regional administrator. In many federal agencies, including the SBA, the regional administrator is a political appointee; that Neglia knew nothing about small business mattered not at all. On October 1, 1981, Nofziger sent a memo to SBA Administrator Michael Cardenas, saying, "We would like Peter Neglia appointed as SBA Regional Administrator." Underneath, Nofziger had written by hand, "Mike—These are very important to us politically—Lyn." Neglia got the job on November 1.

Neglia was the sort of person who was always well liked, if not particularly respected. Current and former SBA officials were staggered when he was indicted, and later convicted, for taking a bribe from Wedtech, and there is no evidence that he was on the take from anyone else. Minority businessmen recall Neglia as an attentive and sympathetic man. "He's not an evil person by any means," says an official in the SBA's Washington headquarters. "He's just a *schnook.*" But he was not a *schnook* of no account. The regional administrator of New York is always an important figure in the SBA, since so many of the agency's beneficiaries are concentrated there, and in 1984 Jim Sanders would make Neglia his chief of staff. In the backwaters of the SBA, Peter Neglia, hack though he was, was a hack to be reckoned with.

Even before the fall of 1983, Neglia had proved himself to be a good friend of Wedtech. It was he who had granted the company its April 1982 extension. Neglia was a political creature, and, like Sanders, he understood very clearly that Wedtech sailed under the banner of the Reagan administration itself. Nobody, as Tim Sullivan said, would oppose them. Moreover, Wedtech's story of success against all odds made the whole program look good in a way that the history of no other minority firm could do. And since the entire nature of the 8(a) program was to foster success rather than to serve as an impartial arbiter, nobody *wanted* to oppose Wedtech.

Wedtech responded to Neglia's kindnesses with the common coin of free meals. Federal employees are enjoined, of course, from receiving things of value, including meals, from private citizens with whom the government does business, and conscientious civil servants often refuse to go out at all with contractors, even if they pay for their own meals. But Neglia wasn't a civil servant; he was a political appointee, and, like a great many such creatures, he was looking for a star to hitch his wagon to. Wedtech was a star.

The Wedtech men, like a lot of Americans, tended to split their tickets, going with the Democrats at the local level and the Republicans nationally. Bernie Ehrlich was one of the in-house Republicans, and Ehrlich had been trying to bring the state chairman, George Clark, into his network of contacts. Ehrlich often turned up at Joe Neglia's monthly lunch in Manhattan with Clark, George Bush's brother Jonathan, and other second-string Republicans. Ehrlich thus came to know Peter Neglia socially, and found that Neglia was happy to have him pay for meals in such old-fashioned haunts as the Villa Pensa, a restaurant in Little Italy where Ehrlich ran a tab.

Mario had first spoken to Neglia in July about Wedtech's remaining in the 8(a) program. Neglia, in turn, raised the matter with a staff member in the office of Jim Sanders, the SBA administrator. On September 12 the SBA's district office recommended that Wedtech be removed from the program when its extension expired in one month, and two days later sent John a letter to that effect. Soon after, Wedtech received a letter from the Army's Tank Automotive Command, TACOM, stating that the firm's loss of 8(a) status would exclude it from consideration for future M-113 contracts. It was a grave moment. It had become clear to all the principals, after a moment of euphoria, that Wedtech would be no more able to survive in the competitive marketplace than would most other 8(a) contractors. In recent months Wedtech had gone zero for three on competitive bids. The company could flourish only in a political marketplace.

At a dinner at the Villa Pensa, Mario and the General told Neglia that he had to help them find a way to stay in the program. When Neglia asked how the company planned to overcome John Mariotta's loss of majority ownership, Mario suggested that the principals would vote so many stock options to John that he would regain at least a theoretical majority of the shares. Neglia said that he would try the idea out on his legal people. He also promised to get the extension prolonged one more month.

In September, the company received a "bridge letter" providing the additional extension. Bridge letters were a new form of abuse occasioned by the forced graduation process. Compliant bureaucrats supplied them to give firms enough time to dream up excuses for staying in the program. The letter, in turn, permitted Neglia to send a letter to TACOM telling the command to hold its horses, since Wedtech remained in the set-aside program.

But Wedtech still needed more time to slip out of the straitjacket it had donned, because Neglia had learned from his regional counsel that Mario's plan of giving John stock options would not fly. Mario and Ehrlich pleaded for another two months, and Neglia came through again. On October 21 Wedtech received yet another extension, this one postponing the graduation date until January 16, 1984. That was all the time Wedtech needed.

The pontoon contract, unlike the six-horsepower engine, was never meant to be set aside for a minority firm: it was too big and too important. The Navy expected to spend slightly more than $400 million on the program over the next five years, and no contract of that size had ever been reserved for minority firms. In the normal course of things, the Navy set aside contracts for services, and humble ones at that, rather than for goods, particularly goods that had to be seaworthy. With its dynastic and blue-blooded tradition, the Navy took an especially dim view of minority contractors. "The joke around here," as one naval officer puts it, "is if it's got more than two moving parts, you've got to think about it." That very summer, it's true, the Navy had awarded a $40 million contract to build steel cargo containers to a minority firm, United Chem-Con (whose owner was later indicted for winning the contract through much the same corrupt tactics as Wedtech was accustomed to use). But the pontoons, though part of the same Sealift program as the containers, had more than two moving parts.

The pontoons were motorized bridges whose function was to shuttle cargo between ship and shore in areas too shallow or dangerous for a large craft to berth at the water's edge. Each pontoon consisted of twenty-one steel boxes welded together in seven rows of three. Each box was five feet long and wide and seven feet deep. The pontoons were very large but very simple, and the technology used to build them had been developed before World War I. The most complicated parts of the structure were the three rear nodules, which contained diesel-powered water jets to maneuver the entire device. Even these scarcely qualified as space-age technology. The principal contracting problem was that installation of the pontoons on what were known as mobile prepositioned ships—part of the new "600-ship Navy" that Navy Secretary John Lehman had been eagerly touting—was to begin in the fall of 1984. Time was already short.

Possibly owing to the United Chem-Con contract, the Washington consultants who sniff out potential 8(a) contracts—"barracudas," John called them—sent word back to their clients that the greatest windfall in set-aside history might be in the offing. The contractors, in turn, started lining up political support, in the accepted manner, and storming the bureaucracy. In mid-June the Navy received letters from both of Nevada's senators and its lone representative, inquiring about the contract on behalf of a company called Univox, one of the largest and best-known firms in the 8(a) portfolio. In mid-August, Acting Assistant Secretary of the Navy Everett Pyatt, in whose office virtually the entire procurement process was run, wrote back to say that the contract was not being considered for the 8(a) program. Pyatt's letter mentioned the importance of competition for so large a contract, though a consideration no less important was the generally depressed condition of the American shipbuilding industry at the time. With so many shipbuilders idle, the Navy was not about to create still more capacity.

A few weeks later Lee Engineering, an 8(a) firm based in San Francisco, heard the glorious news. The firm's attorney, Dennis McQuaid, called Richard Ramirez, the head of the Navy office charged with finding contracts for small and minority businesses, and asked about the pontoons. Ramirez, he recalls, responded with "the strongest confidence." Despite the Navy's official policy, Ramirez said, the contract was likely to be set aside.

Frank Lee, the Chinese-American who had founded Lee Engineering, looked at the pontoon contract and saw the fruition of years of hard work. He was a naval architect, trained in the design department of the Navy. In 1980 he had started his own firm, joined the set-aside program, and started working his way through increasingly large jobs. He had just completed an extensive retooling of the battleship *New Jersey,* and the Navy had made it clear to him that greater things were in the offing. It was clear to Lee that the pontoons would require marine-engineering expertise, and his was the only firm in the 8(a) portfolio licensed to do such work.

Lee decided to abandon all of the little contracts he had been pursuing in order to devote himself and his firm to landing this great catch. He learned everything he could about the pontoons. He began to work up preliminary designs. He sought out partners. Since he had no experience in manufacturing, he cemented a partnership with San Francisco Welding, an experienced shipbuilding firm that also had access to the necessary facilities. He threw everything he had into the effort—first, all of his own money, then the money his parents had placed into an account for his children. Lee had convinced himself that the contract was his.

But he was not alone. A few days after Ramirez heard from McQuaid, he heard from a Puerto Rican group headed by Luis Ferré, former governor of the island. Ramirez warned Assistant Secretary Pyatt that Ferré would be meeting with Vice President Bush to press his case and would emphasize the Caribbean Basin Initiative, a new version of Operation Bootstrap, to which the Reagan administration had committed itself. Within a few weeks, Ramirez had also heard from a concern in Philadelphia called Medley Tool, and a company in Texas apparently represented by an old friend of the Vice President's, Jose Martinez. And the regional administrator, in each case, was pushing the cause of his local client.

At this point Wedtech was not even in the picture. But Stephen

Denlinger, who was secretly receiving several thousand dollars a month from Wedtech, was scoping out the politics. Denlinger spoke regularly to Ramirez and to others in the Hispanic network, especially Robert Saldivar in the 8(a) program. The battle that was shaping up over the pontoon contract was the most intensely political Denlinger had ever seen in the 8(a) program, and the contract hadn't even been set aside. Nothing this big had ever come along before. If Wedtech was to have any hope at all of cracking the inner circle of power where the award would be made, it would have to enlist every connection it had.

In the memo he sent to John and Mario in early October, Denlinger had listed, under "Actions Required," seven separate efforts to influence the Navy, the SBA, the political forces, and the 8(a) competition. Neglia and the "top levels of SBA Central Office" would have to pressure the Navy into setting aside the procurement; and then the politicians and the competitors would have to unite behind Wedtech as the prime contractor. It was clear that the competition couldn't be crushed; it would have to be co-opted. Wedtech would agree to subcontract portions of the $300 million program to the Puerto Rico, Texas, and California groups, thus satisfying the Vice President, former Governor Ferré, the SBA, which wanted West Coast delivery, and the political sponsors. "Project would have strong Hispanic focus in three key states . . . and Puerto Rico," Denlinger wrote. He added that Republicans, including Senators Alfonse D'Amato, John Tower, Pete Domenici, and Pete Wilson, and the California governor, George Deukmejian, as well as such Democrats as Representative Addabbo, could be expected to support a team led by Wedtech.

Many strings would have to be pulled. And it was Mario, operating behind his curtain of tact and diplomacy, who would be the master puppeteer. It was the kind of power, subtle and unseen, that he liked to exert. Mario sent off copies of the Denlinger memo to Wallach and to Nofziger & Bragg. And then, on a Sunday morning in late October, he and John flew down to Washington for a meeting that Denlinger said he would arrange with Richard Ramirez. Denlinger met them at Dulles Airport and telephoned Ramirez at his home in the horse country of northern Virginia. It was critical, Denlinger said, that they speak with him. Ramirez was just about to leave town, but he told them to drive over.

Ramirez was a pudgy man in his middle forties with a thick mustache and an ingratiating manner, a manner that left a telltale impression of complicity. He was a man of somewhat elastic identity. Though of Mexican descent, Ramirez was born and raised in Washington, where his father had been a federal procurement official, and he proudly admitted that he spoke no Spanish at all. But after a stint in Vietnam he had landed, on the strength of his last name, a consulting job with LAMA. Ramirez made a poor "ethnic" lobbyist, and Jose Aceves, LAMA president at the time, referred to him as "Ramirezstein," on the grounds that he seemed more Jewish than Hispanic.

Ramirez also had a business that marketed such patented products as Ram Chaps, a leather garment that could be fastened to the front of a motorcycle and then snapped onto the rider. He was an entrepreneur, a guy on the make, looking to parlay what he had—including his demographic category—into something bigger. The goal was money, not ethnic status, and Ramirez developed a very low opinion of the posturing and moralizing in what he called Minority Land. Nevertheless, Ramirez was not a man to look a gift horse in the mouth, even if it was grazing in Minority Land, and when his last name and his association with Aceves got him a job at the SBA, he took it.

In 1979 Ramirez left the SBA to become head of the small and disadvantaged business office, or SADBU, at NASA, and then, a few months later, for the SADBU position in the Navy, an impressive leap up the ladder, given Ramirez's inexperience and the size of the job. By the time he left, in 1984, the Navy would be procuring $3.5 billion a year in goods and services from small and minority businesses. The job gave Ramirez enormous stature in the minority community, if not in the Navy itself, since it was he who brought potential minority contracts, and even contractors, to the Navy's attention, though he could exercise no formal control over the ultimate procurement decision. Ramirez could help make or break minority firms, and it was no surprise that he had several consulting clients in the 8(a) portfolio when he came to the Navy. What is surprising is that the Navy allowed him to keep the clients, a blatant conflict of interest.

Ramirez had already helped one of those clients, United Chem-Con, which had received the cargo container contract that summer. He had suggested the company to a congressman looking for a minority-business contract for his district, though he's not sure that he mentioned his consulting arrangement at the same time. In fact, United Chem-Con had paid Ramirez over $120,000 in cash, as he later admitted in a guilty plea with federal authorities in Pennsylvania, where the firm was located. He may also have been peddling his services to Wedtech's competition. Dennis McQuaid, the lawyer for Lee Engineering, says that a low-level official for San Francisco Welding had been shocked to hear Ramirez say over the telephone that "he would be receptive to receiving compensation to make sure something went their way." Ramirez was a bit like Mario: he did whatever he had to in order to get ahead in a corrupt world, and he did it with a smile.

Denlinger didn't know about United Chem-Con, but he was certainly aware of what he calls Ramirez's "longstanding reputation for that kind of thing." Not long before that day in October, he recalls, a friend had told him of the time when Ramirez had pulled a big wad of hundred-dollar bills out of his pocket and said, "This is how things get done in Washington." It may have been this incident, Denlinger says, that "cemented my own thinking." Denlinger told Mario that he understood that Ramirez was a purchasable commodity.

When the three men arrived that Sunday morning, Ramirez recalls giving them "a generic briefing as to what the politics were that were involved." It was unnecessary. "They seemed to have the whole game plan. They knew about it, they were going to have it." Ramirez was especially impressed that Mario knew Everett Pyatt had been waiting for months to become permanent, rather than acting, assistant secretary, and implied that that was a card Wedtech could play.

At some point, Ramirez recalls, Denlinger asked whether he could pluck on Ramirez's guitar in the kitchen, and John excused himself to go to the bathroom. Ramirez was left alone with Mario. "How can we help you?" Mario said, casting a look at the battered bachelor's couch that Ramirez, who had split up with his wife, was sitting on. "I don't know," Ramirez replied. "I feel like I've just given you a $100,000 briefing." That was the high sign, and Mario recognized it, just as Fred had with the Teamsters. The two men fell to negotiating, and agreed on $60,000 in cash, payable in two installments.

That, at any rate, is the way Ramirez recalls the events. According to Mario's testimony, once the two men were alone Ramirez said, "It's going to be a difficult battle, but I can be of help to you." In meetings with Secretary Pyatt, Ramirez said, "he could say good things about Wedtech and Wedtech's capability . . . Then he said, 'In order to do that I will need some financial help.' " The two stories seem to amount to the same thing, but Ramirez angrily denies Mario's version. "It wasn't a bribe," says Ramirez, who confessed to conspiracy to commit bribery rather than to bribery itself. "I've never asked for money. But when people are willing to offer it, and they think I'm providing a service to them, fine." Ramirez's gloss verges on the artful, since the "$100,000 briefing" line was meant to be construed as an opening gambit. But such is the human need for self-justification that Ramirez insists he neither solicited the money nor promised anything in exchange. He just accepted a share in the American Dream.

Paying Richard Ramirez for his information and his influence was, of course, a very bad thing. But in this matter, as in so many others, Wedtech was playing the role of the clever but uncouth student. Ramirez was very far from being the only Navy official selling himself to a contractor at the time. Indeed, the fact that Mario was paying the creator of Ram Chaps, as opposed to someone who genuinely counted in the Navy upper echelons, is a perfect instance of the competitive disadvantage suffered by the company.

The contractors who ran the show didn't even have to pay for their secret information; they simply hired former Pentagon officials who used their contacts to get what they needed on a strictly friend-to-friend basis. The buddy system was immemorial; what was new was the kind of transaction in which Ramirez was involved. And the Navy of Secretary John Lehman was just the place for Ramirez's entrepreneurial gifts. Lehman had denounced the procurement bureaucracy as "a socialist culture," and had set out to dismantle it in favor of a marketplace culture. The Navy thus turned into one of those go-go institutions of the Reagan years, when the ancient, creaky machinery was junked in favor of what was supposed to be the streamlined apparatus of competition.

In fact, as the subsequent federal investigation Ill Wind revealed, capitalism didn't replace socialism so much as money replaced friendship. As elsewhere in the Reagan administration, free enterprise culture degenerated into cash culture. The old boys hired "consultants" to pay for the information and influence they could no longer get for free.

With the old socialist procurement bureaucracy largely abolished, ultimate power over the tens of billions of dollars spent annually by the Navy rested in the office of Secretary Lehman and his two closest aides, Assistant Secretary Melvyn Paisley and Everett Pyatt. If you wanted to get a hearing, in other words, you had to go to the top. And contractors far more powerful than Wedtech apparently found a friendly reception there. In 1985 a Defense Department official sent a memo to Defense Secretary Caspar Weinberger stating that contractors had a "direct link" to classified budget documents through "leakers" in Lehman's office. Weinberger never acted on the memo.

SEVENTEEN

"You People Are Crazy"

WEDTECH was never the sort of place where responsibilities were divided according to a rational plan and information was pooled in regular meetings and tasks delegated along a chain of command. But the complexity of the events of the fall of 1983, the need to do several large things simultaneously, had elicited an unusual degree of forethought from the insiders. And so, while Mario was handling the Navy and the SBA in Washington, Tony had been given the primary responsibility to work with the lawyers to skin the cat of 8(a) membership.

The three-month extension had given Tony and the Squadron Ellenoff attorneys desperately needed time; now they had to come up with a plan with enough plausibility to permit the SBA to do what it was inclined to do without making obvious its partisanship for Wedtech. There was nothing for it, apparently, but to find a mechanism to transfer enough shares back to John so that he would regain the appearance of majority control.

The transfer, of course, would have to be a sham. Fred, for one, was not about to yield up millions of dollars of equity so that Wedtech could stay in the 8(a) program. On the other hand, if John did not really control the company, then Wedtech would be subverting the essential purpose of the set-aside program. The SBA was already going to have to overlook the company's ready access to investment capital, as well as the wealth of its principals. The speciousness of the stock transfer thus could not be too blatant.

On Friday, November 4, all six of the insiders gathered around the speakerphone on the enormous desk in John's office to conduct a conference with the attorneys from Squadron Ellenoff. On the other side, Arthur Siskind and Jeff Rubin were joined by Ira Scheinfeld, Squadron Ellenoff's senior tax partner. In the course of the conversation a plan was sketched out. The company principals, above all Fred, who owned by far the largest block of shares, would agree to transfer stock to John. John was to begin paying for the stock two years later. But Siskind agreed to include in the contract a series of provisions that would ensure that Mariotta would have to default on the payment so that the stock would automatically revert to its owners after the two-year period—at which point Wedtech would have finally outgrown its need for protected status.

There was only one problem, assuming that the SBA would look the other way, and Mario, according to court testimony, posed it directly to Arthur Siskind: "How can we be sure that John will default?" Siskind responded, "You're going to have to trust each other." Mario, however, was not inclined to trust John with several hundred thousand dollars' worth of his equity, and he said into the speakerphone, "Can we have some kind of side agreement to guarantee that John will default?" To which Siskind, as Tony recalls it, said, "If you do it, just don't tell me about it, because I can't know about it." At this point, says Tony, John "stood up, describing to them blow by blow as he shook our hands and agreed to default in January 1986. We all stood up and shook hands and said, 'Do you hear this, Arthur? This is our agreement. We want you to be a witness.' " Siskind absolutely denies that the side agreement was mentioned in the course of this conversation.

On the following Monday, Wedtech called a meeting in a banquet room of the Helmsley Palace Hotel in midtown Manhattan—this was the new, upscale Wedtech—to discuss the ramifications of the stock purchase plan. At first Bob Wallach took the floor to explain what everyone present already knew: Wedtech had to keep its protected status in order to win the pontoon contract. Then Siskind and Scheinfeld explained how such a plan might be structured, and discussed the tax consequences of the expected default. After further discussion Wallach asked the question

Mario had asked over the phone: Can we have a secret side agreement stipulating default? Squadron, Tony recalls, said unequivocally that they could not. At this point John, according to Tony, repeated what he had said before: *"Tateleh,* you trusted me for a million dollars in the past [referring to Wallach's stock], you could trust me to default."

Squadron says that he could not have made such a comment to Wallach, since he hadn't attended the meeting. "I stopped for not more than ten minutes," he says, "and there was no substantive conversation. At that point everyone was just saying hello and goodbye." The founding partner of the law firm says that he would scarcely have been aware of details of the stock purchase plan; he had, he says, a great many more important things to attend to. Yet both Mario and Tony recall him as an active participant in the Helmsley Palace meeting, and Tony recalls Squadron's position—between Wallach and Siskind—at the formal lunch that followed the meeting. "I am absolutely a hundred percent sure he was there for the whole meeting," says Tony.

Siskind, who was present, denies that the exchange took place. Later, he says, both Fred and Tony approached him about a side agreement, and he told them that it would be illegal unless it was disclosed.

Curiously, however, Siskind does not deny that he and the firm understood quite clearly that nobody wanted to have John Mariotta end up owning his stock, and that Squadron Ellenoff was looking for ways to build default into the agreement so as to nullify its expressed purpose. Indeed, ten days after the conference call, having put two associates in the tax department to work on precisely this problem, Siskind received a legal memorandum stating, "You have indicated that it is desirable for Mr. John Mariotta to obtain a majority equity interest in Wedtech Corp. for a limited period of time." The memo goes on to mention the forfeiture provisions of which Siskind had spoken.

Squadron Ellenoff is not quite certain whether it should be embarrassed by the memo. Siskind says that it represented nothing more than "brainstorming" by two relatively junior members of the firm, and was not accorded much weight, though it was obviously a response to Siskind's request. On other hand, Ira Sorkin, who was on leave from the firm during this time, argues heatedly that the memo was simply standard lawyer's work. "We had no idea what the SBA would or would not accept," he says. "At the time of the memo, giving the stock to Mariotta and letting him hold it for two years was just another alternative that the SBA might accept. When it became clear that the SBA would not accept it, we then went to the plan that was ultimately approved by the SBA."

Indeed, it's clear from memoranda that Wallach sent to the principals that he assumed that Wedtech was staying well within the boundaries of the law. "The attorneys," he wrote after the November 7 meeting, "will undertake to prepare a proposal that will accomplish the transfer of equity in a manner which will be both lawful and congizant of the tax liability potential involved." "Lawful," in this case, meant nothing more than whatever the SBA would accept; since the SBA ultimately did accept a form of the agreement, the only sham element was the side agreement, of which Siskind, Squadron, and Wallach claim to have been wholly ignorant.

But the side agreement itself was something of a will-o'-the-wisp. What the lawyers say they did not know was that the Wedtech principals had shaken hands on this undisclosed rider to the transaction. If they did know, and agreed not to disclose the understanding to the SBA, then they were clearly parties to a fraud—thus their vehement, if not altogether convincing, insistence on their ignorance. Siskind would be named as an unindicted co-conspirator in the Biaggi trial. But even if they did not know, the attorneys fully understood that the principals never intended to give up their stock, and had structured a deal in which they would not have to do so. It was not only the side agreement that was not disclosed to the SBA; it was the intention embodied in the side agreement.

Squadron Ellenoff understood, as Squadron himself puts it, that "the SBA regarded this company as a feather in its cap and was going to do everything possible to keep waving that feather." Squadron had seen Neglia virtually campaign for the company at a meeting with the EDA in June, and everyone knew of the regional administrator's close relationship with Mario and Bernie Ehrlich. The attorneys understood, as their clients did, that the goal of the exercise was to stay close enough to the letter of the 8(a) regulations, while completely ignoring their spirit, so that the friendly bureaucrats could give their stamp of approval. The goal was to get inside what the SBA would be willing to construe as the foul lines of 8(a) membership criteria. Squadron Ellenoff, after all, was scarcely obliged to take the rules more seriously than the agency itself did. "You want to know if I would have approved it if I were sitting in Washington looking at this thing?" Siskind asks. "I probably would have turned it down, but that wasn't my position."

Even Neglia found transparently specious the initial drafts produced by Siskind and others. Throughout November, Ehrlich relayed to Neglia the draft agreements that came in from Squadron Ellenoff, and Neglia, apparently after speaking with his regional counsel's office, returned them for more work. For one thing, the conditions under which John would default—if the company did not, for example, achieve stratospheric profits—were too obviously designed to sabotage the agreements. Siskind rectified this problem by eliminating the most implausible of the conditions while nevertheless agreeing to structure the deal with an eye to the consequences of default.

The stock purchase plan, as it was ultimately composed in December, looked very much like the sort of nonbinding option arrangement that Neglia had said earlier the SBA could not accept. The shares were not even to be delivered to John, but were to be transferred to an escrow agent—Squadron Ellenoff. John, in turn, would pay no money up front, thus incurring no loss should he welsh on the deal, a stipulation unheard of save in option contracts. Only after two years would John dole out his first dollar, and then he would make annual installment payments over another ten years, which was a good nine years longer than Wedtech could reasonably expect to stay in the set-aside program. He did not, as in a futures contract, bind himself to buy the stock at a fixed price, but only at the market price prevailing at the time of purchase. And as if all that weren't preposterous enough, the stock that John was proposing to buy was then worth $36 million. John Mariotta was a man whose sole legal source of income, aside from a salary of $100,000, was the *sale* of Wedtech stock.

No matter; Neglia had told Ehrlich that the plan looked seaworthy. On December 27, Fred, Mario, Tony, and Larry Shorten signed over all or most of their stock to John, secure in the knowledge that they would be getting it back in two years' time. Others, including, curiously enough, Bob Wallach and Squadron Ellenoff, had refused to sacrifice their control over their stock for the company's well-being. At first, Biaggi and Ehrlich had also refused as well, thus potentially wrecking the deal. The problem wasn't Ehrlich; it was Biaggi, who was acting, as far as the other insiders could tell, from pure greed. The two-year period, Biaggi argued, would extend one extra year the period during which securities regulations would prevent him from selling the stock.

Finally, after weeks of pleading, primarily by Mario and Tony, Biaggi agreed to a proposal that John buy half his stock after a year, and the rest a year later, a provision that would, of course, start the default a year too early. As it turned out, Biaggi agreed to a postponement at the end of the first year. Biaggi and Ehrlich also refused to turn the stock over to Squadron Ellenoff, whom they hated for their thoroughly merited air of professional superiority and for having cut them out of Wedtech's future. The SEC was told that all of John's stock had been delivered to the escrow agent, but, as Squadron Ellenoff knew, that was not the case.

December 27 was a great day for the boys from Wedtech. Along with their fancy Fifth Avenue law firm they had devised a way to do what had seemed inconceivable a few months earlier. Of course the SBA still had to approve the plan, but Neglia had promised to steer it through the bureaucracy. After all those meals at regular-guy hangouts like the Villa Pensa, Ehrlich took Neglia out for dinner at the Palm, New York's finest steakhouse. It was an expensive meal, but Neglia's effort had been worth a lot more. Ehrlich had $1.8 million in Wedtech stock, and Peter Neglia had just protected his investment.

By the time Tony had begun scraping together $30,000 in hundred-dollar bills to make the initial payment to a consultant who was acting as Richard Ramirez's bagman, the San Francisco firm Lee Engineering had made every earnest of its faith in the integrity of the set-aside system. The company's Washington consultant, Julien Zuke, had met with Jim Sanders and other SBA officials, not to indicate "White House interest" but to press the merits of Frank Lee's case. It hadn't occurred to Zuke to "line up political support." He recalls, "It wasn't felt to be necessary, since everything on the surface appeared to be" on the up-and-up.

Zuke was not altogether naïve. He knew that the administration was trying to prove its bona fides to Puerto Rico, and suggested that Lee form a joint venture with the Puerto Rican group represented by former Governor Luis Ferré. In mid-October Dennis McQuaid and Frank Lee traveled to Puerto Rico, signed an agreement with a firm called Puerto Rico Dry Dock and Marine Terminals, Incorporated, and sent it to Richard Ramirez and to the SBA. Both from SBA headquarters and from his regional administrator, Lee had learned that the procurement, if it was set aside, would be divided between an East Coast source and a West Coast one. With facilities now established on both coasts, Lee felt that he would win at least half the contract.

In fact, Lee was a dark horse from the very start. The favorite inside the 8(a) bureaucracy in Washington was Univox, the firm championed by Senator Paul Laxalt of Nevada, a close friend of the President's. The rule within the program was that whatever qualified firm asked first was the winner, and Univox had asked first. More important, John Grayson, Univox's founder, was a friend of the new head of the 8(a) program, Henry Wilfong. Wilfong, like Ramirez, was a former businessman with a highly developed sense of politics. To him the equation was overwhelming. "If this guy is right," he says, recalling his thoughts at the time, *"and* he's got Laxalt, why aren't we just giving him the contract?" Wilfong, however, was to be systematically cut out of the decision-making process.

Wedtech inserted itself into this process at a stage so late that, had it been any other firm, it would have been eliminated from competition. But as a great player, they say, raises the level of his game to meet his opponent's, so Wedtech opened up with a degree of ferocity no one else had even imagined. It was prepared to destroy those adversaries it could, and co-opt those it couldn't. Only a few weeks after Frank Lee had traveled to Puerto Rico to forge his joint venture, John and Mario, unbeknownst to Lee, met with Ferré to appeal for his support on grounds of common ethnicity. That had been number six under "Actions Required" in the Denlinger memo—"meet with principals in Puerto Rico, Texas, and California to formulate the basic structure of the co-production program." Ferré then came up to New York to tour the Wedtech facilities. Although Ferré never became an outright Wedtech advocate, Mario felt that he might be willing to take a back seat as subcontractor to Wedtech.

On October 24 the insiders attended a $500-a-plate Republican fund raiser at the Grand Hyatt Hotel hosted by Vice President George Bush. Mario had seen to it that the company purchased a table. During cocktails Mario and Ehrlich walked over to Neglia, and Mario drew him aside. "We have found a contract in Washington that looks like it can be obtained for Wedtech," and, so saying, pulled from his pocket and unfolded the two-page memo he had received from Stephen Denlinger. ("Support from three SBA RAs [regional administrators]," the memo had suggested. "Neglia (NY), Lopez (TX), and Castillo (CA).") Neglia took one look at it and said, "You people are crazy."

Tony, who was present, recalls that Neglia then said that the Vice President himself had already promised the contract to the Puerto Rican group. The state party chairman, George Clark, then said, according to Tony, "Well, let's bounce it off Bush." Clark had arranged for the group to be introduced to the Vice President. They had, after all, anted up. They were brought to a private room, where they waited until Bush walked in and greeted them. Exactly what happened next is not clear. Tony recalls hearing a conversation about the pontoons and Bush's saying, "I'll see what I can do." But Tony was standing at the edge of the conversation, and Mario, who was in the middle of it, does not recall this exchange.

Mario focused on influencing the people he could reach. Throughout November, while Mario and the General were pressing Neglia to use his influence on the stock transfer problem, they were also turning him around on the pontoons. They would take care of their end; he would take care of his end. And Neglia responded. He reached an agreement with the Philadelphia regional administrator that Wedtech would ultimately share the contract with the Philadelphia contender, Medley Tool and Die. Mario himself called an SBA official, now in Dallas, who had been a key supporter during the engine contract negotiations. Mario invited him to New York, where another handshake agreement was worked out: Wedtech would agree to subcontract work to the Texas consortium, and the SBA official would drop his aggressive support for the group. All the "Actions Required" were being crisply executed.

At SBA headquarters in Washington, Wedtech selected its friends carefully. Rather than deal with Wilfong, whom Mario and Stephen Denlinger took, probably rightly, to be the leader of the black contingent of the ethnically divided 8(a) bureaucracy, Wedtech paid its court to Wilfong's Hispanic deputy, Robert Saldivar, who was considered a highly competent official and something of a favorite of Sanders'. Ramirez, who met with Saldivar frequently in the ordinary course of business, began to drop Wedtech's name into these conversations, according to Saldivar's congressional testimony, presumably implying that the Navy, should it set the contract aside, would favor the South Bronx firm. Ramirez was also doing what he could inside the Navy by speaking with officers associated with the pontoon procurement, though he does not seem to have mentioned Wedtech. As one of the officers recalls, "Ramirez's approach was 'Pyatt wants a big 8(a) contract, and you guys are the biggest target.' "

Wedtech's jockeying inside the SBA would come to nothing, of course, if Pyatt could not be persuaded to change his mind. In early November, Jim Sanders personally requested a briefing on the pontoons by Pyatt's office, and on November 8 he wrote to Navy Secretary John Lehman, asking for "your personal intervention to reverse the decision against 8(a) participation" made by Pyatt. Sanders had never made such a request before. He had been, he says, under pressure to get the contract set aside from the regional administrators, including Neglia, and from the 8(a) bureaucracy.

It was the sort of letter bureaucrats write to mollify the restless. Pyatt had made his position clear. This was a job for a big, experienced contractor, and he had plenty of idle shipyards to choose from. The secretary was committed to getting the shipbuilding industry back on its feet. And yet a force field, an almost palpable atmosphere, was beginning to close around the deputy assistant secretary for shipbuilding and logistics. Wedtech's retainers, as directed by Mario, were filling the air with the charged ions of political pressure. Ramirez was talking about the ramifications, the alignment, the big guns who were taking aim. Mark Bragg and Lyn Nofziger were dropping by Pyatt's office in Crystal City,

Virginia. Perhaps—it's not clear—the secretary himself had said something.

The pattern of influence was becoming denser and more complex, linking Wedtech's two targets—the SBA and the Navy—to each other. Several weeks after the Sanders letter, Ramirez received a call from the Navy general counsel, Hugh O'Neill. The White House wanted to talk about the pontoon contract, said O'Neill, and Ramirez should get himself over to the Old Executive Office Building. At the meeting, Ramirez recalls, were SBA chief of staff Robert Lhulier, Peter Neglia, Peter Terpuluk, another key SBA regional administrator, and "a White House person"—Ramirez can't recall who. The SBA, Ramirez was told, felt that Wedtech could do the job as prime contractor, and that it was time for the Navy to stop avoiding the issue. Pyatt, said one, was in "a sensitive position" and "shouldn't entertain stopping this thing."

Ramirez already knew that Wedtech was heavy. Now he was really impressed. The whole SBA seemed to be behind the company. Lyn Nofziger's name had been bandied about. The meeting seems to have had the desired effect, for Ramirez, the consummate politician, returned to update Pyatt on the new charge in the atmosphere. "I said, 'Politically, you've got a problem.' " The problem, Ramirez explained, was Nofziger, who appeared to be placing his mighty heft behind this one contractor. Pyatt seemed to know all about Nofziger already. He reiterated his opposition to the set-aside, but Ramirez thought he detected the tones of Brer Rabbit: "Please don't throw me in that briar patch, Brer Rabbit."

On December 8, Pyatt took one small but irreversible step into the briar patch. Exactly one month after Sanders had written to Lehman, Pyatt responded with a five-sentence letter stating that "the Naval Facilities Engineering Command (NAVFAC) has been instructed to consider your nominee for the production of non-powered causeway units and related components for FY 84. It is anticipated that $3–4 million could be committed to the 8(a) Program in this area."

It was a token, really, and perhaps this letter too was intended only to mollify the restless. But it didn't work. When Mario heard about the letter—the day before it was sent—he said that Wedtech would not settle for peanuts; it wanted the whole contract or nothing at all. They were getting closer and closer to working out a stock transfer solution; a draft was already circulating. It was all coming together, and Mario's blood was up. The pressure only intensified.

Four years later Wedtech's procurement activities would be investigated by a congressional committee headed by Michigan Senator Carl Levin. Pyatt told the Levin committee that he had been persuaded by

Sanders to set aside the nonmotorized portion of the contract; but, as the committee's report pointed out, there is no evidence that he had spoken with Sanders as of December 8. The week after the letter, though, Sanders did come to Pyatt's office, for the first and only time in his career, to make one last pitch for the whole kit and caboodle.

It was obvious to Sanders that Pyatt was not very happy with his own decision. "I felt that he was kind of the Reluctant Dragon," says Sanders. He left the meeting assuming that Pyatt was committed to going competitive with the bulk of the contract. "*I* was concerned about the motorized portion of the contract," says Sanders, though he doesn't recall whether he expressed his doubts to Pyatt.

But there were larger forces at work than Jim Sanders. Pyatt also told the Levin committee that he had never discussed the pontoon contract with Lyn Nofziger or Mark Bragg; in fact, that he had not even met either of them prior to the awarding of the contract. But neither of these statements seems to be true. Earlier in 1983, says the Washington political consultant David Keene, Nofziger had arranged a meeting in Pyatt's office between the three men and Keene's client, Jesse Calhoun, head of the Marine Engineers Benevolent Association.

Pyatt had been named acting assistant secretary that summer, but his nomination for the assistant secretary's job had been held up for political reasons; this was the "sensitive position" about which Ramirez had been warned. Calhoun's union had been one of several forces blocking the nomination. The meeting, intended to bring about a rapprochement, was not a conspicuous success. Pyatt, Keene recalls, had said, "I would appreciate your support." Calhoun, who felt that Pyatt had not supported his members on some key issues, answered, "I'll die opposing you."

Ramirez, moreover, recalls "numerous telephone calls from Nofziger and Bragg" to Pyatt's office in November and December. The magnitude of the contract had taken the firm's lobbying efforts from the Mark Bragg level to the Lyn Nofziger level. Pyatt's schedule, which was obtained by the Levin committee, listed three meetings between the two men during the fall, though one or more may have occurred before the Wedtech lobbying effort. Ramirez recalls seeing a breakfast between Nofziger and Pyatt listed on the latter's daily agenda.

Perhaps Nofziger felt that he was not obtaining satisfaction, for in the middle of December, soon after Pyatt had agreed to the token set-aside, the former Reagan intimate requested, and received, a meeting with Navy Secretary Lehman, a man famous for his acute sensitivity to political alignments. Lehman told the Levin committee that Nofziger proselytized for Wedtech, though he says that he merely referred the consultant back to Pyatt. As the year came to an end, and the pressure increased, Pyatt may have felt that he was running out of room.

PART FIVE

The Glamour Years

EIGHTEEN

The Double Steal

BY THE FINAL DAYS of 1983 everything seemed to be accelerating, as the United States government adapted itself, with a remarkable flexibility, to Wedtech's timetable. The SBA was pressing the Navy, through Ramirez, to agree to the set-aside and to do it now. Wedtech's 8(a) eligibility was to run out on January 16, 1984. For the same reason the company's application for an extension would have to be whipped through the normally comatose SBA bureaucracy like the perfect triple-play ball.

After the December 27 agreement on the stock purchase plan, the associates at Biaggi & Ehrlich—the ones who actually did the firm's legal work—spent a week getting the documents in order, and delivered them to the SBA district office on January 4. The stock purchase and escrow agreements were accompanied by a legal memorandum, written by a Biaggi & Ehrlich associate, that included, among its most salient arguments, the observation that "the transfer of stock was paid in United States currency, and hence, there is real consideration." Beyond that, the four-page memo contained no serious attempt to justify the jerry-built structure Squadron Ellenoff had erected, nor was any justification necessary.

It was still January 4 when the New York district director sent a letter to the assistant regional administrator for minority small business, stating that his office had "recently" received the Wedtech documents, and had decided, after "reviewing all documents," to recommend an extension. It took David Elbaum, the district counsel, one additional day to "review" all the documents and conclude that the stock purchase was valid and enforceable. Of all the other perfectly valid reasons for kicking Wedtech out of the program, Elbaum said nothing. He told the Levin committee that Neglia had summoned him to his office the day before and instructed him to pass only on the validity of the contracts and to hurry up about it, since "there was a conference of some kind in Washington with regard to a contract for Wedtech."

The charade continued on January 5 with a letter from the assistant regional administrator to Neglia, recommending an extension for Wedtech. Neglia didn't need much time to ruminate on the issues. He knew from Mario and Bernie Ehrlich that the Navy might assign the pontoon contract to the SBA any day, and that Wedtech would have to be securely in the program when that moment came. He knew also that Wedtech's extension came to an end on January 16. And so it was on that very same January 5 when Neglia wrote to Henry Wilfong, the administrator of the 8(a) program, "I approve an extension of three (3) years . . . to expire on October 11, 1986."

The Navy, in the person of Everett Pyatt, was falling into line at nearly the same moment. At the end of December, word had gone around the Navy's Sealift command that a briefing on the pontoons would be held in Everett Pyatt's office on January 4—the conference which Neglia had mentioned to David Elbaum. Very few Navy officials knew of Pyatt's December 8 letter, and as they walked into the meeting the officers assumed that the SBA's importunities had been ignored. They were expecting a standard briefing.

"Normally," says an officer who was present, "when you go over to brief somebody, you say, 'This is a causeway, this is what it costs, this is why we need it.'" Instead, says the officer, Pyatt stunned him and everyone else in the room by saying, "I think we should go 8(a)," and challenging them to argue otherwise. Nobody knew what to say. There were about a thousand reasons, but it suddenly seemed pointless to mention them. "The impression I got," says this officer, "was 'Hey, this guy's already made up his mind.'" And he had. Two days later, and one day after Neglia's letter approving the extension, Pyatt sent a letter to SBA Administrator Jim Sanders, stating that "I am pleased to advise that the Department is willing to entertain the placement of the entire current year program for contracting with your agency."

Sanders says that he was surprised by the news, since Pyatt had opposed the set-aside only a few weeks earlier. The uninformed Navy, however, was stunned. Pyatt wasn't one of them, of course, and thus couldn't be expected to share fully the military hatred of political meddling; but he was a civil servant, not a political appointee, and he had gotten the job precisely because of his reputation for toughness and his willingness to stand up to contractors.

What had turned Pyatt around? Was it Lyn Nofziger's influence over his "sensitive position"? Assistant secretary for shipbuilding and logistics was the single most powerful procurement job in the Reagan Pentagon, because the Navy, in the early 1980s, had been granted practically a blank check for expansion. The job was a giant political plum, but Pyatt was not only a career civil servant but was registered as an independent, a sin of no small account in the partisan and ideological atmosphere of the Reagan White House. Pyatt had the strong backing of Navy Secretary Lehman, but was opposed by both Jesse Calhoun of the MEBA and the political types who looked on Lyn Nofziger as their godfather.

The meeting Nofziger arranged with Calhoun shows that he was doing his best to help Pyatt's nomination, or at least to make Pyatt feel that way, though Nofziger believed with a singular intensity that loyalty to the cause was the only currency that bought good government jobs. And Pyatt's dissimulation about his contacts with Nofziger have raised suspicions on that score. Moreover, in what was probably only a coincidence, the White House ultimately forwarded Pyatt's nomination to the Senate on April 16—the same day that Wedtech signed the pontoon contract. The question thus arises: Did Nofziger and Pyatt strike a corrupt bargain in which the one was exchanged for the other?

The Levin committee found no evidence of a quid pro quo, though it concluded that Pyatt's testimony "contains serious inconsistencies and contradicts relevant documents." And John Herrington, who as assistant to the President for personnel in early 1984 refereed the political battle over the Pyatt nomination, says that he never heard from Nofziger, who was an old friend, or from Bragg or even Calhoun. The opposition, he says, came largely from the political appointees serving Defense Secretary Caspar Weinberger.

The question itself probably bespeaks the mistaken obsession with the smoking gun. The dragon may not have needed a quid pro quo to quiet his snorting. The growing intensity in the atmosphere may have been signal enough for a man in a sensitive position. It may have been enough that Pyatt felt that making Nofziger happy could be helpful to his own future; it may have been enough that Richard Ramirez had preached the political virtues of acquiescence. Whatever it was, some calculus of hope, fear, and resignation seems to have made Everett Pyatt do something he had refused to do a few months earlier, something that could not be explained, but only commanded.

At first the Navy hoped that Pyatt's January 6 letter did not represent an irreversible position. Admiral T. J. Hughes, of the Sealift Command, chose to interpret the letter literally. Since the Navy was only "willing to entertain" the set-aside, he requested a second, far larger meeting on January 19 to hash out the issue. His office prepared a memo explaining, in Pentagonese, that at Risk N—the normal sequence associated with 8(a) procurements—the pontoons would never be ready on time, and that, in fine, the idea was sheer madness.

A synopsis of the January 19 meeting makes it painfully clear that Hughes's strategy was doomed. "VADM [Vice Admiral] Hughes stated purpose of meeting—to reclaim decision to set aside the FY 84 SFFP 'Causeway' procurement for Small and Disadvantaged business." The scheduling problems were then detailed at tedious length. Pyatt asked whether a more sophisticated contractor could build the powered units, with an 8(a) firm assembling the whole. "Ans: No." Then "Mr. Pyatt asked if anyone knew of an alternative steel fabrication oriented procurement that could be offered to SBA in lieu of this one. No one responded." And that was that. "Summary Understanding: Proceed with 8(a) . . ."

Meanwhile, the other strand of the double helix, the extension application, had curled out of the safe confines of Peter Neglia's office, and beyond the immediate sphere of Wedtech's influence, to the SBA's office of general counsel. Now the company would have to depend for its future on some combination of the favoritism shown it throughout the agency and the timidity and incompetence with which the SBA was rife.

On January 5, the same day that Peter Neglia had given Wedtech's application the high sign, Robert Webber, the SBA's general counsel, received a stack of papers as thick as a phone book. Webber handed them to a lawyer in his office for review, as was his custom. Webber says that the name Wedtech meant nothing to him, though several SBA officials say they had discussed with him the vexing question of whether the firm could retain its 8(a) eligibility. Webber does concede that he knew that no 8(a) firm had ever before gone public and sought to remain in the program.

When the lawyer to whom Webber had handed the Wedtech telephone book reported back several weeks later that the arrangement seemed fine to him, Webber says he simply accepted the opinion and sent it on. Though he was ultimately responsible for approving the plan, he says that he knew almost nothing about it. He understood that the stock was to be held in escrow, but he considered escrow tantamount to owner-ship. He was ignorant, Webber says, of the two-year waiting period or the ten-year payout. "If I had known that," he says, "I would have said immediately that something was wrong."

The approval wasn't ready by January 16, so Wedtech received yet another brief extension. By January 20, the day after Pyatt had banished the last doubts about the set-aside, the general counsel had produced a draft of a note giving the transaction a clean bill of health. Webber, who has since retired, is baffled, and above all humiliated, by his own actions. "In my whole career," he says bitterly, "I never did anything I had to regret, and this had to come along at the end." Webber has been accused of falling into line before Wedtech's power, but he insists that the expla-nation is simpler: "I fucked up."

The approval still had to clear Sanders, who says that he had been aware of the discussions about Wedtech without actually taking part in them. Sanders issued his acceptance of Neglia's decision of January 5, and on January 25 Robert Saldivar sent Wedtech a letter formally grant-ing the extension. Sanders has since thought of any number of sound reasons for his swift decision to approve the extension. "I think that there was by that time a kind of inertia or a momentum by the firm and by those that were involved with them," says Sanders, "almost as a bank does when someone gets deeply in debt to them—we've got to see these people succeed."

Sanders also says that he was given false and inadequate information. And then, he suggests, "I'm sure it melded into a hundred other deci-sions I made that week." Finally, he says, it seemed "kind of silly" to penalize the company for its own success. But wasn't it precisely that success which made Wedtech the perfect candidate for graduation? "Strangely enough," Sanders says, "in those debates no one presented that argument, which I think is overwhelming in retrospect." Still, San-ders admits to a feeling something like Webber's, only less so. "That's the one decision I think I clearly made a mistake on," he concedes.

An SBA official puts the matter succinctly: "We weren't looking for a way to say no," he says. "We were looking for a way to say yes."

. . . .

Wedtech was now two thirds of the way home. The company had cornered its victim; there remained only the final act of predation. Pyatt had not awarded the contract to Wedtech; that was the SBA's job, and from the very beginning the SBA had said that it planned to spread the work around the country. Sanders had even created a committee, including Saldivar—though not Wilfong—to figure out how to divide the spoils fairly, much the way that savvy Pentagon procurement officials make sure that subcontracting work goes out to as many congressional districts as possible. The committee had come up with half a dozen or so potential minority contractors. And then the candidates began to disappear.

Or rather, as they said in the heyday of Latin American death squads, they were "disappeared." Frank Lee still thought he had the inside track. He knew that Wilfong was backing Univox, but Irene Castillo, the SBA regional head in San Francisco, assured him that Wilfong would not have the final say. Castillo and her staff had been encouraging Lee from the very beginning. In early January, Lee returned to Washington with his lawyer, Dennis McQuaid. There they received what appeared to be further encouragement from Sanders and Ramirez. On January 9, three days after Pyatt's letter to Sanders, Lee was asked to attend a meeting without either his lawyer or his consultant. At the meeting, Wilfong abruptly informed Lee that "a big contractor" had already been chosen for the job. But the Navy, he said, had a special job reserved for Lee himself; he was to be a consultant who would oversee everything. The job carried heavy responsibility and would be a great opportunity for Lee, though not, unfortunately, for his company.

Puzzled but still hopeful, Lee consented and went home, awaiting further news. He never heard from the SBA again. Castillo testified that Sanders stopped returning her phone calls. (Sanders denies this.) Lee had gambled everything, and now he lost everything, including the money set aside for his children. Unable to repay the loans he had contracted, he filed for bankruptcy. His wife, who had told him that he was a fool for putting all his eggs in one basket, left him. His home was sold, and he moved, alone, into a small apartment. And he was unable to retrieve his firm, which at one time had employed two hundred people, from Chapter XI. It would be several years before Lee could begin to put his life back together.

Henry Wilfong already knew very well that "the big company" was not Univox. John Grayson had called him around the end of the year to recount a phone conversation he had just had with his consultant, Mark

Bragg. Grayson said that Bragg had advised him to forget about the pontoon contract; it was being decided at the level of the White House. Bragg had spoken of Nofziger's involvement with Wedtech, including the stock the two men had received, and left the strong impression, at least on Grayson, that money was talking. Wilfong, probably delighted to get some dirt on Wedtech, had immediately called Sanders and asked for a meeting, though it was a Saturday. "I explained to him very clearly that it was high political, and that we're talking about allegations of bribery and messing up with the system," Wilfong recalls. "And Jim said to me, 'He [Nofziger] is a private citizen. It's not our responsibility.' " Sanders says resolutely that Wilfong, whom he later replaced with Robert Saldivar, has simply invented the meeting.

And so, like ten little Indians, one company after another fell. The contestants from the Gulf, in Texas and New Mexico, simply melted away, nobody seems to know why. By and by only two remained. On January 25, the very day that the SBA extended Wedtech's 8(a) term, Sanders and Saldivar met with the Navy to report that Wedtech and Medley Tool and Die, the Philadelphia company, had been selected to perform the contract.

But whatever dread disease had visited Wedtech's other adversaries befell Medley as well. Negotiations between the two firms over the divvying up of the contract began in early February. But after several weeks the Defense Department informed the SBA that an old investigation of Medley had started up again. Mario already knew as much, for Bragg had told him so. At the end of February, Elijah Medley, the company's founder, agreed to pull out of the discussions, which by then were nearing their conclusion. And then there was only one little Indian.

Wedtech was now the last contestant standing in the elimination match for the pontoon contract. Yet despite the almost dizzying sense of victory, the company had not been able to sign on the dotted line. Wedtech came very close to demolishing itself after it had knocked off everyone else. In early February, NAVFAC officials made a three-hour site visit to see for themselves the company the SBA had selected to build the causeways. Normally they would have conducted an exhaustive survey while auditors scrutinized the company's books. Neither complete survey nor scrutiny was carried out, for the Navy was slipping behind schedule, and Pyatt's office was bent on awarding the contract.

The report from the site visit made strange reading. The author observed that Wedtech's 149th Street facility "was recently acquired and is just a shell of a building. Roof is not finished, no facilities inside, such as heat, light or sanitary fixtures." Pyatt had said at the January 19 meeting that the Navy would not consider a contractor without finished facilities. The report concluded, "Contractor can technically and physically do the job. However, he cannot meet the schedule." The schedule, of course, was paramount.

But by now NAVFAC understood that the top brass wanted Wedtech, and unless the NAVFAC people could prove that the company couldn't do the job, it was best for them to keep their head down. Pyatt ignored both their memo and a comparable one six weeks later. After Medley dropped out, Wedtech submitted a price to the Navy that was $12 million over the $24 million at which the Navy had priced the initial contract. It was clear, as it had been with the engine contract, that Wedtech could not dream of building the pontoons without taking a ruinous loss. Yet another NAVFAC official wrote yet another memo to Pyatt suggesting that "prompt termination of the Section 8(a) consideration" was the only way to ensure that the Navy got its pontoons on time. Instead, Pyatt instructed Ramirez to try to wangle the difference out of the SBA, as the Army had done with the engine contract. But the SBA declined to feed its business development budget into the Wedtech maw a second time around.

Mario was spending almost all of his time with his contracts staff in Davisville, Rhode Island, duking it out with the NAVFAC pricing people. But the Navy was not about to make it easy for Wedtech. Mario dropped the price the company said it needed, and then he dropped it again. On March 28 he simply capitulated and accepted the Navy's price. The $24.5 million figure was insanely, ruinously low, but a bond offering was coming up the following month, and everyone knew investors wouldn't bite unless they could see a signed contract. The proceeds from the offering could be used to tool up for the pontoons, because the stock offering, what little of it remained, had been used for the engines. Anyway, the gravy would be found in the out years. Mario had won an understanding that the Navy would practically guarantee Wedtech the contract options for the two following years. It was a deal by virtue of which the Navy and Wedtech locked each other in a self-destructive embrace.

On April 23 Wedtech held a gala press conference at 595 Gerard to announce the receipt of the pontoon contract. Everyone was there— Senator D'Amato, Peter Neglia, Robert Garcia, even the now normally Wedtech-shy Biaggi. "Wedtech," Senator D'Amato told the crowd of excited employees and local media people, "is living proof that if you work hard, are dedicated, and willing to compete, you can succeed." Representative Biaggi thanked Senator D'Amato for his efforts. Representative Garcia piped up on behalf of his native South Bronx.

Commander Thomas Troy from Naval Operations was there too, along with Captain David de Vicq, who had conducted the site survey a few months earlier. At one point during the signing, de Vicq gave Troy a nudge and pointed to some shelves covered with sheets. "Know what those are?" asked de Vicq. "Those are the engines they haven't delivered to the Army." Troy, who had never heard a word about Wedtech's problems with the engine contract, was startled. He remembers thinking, "I hope we're not making a terrible mistake."

NINETEEN
NINETEEN

A Deal, a Miracle, and Another Deal

THERE WAS NO LIMIT. That was the moral that John and Fred and Mario and Tony had deduced from the experience of the past few months. If you were bold and relentless, if you didn't shy away from power, there was nothing you couldn't get. Once they had all suffered from a sense of injured merit; now it was clear that merit had nothing to do with it. Mario had mapped out a strategy based on pure politics, and seen it all come to pass. Even Mario had never expected Wedtech to win the pontoon contract all by itself, and now the company was looking at $300 to $400 million worth of work, maybe more, over the coming years. What Bob Wallach would delicately refer to as "the general ally structure" had proved that it could pulverize the competition.

Amazing things were happening to the little company with the persecution complex. Wallach, who had always awed this little ring of immigrants and dead-end kids with his tales of life inside the White House, announced in late January that he was going to be drawing even closer to the heart of power. The President had nominated Ed Meese to be Attorney General of the United States. Since they thought of Meese as godlike, the Wedtech boys would have been shocked to learn that he had essentially been kicked upstairs by the White House inner circle, who had rolled their eyes for the last three years as Meese oozed his special brand of tar into the policy-making gearbox. What mattered, in any case, was that the nomination afforded Bob Wallach an opportunity to insinuate himself into Ed Meese's daily life. When Wallach had heard the news, he wound up his practice in San Francisco and sublet his apartment. Bob Wallach was moving to Washington.

Wallach felt that his moment of destiny had come. Eight months earlier this one-man fan club had written to Meese, "I believe you have the potential to become the greatest Attorney General in the history of this country." As for Wallach himself, all he had ever wanted to do was help; now he had the opportunity to help on a truly national scale. He and Ed would do it together; that's how Wallach thought of it. Together they would do justice and vindicate the maligned Reagan administration and Meese himself. Wallach had come a long way in the last few years; he had created a space for himself in Washington. Now he would occupy that space. He would become one of those prominent, dignified characters whom others pointed to with a knowing nod. Exactly what he would do Wallach himself may not have known. But his dear friend was now venturing into a field in which he himself was deeply versed, and he knew that Ed would need him by his side.

Meese could not become Attorney General until he had been confirmed by the Senate, and it was clear from the initial reaction to his nomination that the Democrats on the Senate Judiciary Committee were going to use the confirmation hearings to explore the reactionary views for which Meese had become notorious. Meese would need counsel, and Bob Wallach had assured him from the very first day that he would drop everything to serve as his attorney. This was where Wedtech came in. In recent months Wallach had made a point of mentioning the high cost of maintaining his "presence" almost every time he talked with the Wedtech boys. He was flying back and forth across the country; he was entertaining the immortals in Washington; he was supporting his family. And now he was giving up his practice. His needs were growing, and his income was shrinking. The $150,000 he had received in September was long gone.

Late the previous year Wallach had learned that Mario Biaggi and Bernie Ehrlich had received millions of dollars in stock more than he had, and he had reacted furiously, though always in that ominously quiet tone of voice of his. How could they put so much faith in Biaggi and

Ehrlich? Hadn't he brought them Squadron Ellenoff to replace those two? They were Wedtech's past; they were nobodies. He, Bob Wallach, had made them household names in the household of Ronald Reagan and Ed Meese. And he had gotten *one* percent of the company. Wallach had been placated only when John and Mario had agreed to give him 50,000 stock options. But options were for the future, and Wallach needed money now.

In the first days of February, Wallach sat in John's office and explained that he would be forgoing his livelihood to represent Ed Meese, gratis, in his confirmation hearings. In effect, Wallach was asking Wedtech to subsidize his representation of Meese. He already had a standing agreement, ratified by the board only a few days earlier, to receive another $150,000 in quarterly installments during the coming year. Now Wallach said he needed the whole amount immediately. It was a lot of money, and at just that moment the cash being generated by FHJ Associates was going to repay Pat Simone. The company's legitimate resources were being thrown into the effort to persuade the Navy that Wedtech could indeed build the pontoons.

But Bob Wallach was a very important man, and Ed Meese was an even more important man. It wasn't clear whether or not Wallach had played a key role in the pontoons; he certainly said that he had. The very next day Tony handed Wallach a check for $150,000. Everyone assumed that Wallach would give Meese to understand that Wedtech had covered his legal costs. Meese would be in their debt. Maybe the men at Wedtech can be excused for reasoning thus, since fees-for-influence represented the sort of transaction that, as they understood it, governed life in Washington, as it did in the Bronx. In fact, there is no evidence that Wallach told Meese of the payment.

One month later Wallach sent Wedtech a present that went a long way toward earning his fee. He had persuaded one of the President's speech writers that the inspiring example of little Wedtech might afford the President some political advantage. He called up John to say that Mr. Reagan, who two years earlier had listened to John's litany and pronounced it good, would repeat his blessing. The President of the United States would praise John Mariotta before the entire world. It was like a gift from heaven.

The wayward little company from the South Bronx had something important to offer the man who ran the nation. On the merely financial level, the Wedtech boys were dependable givers. They had taken a table at George Bush's campaign dinner back in October. They were, in fact, spending tens of thousands dollars to back their friends, Republican and

Democratic, national and local, and of course secretly and illegally reimbursing themselves through FHJ. Wedtech was a government contractor, and like any other member of the species understood very well who buttered its daily bread. For the presidential speech, which was to be given on March 6 at the Waldorf-Astoria Hotel, company executives bought two tables of ten, at $1000 a plate.

But $20,000 was not going to buy Wedtech a mention in a presidential speech. Wedtech was proof positive that Mr. Reagan's policies were working. Wedtech was precisely the kind of symbol the President needed to refute the Democratic argument that, for all his personal geniality, he was the author of a massive and inhumane transfer of wealth from the poor and middle class to the rich. The President needed stories like that of Wedtech to demonstrate that his policy of encouraging "initiative" by reducing welfare payments and lowering regulatory and tax barriers had helped rather than harmed the poor.

The evening of March 6 was a sublime moment in the history of Wedtech. In practical terms, it was the moment when Mario agreed to buckle under to the Navy and accept a contract that could bankrupt the company, but no matter. All the insiders were at the Waldorf-Astoria, as were Wallach and a few other of the most important Wedtech friends. After dinner the President warmed up the crowd with his ritual denunciations of Jimmy Carter and all his kind. Then he turned to the "conscientious and hard-working individuals" whose values the Republican Party had sworn itself to uphold, and as he did so a spotlight swung through the crowd to pick up a thick-chested man with high-waved hair and tinted glasses. "One such person," the President said, "is John Mariotta, who's providing jobs and training for the hard-core unemployed of the South Bronx . . . And what gave Mr. Mariotta the courage to keep going when others quit? He tells us it was his faith in God. Now, his faith has moved mountains, helping hundreds of people who'd almost given up hope.

"People like John Mariotta are heroes for the eighties."

As soon as the speech ended, the freshly canonized hero for the eighties was surrounded by well-wishers and the press. John launched into his spiel about the spear chuckers and the Twilight Zone and so on, the press scribbled, and then, the moving finger of destiny having writ, moved on. But Wedtech was quick to exploit the moment. The 1983 annual report, Wedtech's first as a public company, featured on the cover a sea of brown and black faces in Wedtech blue crowding the shop floor at 595 Gerard, and on the inside a picture of the President of the United States standing at a lectern, and beside him the printed text of his remarks on Wedtech and on the heroic Mr. Mariotta. On the outside, the dream; on the inside, the royal blessing. It was a formidable combination.

Since the previous fall Wedtech had been, more or less, a six-man operation. More or less, because it wasn't at all clear what the most recent arrival, Richard Bluestine, thought he was doing there. For all the others, Wedtech was a life-consuming experience. The previous summer Mario had collapsed from exhaustion. And to find John or Tony or Larry Shorten at his desk in the middle of the night was nothing. Wedtech was not so much the company these men worked for as the race car they had been strapped into. For Richard Bluestine the company seemed to be a distraction from his golf game. In February or March, when John brought everyone up to the new coating facility in Mount Vernon, he walked into the corner space that would one day serve as his office and said, "And this will be my desk over here, and I can get up and look out my blinds, and I can see my beautiful lawn—and I can watch Bluestine putting!"

Bluestine walked around 595 Gerard, when he was there, with a put-upon expression, as if he were embarrassed to be consorting with such lowlifes. He was not a tactful man, and he was prone to begin sentences with "When I'm president . . ." But Bluestine seemed to want to run the company without having to work. He received a big salary, a fancy title, a huge chunk of stock, and a $900,000 loan guarantee, but he barely even said hello to his colleagues in the hall. Possibly he had never wanted to do more than pick up his welcoming present and leave. He did not, in any case, last long.

In early April, at one of the endless political fund raisers that Mario attended and that the others occasionally sat through, Bluestine's wife began prattling about her marvelous new wealth. Oh, she said, it was so wonderful to have furs and diamonds and a Porsche and their grand condos, in Vermont and in Boca Raton. But her husband was pulling down only $125,000 a year in salary. What the others suddenly realized was that Bluestine had treated the $900,000 loan Wedtech had guaranteed to defray the taxes on his stock as just so much funny money. He had received the stock on a ten-year installment plan, and he was drawing down the loan each year to pay that year's taxes. By cheating, he had prevented Wedtech from reducing the size of its guarantee. That was going too far.

Tony waited a week or so until the April 15 tax filing deadline passed, and then told Bluestine that he needed to see his returns for the "due diligence" work on the upcoming bond offering. Bluestine stalled, and then tried to fob off on Tony a series of worksheets with columns of numbers on them. That was proof enough. It was unanimously agreed that Bluestine would be fired. He was given a ten-year "consulting" contract, though it was fully understood that he would never work at the company again—and he never did.

It was, indeed, the year of campaign fund raisers, of the big bite from needy politicians. Nineteen eighty-four represented the convergence of Mario's efforts at cultivating the political forces and Wedtech's emergence as a big company with real money at its disposal. It was a time for giving: to the President, to the Chairman—Joe Addabbo—to candidates in New York and the Bronx, like Borough President Stanley Simon. Politicians lived by the quid pro quo. You give to get; that was the rule.

Bobby Garcia was always on the asking end that spring. Garcia hadn't given all that much, not compared with his colleagues Mario Biaggi and Joe Addabbo or with Senator D'Amato, but he expected suitable recognition nevertheless. And he expected more from Wedtech, since the company was on a level by itself among Hispanic-run firms in the South Bronx. Mario and John went to every Garcia function; Mario, especially, had become a frequent visitor at Garcia's offices in the Bronx and in Washington. And the money was always there. In mid-February, at the congressman's express request, Wedtech bought three tables of ten each, at $75 a ticket, at a Garcia fund raiser.

Mario had never thought of Garcia as a dishonest politician. Back in 1980, when he married Jane Lee, Garcia had accepted unsolicited wedding gifts of $1000 from John and Jenny and $200 from Mario and Conchita, but those had been gifts, not bribes. The following year he had solicited a $4000 loan from John. The company had given another $4000 and then some toward the construction of the Crossroads Tabernacle Church, whose preacher was Garcia's sister, Aimee Cortese. These were relatively modest requests. But the congressman had something in common with Bob Wallach: he was living beyond his means.

In retrospect, the whole thing would be blamed—by Garcia's friends—on Jane Lee. Garcia, or so it is widely felt in the South Bronx, was a man of simple tastes, humble despite his eminence. His rumpled suits seemed to clothe his very person with integrity. He never, it would be said again and again, forgot his roots. Then he forgot them. In his first term as a congressman, Garcia fell in love with the very attractive and very much younger Jane Lee Matos, who had reverted to her maiden name after divorcing her first husband. She was an aide on the House Census

Committee, of which Garcia was a member, when they first met. The congressman left his wife to move in with her, and then he married her.

Jane Lee was everything Garcia was not: worldly, sophisticated, and materialistic. She came from the horsey set of Puerto Rico, a class that thought of itself as a distant outpost of aristocratic Spain. With the ambition of a Lady Macbeth—or so the story goes—she set out to reshape the former South Bronx choirboy, and in the process make the two of them the power couple of Puerto Rico.

Jane Lee Garcia also wanted power. In 1982 she replaced—and perhaps unseated—Lou Benza, Garcia's administrative aide, to take the job for herself. (Benza then took a job with Mario Biaggi.) She frequently flew back and forth with the congressman to Puerto Rico, where she was on excellent terms with Governor Rafael Hernández-Colón, or to a resort near Santo Domingo, in the Dominican Republic. The two lived in the manner appropriate to their standing rather than to their income. With her congressional job they earned $120,000; they needed twice as much. Garcia's account was always overdrawn, once by as much as $14,000, but the banks never bounced his checks. He was a congressman and, perhaps not coincidentally, a member of the banking subcommittee.

The crowning blow to their finances came in January, when they closed on a horse farm in upstate New York, the sort of genteel retreat that would prove to Bobby Garcia's old friends that he had lost his head. A veteran, Garcia applied for and received a 100 percent Veterans Administration mortgage, though the VA supplies mortgages only to help veterans buy primary residences. The farm cost $150,000, plus the thousands of dollars the new owners spent on horses and on improvements. Perhaps because their finances were now strained beyond the capacity even of friendly bankers to accommodate, Jane Garcia left her job and established herself as—what else?—a consultant. Someone in the family was going to have to cash in.

In the middle of May, Garcia began leaving messages for John and Mario. The messages said that he wanted to talk about the pontoon contract, about sharing some of the work with a firm in Corpus Christi, whose congressman, Solomon Ortiz, was a friend. John was out of town and Mario returned the call. Garcia asked Mario to meet Jane and him for dinner that evening at Lello Ristorante, an elegant Italian spot at 54th and Park. Over drinks Garcia companionably asked Mario to tell him about his background, and then Garcia spoke of his own humble beginnings and of the stature he had now attained. Mario talked about the pontoons, about the critical need to win the option contracts for the ensuing years. Jane Garcia said that she had gone to school with a good friend of Secretary John Lehman's; perhaps, she said, she could introduce him to the Wedtech people.

The three were well into dinner when Garcia broached the real subject of the evening. "You know," he told Mario, "Jane has been doing public relations work for a number of firms. I think she would be very good for Wedtech as well." Mario was completely taken aback; he thought he had been invited to dinner to discuss the pontoons, not to give a bribe to the Garcias. He had thought that Garcia was different from Biaggi and from all the others who had their hands out. He had identified, in a way, with the Hispanic congressman. "Bobby," he said, "that sounds crazy." Mario explained that Wedtech was not in the kind of business that needed public relations. Well, said Garcia, maybe we can find some other way to do it.

Garcia asked how much Wedtech paid its consultants. Three or four thousand a month, Mario said. That would be fine, said Garcia; Jane would serve as a consultant to Wedtech at $40,000 a year. At this point Jane Garcia chimed in with the suggestion that the money be sent to a very close friend of hers in Puerto Rico, who would then forward it to her. Apparently the Garcias had thought the matter through in advance. Mario agreed, and Jane then spoke of the connections she and the congressman had that might be useful to Wedtech. Mario paid the bill—$217.25—and walked out of Lello's in a daze.

Four days later John, Tony, and Larry Shorten each gave $1000 to Garcia's campaign fund. Mario had already given the limit, and Fred, characteristically, refused to give at all. Then in July, Jane Garcia called Mario to give him the phone number of Ralph Vallone, a lawyer in Puerto Rico who would serve as the middleman. Mario called Vallone, who knew all about the agreement, and said that Mario should send $4000 a month. When Mario protested that he had just jacked up the rate $8000 per annum, Vallone ascribed the difference to expenses. Mario shrugged and agreed.

TWENTY

Anchors Aweigh

NOTHING—neither the President's blessings nor the operations of the general ally structure—could ultimately save Wedtech from the consequences of its rashness. The company had gone after the pontoon contract out of sheer, unthinking ambition; now it was like a man at an auction who suddenly finds that he's holding the winning paddle and wonders how in the world he's going to pay for his bid. For the next two and a half years the Wedtech insiders would do everything possible to escape from the consequences of their miraculous victory; and while they would trump their own doom again and again, eventually they would fail. By the time they turned the corner on the pontoons, it would be too late.

The Army had proved fierce in defending the integrity of its procurement process, and then perfectly mild once it came to administering the contract; with the Navy, it was the other way around. The Dr. Keenan of the Navy, at least as the Wedtech principals saw it, was the pontoon program officer, Captain David de Vicq from NAVFAC. They were probably right in thinking that de Vicq had taken a dim view of them from the start, though they were probably wrong in attributing his impatience to prejudice. De Vicq had had the dubious privilege of a ringside seat throughout the procurement process. He had been brought in to serve as program manager for the pontoons, and he had assumed that the pontoons would be awarded to the most competitive bidder. He had sat through the January 19 meeting in Everett Pyatt's office, and had watched Pyatt unaccountably knuckle under to the SBA. Suddenly he had been presented with Wedtech as a fait accompli.

De Vicq had conducted the site visit in early February and had seen the roofless shell that Wedtech had described as its manufacturing facility. He knew that the contract had been rushed through without a pre-award survey, that the company had agreed to a price that could bankrupt it, that it had fallen behind on its production of engines for the Army. He knew, in other words, that he had been handed a practically hopeless situation and would have to make the best of it. The first pontoons had to be ready in October in order to accommodate the schedule of the Navy's fleet.

Worse still, Captain de Vicq was a man shaped by character and experience to be Wedtech's nemesis. He was an intensely serious man, laconic, tight-wound, as if he had only barely banked his internal fires. He was lean, spare, with close-cropped blond hair and prominent eyes behind metal-rimmed spectacles. De Vicq had spent his career supervising massive construction projects for the Navy, including the base at Diego Garcia, in the Indian Ocean. And he was an educated man; he had received his master's in civil engineering at MIT. He was difficult, uncompromising, and extremely capable, or so his colleagues felt. In short, Captain David de Vicq was a sort of Spartan, an unclubbable man in the cozy and class-conscious world of the Navy.

From the beginning, de Vicq singled out Mario as the person to talk to. He was attracted, as were a great many people both before and after him, by what he recalls as Mario's aura of sincerity. Mario told de Vicq that he had been a teacher at a business school, and the military man, with his respect for authority, assumed that he had found someone he could trust.

Whenever he visited the South Bronx, which he found himself doing with unconscionable frequency, Captain de Vicq would ask Mario when they were going to get the electricity installed in the 149th Street facility, and when quality control was going to get fully staffed, and when he was finally going to see a schedule in which the immensely complicated process of executing a $24 million contract would be broken down into milestones, with a time allotted for reaching each one. He would ask, and

Mario would say, "Soon." There was always a plausible reason for the delay; it was always under control; it was always just about to be resolved. Mario made a point of agreeing with everything de Vicq said. And de Vicq, at least at first, believed him. It's a weakness with many military people: they tend to believe what they are told.

Wedtech wasn't so much incompetent as hopelessly unprepared and thoroughly overwhelmed. It was preposterous even to imagine that a little company with absolutely no experience, no facilities, and no trained employees could build ninety-foot pontoons to military specifications and get the first one delivered in six months. Wedtech had already fallen way behind on the Army engines, and would not deliver the first batch until late 1984. But the pontoons were vastly more complicated than the engines. Mihai Soiman, who was placed in charge of solving the engineering problems, estimated that he would have to make three thousand separate drawings before the first causeway could be bolted together.

The company could hardly be faulted for lack of effort, since from the moment the starter's pistol went off everyone began working eighteen hours a day. John had to buy millions of dollars' worth of equipment and had to hire hundreds of employees. He and others scoured shipyards along the East Coast in search of qualified welders, and agreed to put up not only the new employees but their families, at tremendous cost, in hotels and other temporary housing. Anyone in the greater metropolitan area who could pass a welding test was signed on and then trained by the more experienced workers. And the company had to find engineers—for which the Russian Overground Railway was tapped once again—quality-control experts and support staff. Long gone were the days when John visited the local churches and insisted on establishing a sturdy spiritual bond before hiring a new employee. Wedtech more than doubled in size in a year's time, a rate of growth that would cause chaos in any company.

There is also the inescapable fact that Wedtech, as always, was working at cross-purposes with itself, at once the entrepreneurial dream and the den of thieves. The 149th Street facility had to serve the dual purpose of providing the company with a place to build pontoons and providing the principals with enormous quantities of cash. Even with the Navy riding the company as hard as it could, the work at 149th Street was going slowly. The project had turned out to be far more costly and complicated than anyone had realized, especially in the matter of plumbing and electricity. Wedtech had publicly projected a cost of $3.8 million to turn this gigantic roofless shed into a pontoon factory; the ultimate cost was to be more like $10 million.

Most of the huge discrepancy actually had to do with unanticipated expense, but the rest could be ascribed to ulterior motive. After the secret deal concluded the previous fall, Pat Simone, according to Mario, Tony, and Fred, had hired contractors willing to submit inflated invoices and kick back the surplus. There were wheels within wheels in the kickback scheme. One of the contractors, who had been hired to do the electrical work, was Reynaldo Berney, a brother-in-law of Mario's. What Mario neglected to tell the others was that Berney had agreed to give him a 20 percent share of his business's profits. This constituted one of the earliest instances in which one Wedtech insider cheated the others.

At a time when any sensible, or legitimate, company would have been desperate to hold down costs, the Wedtech insiders turned the pontoon facility into a bonanza. Simone had handed over the first $100,000, in cash, by the end of 1983. Over the course of the following year he would give Tony another $200,000, keeping $100,000 for himself. By the end of 1984, $1,179,690.80 would be deposited into FHJ, most of it from kickbacks on construction at 149th Street and other sites.

Tony had long since relieved Ceil Lewis of her responsibility for controlling the FHJ account. Even John, her mentor and protector, admitted that Ceil was a hopelessly disorganized bookkeeper. When someone told her to write out a check on the account, she would record the transaction by pulling a slip of paper out of her drawer and scribbling a number and a date on a corner, as if she were trying to hide the information even from herself. Sometimes she would write the figures at the bottom of a grocery list.

The system, by now, was well greased. When a check came in from one of the shell companies used by Simone, or from Berney or Henry Zeisel, Tony would log the amount on a running total he kept on a yellow pad in his perfectly neat handwriting. A sum would then be added to the accounts of those who shared in FHJ at a fixed ratio. During the brief Bluestine era, Fred and John had each received a quarter of the FHJ take, with an eighth apportioned to Mario, Tony, Shorten, and Bluestine. Thereafter the ratio had become 27.5–27.5–15–15–15. When a payment would be made through FHJ—for example, the monthly bribe to the union—Tony would debit each account proportionately. The account was also used for the reimbursement of political contributions. Thus, Tony wrote at the left edge of his yellow pad "Political Contrib. paid by M. Moreno (300, 500, 1000, 12,000)," then added back the $13,800 to Mario's account and subtracted from each of the five an amount determined by that person's share.

The most common entry in Tony's FHJ books was "Dist. to . . ." followed by the name of one of the five. Then Tony would simply subtract the amount from the individual's running total. Sometimes the least extravagant had to bankroll the most. John tended to view the FHJ money as inexhaustible, and often ran a negative balance. At one point Fred was $50,000 or so in the black, and John about equally deep in the red, and Fred demanded a settlement. John, who had no idea how to balance a checkbook, and who in any case could not conceive of FHJ as a source of debit rather than credit, told him to take a walk.

A good deal of the FHJ money went out in the form of cash, either to the five shareholders or to the union or other special beneficiaries. This was where Ceil, now reduced to the status of resentful gofer, came in. Someone, usually Tony or Mario, would call up Ceil and tell her to raise some thousands of dollars in cash through FHJ. Ceil would then call Bibi Figueroa, one of Wedtech's friendly bankers and an assistant manager at the Banco Popular, and say that she was sending someone down to cash a check. Ceil, who did not drive, would give a check, made out to cash, to the company driver, Frank Morales, and tell him to head over to the bank. Over the years Morales ferried hundreds of thousands of dollars from the Banco Popular branch at Bruckner Boulevard without, apparently, ever lifting a single greenback for himself. For those recipients who did not require cash—for example, charities—Lewis would instruct Morales to cash the check and then use it to purchase a bank check made out to the beneficiary. This was an innovation devised to reduce the number of FHJ checks wafting into the hands of strangers.

Ceil never gave Morales checks for more than $9500, since banks must report distributions of more than $10,000 to the Treasury Department. The restriction became awkward at moments when the company had to raise a great deal of cash quickly. Then Morales would be back and forth to the bank every day, with his $9500 in crisp hundred-dollar bills. At hectic moments Ceil would send him over more than once in a day, thus putting Wedtech over the $10,000 limit. The bank, however, did not report the transactions as required, owing perhaps to the cash gifts that were presented to Bibi Figueroa. When Wedtech needed a friend, it always found one.

By the late spring, hundreds of workers were cutting steel in 149th Street, and Berney's electricians were finally replacing the vast caravan of generators that went snaking out the doors. But Wedtech hadn't even located a waterside facility it could use to assemble the metal cubes into ninety-foot causeways, test their seaworthiness, and send them on their way. Simone, once again, came to the rescue. Farther north from the 149th Street building, in his own neighborhood of Hunts Point, Simone found a former fish-packing plant once operated by the Vita Herring company. A minority food-service company now occupied the building, but the large parking lot, which lay along the East River, was unused. On June 5, John, Mario, and Bernie Ehrlich visited the site; it looked perfect.

It *was* perfect, except for one thing: the property belonged to the city and could not be leased without negotiating New York's regulatory labyrinth. The contract would have to be thrashed out with the Department of Ports and Terminals, which regulates New York's waterfront property, and then approved by the Board of Estimate, a body which at that time passed on all major contracts signed by the city. Wedtech would have to reach out and touch someone, and it would have to do it quickly, since the Navy, in the person of Captain David de Vicq, was already growing restive.

Into this breach shambled the stout and mumbly figure of Bronx Borough President Stanley Simon. Simon had been among the first to educate Wedtech in the petty self-aggrandizing of public officials. Back in April 1981, the company had needed Board of Estimate approval to purchase from the city a building on Gerard Avenue. One of the few remaining responsibilities of the borough president at the time was a seat on the board, which has since been abolished. Simon told Mario that he would shepherd the loan through the board if Wedtech would hire his brother-in-law, a hapless gentleman named Henry Bittman. Bittman could work only four days a week, since Simon had already gotten him a no-show government job for which he had to sign in on Fridays. Wedtech nevertheless hired Bittman as a $15,000-a-year payroll clerk, and padded his salary, at Simon's request, with an additional $4000 to $5000 from a subsidiary company. Two years later Simon said that Bittman had been forced to leave his government job, and therefore needed a $10,000 raise. The Wedtech boys dutifully complied.

Stanley Simon was the quintessential hack, the creature of a system so corrupt that everywhere he looked he saw only reflections of his own pettiness and greed. The system was the Democratic Party machine that, to one degree or another, had controlled New York City politics for the previous 125 years. It was a system almost noble in its antiquity, though, unbeknown to Simon, its organs had decayed over the generations and it was just about to tip over and die. Once there had been good bosses and even great bosses, such as the former Bronx Democratic chief Ed Flynn; now, with the working-class immigrants who had been the machine's fuel moving up and moving away, the machine had lost much of its purpose. Once the bosses had ministered to a flock; now they ministered to themselves.

Simon, born in a working-class family, had grown up inside this apparatus, and had never troubled to look beyond its confines. He became a
precinct captain, the lowest order of functionary in the hierarchy of
member, captain, district leader, party boss. Simon attached himself to
his district leader, who was also, by tradition, a state assemblyman, and
when he graduated from law school, Simon took a job on the man's
statehouse staff. After a Bronx Jewish Democrat left the City Council,
New York's principal governing body, Simon was given the man's seat by
his county leader. And in 1979 the new county leader, Stanley Friedman,
whom Simon had courted assiduously, selected him to be Bronx borough president when the incumbent resigned to pursue higher office.
Given the nearly nonexistent powers of the job, practically anything
qualified as higher office.

Stanley Friedman and Mario Biaggi were big men, at least in their own
worlds, men who alternately bullied and charmed everyone in their path.
They would ultimately be convicted of using their power to corruptly
gain millions of dollars. Another county leader, Donald Manes of
Queens, was accused of looting entire departments of the city government, though, like a noble Roman, Manes drove a knife through his heart
before the government had finished drawing up an indictment. Simon,
on the other hand, brought pettiness to the level of the microscopic.

The borough president was well known as the cheapest man in the
Bronx. When public school students were sent to one of the Young
People's Concerts at Lincoln Center, Simon demanded that his daugh-
ters, Suzette and Lorette, be given free tickets. "If you sat in a restaurant
with him," says Arthur Levine, a reformer and one-time Simon ally, "he
would outwait you for the check. I have never seen that man pick up a
check. The only reason he has ever put his hands in his pocket is to
scratch his balls. The man is an absolutely incredible *schnorrer,*" a Yiddish
word that means "moocher."

Simon devoted himself heart and soul to objects too trivial for all but
the smallest men to dispute. He was diligent about installing supporters
on community boards and school boards, which constitute the lowest
level of local government in New York. "He was into everything," says a
former Bronx political organizer, "the synagogues, the churches, the
schools. He completely infiltrated the Hebrew Home for the Aged,"
where his wife, Irene, sat on the board. Everything was on a tiny scale,
both the favors Simon gave and the benefits he exacted. The Bronx
borough president expected people to pay for his breakfast—constantly.
He had an aide, Ralph Lawrence, who testified in court that he was
treated like a lackey and was expected to kick back part of his salary in the

form of theater tickets, pin money, cups of coffee. Simon would give the man a raise, and then keep most of it for himself. The Wedtech people assumed that Simon had the same relationship with Henry Bittman.

Simon was widely considered an incompetent manager, a man too obsessed with accumulating authority, and too afraid of delegating it, to devote himself to the business of running the Bronx. Stanley Friedman thought Simon so unequal to his modest responsibilities that he assigned a loyalist of his own to sit outside Simon's door all day long to make sure he didn't screw up. The Wedtech boys might have found a sharper instrument than Simon, but they had worked with him before and found him suitable. And Simon sat on the Board of Estimate, and it was the Board of Estimate that they needed.

Immediately after the visit to the waterside site, Ehrlich called Simon and said that Wedtech needed help. Simon then instructed Kathy Zamechansky, the titular head of the economic development arm of the borough president's office—the office was, in fact, controlled by Stanley Friedman—to call City Hall and get Wedtech the lease, instantly. Events that normally take weeks or months were now completed in a matter of hours. Zamechansky called an official with the city's Division of Real Property, who set up a meeting that afternoon at City Hall. A Biaggi & Ehrlich associate was packed off to the borough president's office to pick up documents and maps. Susan Frank, administrator of the Department of Ports and Terminals, agreed to attend on short notice. Simon himself even showed up to introduce the parties to one another. And so did a representative from the Hebrew National company, to which, awkwardly enough, the city had committed the entire property, formally known as 1 Loop Drive, only one month earlier.

The status of the property was, in fact, thoroughly unclear. The Vita Building had been leased eighteen months earlier to Henry Thomas, an 8(a) contractor who had begun supplying ration kits to the military. But the building turned out to be everything short of haunted, and Thomas had had to spend so much money repairing it that he had fallen months behind in payments on his lease. By early January the city had begun eviction proceedings against Thomas, and after several delays began shopping the property to prospective tenants. In May, Hebrew National agreed to lease the building and move part of its operation there from Queens. Then Wedtech found the property. By the time it did so, in early June, Hebrew National remained an obstacle, even though Thomas was almost out of the way.

At the meeting that Simon had convened in City Hall, Hebrew National did agree to relinquish its claim to most of the parking lot, but this still left dozens of matters to be resolved, not least of them the obtaining of Board of Estimate approval. Ehrlich, however, insisted on moving immediately to price negotiations. Susan Frank, of Ports and Terminals, agreed. There followed, according to trial testimony, a discussion of about one minute's duration. Frank said the city expected approximately $100,000 a year. Ehrlich said Wedtech couldn't afford more than $50,000. That's fine, said Frank. Ehrlich had just earned four months' worth of his retainer in a matter of moments. And that wasn't all. When Ehrlich said he needed a letter of commitment that very day, Frank volunteered to drive the Biaggi & Ehrlich associate back to her office, draw up the papers, and sign them then and there.

It only remained for the city to work out the lease and for the Board of Estimate to approve it. Ehrlich and Simon's aide, Kathy Zamechansky, began bombarding city officials with calls. Zamechansky would invoke the names of Simon and Friedman; if it came down to a conflict between Wedtech and Hebrew National, Zamechansky said, Simon wanted Wedtech. Ehrlich strutted around the Board of Estimate with "that uniform, and the hat cocked at a cocky angle," a city official recalls. He made sure that everyone knew about the one day a week he spent in the office of Senator Alfonse D'Amato. Low-level government officials constituted the one group that Ehrlich had the capacity to intimidate. The fact is that the city probably would have put the lease together even without all the shouting and strutting, since Hebrew National needed only a small piece of the parking lot, and Henry Thomas had been consigned to oblivion. But it certainly wouldn't have been done as quickly.

The problem with Simon was that, though he was the sovereign of the desperate province of the Bronx, he had very little influence with his peers. Board of Estimate convention dictated that a borough president's pet project never be turned down, but Simon could not get 1 Loop Drive on the calendar. A meeting in mid-June was deemed too early. Just before the next scheduled meeting, two weeks later, Donald Manes, in a fit of pique at seeing Hebrew National move from his borough to Simon's, struck the issue off the calendar. Everyone was furious at Simon, above all Biaggi, who felt that he and Ehrlich had engineered everything to date. Biaggi called Simon and threatened to withhold his support in next year's election—a terrifying prospect for the borough president.

But a borough president's pet project was never allowed to languish for long in the Board of Estimate. The lease was finally put on the calendar, and at the next convening of the board, in mid-July, it passed with very little further discussion. Henry Thomas made a brief speech, which was duly ignored, and Wedtech had its waterfront property. A good deal of wrangling ensued, including the eviction of Thomas in September, but Wedtech got its waterfront site in time to hold off the Navy.

TWENTY-ONE

Pyrrhic Victory at Sea

BY THE MIDDLE of 1984 Wedtech was traveling along two trajectories. In what might be called its inner trajectory, the company was trying, and failing, to cope with the consequences of its ruinous victory in the pontoon competition, and was skidding steadily downward as the gap between income and expense widened. This was the simple truth about Wedtech, though it was a truth too painful to be acknowledged even by the few who understood it. In its outer trajectory, which everyone save a few gimlet-eyed Navy officials took for the truth, the company was rising like a rocket, shooting up into the rarefied atmosphere where the billion-dollar companies dwell. In April, *Inc.* magazine ranked Wedtech as the third most profitable company among America's hundred fastest-growing concerns. The editors of *Inc.* can scarcely be blamed for following the outer trajectory. Wedtech wasn't making a profit at all and never would, but Tony had begun to doctor the books by adding hypothetical contracts and underestimating projected expense.

With the pontoon contract and the semiguaranteed options safely in hand, Wedtech discovered that finding money was a cinch. Bank Leumi had rolled over Wedtech's line of credit to provide a fresh $20 million. The city of Mount Vernon had floated $5 million in industrial revenue bonds in order to help finance Wedtech's acquisition of a facility to accommodate the coating division. And on June 22 Wedtech's banker, Moseley Hallgarten, in conjunction with Bear Stearns, successfully sold $40 million worth of corporate bonds.

The money represented a great opportunity. Perhaps if John and Mario had been able to ignore the siren song of the pontoon contract, of take-whatever-you-can-get, Wedtech might have been able to devote the tens of millions it raised to expanding its engine-manufacturing capacity or transforming the coating division from an enormous high school science project to a commercial proposition. Instead, the money simply disappeared into the pontoon program.

Mario was also beginning to put some heavy cash into his pocket. His combined salary and bonus had gone from $80,000 in 1983 to $262,000 in 1984. He had his half a million dollars from the stock sale, another half million from stock he sold in September, his cut of FHJ, and several hundred thousand dollars flowing from his secret deal with his brother-in-law Reynaldo Berney. Though his love of wealth had nothing of John's obsessiveness nor of Fred's casual rapacity, Mario had begun to revel in the good life. He started to dress well, though he was a mere mud hen compared to Conchita, who was never known to wear the same dress twice. Conchita had converted two bedrooms in her house into walk-in closets, where her wardrobe was arranged with the care normally accorded the costume collection of a major museum.

This house, in fact, was Mario's great achievement. Back in 1981 Conchita had purchased the big brick house on Sedgwick Avenue at the very northern tip of the Bronx for $89,000. It was already the biggest private dwelling in the neighborhood, a three-story cube with a Spanish tile roof. With his new wealth, however, Mario began to turn this pile into the petty fiefdom of a Latin American industrial magnate. He added an elaborate wrought-iron fence with a swinging gateway controlled by an electronic security system, the sort of bricked drive associated with English manor houses, an incongruously carpeted walkway, and a thickly blooming shrub garden dotted with benches, urns, and a statue of a naked nymph or some other antique female. He built a greenhouse for a sort of indoor tropical rain forest. The greenhouse alone came to $300,000.

Mario's one unparalleled achievement in the field of extravagant decoration was what he called "the grotto," which, it is probably safe to say, was the finest item of its type in the Bronx and the greatest of the many Wedtech swimming pools. Mario spent half a million dollars carving the grotto out of the schist under the house. No one enjoyed it more than Mario—certainly not Conchita, who did not know how to swim. Sometimes when Mario would arrive home at two in the morning, exhausted and tense, he would strip off his clothes and glide through the dark water.

Mario was often exhausted and tense, though it would have violated his code of decorum to show it. The year before, he had collapsed and almost died. Mario could not forget about what he was doing; he was afflicted with self-awareness. He knew that he hadn't left when he had had a chance; now he was in far too deep even to contemplate escape. Wedtech was his life. John Mariotta and Bob Wallach and Bernie Ehrlich were his good friends. He loved the whispered conversations in congressional offices, the tacit understandings, the sense of standing at the center of a vast web of influence. He loved the complexity of it all. But it was a life that took its toll. And the cash and the clothes and even the pool did not dull the sharp edge of anxiety.

Mario found his escape in cards. Since the beginning of the year he had begun to spend a lot of time in Atlantic City, at the condo he owned in a building called the Ritz Tower. He wouldn't so much visit the casinos as vanish inside them. Tony, too, was becoming a heavy gambler, but Mario was an addict. When he and some of the others went to the casino together, Mario would stay while everyone else got up to go to dinner or a show. He could sit at the blackjack table all evening, all night, and into the morning. And he lost big—sometimes $50,000 in a weekend, even $100,000. The losses pained him, but during those long hours in the big, dark theater he could be alone with himself. "It was," he would later testify, "the only place where my anxieties could go away."

In mid-July, right after the Board of Estimate approved Wedtech's lease to 1 Loop Drive, John and Mario, along with Jenny and Conchita, gave themselves a vacation in Rome. Tony had been in Israel looking over the Carmo plant, and he and his wife, Cynthia, flew to Rome to join the group. John was playing the last of the American plutocrats, drawing up bucketfuls of cash from his apparently bottomless well. He and Jenny were buying furniture for the Condado Bay apartment, and he had hired a stretch limo to sit in front of the hotel and take them all to shops and restaurants. The grandee from the South Bronx kept the generally idle driver ecstatic with daily tips.

After a week Tony went home, and John and Mario traveled to Milan to visit the factory of Figlia di Stefano, a company that manufactured forgings for the six-horsepower engine. Fred and John, on an earlier visit, had worked out a system whereby the subcontractor added $4.00 to the price of each kit of forgings, and then kicked back the sum to Wedtech, a minor scam that netted about $100,000 over the years. It was nothing unusual: Fred had worked out similar scams with many of his suppliers, including a firm in West Germany. From Italy, John and Mario continued their vacation in France and then England. In London they got word that Captain de Vicq's threats were becoming more frequent and that the pontoon program was in jeopardy.

They raced back to contain the situation. By now, however, Mario's lies or unfounded hopes had become threadbare, and de Vicq had stopped listening. So had Colonel Donald Hein, who ran the New York regional office of the Defense Contract Administration Service, or DCAS. Hein got into the habit, more or less to humor himself, of telling Mario what he would like to hear, and then waiting to hear just that some while later. It was not a joke that Hein especially enjoyed. At one point, after hearing different stories from different officers, the DCAS officer marched into Mario's office and told everyone except Mario and two others to leave. To the remaining three he said, "Stay in this office until you get your story straightened out. When you're ready, come and knock on my door." Hein then left, and listened to the uproar as the three accused one another of screwing up.

By August, two months from the date when Wedtech was to deliver the first pontoon, relations between the company and the military had reached a low point. The wagon train of electric generators had been pumping fumes back into the building, creating a noxious atmosphere that violated OSHA workplace regulations. Hein even considered removing DCAS employees from the facility for their own safety. De Vicq was telling colleagues and superiors in the Navy that Wedtech had demonstrated its incompetence beyond a doubt, and that the 1985 options should be let for competitive bidding. John and Mario, for their part, were convinced that de Vicq was Dr. Keenan all over again, a racist who would be happy to vindicate his prejudices by destroying the company.

At this point Wedtech made a strategic purchase that placated the Navy just a little. In April, when Wedtech's old friend Richard Ramirez was preparing to leave Minority Land to return to his first love, making money, he had called up Mario to make a typical proposition. "When I leave here," he said, "I'll put something on your plate that will make your day. If it doesn't work, don't pay me." The previous summer, Ramirez had been flown to the Upper Peninsula of Michigan to look at a bankrupt shipyard, Upsco, in the remote town of Ontonagon, on the shore of Lake Superior. State authorities were desperate to find someone to get the shipyard, which had been the principal source of employment in a depressed area, up and running once again. Ramirez knew that Wedtech was equally desperate for immediate shipbuilding capacity. In short, he'd be doing everyone a favor, himself included. Mario agreed that if Wedtech bought Upsco out of receivership, Ramirez would get $120,000, payable monthly over two years.

In June, John and Mario went out to Ontonagon and discovered that Upsco was a steal, a shipyard that needed nothing but capital to start doing what Wedtech could not yet do in the Bronx. Wedtech submitted a bid of $5.3 million for more than $20 million worth of plant and equipment. Another firm had already entered a bid for the shipyard with the bankruptcy court, but proved unable to supply the needed cash by the July 30 deadline. Wedtech, still flush with the proceeds of its debt offering, had no trouble coming up with the scratch, and closed the deal at the end of August. Within weeks, Upsco's highly professional work force had been reassembled and been put to work constructing the pontoons. De Vicq used to marvel at the efficiency of the Ontonagon shipyard and bemoan Wedtech's inability to do half as well in the Bronx.

The one unmistakably Wedtech element in the shipyard purchase was the role played by Richard Ramirez. Ramirez took the $120,000 as a finder's fee. But the actual work on the deal was performed by a consulting firm he had joined, Gnau, Carter, Jacobsen. Ramirez decided it would be the better part of discretion not to mention to his employers that he had cut a separate deal with Wedtech, and he even went so far as to have his Wedtech checks laundered through his bagman, Carl Jacobson (no relation to the firm). At the conclusion of the deal, Wedtech paid Gnau Carter $125,000. And the principals of the firm, unaware that Ramirez was already getting his cut from Wedtech, rewarded him with a third of the fee. Ramirez thus walked off with about $160,000 for a property he had been shown while working for the U.S. government. It sure beat Minority Land.

In late August, Everett Pyatt's new deputy for 8(a) matters, Wayne Arny, called a meeting of Navy and SBA officers to discuss the pontoon options. The NAVFAC officials complained harshly about Wedtech's performance, but the SBA, whose own judgment was on the line, stoutly defended the firm. In the normal course of things Arny, a former career Navy man and pilot in the Vietnam War, would have sided with his professional people in a disagreement with the SBA over matters of contract compliance. Instead, Arny did something very unusual: he asked a Navy officer from another command, Captain Charles Piersall, to prepare an independent report.

Arny later testified to the Levin committee that he was simply trying to adjudicate between the two sides. Piersall's impression is that Arny had lost faith in the whole system, though it's not clear why. It is also true, however, that the criticism coming from de Vicq and other NAVFAC officials, if unchallenged, almost certainly would have precluded Wedtech from receiving the options, thus leading to the company's bankruptcy. And Pyatt, having crowned Wedtech with this laurel in the face of universal opposition, may not have been in a position to permit the company to fail.

John, Mario, and the others now proceeded to do to Piersall what they had already done to Hein and de Vicq. "These guys put on a dog-and-pony show," says Hein. "Everything was cleaned up, and everything they briefed him on was bullshit." Piersall himself insists that he was neither pressured by Arny nor conned by Wedtech. Whatever the reason, his report, issued at the end of September, concluded that many of Wedtech's problems could be traced to poor coordination among the supervising agencies, as well as slow deliveries from the Navy of the pump used to power the causeways. In a covering letter, Piersall assured Arny that Wedtech would complete its first article test the following week, with the first pontoon to be delivered by October 15. "This critical milestone," he wrote, "will demonstrate Wedtech's capability."

Wedtech required only a few days to demonstrate its capability. On October 9, Mario wrote a letter informing NAVFAC that the company could not deliver the first causeway until early November nor the tenth until the end of December, a full month later than planned. In fact, the situation was even worse. By mid-November de Vicq reported that Wedtech was slipping still farther behind, and that the first finished causeway could not arrive before mid-December.

It was now painfully obvious that the pontoons were more likely to destroy Wedtech than to enrich it. The tooling-up costs had swallowed almost the entire bond offering—this for a contract worth $24.5 million —and Tony and Larry Shorten had had to renegotiate the credit line with their bank consortium to raise their limit from $20 to $30 million. The 149th Street facility was now in full use, with the huge steel cubes for the pontoons dangling from a wilderness of cranes and a conveyor belt hung from the ceiling. If de Vicq wouldn't relent and recommend that the options be granted, Wedtech would be stuck with about $25 million worth of equipment and with no prospects for the future. Everyone felt that the company had made enormous strides in recent months, training several hundred semiskilled and unskilled workers, organizing an assembly line, and drawing up the detailed documentation required by the Navy. Wedtech *deserved* those options. But de Vicq had to be persuaded— or something.

Fred had a characteristic idea. One day in early November he came charging down the hallway at 595 Gerard after a conversation with de Vicq. "I got to him!" Fred roared. "The man can be bought. I tell you, I had him eating out of my hand." Fred said de Vicq had given him the impression that he would lay off Wedtech in exchange for a promotion. Everyone was very excited, and the speakerphone in John's office was switched on and a call placed to Wallach. Fred asked Wallach whether he could do anything to get de Vicq promoted. Wallach said that he would see what he could do.

Wallach must have liked the idea, though he adjusted it in his own mind to something more delicate. During "a candid discussion" with de Vicq, he wrote in a memo soon after the conversation, "Wedtech's general ally structure" ought to be "gently indicated so that he understands that we will view favorably with all we know his efforts to legitimately conclude this agreement and fulfill the Navy's responsibilities to the public." And should the captain stubbornly refuse the bait, Wedtech officers should threaten to send to Pyatt a letter complaining of mistreatment. The meeting does not appear to have been held, though Fred broached the idea of a quid pro quo with de Vicq. De Vicq told Fred to go to hell.

On November 19, a month after Wedtech had missed its "critical milestone" and with no finished pontoon in sight, Wayne Arny decided he'd seen enough. Earlier in the month Mark Bragg had succeeded in getting Arny to pay a visit to the South Bronx, to take The Tour and witness the remarkable progress being made at 149th Street. Arny had always been receptive to the Wedtech point of view. Now he wrote a letter instructing NAVFAC to proceed immediately to award the 1985 options to Wedtech. What's more, he wrote, the command should simply tell Wedtech to start building, and negotiate the price at some point in the future. When de Vicq saw the Arny memorandum, he was floored. Nothing short of an emergency at sea was supposed to justify a "letter contract," as such a document was called.

It was obvious what Wedtech would do once the restraints were removed: squander an insane amount of money, and then stick the Navy with the bill. As of that moment, in fact, Wedtech wanted $68 million to execute the options, and the Navy was offering $42 million. Arny had given Wedtech the opportunity to euchre the Navy out of $26 million. At a meeting with Hein and his staff, a disgusted de Vicq spluttered, "This letter is ridiculous, and I just won't do it." "No one in this room will do it either," said Hein.

Arny had gone too far, and he was forced to back down. De Vicq complained to his superior, Admiral John Paul Jones, Jr., who sent Arny the sort of blisteringly polite letter that the uniformed military writes to deputy assistant secretaries. Then Jones's superior complained to Pyatt, and Arny backed off, directing NAVFAC to proceed to immediate negotiations with Wedtech. As the end of 1984 rolled around, Wedtech's contract people were back in Davisville, Rhode Island, where they had been not many months earlier, once again trying, and failing, to get the Navy to come up to a price the company could make some money on.

TWENTY-TWO

Paying the Piper

ASIDE FROM the irascible Fred Neuberger, everyone at Wedtech understood that political influence was a very expensive commodity. Over the years the company would spend millions of dollars, legally and otherwise, on its lobbyists and consultants and friendly politicians and civil servants—over $900,000 in fees to Biaggi & Ehrlich, over $700,000 to E. Robert Wallach, $569,000 to Gordon Osgood of the Army, $500,000 to Nofziger & Bragg, $175,000 to Stephen Denlinger of LAMA, and so on. Many millions of dollars of stock and stock options were thrown into the pot, too. These payments were a serious drain on capital and on equity, but without them, there would have been no Wedtech.

At certain moments, normally soon after public offerings and the announcement of large contracts, Wedtech had to pay the piper. One of these moments was the fall of 1984, when the company seemed to be flush with its debenture offering and its pontoon contract. In fact, the insiders were struggling to keep Wedtech from being crushed beneath the financial weight of that contract, but that was scarcely obvious from the outside. The first to bury their snouts in the trough were the Bronx contingent. Within days after the Board of Estimate's approval of the lease for 1 Loop Drive, Bernie Ehrlich complained to Mario that Stanley Simon had been useless, and that he and Biaggi had had to go to bat to save Wedtech, especially with the Queens borough president, Donald Manes. The work, said Ehrlich, had been worth $50,000. Mario accepted the figure, as did the other insiders, and at a meeting in the congressman's office in the Bronx, Mario agreed to make the payment.

Simon himself, as usual, made his demands more indirectly. It was time, he said, for his brother-in-law Henry Bittman to get another raise, to $35,000, even though Wedtech had jacked up his salary to $25,000 only nine months earlier. Mario argued that Bittman would then be earning about twice what the other payroll clerks were getting without even doing a competent job. "He deserves it," said Simon, who had, at best, a foggy idea of merit. After conferring with Tony, Mario offered a $5000 raise instead. Simon agreed, and on August 1 Henry Bittman became a $30,000-a-year payroll clerk.

And then there was Bob Wallach. Wallach had expected to spend a few months defending his friend Ed from misguided liberals in the Senate, and then mount to a splendid new status. The hearings, at first, had gone very well. Not only did he spend much of every day with his famous friend; he sat by his side in the Senate or scurried between the Congress and the offices of his friend and co-counsel, Leonard Garment. He sent a breathless note to his friends at Wedtech congratulating himself on the smoothness of the hearings and imploring them to follow the advice he had given Ed: " 'Don't get cocky.' 'Stay humble.' . . . Much of what has been accomplished has been because of who you are, your enormous dedication to the company and to the community, and your obvious dedication to a quality product. Those are rare combinations of qualities in this day and age (tragically)."

As it turned out, Wallach had lit the victory cigar a trifle early. In April a special prosecutor was appointed to look into allegations that Meese had received financial favors from friends whom he had then appointed to federal jobs, and had failed to mention some of these benefits on financial disclosure forms. The allegations were remarkably similar to those later investigated by the 1987 independent counsel, and the results were the same: Meese saved his own head from the chopping block through sheer, insuperable heedlessness. He had simply forgotten, he insisted, about a $15,000 loan to his wife from a friend whom he had later made his personal assistant. That four officials of a bank which had graciously permitted Meese to ignore prompt loan payments had received federal jobs was pure coincidence.

It seemed inconceivable that the man could be so unwitting of the consequences of his own acts, and a number of senators later said so. It was terrifying that such a man could become Attorney General. But that wasn't the question. In September, the independent counsel, Jacob Stein, announced that he had found nothing in Meese's behavior that demanded indictment.

Now that it was clear that Meese's confirmation was only a formality, Wallach began agonizing in front of all his most important and prestigious friends about whether or not he should take on a central role in the Meese Justice Department. Both Leonard Garment and Howard Squadron recall Wallach asking them whether he should become Meese's chief of staff, or perhaps take some other job. It wasn't at all clear what he would do, though it was obvious that the Chagall angel, as Garment thought of him, was suffering from intensely earthly ambitions. Wallach knew that he might feel constrained in a government job, that he would be a liberal in a conservative administration, that he would have to take a big cut in salary. The possibility that he simply might not be wanted did not occur to him.

Wallach was not in the habit of communicating his self-doubt to his friends at Wedtech. On the contrary, he was wont to magnify his powers, and thus to enhance the value of the protective cloak he threw around them all. Mario and John, the two minority members, were his friends at the firm, and it was to them that Wallach did most of his boasting. A few weeks before the Stein verdict, Mario testified, Wallach took his two friends to lunch at Mel Krupin's, a Washington power hangout. Wallach made a point of greeting his friends Lyn Nofziger, James Baker, and the real estate potentate Howard Bender. After lunch Wallach took them back to his Georgetown apartment and said that he expected to be entering the Justice Department as Ed Meese's chief of staff. Since he would not be able to accept money from the company once he had gone to work for the government, Wallach said that he would like $500,000 as payment in advance for help he would be giving them over the next two years.

Mario testified that he was taken aback and said, "Bob, how would this look? This is like an illegal payment." Wallach answered dismissively that he would check with an ethics authority, but that he didn't see a problem. Several weeks later, at a lunch at Wallach's favorite haunt, the Four Seasons, he repeated the $500,000 request. John and Mario had already related the story of the first meeting to Fred, who of course had hit the ceiling. So Mario tried to convince Wallach that $300,000 would be plenty. In effect, he would be prepaid for 1985 and 1986 at the same rate at which he had been prepaid for 1984, back in February.

Toward the end of October, Wallach came up to 595 Gerard to settle his future. Sitting in John's office, he asked for the $300,000 in a lump sum, and John agreed. Mario was still hoping to stretch the payment over time, and rushed down the hall to Tony's office to ask him to join the group. When Tony arrived and asked Wallach why he should be paid in advance for both years, Wallach explained that he was going to take a job with the Justice Department—the job as Tony recalls it was the full-time chairmanship of an advisory commission—and he would be legally prohibited from receiving fees from Wedtech once he did so. Nevertheless, he said, as a member of the Justice Department he would be "going through the front door," and he would be even more able to help Wedtech than he had been before.

As a matter of accounting, Tony said, he would like to have Wallach ascribe the payment to the purchase of the Upsco facility. Wallach had not worked on the purchase, but, then, he hadn't asked for any explanations the previous September when Tony had him attribute the $125,000 payment to work on the public offering. Wallach agreed without comment. This done, there was nothing further to discuss. On October 27 Tony gave Wallach a check for $300,000.

The $300,000 payment, which later constituted the principal charge against Wallach in his 1989 trial, appears to have been one of Wedtech's straightforward transactions. Wallach, essentially, was selling a government office he expected to receive. Certainly the story Wallach told at the trial, that by the fall of 1984 he was worn out and hoping to take a job as dean of the University of Hawaii Law School, and that Wedtech, and above all Fred, prevailed on him to stay with the $300,000 offer, had the ring of the preposterous. But with Wallach, no transaction was altogether clear-cut. Unlike a Lyn Nofziger or a Mario Biaggi or a Stanley Simon, Wallach did not conceive of life as a great favor exchange. In the windy plain of idealism on which he consciously lived, Wallach thought of even his most selfish acts as fundamentally selfless.

It is impossible to know what Wallach was thinking when he made this transaction, which ultimately destroyed him. The fact is that Wallach was desperately torn between public and private life. A memo he wrote to Meese the following May, when Wallach was already working as a self-appointed screening committee for Justice Department positions, expresses his anguish in typically elliptical, if revealing, language: "More and more, as this time has elapsed, I have been struggling with my own

TACOM in January 1984, the Wedtech principals briefly considered becoming part owners of his firm. The idea was rejected, and the monthly payments continued, and even grew. Osgood could do them no good from the outside, but John had allegedly promised him half a million dollars, and John believed in paying what you promise. In 1983 Wedtech had paid Osgood $101,942.23. In 1984 the figure rose to $231,401.98, and he had a leased Mercedes, just as the insiders did. The only difference was that now that Osgood was a private citizen, Wedtech could make payments to him personally as well as to his company.

Finally, there was Stanley the *schnorrer,* the politician who never had enough. Simon had wangled his breakfasts and lunches; he had made Henry Bittman one of the world's best-paid payroll clerks. He had also exacted favors in the more orthodox form of political contributions. In October 1983, Wedtech gave Simon's campaign $1250; in February of the following year the company gave his political base, the Riverdale Democratic Club, $1000. And in April 1984, Simon instructed Mario to make a $5000 contribution to his campaign. This gift enabled Mario to join something called the President's Club, along with a number of other large contributors who assumed that they had been granted entrée to one of those elite bodies limited to chief executive officers. In fact the president of the title was none other than Stanley Simon, president of the borough of the Bronx. Another member of the club was Pat Simone, and another was Ivan Irizarry, formerly with the SBA and now with the New York National Bank.

But unlike the Alfonse D'Amatos of this world, Stanley Simon also took cash. Over the years Simon had developed a number of devices for making other people pay for his expenses. The distinguishing feature of these schemes was a peculiar combination of shamelessness and niggardliness. There was, for example, the Simon tab. At a number of restaurants in his neighborhood of Riverdale, most of them coffee shops or delicatessens, Simon's meals, according to testimony by Ralph Lawrence, would be deducted from a running total, or tab.

The trick, however, was that the money for the tab came not from Simon but from benefactors whom he would designate, most of them developers and businessmen who were all too happy to purchase Simon's friendship at so cheap a rate. Alternatively, Simon would cash a check at his long-time haunt, Angelo's, whose owner would then turn to one of the members of the Simon fund for remuneration. Wedtech now became a sustaining member, and Ralph Lawrence, Simon's advance man, porter, and all-around slavey, often showed up at the company's doorstep to pick up a check.

Fred also testified that just before Christmas 1983, Simon asked whether Wedtech could pick up the meal expenses for a trip he and Irene were taking to Mullet's Bay, in St. Martin. "What do you want me to do?" asked Fred; "get a letter from the headwaiter every time you pay for a meal?" After the vacation Simon called to say, "Forget about it. It was taken care of."

Simon also permitted Wedtech to become a principal funding source of his gambling activities. The borough president had developed a method of playing the dice which he called "progressive betting." By playing the odds with dogged patience, he could stay at craps tables for hours, and walk away with maybe $100 in winnings. Simon loved going to Atlantic City, and he would appoint himself den mother to, say, a group of Bronx senior citizens. On the bus to the casinos Simon would collect a pool of about $100, taking care not to waste any of his own money, and then head off to the tables for a long afternoon of progressive betting.

Simon had probably never known a gambler like Mario Moreno. In the plush-and-satin world of the Atlantic City casinos Mario, a big and very dependable loser, was treated like a sheik. Stanley Simon looked at the princely Mario and saw a source of perpetual fun. He prevailed on Mario to get a line of credit at the Golden Nugget, which he could then use himself. Once he found that Mario was obliging, Simon began pestering both him and Ehrlich to go to Atlantic City with him. He was not only a *schnorrer* but a *noodge,* and Simon sometimes *noodged* his friends at Wedtech half to death. And it wasn't always nickel-and-dime stuff, either. On one trip to Atlantic City in late 1985 Mario found rooms for the Neglias, Ehrlichs, and Simons, bought dinner for everyone, took them all to hear Neil Sedaka, and seems to have spent much of Friday and Saturday nights handing out black $100 chips to Simon and his wife, Neglia's wife, and Ehrlich's wife. Simon must have been feeling giddy enough to abandon progressive betting for the nonce, because Mario recalls giving the Simons about $3000 on Saturday night alone.

In Wedtech Simon saw a kind of casual wealth and extravagance that he could have scarcely known before. Perhaps this was what emboldened him to do something that seemed very much out of character. During the period in mid-1984 when Wedtech had had the greatest need of him, Simon had asked for little beyond the usual petty gifts. Now, in the fall, for reasons that are not clear, Simon raised his sights to the level of the grandiose. The borough president made his move at one of the benefits he attended almost around the clock, an outing for the Hebrew Home for the Aged at the Yonkers Racetrack on November 14. Fred was there with his wife, Eileen, and naturally shelled out $50 or so for Simon to bet on the ponies.

Later in the evening, Fred testified, Simon sat down for a chat. "He pulled me to the side and said he is running a re-election campaign that is a very hard-fought campaign and he needs help. So I said, 'Well, what kind of help do you expect?' So he said he needs, again I don't remember, $75 or $100,000. And I told him this is ridiculous, we can't do that. Besides, I told him, it's illegal for a corporation to make a contribution to a campaign. So he said, 'Well, do it in the form of churches and some other expenses.' So I said, 'The best I can do is $50,000.' So we settled for that."

Even Simon's enemies cannot easily picture him coolly demanding so large a sum of money. It's one thing to be a *schnorrer;* it's something else to be an extortionist. Simon didn't seem to have it in him. Yet the fact is that within a few weeks Ceil Lewis had begun issuing a stream of checks for Simon and subtracting them from a $50,000 credit. Even Simon conceded that the credit existed, and at trial argued that Fred had spontaneously offered a campaign contribution of that size while making a condolence call several days after the death of Simon's father—a claim oddly similar to the one Wallach would later make, and every bit as implausible.

What gives the story of the bribe the unmistakable Simon tang is that the $50,000 was arranged in the form of a tab. Rather than demanding a stack of fresh bills, as Richard Ramirez had done, Simon converted Wedtech into a sort of automated teller machine. One day in late November, Ralph Lawrence showed up at Ceil Lewis' office behind the coffee room on the first floor of 595 Gerard. Lewis had to come out from her desk to receive visitors, since she always locked the door to keep prying eyes away from the FHJ books and prying hands from the wads of bills in the petty cash box. Lawrence said he had instructions from his boss to pick up a $500 check made out to cash—the first debit against the $50,000 tab. Since the FHJ account happened to be empty, Lewis made out a check on her own account and later reimbursed herself from FHJ.

It took Simon only a year to exhaust the account. Lewis wrote out thousands of dollars' worth of checks to the delicatessens and coffee shops and greasy spoons that Simon used both for himself and for the victualing of the enormous volunteer army he conscripted for his electoral campaigns. She wrote out checks to his clubhouse and to sympathetic clubhouses and to his bewildering array of campaign committees.

The Simon campaign received a $10,000 contribution from Fred, $5000 from John, and $2000 from Ceil Lewis herself. At the borough president's direction she wrote out large checks to synagogues, yeshivas, nursing homes, and all the other institutions to which Simon had assiduously paid court over the years. The local rabbinate, which enjoyed tremendous moral authority over their largely elderly and politically active congregants, formed a key part of Simon's vast electoral apparatus. One member of Simon's entourage, Rabbi Israel Greenberg, of the Beth Jacob Miriam girls' school, became Ceil's political escort, squiring her to campaign lunches, benefits, and fund raisers. Wedtech not only bought tickets for these events, but often paid for the food.

In early 1985 Simon said that he and Irene wanted to go to Atlantic City, he wanted the keys to Mario's apartment, and he needed some cash. Simon might have been happy with several hundred dollars, but Mario told Ceil Lewis to get together as much cash as she could, which in practice meant $10,000. When Lawrence arrived the following day, Ceil unlocked the safe, pulled out a large white envelope, and handed it to the borough president's factotum. Lawrence took it without a word, stuffed it into his inside jacket pocket, and left.

Simon continued receiving money from Wedtech, in cash and in checks, directly and indirectly, in driblets and in big chunks, until he finally went over the top around the time Ceil Lewis shelled out $500 so that Bernstein's delicatessen could cater his annual Chanukah party. And when it was over, Simon didn't ask for more. That, after all, would have smacked of extortion rather than contributions made in exchange for expediting the political process. It wouldn't be right. "The amazing thing about Stanley," says a man who has known him for years, "is that he's a *schnorrer* to such an extent that I firmly believe he never thought he was doing anything wrong."

TWENTY-THREE

Near-Death Experience: IV

THE GODDESS OF RETRIBUTION, whom the Greeks called Nemesis—and whom men invite when they overreach themselves—began to visit the unstoppable little company in the South Bronx during the summer of 1984. Had they not grown so arrogant, the Wedtech men might have realized that their course was leading to catastrophe. But when they beat back this challenge, they grew all the more convinced of their invulnerability. Whom the gods would destroy . . .

Retribution came in the form of John Grayson, the black businessman whose company, Univox, had lost out in the rigged contest for the pontoon contract. Soon after Wedtech walked away with sole possession of the contract, Grayson had spoken with his old friend Representative Parren Mitchell, chairman of the House Small Business Committee. The SBA, Grayson recalls saying, had violated its own rules. He himself should have won the contract, he said, since he had applied for it first. And Grayson then recounted to Mitchell the conversation he had had with Mark Bragg at the time of the award: the White House was calling the shots, Lyn Nofziger was throwing his weight around, and so on. Grayson had told Bragg, according to Denlinger, that he would get back at Wedtech if he was boxed out of the contract. (Grayson denies having said so.) Now, perhaps, he was evening the balance.

A liberal black who represented the Baltimore area, Mitchell had been a leading advocate of civil rights and especially minority business issues, and a thorn in the side of several administrations. Within the 8(a) community he was also understood to be a champion of black entrepreneurs at a time when the Reagan administration was clearly trying to play to the Hispanic gallery. And Wedtech was the prime instance of the administration's favoritism. If Grayson was right, it was favoritism of the worst kind. It is unlikely that in the summer of 1984, with a presidential election four months away, the congressman never gave a thought to the political value of exposing the cynical and all-too-characteristic horse trading of the President's old pal and campaign operative Lyn Nofziger. On the other hand, had Mitchell been a Republican and simply sat on the story, it would have constituted an even more grossly political act.

Mitchell was an ardent advocate but scarcely a confrontational one. He was not the kind who bangs gavels and hurls maledictions. Not once, in fact, had he asked his chief investigator, Tom Trimboli, to look into a specific instance of abuse by an 8(a) firm. Now, however, in late June or early July, he told Trimboli about the rumors he had heard, without mentioning their source, and asked him to do just that.

Tom Trimboli, unlike his boss, had the prosecutorial fire in his belly. Trimboli had been exposing the manifold stupidities of the 8(a) program since Joseph Addabbo had asked him to look into the set-aside system in 1975. He knew as well as anyone how thoroughly the system had been corrupted by political considerations, and he derived an essentially non-partisan pleasure from proving it. He was fast-talking, aggressive, and inclined, as investigators are, to believe the worst. In this case, he had found the worst. Trimboli knew from past investigations that files had a way of disappearing between the district SBA office and Washington. So he took a step that must have struck fear into more than one heart: he told the SBA that he would be arriving in the New York district office at noon on July 27 in order to obtain files on an 8(a) firm. Which firm, he wouldn't say.

That morning Trimboli and an aide, David Robinson, took the shuttle to New York. When they arrived at La Guardia, Trimboli called another staff member back in Washington and instructed him to proceed, as planned, to the congressional liaison office at SBA headquarters, there to await another call. It was a miserably rainy morning, and Trimboli's cab, or good measure, had a hole in the roof. When the two men arrived at the ugly government building at 26 Federal Plaza, they went directly to the office of the district director. Trimboli picked up a phone and called his staffer at the SBA office in Washington. With the precise coordination normally associated with FBI sweeps, Trimboli then presented a letter to the district director at exactly the moment his aide was handing the original of the letter to the congressional liaison director, Janine Perrignan.

The letter requested all documents pertaining to Wedtech's involvement in the set-aside program, a roster of all SBA officials who had dealt with Wedtech within the program or who had helped the firm receive loans or contracts, and "a list of all and any agents"—consultants—"who may have appeared before the SBA on such concern's behalf since March 1, 1981 . . . It would be appreciated," the letter continued in an unmistakably threatening tone, if the request for 8(a) documents "be considered as immediate."

Surrounded by nervous bureaucrats, Trimboli then walked into the file room with the director and watched him remove the Wedtech materials. He and Robinson had each brought a big legal briefcase, assuming that they could fit everything in and cart it off themselves. But the material was mountainous. Jack Mitchell, the regional SBA counsel, gave them yet another satchel. Still more material was boxed up and sent off to the Small Business Committee. Only a few hours after he had arrived empty-handed, Trimboli left, still surrounded by shuffling bureaucrats, now bowed down like a pack horse.

Then he got home and opened up his presents. "Republicans," he says, "are great. They document everything." Trimboli was the first but by no means the last investigator to stumble into the Wedtech archives and feel like Howard Carter coming on the throne room in the great tomb of Tutankhamen. He saw the April 8, 1982, letter from Nofziger to Meese; memos from Jim Jenkins, Pier Talenti, Henry Zuniga, and others; documents describing the White House meetings during the engine contract negotiations; letters from Mario Biaggi's law firm to the SBA; stock records and references to the progress payment issue and to the firm's 8(a) eligibility; and innumerable signs of the SBA's favoritism. The documents cast an appalling light, even by the debased standards of the 8(a) program, on both Wedtech and the SBA.

A lot of necks were on the line, not least of them the tender, thirty-seven-year-old neck of Peter Neglia. The regional administrator's office was just one flight up from the district office, so Neglia, in all probability, had heard about the rape of the files while it was in progress. The regional administrator must have had the cold sweats at the thought of a hostile congressional investigator wading through evidence of his long campaign of advocacy for Wedtech. Neglia had already begun talking to Bernie Ehrlich about a job at Biaggi & Ehrlich when he left government service, as planned, at the end of the first Reagan term. The investigation could wreck not only Wedtech but his career. Neglia telephoned Mario and said that the company was under siege from hostile forces.

Mario seemed to like crises, which was just as well. In a flash he would summon the angels, archangels, principalities, and powers who coursed through the Wedtech heavens, and send them off on their errands. At just this moment Mario already had a perfectly serviceable crisis on his hands, what with Captain de Vicq growing short-tempered, and 1 Loop Drive still in the hands of Henry Thomas, who had not yet moved out. Now he had a big Washington problem, the kind that only he, of all the insiders, could deal with. He told the others what was heading their way, and then, with Tony Guariglia in tow, he climbed on the shuttle.

Mario always stopped by to see Mario Biaggi first when he went to Washington, if only as a matter of fealty; but Biaggi wasn't in, so Mario and Tony went to Bobby Garcia's office. In recent days Mario had been talking to Garcia about a contract, worth up to $80 million, to manufacture letter-carrying boxes for the post office. This was one of the few areas where Garcia had any pull, since he sat on the House Postal Services Committee. Now Mario told Garcia that they had to move fast on the postal contract. In one of those moments which still gave Mario a charge, Garcia simply picked up the phone and asked for William Bolger, the Postmaster General. Bolger wasn't in, but Garcia promised Mario that he would pursue the matter.

Then Mario turned to the recent raid on the SBA's files. It was an outrage, he said; some kind of witch hunt. Garcia listened gravely and said that he would talk to his friend Parren Mitchell. Mario said that he knew election time was coming up, and Wedtech wouldn't forget its friends. Within the next three weeks Tony and his wife gave Garcia's re-election fund $3000; Larry Shorten and his wife gave another $3000; and John and Jenny gave $2000.

Mario's counterassault started even before Tom Trimboli could open his trophies. Within minutes of Trimboli's return to Washington, Stephen Denlinger of LAMA was on the phone. Trimboli had no idea that Denlinger was on the take from Wedtech, supplementing his LAMA income with monthly payments that would amount to between $175,000 and $200,000. So he was nonplussed to find Denlinger yelling at him over the phone about this "outrageous affront to the flagship of Hispanic business." Trimboli told him to talk to Mitchell if he was so upset. A few days later Trimboli got a call from Representative Addabbo, with whom he had remained on the best of terms. Ehrlich had called the Chairman, on Mario's instructions, and had told him in a panic that some congressman was out to destroy Wedtech. Trimboli explained that the company may have committed some serious infractions, including conflict of interest on the part of Mario Biaggi. Take it wherever it goes, said Addabbo.

This was not, however, what Ehrlich understood Addabbo to say. The General was not the most clear-headed of soldiers and was prone to fits of panic. After talking with Addabbo once again, he reported to Mario that the Chairman had received assurances that Wedtech was in the clear. Several days later Mario, furious, called Ehrlich to say that he had just talked to Denlinger, who said that Trimboli was bent on mayhem. Where the hell did Ehrlich get the idea that there was nothing to worry about? Apparently Ehrlich had misunderstood. That was it, as far as Mario was concerned. Ehrlich's role in the assault on the Small Business Committee came to an immediate end.

The angels and archangels were getting shot down. Denlinger tried to pressure Representative Mitchell by visiting his office with an entire delegation of Hispanic businessmen in tow, all of them supposedly up in arms about this outrageous affront. Mitchell testified that he told him to cut the crap, and added that the charges were serious ones. Quite the contrary, says Denlinger; Mitchell was "very receptive, very concerned," and said he was hoping to solve the problem without bloodshed. But Mitchell didn't call Trimboli off, and was polite but noncommittal with Garcia and Biaggi. Neglia had said that the investigation could get Wedtech bumped out of the 8(a) program, thus perhaps canceling the pontoon contract; now it looked as if the company was staring doom in the face.

At the end of September, Mario was called to a dinner at the Villa Pensa with Ehrlich and Neglia. Before the food was served, Neglia reached into his inside pocket and withdrew a letter, marked "Confidential" and dated September 25, which Neglia said that Mario could read but could not keep or even copy. Wedtech's files, after all, could no longer be considered secure. It was a letter from Parren Mitchell to Jim Sanders of the SBA, asking a dozen questions whose very premises showed a disconcertingly high degree of familiarity with Wedtech's inside game. Neglia was every bit as frightened as Moreno. Sanders had instructed him to provide Mitchell with answers within a week.

What none of the men sitting around the table and drowning their woes in strong drink understood was that the letter meant the threat had

already begun to fade. After he had sifted through the boxes and box
of documents, Trimboli had gone to Mitchell to discuss his findings in
detail. Wedtech looked to be a rich harvest of thorns and brambles, but it
wasn't quite clear who should do the gathering. Certainly a full-blown
Small Business Committee investigation would make political hay, if
that's what Mitchell was after, but Mitchell didn't want to turn his committee into a courtroom. Perhaps, like so many others, he had glimpsed
Wedtech's general ally structure, and decided the battle wasn't worth
fighting. But the allegations against Wedtech would be so far-flung—
including even the company's acquisition of an Israeli subcontractor—
that the investigation would swallow up the committee's resources.

The problem was, if not Mitchell, then who? You couldn't very well
turn the material over to the Justice Department and ask an administration that considered Parren Mitchell an implacable foe to investigate its
own poster child; not, in any case, with Ed Meese soon to become
Attorney General. Meese, after all, was one of the alleged culprits. Mitchell decided to turn the material over to SBA Administrator Jim Sanders,
who could initiate an investigation of his own. This, too, carried the risk
of a cover-up. "We felt uneasy about it," recalls Trimboli, "but I think at
that time Parren felt it was the only option left." Trimboli drew up a
letter detailing his areas of concern, gave it to Mitchell to sign, and sent it
to the SBA on September 25.

Incredibly, Neglia would succeed in sitting on the Mitchell letter for
six months before yielding up a feeble and evasive answer. But at the
time the letter was issued, the investigation looked as if it could level the
company. Wedtech had to get to Parren Mitchell, and its congressional
lineup had already advanced to the plate and struck out. But sometimes
good things come from the most unexpected places. A few days before
Mario read the fateful letter, he received a visit from Richard Strum, a
middle-aged tough guy whom Wedtech had hired the previous year to
estimate bids on military contracts, and later invited to create a network
of marketing representatives to sniff out contracts for Wedtech at military bases around the country.

Strum had heard that Wedtech was on the grill, and when he knocked
on Mario's door he had a proposal that might save the company and earn
him a large piece of change. One of Strum's marketing reps, and an old
pal, was a gentleman named Anthony Loscalzo, whose occupation, as far
as Strum could tell, consisted of buying drinks and dinners for Army
procurement officials at the Sundance Bar, just off the edge of the arsenal in Rock Island, Illinois. Loscalzo, Strum told Moreno, had once
worked with two Baltimore lawyers and prominent citizens named Clar-

ce and Michael Mitchell, and remained on intimate terms with them. The Mitchell brothers, not coincidentally, were cousins of Parren Mitchell. It occurred to Strum that for a fee large enough to accommodate himself, Loscalzo, and the Mitchells, Representative Mitchell might be persuaded to cease his huffing and puffing. Moreno was willing.

And so began yet another walk on the wild side for the respectable Wedtech Corporation, a firm that, try though it would, could never quite rid itself of its sleaziest retainers. Way out at the extremes of peril, where the company was forever daring to go, there was always a gang of desperadoes all too ready to help. Richard Strum, for example, was a man whose résumé included, prior to his stint at Wedtech, a two-year stretch in the Allenwood federal prison camp, where he had been enrolled for wire fraud. That, apparently, had not cured him of his taste for felony, since Strum conferred membership in his marketing network in exchange for kickbacks. Strum never came into big money, by Wedtech standards, but he did manage to skim a total of $150,000 out of the monthly compensation he paid to his consultants, including, he testified, Anthony Loscalzo. Strum reported to Fred, and Tony later came to wonder if Fred had skimmed off some of Strum's skim.

Strum now proceeded to recruit his own Dirty Dozen. First, he testified, he spoke to his pal Loscalzo, who suggested that Strum call the Mitchell brothers directly. The Mitchells refused to return Strum's calls, so he then tried Leonard Lockhart, Jr., a businessman who happened to have shared his cell at Allenwood. Strum had gotten Lockhart a $5000-a-month fee to serve as Wedtech's consultant in the Baltimore-Washington area, on the grounds that Lockhart was tight with local politicians. Lockhart, Strum testified, had been kind enough to kick back a portion of the fee.

The sequence of events that followed was all too predictable. Lockhart said that if there was any money in the transaction, he would be glad to offer his services. Strum went down to Baltimore on September 24, met with Lockhart, Lockhart's father, and a local state politician, and was put in touch with Michael Mitchell. For a sum of money that Strum recalls as either $25,000 or $50,000, payable as a retainer to his law firm, Mitchell said that he could do what had to be done. Strum had hit a home run. He then called Loscalzo to tell him that he had scored, and Loscalzo graciously offered him half of the one third of all referral fees that Loscalzo said he received from the Mitchells.

By now Neglia had shown Mario the letter from the Mitchell committee, and Wedtech was desperate for help. And so when Strum reported back on his field trip, John and Mario agreed to go to Baltimore immediately to meet their saviors of the moment and supply them with a wad of bills to be divvied up, kicked back, laundered, and who knows what else. A meeting was arranged in the Mitchells' law office for the evening of October 1. Mario and Michael Mitchell did most of the talking, and after the traditional pious rehearsal of Wedtech's history, Mario got right to the point. The investigation had to be stopped, and stopped now. Mitchell said that he already knew all about it, could get Wedtech a copy of the letter Neglia had been afraid to hand over, and, for $50,000, payable immediately, could deal with the situation. The part about the letter cinched it for Mario. If the Mitchells could get a copy of the letter, they must be on the inside. An agreement was drafted right then and there, describing the payment as a retainer for legal services. Everybody went home, and on the following day Tony cut a $50,000 check, and Mario Rosado, the Pentecostal minister, was dispatched to deliver it to the Mitchells.

The Mitchell brothers proceeded, as far as is known, to do nothing whatever to make good on their promise to Wedtech. There is no evidence that they ever sought to influence their cousin, much less pay him off, to stop the investigation. The Mitchells' inaction raises the intriguing question of whether the brothers had Wedtech spotted as a mark from the word go, and took the money—up front, of course—with no intention of making good on their promise. This explanation, though it has the appeal of poetic justice, seems unlikely, if only because it would be in the Mitchells' interest to keep Wedtech healthy. Possibly the brothers did speak to their cousin, and were told to back off, or were reassured that all was well. A likelier explanation is that the Mitchells learned, through their contacts in the SBA, that the agency was going to bury the investigation, and it would die without any help from them.

The Reagan SBA had become so politicized and so adversarial that Tom Trimboli considered himself fortunate when he got a phone call returned. The one person in Jim Sanders' office with whom Trimboli could deal on a nonpartisan and noncombative basis was Janine Perrignan, which was why he had posted a staff member in her office for the July 27 raid. The boxes of documents that Trimboli could not carry had been sent to Perrignan's office, and when they arrived she started to read through the material. What she saw was so troubling that she called another official. Together they found, among other things, memos documenting calls from the White House to the SBA, and notes of conversations in which Peter Neglia told his staff of discussions he had held with

White House officials. The Mitchell committee was clearly onto something; at the very least there was the appearance of a conflict of interest.

Perrignan then did the natural thing. She went to Robert Turnbull, a confidant of Sanders' within the agency, and told him what she had found. This was the same Robert Turnbull who had been Nofziger's man in the SBA, and who had kept Meese's office informed of the early negotiations over the engine contract. Perrignan told Turnbull that she was very disturbed by what she had seen, and added, "I have to send these documents to the Hill, but I've made copies of the ones that I think Jim [Sanders] ought to be made aware of." Perrignan added that she didn't think the inquiry was going to go away, and that the wisest policy might be to refer the matter to the agency's inspector general and inform Mitchell that they had done so. Turnbull simply took the material intended for Sanders and said, "We'll get back to you."

So Perrignan waited and heard nothing. Finally she received a call from Trimboli saying that the committee had decided to hand the matter over to the SBA. Trimboli said he would send her a copy of the September 25 letter, because that was the only way he could force the agency to follow up on it. The letter should have been sent to Perrignan from Sanders' office, but hadn't been. After waiting several days, Perrignan went in to Turnbull's office and said, "Have you responded to this letter?" Turnbull was livid. "How did you get this letter?" he shouted. "It was a personal letter to the administrator." Perrignan explained how she had come by the document. "Don't worry," said Turnbull, ending the conversation. "It's being taken care of. It's got nothing to do with you."

As the weeks went by and nothing was done, and Trimboli kept calling to ask when he was going to see some results, Perrignan began to suspect that the investigation was being stalled. She had gone to Sanders early on and repeated what she had told Turnbull, and pointed out that if the SBA failed to cooperate, the Congress would accuse the agency of stonewalling. Now she found Sanders inaccessible. Every time she walked down the hall toward the administrator's office, Turnbull seemed to be dogging her steps. And then the election intervened, and then there were preparations for budgetary hearings, and Sanders was busy trying to spare the SBA from the complete extinction David Stockman had recommended. Soon it was early 1985, and still there was no word on Wedtech.

By November 1984, Peter Neglia was in a perfect position to protect himself, since Sanders had made him his chief of staff, a job he rotated among his principal regional administrators. Neglia controlled practically everything and everyone Sanders saw, a role that made him even more valuable to Wedtech than he had been before. But as far as Perrignan could tell it was Turnbull, not Neglia, who was responsible for the stonewalling. It was Turnbull who ran the agency, especially now that Sanders was preoccupied by seeing to his own survival. Turnbull's political connections gave him a status unconnected with his position, and he had the agility, as Perrignan saw it, "to do things without leaving his fingerprints." Turnbull had bragged to her that it was he who had gotten Michael Cardenas, Sanders' predecessor, fired in the spring of 1982.

Turnbull was a charming man who seemed to have an in with everyone —the White House, the Congress, and with Sanders and Neglia, both of whom appeared to admire his political skills. It became clear to Perrignan that Turnbull was concerned with protecting the White House— and perhaps himself—and that he had managed to convince the ever-attendant Sanders that the investigation was a put-up job that could be safely ignored. Sometimes Perrignan even wondered whether Turnbull was subtly nudging Sanders over the cliff, for she heard him counsel the administrator to stand up to Stockman and his adversaries in the White House and to do it publicly. Perhaps he would do to Sanders what he had done to Cardenas.

A political amateur himself, Sanders was naturally inclined to take Turnbull's advice. But he had his own reasons for wanting the investigation to go away. Wedtech, more than any other firm, had made the whole 8(a) program look good. The President had personally endorsed the firm, and every quarter it had churned out was further proof of its fantastic success. Sanders had given the company his own imprimatur, not least when he approved the stock transfer plan in January 1984. He had stood up for the company before the Army and the Navy. An investigation into Wedtech could make the 8(a) program, the SBA, and Sanders himself look bad. His position was not very different from that of the Navy's Everett Pyatt. So Sanders made sure that no investigation was conducted. He refused to hand the matter on to his inspector general and, as he says himself, "I didn't tell my troops to hurry up."

Sanders had every reason to believe that the investigation was serious. He had received the July 27 letter, with its urgent and threatening tone; he had heard from Perrignan that the files contained worrisome disclosures; and he had read the September 25 letter, which included pointed questions about White House involvement, SBA favoritism, the undisclosed use of consultants, and so on. He knew at first hand of Wedtech's considerable political influence. But Sanders persisted in seeing the inquiry as a run-of-the-mill attempt by a liberal Democrat to embarrass a

Republican administration, or racial posturing by a black leader irked by the success of a Hispanic company. The letter was just a fishing expedition, a collection of leading questions that had no foundation. Sanders now says that he had no idea at the time that Trimboli had based the questions in the letter on a thorough dredging of the SBA files. Perrignan, however, had told him just that. Perhaps Sanders wasn't listening.

And so the SBA administrator simply refused to cooperate with the House committee that had jurisdiction over his agency. To the July 27 letter asking for a list of the company's consultants, he sent a response mentioning Bernard Ehrlich and Howard Squadron, but not Nofziger and Bragg. And though he formally instructed Neglia to prepare some kind of reply, Neglia must have quickly realized that the whole matter could be safely dropped. Even with Neglia by his side after November, Sanders apparently said nothing.

By March 1985, Tom Trimboli had lost patience with the SBA, and he called up to ask for a briefing on what he assumed was a current investigation. After some further delay, Bob Turnbull showed up at the Small Business Committee office. "Well," Trimboli asked, "have you folks finally finished this investigation?" "Investigation?" said Turnbull. "There isn't any investigation." Then he smiled his ingratiating smile and asked blandly, "What are you actually looking for?" Trimboli had reached the furthest edge of patience. He fixed the man with his most baleful glare and said, "The truth." Turnbull's jaw dropped open, as Trimboli recalls, "like no one had ever asked him for that before"—not an altogether implausible conjecture. After a few excuses, Turnbull promised to deliver an answer.

Turnbull returned to the SBA building at L and 14th streets, told Janine Perrignan that everything had been ironed out, and then told Neglia that the stall would have to come to an end. The SBA would have to answer the twelve terrible questions. Indeed, on March 7 came another letter from Parren Mitchell, angrily demanding some answers. And now the whole chain of events from late September was repeated. Neglia called Mario to say that the investigation the Mitchell brothers had supposedly killed was being revived. Mario, in turn, called Strum to ask what his friends in Baltimore had done for their $50,000. Strum went down to Baltimore and told Michael Mitchell what had happened. If Mitchell was chagrinned, apparently he didn't show it. Another $10,000, he said, and Wedtech could sleep soundly. Strum told Mario, and another $10,000 check was sent on its way. There is no evidence that the

Mitchells did any more to earn this check than they had done for its predecessor.

While the Mitchells were once again ripping off Wedtech, Peter Neglia was pressing ahead with the hard work of deceiving the House Small Business Committee and his own colleagues. Over the course of several days Neglia sat down with regional and district officials to provide answers to Trimboli's questions. The officials had, by and large, the same motives Sanders had to find Wedtech not guilty, and, with Neglia's gentle guidance, they managed to do just that. They found no evidence of "preferential treatment" by any SBA official, despite the speed with which the 8(a) eligibility issue was whisked through; no evidence that SBA officials had taken action at the behest of the White House, despite the White House basement meeting; no evidence of influence exerted on SBA employees by "agents who were former employees of the White House," and on and on. In fine, the company was blameless.

The inquiry that had begun with Trimboli's G-man assault had ended in farce. The SBA "investigation" had been conducted by the man who ought to have been its principal target, and had included no interviews and no attempt at all to get behind the official façade of the documents themselves. When Trimboli received the SBA's official answer, in early April, he was flabbergasted. He was also completely helpless. There could be no thought of appeal to the White House. The General Accounting Office did not then, as it does now, mount criminal investigations. The SBA had scrutinized itself and exonerated itself. Here was a scandal, of proportions no one could guess, that the world would never hear about. A more pugnacious legislator than Parren Mitchell might have called a press conference and issued denunciations, but Mitchell was content to let the matter pass. Perhaps he *had* had a chat with his cousins Michael and Clarence. According to a story Neglia told Mario, Representative Mitchell had visited Sanders to reassure him that a pro forma response would be quite satisfactory. It would "close the file" and need never see the light of day. Mitchell denies the story, and those who know him find it unlikely.

If the Mitchell brothers did nothing more than preach the virtues of Wedtech to Uncle Parren, as Tony Loscalzo called him, then they may have earned their $60,000. The same cannot be said for an additional $50,000 payment that Wedtech made during the time when the Mitchell letter was gathering dust. In late 1984 Loscalzo reported from his command post at the Sundance Bar that the Rock Island Arsenal would be setting aside a contract for a decontamination kit, known as the M13, to be used by soldiers in the event of chemical warfare. The contract, said Loscalzo, could be worth millions of dollars. Wedtech accordingly asked the SBA regional office to issue a search letter, the document by which a contractor formally gets in line for an 8(a) contract. It turned out, however, that a Cleveland firm run by a former football player, Ernie Green, had had a search letter issued a month before. And the rule in such matters, as Henry Wilfong had pointed out in the case of Univox the previous fall, is first come, first served.

Tony Loscalzo, according to Strum, was not a man to be fazed by niggling considerations of the law. It occurred to him that maybe the Mitchell brothers could work their magic in reverse. If they could make Uncle Parren stop an investigation, maybe they could make him start one. Why not, he suggested, call the Mitchell brothers and get a Small Business Committee investigation started into allegations—heretofore nonexistent—that Ernie Green was a front for white businessmen? Get him knocked out of the box, and Wedtech, second in line, eats Green's lunch. Good idea, thought Strum.

In late February, Strum flew down to Baltimore to broach the idea with Michael Mitchell. For another $50,000, said Mitchell, we can do the job. At this point the Mitchell brothers were still looking like magicians, and Wedtech had paid a lot more money for a lot less help in the past, so on February 26 Wedtech cut another check for $50,000. Once again, Loscalzo got his third and Strum his sixth. It was good business all around, save for one thing. The Mitchell brothers limited their dirty work to making two phone calls to an Ohio congressman who was an old friend, suggesting that he look into rumors that Ernie Green was a front man. Apparently their skullduggery was limited to their relationship to their client. There was no investigation, though the Army ultimately declined to award the contract at all.

TWENTY-FOUR

It's Morning in America

BY THE BEGINNING of 1985 Wedtech was one of the largest manufacturing concerns in New York City, and of course a colossus in the Bronx. The previous year, in numbers that were of course inflated by Tony's creative calculator, Wedtech had done $72 million worth of business, an increase of 166 percent over the year before. The company was expanding across the Bronx—595 Gerard Avenue, 149th Street, and 1 Loop Drive for the pontoons, 112 Bruckner Boulevard for engine manufacture, 601 Cromwell Avenue for inventory and shipping, and 350 Gerard, where work was beginning on another facility for the six-horsepower engine. The hundreds of new employees included not just welders and engineers but accountants and payroll clerks, quality-control experts, even managers. Local politicians made Wedtech a stop on their pilgrimage. Wedtech had become a powerhouse without sacrificing the air of sanctity that befits a cause.

Nobody ever forgot that the company owed its status, both as powerhouse and crusade, to the solicitude of the Reagan administration. Presient Reagan, who had seen fit to bless John Mariotta not once but twice, had been resoundingly re-elected. The President was their man, and Wedtech had given generously. The executives had, in their modest way, even become Republican fat cats. And so, when the President was to be sworn in for his second term, the Wedtech boys decided to join the giant floating Inaugural party, don their tuxedos, and strut around the nation's capital with all the pooh-bahs and the plutocrats and camp followers and cheerleaders and spin doctors and anointed scribes who swirled around the Reagan administration.

The impetus for the trip came from Wedtech's local Republican connection, Joe Neglia, father of Peter and old pal of the New York State Republican Party chairman, George Clark. The Inaugural would be a nationwide summoning of Republicans great and small, and for an old party warhorse like Neglia it would offer an opportunity to make contacts in the most salubrious, Scotch-soaked of environments. Bernie Ehrlich called Tony and said that the Neglias, father and son, and their wives wanted to attend, along with a group that kept growing and that ultimately included the Ehrlichs, Richard Biaggi and his wife, a Neglia family friend named Ronald Betso, a Bronx developer named Zack Gertler, former General James Rosenbloom, now a Wedtech consultant, other hangers-on, and the whole Wedtech gang, with wives and girlfriends.

The 1985 inaugural was designed to be what the party-giving professionals of the Reagan regime understood to be a modest affair. The 1981 inaugural had given the unfortunate, if not inaccurate, impression that the nation had been delivered to a class of plutocrats, as Ron and Nancy's society friends had descended on the nation's capital in limousines, minks, top hats, and distinctly proprietary expressions. The party had cost $16 million, and the liberals and the media had had a field day. This time the First Lady had cut down on her wardrobe for the affair—it came to only $46,000—and some of the deluxe trimmings had been eliminated from the round of parties. The 1985 inaugural cost only $12 million. Most of the money, however, came not from the taxpayer but from businessmen who, as a *Pravda* correspondent had the ill grace to point out, "expect to be given considerable compensation, for, as the saying goes, 'He who pays the piper calls the tune.'"

The Reagan people arrived once again to stake their claim to the nation's future. There were the Annenbergs and Betsy Bloomingdale and Jerome Zipkin and Oscar de la Renta and Merv Griffin and Charlton Heston and Donna Summer. Ol' Blue Eyes arrived to host the gala on Saturday night, and provided the only truly memorable event of the weekend when a reporter asked whether the other members of the Rat

Pack would be making the scene. Sinatra fixed her with a look of pure hatred. "You're all dead!" he shouted to the stunned crowd of reporters, "every one of you. You're all dead." On Sunday the President himself, a former sportscaster, conducted the coin flip, via television, at the outset of the Super Bowl between the San Francisco Forty-niners and the Miami Dolphins.

The twenty or so Wedtech people missed out on Frank, though they all had tickets for the Kennedy Center gala. Their dinner ran late, and the limo traffic was insane, and they wound up sitting around while the Palm Springs crowd settled in for a night of old-fashioned style. Actually, the whole thing was something of a bust, since the inaugural on Monday was canceled owing to extreme cold, and of course everyone had tickets for that, too. Nothing much happened, except that they all sat in their hotel suites and talked about what a great time they were having. John grumbled a bit, it's true, because somehow he had never gotten a limo assigned to him, as the other Wedtech wheels had. John took this, correctly, as a sign of his declining status within the company, despite his being the President's soul mate.

Of course the company paid for the whole bacchanal. Tickets for the Kennedy Center came to $4800. Wedtech gave a Super Bowl bash in a suite at the Sheraton and had a $2000 dinner on the night of the inauguration. They tooled around in their limos—total cost, $5855—and ran up big hotel tabs—$1000 a couple, more or less. Tony and Larry Shorten put everything on their American Express cards, which they half expected to melt at any moment. Paying for Peter Neglia's hotel room was obviously a dicey matter, so Tony had his secretary call up and reserve Neglia's room in her own name and her husband's. Maybe Neglia felt that he was treading on thin ice; he racked up a grand total of $11.41 in charges above the cost of his room at the Sheraton.

Neglia, or perhaps his father, picked this richly symbolic time and place to ask for the gift he felt he deserved. Of all Wedtech's moles—in the Army, the Navy, the SBA, and the DCAA—it was Peter Neglia who had accomplished the most for the company, though for all his efforts he had received nothing but several thousand dollars worth of food, drink, and hotel suites.

The solicitation was standard Wedtech material, except that Neglia had an agent. Over noontime cocktails after a reception given by Senator D'Amato, Bernie Ehrlich, sitting with Neglia, said to Mario, "As you know, Peter has done a lot for the company up to now and I have told him that you people are going to be helping him after he leaves the Small Business Administration." Of course they would; that's how business was transacted in the real world. The big defense contractors hired whole wings of the Pentagon, and scarcely waited to do so until the resignation letters were stamped. Months before, Ehrlich had spoken of plans to hire Neglia at Biaggi & Ehrlich, and now he suggested that Wedtech pay half of his projected $100,000 salary. "No problem," said Mario.

What was more problematic was that Neglia also wanted some stock, or so Ehrlich said. Neglia remained silent, as if the discussion were no affair of his. Mario explained that public companies cannot simply issue stock to individuals—which neither Ehrlich nor Neglia, lawyers both, apparently realized—but that Wedtech would be happy to offer stock options instead. Given the brilliant future envisioned for Wedtech, the 20,000 options Mario was ready to offer seemed a ticket to El Dorado. Neglia was a believer; everyone was a believer. Within the company, options were considered a sweet reward for good behavior, and management distributed them generously—though the downward trend of the stock price prevented any of the options from ever being exercised.

The only problem was that Neglia couldn't very well have options voted in his name, not while he still worked for the SBA. That would constitute a patent crime, unlike the slightly less blatant crime of agreeing, while still a government servant, to accept money after he retired from a company he had prodigiously assisted. That crime was essentially the opposite of the one for which Wallach was convicted. Neglia said that he would think of a nominee to hold his stock.

The following day, after the canceled inauguration, Joe Neglia, according to Mario, joined the little cabal in the Sheraton lobby and said that Ron Betso had agreed to serve as nominee. Betso had attached himself to Joe Neglia and to George Clark in the hope of making something of himself in the New York Republican Party, scarcely a grand ambition. He was a stand-up guy, and he could be counted on. Then the entire group went off to a $2000 dinner at an Italian restaurant. It had been a wonderful inaugural.

It was morning in America, as the President had said. Certainly it was morning at Wedtech, where the new year held the promise of all the humble pleasures the owners of a minority enterprise could expect—wall-to-wall carpeting, ski chalets, jewelry, English suits, champagne on the Concorde. The boys from Wedtech had availed themselves, one might say abandoned themselves, to that freedom which the President, and the Annenbergs and the Bloomingdales, had pledged themselves to protect—the freedom to make immense quantities of money and live more or less like the people in *Dynasty*. John and Fred and Mario and Tony took their cues from the culture. Never having had any money before, they patterned their millionaire lives on what they saw all around them. They couldn't have picked a better moment to become rich.

Fred and John had become instant millionaires back in September 1983. By early 1985, however, everybody was rich. Much of the wealth was legitimately obtained. They were now officers of a $70 million company, and they paid themselves accordingly, or perhaps a little bit better than accordingly. In 1984 John and Fred had each received $360,000 in salary and bonuses; Mario had received $262,000; Tony and Larry Shorten, $156,000 each. John had sold another $780,000 worth of stock, with an equal amount to come in June; Fred, another $1.2 million, with a million more to come in August, and Mario, half a million, with $400,000 more due in May.

Much of that wealth was not legitimately obtained. In 1984, $1,179,690.80 had been deposited in the FHJ account, either by suppliers like Zeisel or by Pat Simone. In the coming year the figure would reach $2,659,032.95. Some of that money went to payoffs, but most of it was available for the discretionary use of the principals. And most of them had side deals, which they neglected to mention to their colleagues.

Tony kicked off the new year by establishing a company with the characteristically macho name of Ramrod Associates. The company was funded with a loan of $1,359,000 Tony had received from Pat Simone; the funds would be doled out over the years for the construction of a palace in the exclusive WASP neighborhood of Matinicock Point, on Long Island's northern shore. Tony was a man who loved real estate, and he had watched enviously as John and Fred and Mario had built pleasure palaces of their own. Only the year before, he had sold his old condo in Jericho for $250,000 and bought a new one for $360,000. But the Matinicock house was going to have everything: bowling alley, billiard room, exercise room, pool, cabana, the works. It was the kind of palace they feature on *Lifestyles of the Rich and Famous,* and it was the joy of Tony's life.

All of the Wedtech boys had sunk their money into real estate: it was showy, it was solid, and it was a good investment. And when you're taking in a lot of illegal cash, real estate is a great way of hiding it fast. Mario, for example, owned a total of seven condos in the Ritz Tower at Atlantic City, valued at a bit over $1 million, though he owned several with John and Tony. He bought a condo in Puerto Rico, which he turned over to his son, and a country home in upstate New York, which he never visited. He, Tony, and Fred also had condos next door to one another near Tampa.

John already had his big, stuffy ranch house in Scarsdale and his condo in Condado, and Fred had a brownstone on Sutton Place, so the tide of cash washing up on their shores could be devoted to private pleasures. Fred spent a good deal of it on girls, but he was also an inveterate investor, and he sank much of his winnings into still more real estate, as well as into a yacht-building firm in England and some little companies in Israel, including one that manufactured safes.

Fred also built himself, at company expense, a magnificent office in the vast, clanking warehouse at 149th Street. Designed by Fred's interior-decorator girlfriend, the office featured an all-marble bathroom, modern furniture, and a separate conference room with a splendid table and leather chairs. It was, in short, "gawgeous." Fred loved this upholstered sanctum so much that he uprooted himself from the craziness at 595 Gerard and lolled in his peaceable kingdom, planning his vacations, for the remainder of Wedtech's history.

By 1985 the thievery had become so common, so casual, that whatever fear and trembling may have once attached to it was long banished. As the flood of cash from 149th Street began to dry up, a new source took its place. The big construction project for 1985 was the renovation of a plant at 350 Gerard Avenue for inventory and shipping of the M-113 parts. The general contractor at 350 Gerard, Mohammed Yaghoubi, agreed to kick back funds in the same manner as Berney, though without the skim taken by Simone. Moreover, Berney and others had also begun building half a dozen launching bays, each covered by a big inflatable dome, on the waterside facility at Loop Drive. The cash came pouring in in unprecedented amounts.

Having jointly stolen from the shareholders for so long, the insiders no longer scrupled about stealing from one another. The others thought that Yaghoubi was a friend of Berney's; in fact, he was another of Mario's brothers-in-law, and he had reached the same kickback-within-a-kickback arrangement with Mario that Berney had. Tony had a deal that Pat Simone had rigged for him. Along with a pal of Simone's known as Sonny, said to be "connected," Tony established a phony firm called Consultants Supreme, which billed Wedtech $150,000 for nonexistent work on the Michigan shipyard. Tony and Sonny divided the take evenly.

John may have had his own thing, too. John was extremely protective of the purchasing department, and above all of the head of purchasing, Mario Gonzalez. The insiders came to suspect that John, who always seemed to have immense quantities of cash, was raking off a portion of the millions of dollars the company spent on supplies. Their suspicions were fueled when John proposed to spend $1.1 million to buy four robotic welding systems that cost only $900,000. It was not, however, the sort of issue that could be raised with the increasingly unstable chairman.

One morning in early January an excited employee came into Fred's office and said that a foreman over at 1049 Washington Avenue, the old headquarters, had gotten into a fight with a worker. Apparently the worker had complained, first to the plant manager at 595 Gerard, Vijay Nair, and then to his shop steward. Nair had refused to discipline the foreman, and now all the workers at 595 were up in arms. It was the kind of ugly situation that required a good deal of delicacy to defuse. Unfortunately, the only person around was Fred. Tony was down at Squadron Ellenoff; Mario was in Davisville, negotiating the pontoon options; and John, the only man the Hispanic shop floor workers would listen to, was at the dentist.

Fred was a man whose idea of employee relations was to bribe union officials to keep the workers in line. His first move was to call Frank Casalino, one of the union officials from whom he had been buying labor peace for years. Casalino had no problem with Fred's suggestion that both parties to the fight be suspended, pending an inquiry. The workers felt otherwise. When Fred went downstairs to the shop floor to explain his decision, the workers started shouting at him in Spanish. If the foreman wasn't sacked, they yelled, they'd walk off the job. Casalino's opinion meant nothing to them, since he had never showed the remotest interest in their welfare.

Their distrust was fully merited. When Fred went back to his office to tell Casalino what his members wanted to do, the union official told Fred to let them go ahead; that way, management would have a pretext to fire all the malcontents. This idea had a good deal of appeal to Fred; he went back downstairs and said that anyone who didn't come back after lunch could consider himself fired. Now the workers were threatening to riot, and Fred called Biaggi & Ehrlich, where he spoke to an associate and instructed him to call Stanley Simon's office and have him call out the riot squad. Within a few hours a squadron of cops, including the borough commander, had marshaled at 595 Gerard.

John arrived from the dentist in time to see squad cars surrounding the front entrance of the plant. He found the loyal Ceil Lewis in her office with her sidekick, Rabbi Greenberg, and they sketched in the picture for him. John then charged down the hall to Fred's office, where he found Fred in a lather, surrounded by police officers. John said that he was rehiring everyone, and Fred told him that he was a moron. The two men screamed at each other; then John raced downstairs and announced to the throng of workers that he was firing the foreman and reinstating the rest of them, and blamed the whole problem on the union. The employees, who had had the union imposed on them, shouted their approval and agreed to leave peaceably. Fred threatened to take John apart limb from limb, and Frank Casalino, who had lost a perfect opportunity to rid himself of bad apples, concluded that the man was a dangerous lunatic.

In the aftermath of the wildcat strike, John made Tony Guariglia the new head of labor relations. It was obvious to Tony that the union had to demonstrate its bona fides to the rank and file. In a meeting with Casalino, Richard Stolfi, and the union's counsel, Tony agreed that the union would start filing grievances, and management would let them win a few. An arbitrator was hired, grievances were filed, management put up feeble opposition, and Casalino and Stolfi succeeded in staving off further challenges to their authority.

In talking to employees, Tony also learned the full extent of Mario Rosado's extortion activities. Rosado, the preacher who had started with the firm in the early days, had been continuing to collect from everyone on the shop floor the compulsory tithe for his supposed good works. John permitted Rosado to lord it over the workers, though whether out of misplaced faith or complicity was never clear. With John's backing, Rosado made good his threat to fire workers who refused to pay up, and to hire and help those who did.

On a Friday, after the paychecks had been handed out, Tony ventured down to the shop floor to watch the preacher in action. He saw Rosado, accompanied by an enforcer, go from one machine operator to another, pocketing cash. When he had seen enough, Tony told the foreman to shut down the machines. He walked up to Rosado and told him in full view of the now silent crowd of machinists that he was fired as of that moment. "If you don't leave right now," Tony added, "I'm calling the cops." The workers, to Tony's amazement, began to applaud.

Tony walked back upstairs and told John what he had done. John went crazy, which only reinforced Tony's belief that John was himself on the take. John demanded that Rosado be rehired; Tony refused, and the others stood behind him. John's vindictiveness now rose to the surface with frightening effect. If my man Rosado is going to be fired, John insisted, then so will one of yours and one of yours. And John literally walked through 595 Gerard firing long-time employees whom he associated with Mario or Fred. He was uncontrollable.

Even after Rosado was fired, he and his enforcer would stand by the window of the check-cashing service used by many of the Wedtech employees, repeating their threats. John's loyalty took the form of a spasm of generosity. He sent a $45,000 check to Rosado's network of charities in Puerto Rico, Fe Acción in Marcha Christos; then he sent two more checks for $10,000 and another for $6000, and a check made out to Rosado personally for $5000.

By the middle of February John had made Ceil Lewis head of labor relations in place of Tony. Over the years Ceil had seen first one of her responsibilities and then another stripped away, but she had never wavered in her loyalty to John. Now she had a job that made her feel important again, listening to the workers' problems and even negotiating contracts with the union. Still, Ceil had no problem with the traditional attitude toward labor at Wedtech. She worked out a system with the union officials whereby workers considered troublesome were promoted to clerical jobs. As management, they no longer enjoyed protection against dismissal without cause, and after a few months had passed they would be fired.

Wedtech, however, was not over its union problems. One of the scams at 350 Gerard was that Mo Yaghoubi would hire nonunion labor but bill for unionized labor. Hiring nonunion labor at a construction site in New York City, however, is an invitation to disaster. The construction trade unions in New York are heavily influenced, and in some cases directly controlled, by the Mafia. Over the years, by force of intimidation, they have gained a hammerlock over local construction jobs, and builders who try to work without them usually receive thinly veiled threats of violence or sabotage. Such was Wedtech's lot.

One day in late March or early April, when 350 Gerard had been under construction for six months or so, two officials of the carpenters' union showed up at 595 Gerard and demanded to speak with Mario Moreno. Mario called Tony into the office, and the two of them listened as a union official named Frank Calciano stormed that he would shut down 350 Gerard, and 595 too, if the work wasn't turned over to his members. Mario offered to hire a few carpenters, but Calciano said that halfway measures wouldn't do. Everyone got a little hot under the collar, Calciano issued several more threats along the people-can-get-hurt line, and the meeting dissolved.

It was clearly time to summon the Italian branch of the company's general ally structure. It turned out, however, that no one wanted to call the carpenters and tell them to knock it off. Mario asked Bernie Ehrlich to talk to Biaggi, and a few days later Ehrlich reported that Biaggi had suggested that they knuckle under. Tony spoke to Pat Simone, who had once had a similar problem until the unions discovered who it was they were threatening. "You're on your own," said the omnipotent Simone.

Fred called Richard Stolfi, who explained that these were not the kind of people to screw around with.

A few days later Stolfi summoned Fred to his office on Queens Boulevard, and then suggested they take a nice little drive, along with Frank Casalino, out of harm's way. They parked on a secluded street, and Stolfi turned to Fred and said that, as a special favor, he would use his influence to get the carpenters off Wedtech's back. However, it would take $150,000 worth of persuasion. When Fred came back and told the others, they howled, and insisted he bring Stolfi down. Stolfi agreed to accept $100,000. It was a lot of money, but 350 Gerard was a gold mine worth a great deal more than $100,000. On a Saturday morning in mid-April Tony met Casalino at a diner in Glen Cove, Long Island, and in the course of breakfast passed him, under the table, a brown paper bag containing $25,000 in hundred-dollar bills.

That was Tony's own money. In order to pay the remainder of the bribe and reimburse Tony, Yaghoubi was instructed to bill an extra $100,000 and then kick the receipts back into FHJ through one of his shell companies, Demo Construction. That money, in turn, was cashed through a series of FHJ checks. Fred then delivered a $50,000 bundle to Stolfi's office, and Tony, who was too busy to be inconvenienced by such trifles, had Casalino drive to his home in Jericho, where he handed him the final $25,000 installment.

Even that wasn't quite the end. Apparently the leaders of corrupt union locals do not sit in council, because soon after the final payment, Tony got a call, this time from Larry Shorten, saying that officials of two more unions, the lathers and the steamfitters, had showed up in his office demanding jobs at 350 Gerard. Tony, peeved by this lack of coordination, told the two gentlemen that Wedtech had already given at the office, and suggested they contact the carpenters for further guidance. That was the last Wedtech heard from rival unions.

TWENTY-FIVE

Near-Death Experience: V

NINETEEN EIGHTY-FIVE was uniquely free of near-death experiences for Wedtech, but there was a very rocky period, around the ides of March, when a number of ominous events converged. It was at this time that the SBA investigation, which everyone thought had been beaten lifeless, reared its terrifying head one last time before subsiding altogether. This was also the moment when corrupt construction union officials kept appearing unannounced in the lobby of 595 Gerard. Moreover, Captain de Vicq, who had seemed to be checkmated, finally managed to get operations at 149th Street temporarily shut down.

De Vicq and his ally from DCAS, Don Hein, had been right all the time; Captain Charles Pearsall, who had minimized their concerns, and Wayne Arny, who had accepted Pearsall's view and awarded Wedtech the options, had been wrong. Wedtech was simply unable to produce an acceptable pontoon. The individual containers, or cans, of the causeway had to be square to within a sixteenth of an inch so that if one was damaged, another could be snapped into place; in effect, they had to be identical.

Wedtech kept turning out cans that didn't meet the specs. Don Hein remembers seeing six hundred defective cans stacked up and rusting behind the 149th Street facility. Not until early 1985 did the company finally present the Navy with a finished pontoon, and when the NAVFAC people examined this first article, they found eighty-eight defects. Some of the cans had even been banged into place with a sledgehammer.

As long as the pontoon facility was closed, Wedtech's expenses remained almost the same, but it produced no revenue. It was a ruinous situation, and Mario and General Ehrlich flew down to Washington to rouse the congressional claque. First, as always, they went to see Biaggi. Mario explained that de Vicq was hell-bent on destroying the company, that he had to be eliminated. Biaggi then called up Senator D'Amato's office to say that he was sending over Mario and Ehrlich.

D'Amato listened to their plaint and then referred them to an aide, Michael Kinsella, who drew up a letter for the senator to send to Navy Secretary John Lehman. The letter singled out Captain de Vicq, who "has unfairly criticized Wedtech for delivery delays," and said that it would be "devastating" for the company to lose the 1985 options, which were still being negotiated. From Senator D'Amato's office Mario and Ehrlich continued their crusade by walking over to Joseph Addabbo's office, where they met with Addabbo's chief aide, Richard Seelmayer, and Ehrlich's National Guard boss, Vito Castellano. Addabbo later called Lehman, or so Ehrlich told Mario.

Whatever the reason, something happened. In March the Navy and Wedtech reached agreement on the $51.5 million figure for the 1985 options, and soon afterward the Navy permitted the company to resume production. The Navy had already sunk a lot of faith, and a lot of time and money, into Wedtech; it was not, apparently, prepared to withdraw.

It was now evident to Tony that the pontoons were bankrupting the company. The losses were growing far too large to disguise; if Main Hurdman's 1984 audit disclosed the magnitude of Wedtech's reverses, after years of supposedly nonstop profitability, stockholders would start leaping over the gunwales before the water washed in. In March, Tony set about saving the company with a form of deceit that no one save a true accounting genius could have devised. It would not have worked, however, without the complicity of outsiders.

A year earlier Tony had tentatively embarked on an accounting process known as pooling. He had added into Wedtech's revenues from its M-113 cooling and suspension kits the additional income from an options contract that the company felt confident of receiving, though it had yet to be awarded. The additional sum was small, and the auditors had not objected. Like a great many techniques in accounting, pooling depends largely on interpretation.

The purpose of pooling is to allow a company to realize revenue on its books before the income is actually received. A firm that makes an enormous up-front investment based on the expectation of future orders, for example an aircraft manufacturer, can add into its pool of contracts some that have not yet been signed. Without the pool it would suffer huge losses, and then, once the new orders kicked in and the initial costs had been amortized, equally large gains. Pooling smoothes out income.

The problem with pooling is that it compels the outside auditor to accept the company's business judgment about unsigned contracts. For this reason pooling is not used by companies in an uncertain market, like those which depend on government contracting. Nevertheless, the auditors had not murmured when Tony had pooled the M-113 options. And so, in March of 1985, Tony took pooling to its logical conclusion, and then a good deal farther. First he added into the books, as of year-end 1984, over $60 million worth of cooling and suspension kits and also external fuel tanks, which the Army supposedly was going to order from Wedtech for delivery to the West German government. In fact, the Army never did any such thing, but Wedtech secured a letter from an official at TACOM, the procurement office where Gordon Osgood had once worked his magic to land Wedtech the original M-113 contracts, stating the Army's intent to make the award.

Thus emboldened, Tony moved on to the question of the pontoon contracts. He did not, as he felt he might have done, pool the entire $300 million or more expected over the life of the contract. Instead, he added into 1984 revenue both the 1985 options that Wedtech had won only a few weeks earlier and the 1986 options. The question was: How much? Tony decided to claim that Wedtech would receive in 1986 the $68 million it had hoped to get for 1985. This was a risky proposition, and it illustrated the extent to which Tony's bookkeeping began to drive the company.

The 1985 options had been so hard-won that it would have been fatally foolish of Wedtech to take the 1986 options for granted. Mario and John decided that it was time to light a fire under the company's nonchalant Washington lobbyists. Wedtech had been paying Nofziger & Bragg $10,000 a month, which was about half what the firm charged most of its clients, though few of them had remained with the lobbyists since opening day. Wedtech had chipped in, of course, by giving the two men over

$600,000 worth of stock. But the monthly payments were often late, and Bragg, who did all the dirty work, often snapped his teeth. He was, recalls Tony, "an absolute piranha. When he smelled the money he went for the veins, and he didn't hide it."

Owing, perhaps, to the paltriness of the retainer, Bragg also took the view that he should not bestir himself on Wedtech's behalf without a good deal of prompting. In recent months Nofziger & Bragg had simply been pocketing its monthly check. After receiving a lengthy memo from Wallach in November, Bragg had written back, "Many thanks for sending us a copy of your novela [sic] on the trials of Wedtech. It moved me to pick up the phone and call the boys to inquire as to what help they needed at this point. As usual, they told me everything is fine. So I am content to wait for the next crisis."

Now there was a crisis, or at least a need, and John and Mario, along with Wallach, flew down to Washington to talk to their idle retainers. Bragg knew what he wanted out of the meeting and had had the foresight to ask Wallach, whom he saw as a competitor, to remain in the sitting room while the others came in to talk. After some preliminary carping about de Vicq, Mario, who always seemed to know the steps when it came to money, told Bragg, "We want you to get more involved." "What are you willing to do?" asked Bragg. Mario and John then went into one of their patented huddles in the corner of Bragg's office, whispered back and forth, and finally emerged to say that Bragg could expect $400,000 if Wedtech got the options at the hoped-for $68 million—as Tony had promised Main Hurdman it would—and $200,000 otherwise. That, said Bragg, was fine.

This caused still more problems, since Wallach was furious when John and Mario told him about what had taken place on the other side of the door. Wallach *was* a competitor. He felt that Nofziger & Bragg was forever taking credit for triumphs he had orchestrated, and ripping off Wedtech by taking money for nothing more than a few phone calls. Wallach testified that he rebuked John and Mario for throwing away more money. But Mario testified, with corroboration from Tony, that Wallach had demanded something for himself, and that Wedtech had agreed to pay him $150,000 if the company received the options.

When the auditors from Main Hurdman came, belatedly, to conduct their review of Wedtech's 1984 books, they found that Tony had pooled in over $150 million worth of unsigned contracts, wildly overstating the company's profits. A year earlier, however, they had accepted the principle of pooling. And Tony had an explanation for each specific instance. There was the letter from the Army, the commitment from the Navy for

1985, and so on. And yet, taken together, Tony's accounting practices created a gaping discrepancy between the inner world of the books and the real world of Wedtech's profits.

Now, at this late date, the auditors said they wouldn't play along anymore. But they couldn't object to the pooling, not without drawing attention to their earlier acquiescence. Instead, they said, Wedtech's bookkeepers had seriously underestimated projected costs on the pontoon contract, thereby inflating current profits. The company, they said, would have to compensate by placing as much as $14 million in a reserve fund. The reserve would be charged against fourth-quarter earnings, creating a sizable quarterly loss for the first time in Wedtech's history.

Tony fumed and raged and told everyone that the accountants were totally out of line, but he knew very well that they were right. His bookkeeping had been a masterpiece of legerdemain. Every quarter he would come to John and explain how he had doctored the books to turn a loss into a profit. John was bewildered but deeply impressed by Tony's wizardry, and once, taking a rubber band in his fingers and stretching it, had said that it was amazing how he could keep stretching the rubber band until it was about to snap, and then a bank loan or a public offering would come along to save the company. In effect, Tony had created a completely fictitious financial profile of the company, and sold it to Wall Street until the very end.

The unrealistic cost estimates were the other end of an equation. Wedtech, like a great many defense contractors, used a bookkeeping format called cost-of-completion accounting, a method that allows firms to calculate income based on the portion of the overall estimated cost that has been incurred. After spending $50 million of an estimated $200 million over the life of a contract, say, a firm will book one quarter of the overall revenues, even if it hasn't received a nickel in progress payments from the government. As with pooling, cost-of-completion accounting permits a firm to show a profit long before its current balance is actually positive.

Tony was playing conjuring tricks with two elements of the equation: the overall expected revenues, which he inflated by means of pooling, and the overall expected cost, which he diminished by a set of questionable or deceptive assumptions. The receipt of the options, he claimed, would allow Wedtech to renegotiate all of its deals with suppliers, because it would now be purchasing in greater bulk; farm out expensive operations and perform the cheaper ones in house; reduce overhead, and scoot down the so-called learning curve. At times he simply lied about expected costs. At the suggestion of John, he persuaded Wedtech's old friend Henry Zeisel, who had first gotten the FHJ pipeline flowing, to state in writing that the pumps he was supplying for the pontoons cost $75,000, when in fact they cost about $125,000. Since each pontoon had two pumps, that was $100,000 per article spuriously forgone.

Not until May 24 would Wedtech deliver to the Navy its first acceptable pontoon. And yet underlying Tony's accounting was the assumption that the company had mastered the production process. The big costs were already in the past. And since the company had completed most of its outlays, it could realize most of its revenue. And Tony had swollen the revenue through pooling.

It was a form of deceit that devastated the company even while saving it. Wedtech kept using up its profits at the very outset of contracts. It beggared the future to sustain the present. When the company actually received a contract that Tony had already pooled, it would scarcely produce any income, since Tony had already recognized most of the profit. He had to pool more and more contracts, steal more and more from the future, in order to provide a supply of income. This was an imperative that everyone called "feeding the beast."

The company's books became unappeasable, and the financial cover-up dominated Wedtech's strategy. This seems to be almost a structural rule in such events: the cover-up becomes the conspiracy. The whole thing had to end in disaster, since sooner or later Tony would have fed into the books every item of revenue even theoretically possible. But, like the others, Tony hoped that some *deus ex machina* would come along to save them just before catastrophe bore down. The rubber band wouldn't snap. What else could you think?

The auditors from Main Hurdman may have faced a dilemma of their own. As in the spring of 1983, nobody had wanted to blow the whistle; better to slide by quietly and hope it all goes away. Now, in fact, Wedtech was a large and swiftly growing client. The company had paid $1 million for the exhaustive audit of 1982–1983. And Tony had been careful to sweeten the pot with several consulting projects, including one to study the company's computer system and another to study the purchasing department, each worth about $100,000. On the other hand, the problem wouldn't disappear. The auditors insisted on a sizable fourth-quarter reserve; Tony refused, unwilling to unnerve investors. Nobody wanted a confrontation, but someone would have to relent. Tony prepared the party line: these people are coming in at the eleventh hour; it's nothing they haven't approved of before; auditors always take the most conservative solution.

Tony's credibility on financial matters was absolute. Moreover, there was a powerful motivation to believe him. The reserve Main Hurdman was requesting, which would be debited against fourth-quarter 1984 income, could not only kill investor confidence, but would violate a covenant of the company's $35 million credit agreement, which allowed the banks to call in the loan if 1984 net income fell below $5 million. It was one of those situations where reasonable men would have to find reasonable solutions. It was one of those situations where everyone wanted the same thing.

At an April 1 board meeting, according to Tony, Joe Takacs, head of the Main Hurdman audit team, presented the case for the sizable fourth-quarter reserve against earnings, emphasizing the firm's, and the auditor's, obligation to the lending banks. It was Howard Squadron who played the role of Solomon, as he had with the EDA subordination issue back in 1983. "This reserve that you're talking about," said Squadron, according to an account by Tony that Squadron, for once, agrees with, "is very subjective." The auditors, said Squadron, were concerned about the $5 million covenant; Tony was concerned about reported earnings. Couldn't a number be found that would satisfy both? Tony says that Squadron picked a number, which he recalls as $4.7 million; Squadron doesn't think that he did mention a specific figure. The logjam, in any case, was broken.

Takacs said that he and a Main Hurdman senior partner who was also present, Roger Cason, would have to call their national office. Forty-five minutes later they returned to say, according to Tony, that $4.7 million was fine, "but let's make it $4.7—something," a something that wouldn't round up to $4.8 million. Squadron suggested $4.728 million. Takacs agreed, and the board formally approved. Frederick Moss of Moseley Hallgarten turned to Tony and whispered, "Is that generally accepted accounting principles?" "No, Fred," said Tony. "It's not."

Almost as soon as the board meeting was over it was agreed that Main Hurdman would be fired. Tony understood that the auditors knew too much, though other board members simply agreed that Main Hurdman had shown poor judgment. At a special meeting of the board on April 12 the decision was ratified, though "the Board noted that this decision was not the result of a disagreement on accounting policy." That same day Main Hurdman did its part by formally approving Wedtech's 1984 consolidated balance sheet. Shareholders were never informed that Main Hurdman had been fired over the dispute. And technically, of course, it hadn't been, since the disagreement had been settled. Wedtech had dodged another bullet.

TWENTY-SIX

TWENTY-SIX

Chinn Music

WEDTECH was now living more and more for Wall Street. For all intents and purposes the company still lived in Minority Land, but it wanted to be judged by the standards applied to grown-up companies. The problem was, the Wedtech boys weren't even sure how grown-up companies behaved. They were like Big Ten freshmen at the dean's high tea. At one point Fred Neuberger had even invited a group of financial analysts up to 595 Gerard for what they thought would be a discussion of the company's plans. After serving cocktails, Fred had called for order and announced that he wanted to see some really generous contributions to this year's United Jewish Appeal drive.

The company had taken its first steps in the right direction in the fall of 1984, when it had hired a financial public relations firm, Kehoe, Savage & White. Fortunately for Wedtech, Jack Kehoe, like Dicky Dyer and Bob Wallach and Jim Sanders and Wayne Arny, had visited the plant and fallen under its enchantment. Kehoe, snub-nosed, silver-haired, and crinkly-eyed, had been born and raised around the corner, an Irish

Catholic working-class kid in a Bronx that was fast disappearing. He had sold hot dogs at Yankee Stadium even after he was married and working at a low-level job on Wall Street. After graduating from Columbia Business School, he had moved up through the brokerage world and started his own firm.

Kehoe knew that the Bronx had gone to hell since he was young, but when he drove out to the old neighborhood to see the Wedtech plant, he was stunned. It was, he thought, like a phoenix rising from the ashes, a grimy phoenix, perhaps, but beautiful in its ugliness. It was an unpretentious place dedicated to hard work, the walls painted a sickly green halfway up, then white; the grungy old doors, the simple offices. Downstairs, those gleaming, computer-controlled machines were working their magic.

Kehoe liked the boys, liked the way they shared responsibility. John rambled incoherently, but the workers loved him, and in any case it was clear that he was chairman in name only. He was "the cultural fabric" of the place. Fred was the engineering genius, the guy who made everything work behind the scenes. Mario seemed to move in a different sphere, and Kehoe barely got to know him at all. On one of his first visits to 595 Gerard, Kehoe had met Mario in the parking lot, and as they walked in together Mario stopped to tell the receptionist that he had just been held up at gunpoint after parking his car. Well, that was Wedtech.

And finally, there was Tony Guariglia, the young man Kehoe would be working with almost exclusively. Kehoe took to him immediately. He was Tony Tough-Guy, brash and swaggering, a know-it-all, but brilliant in his grasp of financial matters. He was almost crudely ambitious, but the lawyers and the bankers and the accountants supported Tony's ambition. It was reassuring to talk to him. Fred and John might be a little crazy, and Mario a little mysterious, but Tony was a disciplined manager, a technocrat who harped on the need to raise the company's professionalism. Tony not only knew how a grown-up company behaved, he could stand up in front of a group of securities analysts and have them eating out of his hand. To a growing body of people, Tony Guariglia *was* Wedtech.

According to the figures it was disseminating to the public, Wedtech was a stupendous success, the Apple Computer of defense contracting. Wall Street, however, had remained oddly demure. In early 1984 the double steal of the pontoon contract and continued 8(a) membership had muscled Wedtech's stock as high as 24 1/4; but in the course of the year, as the initial outlays on the pontoons had depressed the company's earnings per share, the stock had sunk to around 13. Wall Street wanted to see profits, not volume, not even praise from the President. Moreover,

Wedtech had positioned itself as a high-tech firm, since high tech was the hot thing to be, but the coating technology kept receding into the distance. Kehoe felt that the company had to be sold as a low-tech manufacturer, turning out simple, good-quality defense products at the lowest possible cost. He wanted more substance and less sex appeal.

Kehoe believed that Wedtech would be a highly successful company if only it could bring its image in line with reality. Nothing, of course, could have run more counter to the company's entire history, for the company had thrived on manufactured imagery. Bob Wallach, for example, had a characteristic solution to the image problem. Wedtech, he felt, needed to learn to fit in, to communicate with the mighty in their own language. Desperate for approbation, Wallach yearned to have his friends join him in the eminence he had achieved. He was forever sending the boys newspaper clippings about pillars of the military-industrial complex who had just retired, and who might be prevailed on to work with the company.

In April, just after the Main Hurdman problem was solved, Wallach began telling Tony about two very big investment figures he had come to know, men with the contacts and, above all, the credibility to deal with Wall Street and get the stock price up where it belonged. Tony said that he and the others had had it up to their necks with expensive consultants who presumed to tell them what to do. Wallach reassured him that these men were the real article, and that they were very keen to get to know Wedtech. They would be flying in from San Francisco at the end of the month. Their names were Frank Chinn and Rusty Kent London.

"Frankie Chinn?" said Jack Kehoe incredulously when he heard about Wedtech's latest find. It couldn't be the same tiny, frenetic, shifty character he had known in the mid-1960s when they had both worked at the brokerage house of McDonnell and Company, Kehoe as a partner in New York, Chinn as a salesman in San Francisco. Frankie Chinn a dreadnought of finance? Perhaps Chinn had undergone a dramatic transformation since last they had met. Kehoe decided to call a few old San Francisco friends for an update. "Frank's a lot of fun," they said, "great guy to go to a party with, but he moves in a very fast crowd. Drives a Rolls-Royce, no one knows where his money comes from, numbered-account type of guy. If anything goes wrong, don't look for him."

It was the same Frank Chinn. He was a very curious character, Mr. Chinn, an immigrant plugger with an elaborate air of mystery that left much unsaid—how much was anybody's guess. Traders are normally supreme extroverts, so it was strange that few people knew much about Frank Chinn's life. Those few to whom he had spoken about his past

knew that Chinn was born in Shanghai in the 1940s—in 1943, to be exact
—that his family had moved to San Francisco when he was a child, that he
had grown up in a tiny apartment in Chinatown, worked as a shoeshine
boy in a park and a bellhop in the Sheraton. Without graduating from
high school, he had signed on with a work crew and dug ditches in the
Marshall Islands and then sold encyclopedias in Africa and elsewhere in
the Third World. After returning to San Francisco, he had married and
begun working his way up the investment world to his current position of
mysterious eminence. Successful traders often have the working-class
drive to succeed at all costs, but Frank Chinn, at bottom, wasn't so much
a striver as a street urchin.

He made a very odd impression. To Ben Murillo, a fellow broker who
met him around 1970, Chinn called to mind a cartoon penguin—a tiny
man, five foot two, in suit and vest with an umbrella. He wore shoulder-
length hair, he talked ninety miles an hour, and he had been to the end of
the world and back; and yet for all Chinn's raffish talk, Murillo scarcely
felt that he knew him. He alluded, always cryptically, to the lofty circles in
which he moved. He had married a beautiful and aristocratic Egyptian
woman, Shadan El-Shazly, whose father later was allegedly involved with
the conspiracy to assassinate Anwar El-Sadat. Through her, Chinn had
come to manage the money of a number of wealthy Middle Eastern
figures.

Nobody knew how much money Chinn had or controlled, though one
man who opened up a number of accounts for Chinn said that he understood the minimum trading account he would accept was $1 or $2 million. He was a player, as they said along San Francisco's Montgomery
Street, though since he had no institutional affiliation, he was not considered a significant player. But there was no doubt he had a gift; everyone
who heard Chinn talk recognized that. "The trading environment is one
of the grand examples of Darwin's law," says Chinn's friend Hugo
Quackenbush, one of the founders of the Charles Schwab discount brokerage house. "You're either good, or you get wiped out. Frank was a
very brilliant mind in the market. If you weren't as fast as Frank, you
would get trampled." Chinn's gift was intuitive, the gift of someone who
had had to be more alert than others. "He had a sense of market psychol-
ogy," says Quackenbush, "a trader's sense of where the market was
going."

In the bull market of the eighties, when investors and traders seemed
to be riding the crest of an enormous wave, Frank Chinn was surfing way
out at the edge. He invested the same way he talked and moved—fast. By
the late seventies, when he had finished his apprenticeship in San Fran-

cisco brokerage houses and was playing with his own money and that of his alleged crew of rich Arabs, he had focused his investment activities on initial public offerings, whose prices could vary wildly in a matter of hours. Only a few brokerage houses in San Francisco dealt in IPOs, and Chinn had contacts among them whom he could count on to pass the word on offerings that were likely to take wing. Like the arbitrage then being popularized by Ivan Boesky and others, IPOs required a combination of fearless plunging and inside—not necessarily illicit—information. Chinn was very good at it. He claimed to have made $350,000 on British Airways stock that he held for ten minutes.

But Fast Frank had a problem. Jack Kehoe's friends were not the only ones who had noticed that he was not altogether trustworthy. Traders have to trust one another, even if they trust no one else. When a broker lets a trader buy a few thousand shares of a hot public offering, he expects the trader to steer some business his way. One profits on stock, the other on commission. One hand washes the other; it's the trader's way. But Chinn, according to Howard Maierhoff, a broker who dealt in IPOs, was notorious for promising to deliver business and then disappearing. "He was always leading people astray," recalls Maierhoff. "He didn't pay for what he got. I always felt that he was out to screw someone." Maierhoff finally stopped giving Chinn valuable tips.

Chinn seemed to be looking for a higher-stakes game. Around 1980 he met someone with a similar interest—Rusty Kent London. London had made millions investing in real estate in California and around the world. No one was quite sure, for London was a more peripatetic and mysterious character than even Chinn. They made an exceedingly odd couple: Chinn was short and hyperactive and had a smile for everyone; London was tall and taciturn. He was cool and self-contained, undemonstrative, analytical.

And yet, even more than Chinn, London seemed to have come from a Dashiell Hammett novel. He too was a creature of his own devising. London had been born Irving Louis Warth; when his father died and his mother remarried, the boy became Irving Louis Lobsenz. By the time he was leaving for medical school, Warth-Lobsenz had changed his name once again to the semi-Jewish Irving Louis London. And then, in 1983, he went all the way, adopting the moniker Rusty Kent London. Bob Wallach had merely eliminated the capital letters in his name; Rusty Kent London had given himself a succession of aliases.

After medical school, London, instead of going into practice, returned to San Francisco and in 1970 started a water bed company. He wore granny glasses and sported muttonchop whiskers. But London was not content to be an entrepreneur of West Coast life. He started investing in the market. From a very early age London had been interested in probability—not chance, but the rules governing chance. He tried to apply to the movement of commodity prices the principles he had learned in probability theory. Inevitably, he was attracted to gambling.

People often gamble in a way that unconsciously reveals their identity. Stanley Simon played his persnickety, old maid's game of guaranteed trivial wins. Both Mario and Tony spent money at the tables with the reckless abandon of the suddenly, gloriously rich. John, the idiot savant, played roulette, but placed chips on every single number, so that, as he told Tony, he could be sure to get money back every time. Frank Chinn played craps, banking on his nerves and his love of risk.

Rusty Kent London may have been the only person affiliated with Wedtech who profited from gambling. London approached gambling as a logical proposition, and taught himself to beat the system. He played blackjack all over Las Vegas in the 1970s. For London, it was a game of probability, not chance. Blackjack is the card game most susceptible to card counting, a system whereby a player keeps mental tabs on every card that has been dealt from the deck and calculates the odds on receiving any given one of the remaining cards. Card counting was a lucrative hobby, even a fabulous living, for the mathematically inclined, and London became one of its arch-practitioners.

The casinos, however, had banned card counting, and London had gotten himself thrown out of most of them. In the mid-1970s he adopted yet another name, Ian Anderson, in order to stay one step ahead of the gendarmes. He was leading what was practically a double life. As Irving London he dabbled in real estate and the market; as Ian Anderson he authored or edited a series of books on gambling, including *Turning the Tables* and *Making Money*. Neither his editor nor his agent knew who he was, since London conducted the entire publishing venture through a businessman headquartered in Liechtenstein, who deposited the funds in a Swiss bank. Later, as Irving London once again, he even worked out a deal with Caesar's Palace in Las Vegas: London received a take from the steady stream of high rollers he brought in.

By the time London met Chinn he had largely forsaken his old identities and his old look. He was slender and sloping, elegantly dressed, soft-spoken, faintly professorial. He had had the foresight to invest, through limited partnerships, in the booming real estate market in California and across the West. He was also managing money, though in line with his theories, he offered "long-range" advice on market movement, by which he meant up to nine weeks. He came to meet Chinn when a client asked for someone who could guide his short-term investment.

Each man found the other a kindred spirit. London was the scientist, Chinn the artist, within the sphere of investments. They began working real estate deals together, and London drew Chinn out of his hermetic San Francisco life. Ben Murillo would get the occasional phone call from Chinn, who had never seemed to leave the Bay Area once he discovered prosperity, saying he was going off to the Super Bowl with Rusty, or to the fights, or deep-sea fishing, which seemed almost comical. London apparently had awakened Chinn to larger possibilities.

In the fall of 1984 Bob Wallach moved into a large apartment with a view of the Bay in a building that London owned and where he maintained an apartment. The two men, who shared the typical Northern California obsession with health, began to jog together and to discuss their professions. Frank Chinn, a fellow jogger and vegetarian, soon joined the pair. Wallach asked Chinn to invest the entire $300,000 he had received from Wedtech, unaware that by this time the only accounts Chinn was handling were his own, his mother's, and that of the college his daughter was attending. Chinn turned a quick profit.

Chinn and London talked a very good game, and Wallach was impressed. Here, he thought, was the answer to Wedtech's problems with Wall Street. Wallach waxed eloquent about Wedtech's triumph-against-all-odds background, but he seemed to leave the two men cold. Then he spoke about the coating process, and London, the scientist of investment, was fascinated. Suddenly Wallach's company sounded less kooky. Chinn and London agreed to fly to New York. On April 22 a Wallach-gram went off to Tony advising him to "listen carefully to our friends from the West Coast. I feel very certain about their ability to contribute in a meaningful way to the future economic benefit of the company. Try to separate the past from the present. The fact that you have been hounded by hustlers, then and now, does not make everyone a hustler . . ."

The ever-faithful Wallach missed the point: he had put one group of hustlers in touch with another. Chinn and London arrived on April 27, took The Tour, met the principals, and on April 30 went to the offices of Squadron Ellenoff. Perhaps by then they had already taken the company's measure. In any case, they pulled no punches. At a meeting with the five insiders, Chinn and London offered to help Wedtech beat the system. Chinn said that he and London could raise the price of Wedtech stock by "touting" it among their contacts in the brokerage and investment world. Touting, Tony pointed out, was a vague term. What exactly did they have in mind? Chinn said that he could get his people to trade the stock back and forth among themselves, thus increasing volume, which tends to raise the stock price. Moreover, they could serve as a conduit to the market for beneficial inside information, which Chinn knew something about from the receiving end. Everyone agreed that that would be a fine idea.

Tony left the room to fetch Arthur Siskind, brought him back to the conference room, and explained that they would like him to draw up an agreement ratifying the touting arrangement. But Siskind, unlike most of the men sitting in the room, was not accustomed to looking illegality in the eye without flinching. After all, he was a lawyer. Siskind said that the only contract he would draw up was one that stipulated the legitimate financial services that Chinn and London could perform for the company, such as finding new backers and communicating with securities analysts.

In the contract signed later that day, Chinn and London agreed to engage in these services in exchange for 50,000 stock options. The more they raised the stock price, in other words, the greater their compensation. The participants in the meeting understood that the contract, like the stock purchase plan a year and a half earlier, was a legal fiction. Squadron Ellenoff, however, protected itself by insisting on the inclusion of a statement that "the Contractor shall perform all of his obligations hereunder in compliance with all applicable federal and state laws, rules and regulations, including, without limitation, all securities laws." Siskind had put them on notice, which, short of refusing to draw up the contract, was all that he could do.

Howard Squadron says that he didn't stop there. He told the Wedtech boys that the newcomers looked like bad news to him. In fact, none of Wedtech's really knowledgeable friends liked these card sharps who had been enlisted into the ranks. The board member Frederick Moss said that he had heard nothing good about Chinn and London. And after his phone calls to San Francisco, Jack Kehoe called Tony and said, "I'm really uncomfortable with this." Tony cut him short by responding, "There are no choices on this. He's been recommended at the highest levels, and the decision has been made." If Kehoe couldn't get along with Chinn, Tony said, then he would just have to quit—a side of Tony Tough-Guy Kehoe hadn't seen before.

Certainly those at Wedtech, including the worldly Tony, were impressed with their Mutt and Jeff consulting team. Tony, after all, respected nothing so much as a man who knew all the angles. Exactly how many of those angles Chinn and London actually played is not quite clear. An examination of stock records shows a sporadic increase in trading volume in late May and early June, but the only run-up in the value of Wedtech stock occurred, curiously enough, between the end of April, as Chinn and London were touring the premises, and early May. Almost every trading day for two weeks, the price of Wedtech stock rose an eighth or a quarter of a point, from 13 to 14 7/8. Perhaps Chinn and London had started buying shares in the company themselves.

Over the next few months the two did get in contact with friends who were very heavy players in the market and with a number of institutional investors. In the late spring Chinn even visited the Bronx with Ben Murillo and a former partner named David Meid, whom Tony always called the husband-in-law, because he was married to Chinn's former wife. But a number of the people Chinn called to talk up Wedtech say they hadn't heard from him in years. Florence Griswald, who was then running $80 million a year for BA Investments, a subsidiary of Bank of America, was surprised to hear Chinn's voice on the phone, after an interval of five years or so, suggesting that she take a hard look at some stock she'd never heard of. Chinn mentioned that he himself had invested in the company, but not that he had been retained as a consultant. Griswald assumed, she says, that "he wanted me to pump up the price of the stock," and declined to make a buy. (But Tony says that Griswald pledged to buy 50,000 shares at an offering in January 1986.)

The Wedtech boys, in any case, were credulous in matters of fraud and cynicism, and were quickly convinced of Chinn and London's powers of levitation. In mid-June all five insiders agreed to allow the two men to handle the sale of 10 percent of their personal stock and to pay them the difference between $13, the current stock price, and whatever higher price the shares could be sold for. At this point the agreement transferring almost all of their shares to John Mariotta remained in force, but they all knew that that transaction would be dissolved in early 1986.

London continued to be intrigued by the coating process, and asked whether he could see the Mount Vernon facility, where the reclusive Dr. Pinkhasov practiced his alchemy. What he discovered was that the coating business was a shambles. By early 1985 John had essentially exiled himself from 595 Gerard. In Mount Vernon, he fumed over his isolation and took a perverse pleasure in the reflection of his paranoia in Dr. Pinkhasov's. The sole objective of the coating division appeared to be the protection of the secret process. John refused to enter into a licensing agreement, which might have been worth hundreds of millions of dollars; he believed that no sum could justify parting with a formula that might change the world. London found that the coating division had no

Wedtech's state-of-the-art equipment included this laser cutter. (*Copyright 1990 Scott Barrow Inc.*)

The company's amazing coating process had dozens of potential applications; unfortunately, none of them panned out. (*Copyright 1990 Scott Barrow Inc.*)

The spoils of success. John used money siphoned off from the company to build himself a ranch house in Scarsdale. (*Elizabeth Easton*)

Fred installed himself in a brownstone on Manhattan's Sutton Place, as well as in ski chalets and a London town house.

In his stately pleasure dome in the northern Bronx Mario built
an underground swimming pool, known as "the grotto," and a
greenhouse. (*Elizabeth Easton*)

The mighty domain of Bronx auto-wrecking king Pat Simone,
who allegedly ran a kickback scheme on the construction of
Wedtech's pontoon facility. (*Elizabeth Easton*)

In 1984 the Navy awarded Wedtech a $24 million contract to build pontoon causeways. It was to be the company's undoing. (*Official U.S. Navy Photograph*)

Wedtech paid Stanley Simon $50,000 for his help in getting the company this Bronx site for the launching of the pontoons. (*Elizabeth Easton*)

The gang's all here. Pat Simone (left), Stanley Simon (center), Mario Moreno, and Bernard Ehrlich, Mario Biaggi's law partner.

The South Bronx Republicans celebrate at Ronald Reagan's second inauguration. Fred, SBA chief of staff Peter Neglia, who had just agreed to accept stock options and money from the company in exchange for his help, and Neglia's father, Joseph (right to left).

The trial of John Mariotta, Mario Biaggi, and five others, through the eyes of artist Joe Papin.

The end of the road. Wedtech finally went bankrupt, struggled to reorganize, failed, and was sold off, piece by piece. (*Jim Wilson/ NYT Pictures*)

sales force, no samples, no testing equipment, no publicity or brochures, and no plans.

After some time he began asking John, and then Dr. Pinkhasov himself, just when he would be allowed to see for himself how the process worked. Never, he was told. Finally, after much pleading, Dr. Pinkhasov, picking up a bunch of keys, beckoned to London to come along. The first key let them into a locked room; the second, into a second; then a third. After a fourth door swung open, London found himself standing before one of the chambers in which the vapor deposition process took place. He waited for Pinkhasov to show him how the coating worked. But it was the end of the show; it was enough that London had been privileged to see the chamber.

London also became involved, though vaguely, in Wedtech's attempt to sell a vast barge it had inherited along with the Ontonagon shipyard. When Wedtech purchased the shipyard, it had allocated $1.5 million of the $5.3 million purchase price to what was known as the tug barge system. It was the tug barge that had dragged the original shipbuilding company down to bankruptcy. Upsco had contracted with the state of Michigan to build this leviathan ferry, which measured 460 feet by 70 feet, to carry fully loaded rail cars across Lake Superior from Michigan to Ontario. A protracted dispute with the state had prevented the barge and its attendant tugs from being put into use, and had plunged Upsco into Chapter XI.

Wedtech spent well over a year trying to unload this albatross. The barge couldn't be sold for scrap, because it would cost more to cut up than the scrap would fetch. Mario had the ingenious idea of docking it in the Hudson River on Manhattan's Upper West Side and converting it into a restaurant. Failing that, Mario suggested, the whole contraption could be sunk in Lake Superior and used as a fish sanctuary. Mario was not a man without imagination. The government of Yugoslavia expressed interest in buying the thing, and Bob Wallach, Wedtech's in-house foreign policy consultant, fired off some memos explaining the delicacy of transacting business in the Balkans. That deal fell through, too.

Everyone took his turn in trying to peddle the barge. Rusty London also offered some advice about foreign countries, and sent some literature on the barge to several of his wealthy friends. This, too, came to nought. Nevertheless, on July 1, 1985, he submitted an invoice to Wedtech; it said, in its entirety, "For consulting services related to the sale of the tug barge system. Total amount due $150,000." In fact, according to Tony, this was simply a device to convey to Wallach the sum he had been promised after he learned of the planned payment to Nofziger & Bragg. Wallach, he testified, now wanted his money—though the lobbyists hadn't gotten theirs—but because of the ever-impending Justice Department job didn't want to receive it directly. London offered to launder the funds through his company and then pay Wallach in cash, and Tony suggested he ascribe the payment to work on the barge. London received only $100,000 of the funds in a down payment and six monthly installments, and there was no evidence that Wallach received the cash payments.

London and Chinn were highly skilled men, and London, especially, might have had something to contribute to a company like Wedtech. But what they ultimately contributed were techniques to beat the system, like a team of underwater specialists in a terrorist battalion. Tony always admired essentially adolescent intellectual skills—having a head for numbers, for example—and instances of London's statistical wizardry never failed to amaze him. There was the time when Tony was playing blackjack in Las Vegas, and London, who was permitted to play only craps, wandered over for a chat. Tony had fifteen, and the dealer had a five or a six showing, so Tony held out his palm to indicate that he would stick.

"Take the card," whispered London.

"Fuhgedaboudid," said Tony.

"Take the card," said London. "It's a six."

Since London seemed to be paying no attention to the game, Tony assumed he was kidding. "Will you cover my bet if I lose?" he asked.

"Absolutely," said the impassive London. Tony took the card. It was, of course, a six.

London and Chinn arrived at Wedtech at a moment when Tony was moving to the fore and shaping the company with his fatal weakness for the deal, the quick fix, the ingenious short cut. In this, as in so much else, Wedtech was merely imitating its betters, parodying the feverish corporate culture of the junk-bond era. And London and Chinn played to Tony's deft money shuffling. They seemed perfectly schooled in the arcana of money laundering and kickbacks. They reinforced Tony's belief that sophisticated businessmen played the same sort of games he did, only more subtly. Everyone was corrupt. It was all a game, and the goal was to beat the system.

TWENTY-SEVEN

E. Robert Wallach's Excellent Adventure

BOB WALLACH was like the frog waiting to be kissed by the princess. Throughout the early part of 1985 he had been sending his friend Ed those endlessly long, yearning memos in which he made all too clear his passionate hope of joining the Justice Department. They weren't memos, really, these ten- and twenty-page documents, so much as installments in a study Bob Wallach had commissioned from himself, a study of how Ed Meese and Bob Wallach, together, could make the earth a better place to live. There was a good deal of thought and even sense in Wallach's ruminations on the plight of the handicapped and the pursuit of Josef Mengele and the provision of legal services to the poor; but the inherent hubris in them was astounding.

Wallach did not get kissed, of course, but his special relationship with Meese continued. At least once a week, sometimes more often, they had breakfast or lunch *à deux*. Wallach screened prospective nominees and sent to Meese dozens of nominees of his own. For the moment, at least, Wallach would remain Ed Meese's one-man advisory board. The only "rewards" he wanted, he wrote to Meese, were a photograph of himself with the President and the Attorney General, "with each of us holding up our fingers in a victory sign, and with broad smiles on our faces"; the same picture including Ursula Meese, "but we can leave the gestures out, except for the smiles"; a picture of himself and Meese, with gestures and smiles; a picture of the legal team from the Meese confirmation hearing, with the President, no facial expressions or gestures required; and, finally, White House mess privileges, which he had been told were "the most important 'perk' one could have in terms of credibility." He may have gotten the photographs; he didn't get the mess privileges.

Wallach did provide Meese with some genuinely valuable help. He knew that the Attorney General had to place his investments in a blind trust to avoid the appearance of impropriety, and a few weeks before he began speaking of Frank Chinn to Wedtech, Wallach mentioned him to the Meeses. "Bob told me that he had used Frank Chinn as an investment manager for some period of time," recalls Meese, who says he understood, incorrectly, that the period of time was a matter of years, "and that he had had very good experience with him." Wallach said that although Chinn had retired, he would be willing to take on the Attorney General's meager portfolio.

Meese was completely incurious. He didn't ask Wallach about Chinn's investment methods, or look into the man's reputation, or quail at the thought of placing his entire cash holdings of $55,000 in the hands of a stranger. And when Wallach told him that Chinn had a business relationship with Wedtech, it certainly didn't occur to Meese that Wedtech was paying him back for his many kindnesses, real or perceived. "It was a substantial amount of money," Meese concedes, "but most of my life I haven't spent an awful lot of time thinking about money." He trusted Bob Wallach, as Wallach trusted Chinn. And Ursula, says Meese, thought it was a good idea. On May 23, Meese signed a limited partnership agreement with Chinn's company, Financial Management International, Incorporated.

And it *was* a good idea. Over the twenty-one months that FMI handled the Meese Partners account, the $55,000 investment grew at an annual rate of 34 percent. At the same time, though, the Dow Industrial was rising at an annual rate of 37 percent, which may be taken as a further proof of the validity of the "random walk" theory of market investment. Despite the fact that he was holding a blind trust for the Attorney General, Chinn moved Meese Partners swiftly in and out of stocks, gambled on hot new issues, and betrayed his habitual love of risk and split-second timing. Meese has said that he had no idea what Chinn was doing, and there is no reason to think otherwise. Since that time the independent prosecutor has exhaustively detailed Chinn's investment techniques. Meese, however, still denies that Chinn's methods were unorthodox. "I don't know that he was particularly speculative," says the former Attorney General.

By the middle of 1985 the momentum carrying John and Fred to the perimeter of the company they had created, and Mario and especially Tony to the center, had become irresistible. John had largely retreated to the eccentric confines of the coating laboratory. While the incorrigible Dr. Pinkhasov wandered through the realms of pure science, John built himself a palace worthy of the last days of the Austro-Hungarian Empire. He bought miles of heavily brocaded silk curtain material to cover the ceiling-high windows of his office, the display cases in the central corridor, and—the crowning touch—a blackboard in the conference room.

Antique bookcases, credenzas, breakfronts, and the like were carted in to fill John's office and to spiff up the hallways the white-coated lab technicians strode up and down. The sort of chandelier fit for a grand ballroom hung from the ceiling of the tiny entrance foyer. There were Persian carpets and fine armchairs, and one employee recalls that each office had an end table decorated with an array of crystal, which was reflected in a mirror that ran the length of the corridor. John served coffee in bone china to the research guys in $99 suits who came to look over the place for the big high-tech firms. It was John's *folie*, and there was nothing anyone could do about it.

John was turning into a crank and a painful embarrassment at a moment when Wedtech was trying very hard to impress the world with its corporate solemnity. Wallach, who counted John a saint among men, was nevertheless keen to kick him upstairs in favor of someone with better bloodlines. Chinn and London had joined the campaign, for they felt that only a financial pro like Tony could run the company Wedtech was becoming.

In early June Wedtech underwent one of its periodic games of corporate-title musical chairs. Larry Shorten became executive vice president, Tony became president, Mario became deputy vice chairman of the board—an innovation in corporate nomenclature—Fred became vice chairman, and John remained chairman. John felt that he was losing his grip on his own company, which was true, but Wallach, to whom John was devoted, persuaded him to step up for the good of the company. When his turn came to vote in the June 6 board meeting John said, "Yes," and then said, "They're pushing you aside, Freddy." But Fred had never cared enough to fight for power; Wedtech was not an extension of his physical being, as it was for John.

The titles themselves changed nothing, for everyone continued to be responsible to those above him, but the truth was that Tony was assuming a more dominant role. He had replaced Fred, for example, as the contact man with the Teamsters, though this may have come as a surprise to the bankers and lawyers who looked to him for corporate leadership. In June, Richard Stolfi called Tony and said that he and Frank Casalino wanted to meet with him at the diner in Glen Cove. At the meeting, on Saturday morning as always, Stolfi told Tony that he wanted something for himself. He and Casalino, he said, had used the entire $100,000 Wedtech had given them in March to bribe the carpenters, and they deserved some consideration for their help—something on the order of $50,000 to $60,000. When Tony balked at paying out that kind of cash, Stolfi proposed that Wedtech double the monthly ante to $10,000. Wedtech was a big company, after all, and required more attention than it had before, and Stolfi and Casalino had cooperated when Wedtech asked to keep many of its plants nonunionized. Tony agreed. He gave Casalino the usual wad of fifty hundred-dollar bills, and then drove out with the two men to his Jericho home to give them another $5000 of his own cash.

Tony was also working with Jack Kehoe on plans for a trip to the West Coast to make a pitch to institutional investors, and to soothe lingering anxiety over the unprecedented loss in the fourth quarter of 1984. Kehoe was distressed to hear from Tony that Chinn wanted to be involved. Tony had explained that Chinn would be using his global contacts to raise investment funds abroad. Kehoe did not want to be associated with Chinn, and he wrote a letter stipulating that his former acquaintance not be involved in the presentation. But Chinn wanted to work his contacts, and at a meeting in early July, in the refined surroundings of the Plaza Athenée Hotel—the surroundings were growing ever more refined— Chinn gave Kehoe a patronizing speech on the subject of high finance and presented a list of investors he would like to see invited. A number of these figures attended, and several later purchased Wedtech stock or bonds.

The investment meetings were held in mid-July in San Francisco and Los Angeles, and had little discernible effect on the volume or price of Wedtech's stock. They did, however, puncture a little hole in Chinn's ego. The night before the initial meeting Chinn and London drove out to the airport to pick up Tony. They were driving the 1978 Rolls-Royce, of which Chinn was immensely proud—the gamin playing the grandee.

Chinn drove the two into the elegant parking circle of the Stanford Court Hotel, hopped out, went to open the trunk—and couldn't. For hours Chinn fussed and sweated over the locked trunk of his gorgeous car while hotel employees snickered in the background. Tony was growing desperate; all of his clothes and his briefcase with his presentation were locked in the Rolls. Finally, Chinn telephoned a Rolls dealer and got the name of a mechanic. Early the next morning he drove off, and returned several hours later with Tony's things on the seat and a large hole drilled in the center of his trunk.

Afterward, when Kehoe flew home, Tony went to Las Vegas with Chinn and London. Chinn lost tens of thousands of dollars playing craps, Tony lost at cards, and London made money from his computer-driven craps-betting model and told Tony to take the card.

On August 13 Tony and Frank Chinn, the methodical accountant and the charming and cryptic investor, joined the Wedtech board together. After the two men had been voted onto the board, the question of stock options was considered. The insiders had been promising options, with typical abandon, to one another and to all who had served well and truly. All three of Wedtech's law firms—Biaggi & Ehrlich, Squadron Ellenoff, and Tim Sullivan's firm, Dykema Gossett—had been promised options, as had ten individuals, including Ron Betso, allegedly the nominee for Peter Neglia (a crime of which Betso would later be found not guilty).

Mario and Tony had originally planned on awarding themselves 100,000 options each, though it was not clear that the board would agree. One member of the options committee was a retired military man, General Richard Cavazos, who knew very little about business and seemed likely to approve whatever the executives proposed. Another member, Paul Hallingby, a banker from Bear Stearns, was likely to look askance at this act of self-interested generosity. Tony raised this point with Chinn, who agreed to get himself placed as the swing vote on the options committee. Tony could ask for 200,000 options, Chinn suggested, as long as he was willing to compensate Chinn for his vote. The price, said Chinn, would be 40,000 of the options. Tony agreed.

While the board was voting on the options, those prospective recipients who were present stepped outside. Mario and Tony went off by themselves, and Mario said mysteriously, "Don't be disappointed if I get more options than you." Don't be disappointed, Tony answered, if *I* get more. There was a moment of recognition: each realized that Chinn had struck a deal with the other and had said nothing about it. Tony and Mario had themselves a good laugh, and then walked back into the boardroom to find that each had received 200,000 options. Hallingb▪

had, in fact, objected to the number of options awarded; he feared they could depress the stock price if they were exercised in the same period of time. Don't worry, Chinn retorted; *I'll* bring the price back up.

Chinn brought one virtue to the board in addition to his technical sense of the market—his minority status. For Wedtech to comply with 8(a) requirements, a majority of the board had to be minority-group members, and as the board expanded to include powerhouses like Hallingby, the issue of control became important. Alfred Rivera, Wedtech's treasurer, had been placed on the board in late 1983 for just this reason, and in the spring of 1985 General Cavazos, who had been serving as a consultant, had been invited to join the board. Cavazos was Hispanic, but he came from an old and socially prominent family in Texas. (His brother Lauro was appointed Secretary of Education by Ronald Reagan and reappointed by George Bush.) And when General Cavazos' name was submitted, a district-level official in the 8(a) office had had the backbone to say no dice.

Thus the eminently agreeable Frank Chinn stepped to the fore. Immediately after joining the board, Chinn filled out an application to have himself declared a disadvantaged minority. On the question of victimization he went whole hog. He *x*'d all four boxes under "socially disadvantaged": he had suffered "Racial prejudice," "Ethnic prejudice," "Cultural bias," "Social bias." He *x*'d the "Yes" box to indicate that his "ability to compete in the free enterprise system" had been impaired because of the social disadvantages.

"Business in America," he explained, "is predominantly all white and being Chinese has been a liability as my experience in America has been people tend to associate with their 'own kind' and do not evaluate one on their ability, but rather on their physical, social and religious similarities . . . Furthermore, my religious beliefs differ from those of mainstream America and I feel that I have never experienced equal consideration in the business world." Chinn may have been one of the few citizens of the Republic to suffer discrimination on the grounds of vegetarianism.

Chinn's problem was that, despite the lack of equal consideration, he had become fantastically rich, or so he told everyone at Wedtech. He traveled all over the world at the drop of a hat; his son Bobby went to school in London. On a recent credit application Chinn had modestly listed his income at $225,000 and his net worth at $675,000, showing just enough to get his credit limit extended. Chinn faced this problem directly: he lied. On the "personal financial statement" he submitted to the SBA, Chinn listed a salary of $40,000 and a total net worth of $38,739. When Chinn showed the form to Tony, who had seen Chinn sitting behind $100,000 worth of chips at Caesars Palace, Tony burst out laughing. "That couldn't pay for the tires on your Rolls-Royce," he said. The SBA apparently was not convinced either; Chinn was never made an official citizen of Minority Land.

While Frank Chinn and Tony Guariglia and Mario Moreno were stuffing each other's stockings, Bob Wallach was busy saving the world. He had found something even more fulfilling than serving as chief of staff to the Attorney General, something that would satisfy his deepest need for moral greatness. E. Robert Wallach was going to bring peace to the Middle East.

Israel meant a great deal to Wallach. He had cultivated American Jewish leaders, and when he referred to himself as a man who spoke truth to power, he was thinking, among other things, of his self-appointed role in bringing the concerns of these men to the attention of his friend Ed. Wallach had visited Israel and had even had an audience with Prime Minister Menachem Begin. In the course of the meeting, he told Howard Squadron, he had delivered a secret message from the administration. What it was, he wouldn't say. Wallach loved secret messages and the aura of power that surrounds secrecy.

In late May, Wallach's love of Israel and his love of proximity to power converged into a mighty emotional force when a Swiss-Israeli businessman, Bruce Rappaport, approached him for help in effecting a deal for a pipeline from Iraq across Jordan to the Red Sea port of Aqaba. The idea of the pipeline had been batted around in high government circles ever since the onset of war with Iran had made it perilous for the Iraqis to ship their oil across the Persian Gulf. It was a commercial venture that had to do with Israel only collaterally, but to Wallach it was an opportunity to serve his people.

The stumbling block to this multibillion-dollar construction project was the fear that Israel might blow it to flinders. Rappaport, who was a part of the shadowy group of businessmen who on occasion act as virtual agents for the Israeli government, felt that he could guarantee Israeli acquiescence, but only if he could get the U.S. government to participate in an insurance package he was putting together. Through Wallach, whose connection to Meese had become well known, he hoped to gain access to the American foreign policy apparatus, as, in short order, he did.

Wallach called Meese within a few hours of meeting Rappaport. In early June, Meese did his part by telephoning National Security Adviser Robert McFarlane and explaining, vaguely, that a friend had come to him with a project that seemed to be good for the Middle East, and that his shop might want to get involved. On June 24, Wallach, along with Rappaport, went to the White House Situation Room, where he presented the issue to McFarlane. After a thirteen-minute meeting, and without so much as checking their story, McFarlane called up his international finance expert on the National Security Council, Roger Robinson, and told him to come over immediately. Robinson had never before been summoned so peremptorily, and he knew that something big was up. When he arrived in the Situation Room, McFarlane instructed him to do whatever was necessary to get the project done.

Meese professes surprise that his call to McFarlane could have produced any effect whatever, as he does in regard to his office's intervention with the SBA in 1981 and the Army in 1982. Yet McFarlane's full-scale mobilization is only another sign that Meese's proximity to the throne, in a White House dominated by considerations of personal loyalty to the President, gave him an almost vice-regal status. Meese issued no commands. He was the head of the Justice Department, after all, and this was a foreign policy matter. He simply referred the matter to the proper authority. During the six months' pendency of the Aqaba project, Wallach sent Meese a stream of memos on the subject, and probably spent dozens of hours discussing it with him in private. And Meese merely called McFarlane twice, and sent a note to the current Israeli Prime Minister, Shimon Peres. In his own mind, unwitting of the consequences of his own acts, Meese did almost nothing. Yet the entire train of events proceeded on the basis of his name, which he never asked Wallach to refrain from using. In effect, he gave Wallach license to use that forceful talisman.

Wallach himself now embarked on a fairy tale adventure. He met with Jordanian Prime Minister Zeid Rifa'i, with Shimon Peres, and twice with CIA Director William Casey; and each time he would politely ask his colleagues to leave the room so that he could disclose something only the great man himself could hear. He told everyone, and especially his American Jewish friends like Howard Squadron, that he was doing something top secret that might very well lead to peace in the Middle East. He wished he could say more, but it was terribly delicate. He was in London, in Amman, in California, and Washington. He was conferring with the top officials of the international finance wings of the U.S. government. He sent memos to Rappaport and others full of initials and elliptical references to "the big country."

In short order Wallach succeeded in weirding out the straight-arrow Ivy Leaguers in the U.S. government whom he was trying so hard to impress. He wore a yellow rose in his lapel, as always, and carried his leather shoulder bag, and wafted into and out of rooms like a zephyr from California, and spoke from under the vast canopy of his eyebrows in his painfully quiet and solemn tones. Also, he was having too good a time. "He was riveted," says Roger Robinson, by the importance of it all, "and there was a certain fantasy element to this, and trying to be a mover and shaker." As often as he could, he mentioned his good friend Ed Meese and Judge William Clark, the President's close friend, who had agreed to act as a stand-in for the President. Clark, however, stood out when he heard that Wallach was bandying his name around, seriously damaging the campaign for the pipeline.

In the end, the growing disenchantment of American officials with Wallach and with Rappaport had only a little to do with the pipeline's demise. More important was an Iraqi decision to build a pipeline through Saudi Arabia and on to Turkey, cold feet on the part of the Jordanians, Rappaport's disinclination to put up a good deal of his own money, and legal concerns and financial constraints among the concerned U.S. government bodies. The project finally collapsed only at the very end of the year, when Judge Clark told McFarlane's successor, John Poindexter, that the whole operation had become an excuse for private interests to make money—a sort of prefiguration of the Iran-contra events.

Indeed, Rappaport expected to make $200 million a year from the deal, and in August had paid $150,000 into Wallach's account with Chinn, a payment that Wallach hid from the IRS. That figure must have barely covered Wallach's expenses as a global, not merely a domestic, power broker. Adnan Kashoggi could live this way, but Bob Wallach could not. Wallach *had* to make big money from the pipeline: it wasn't coming from anywhere else. He wrote to Rappaport that in order "to appear as a successful and independent lawyer . . . I require an income of $1 million a year." He wanted a piece of the deal rather than a fee. "My real future," as he put it in Wallach-ese, "lies in the percentage of success our efforts achieve."

By the late summer the pipeline was on its way to vaporizing, but E. Robert Wallach was getting bigger and bigger, like a float being readied for the Thanksgiving Day parade. He was becoming a force. He knew people. He was a discreet operative, like his friends Bob Strauss and Max Kampelman, in that border territory where private actors effect public policy. And, as Wallach was also a man who wanted all of his friends to share in his good fortune, to mix with one another and love one another, he sought to bring Wedtech into his enlarging sphere.

Wallach had fixed on the annual Ambassadors' Ball in September, one of the highlights of the Washington social season, as a means to bring Wedtech into the great world. As he jetted hither and thither attending to greater matters, he issued a stream of memos instructing everyone on the significance of the event to the company's future. He had the company purchase two tables, at $5000 apiece, and prevailed on Nofziger & Bragg and his friends Jeff Cohen and Howard Bender—real estate moguls both, heavy hitters, potential Wedtech board material—to buy tables as well. All would be grouped together, creating a power bloc of fifty seats in a prominent spot in the ballroom. "We will have a minimum of five ambassadors, and probably more, available for Wedtech's selection," Wallach wrote to Larry Shorten.

Wallach himself coordinated the guest list. The beneficiary of the evening was the Multiple Sclerosis Society, for which Ursula Meese worked as a volunteer. Mrs. Meese, in fact, was a co-chair of the event. Wallach knew the director of the Washington chapter of the society, and sent her letters with requests to invite dignitaries suitable to Wedtech's needs: the ambassadors of West Germany, Egypt, Pakistan, Israel, Italy, and Canada; Wedtech's own congressional delegation, and several other representatives and senators, plus the president of the American University and his wife. The event was going to be a watershed in Wedtech's history.

Before Wedtech got to any watershed it had to exert its utmost to keep from drowning. The company was finally gaining a measure of competency in its pontoon production. Mario had replaced himself with a veteran of the shipbuilding industry, Rudy Roemer, who had started to turn things around. Roemer had built a metal framework the exact dimensions of the pontoon and bolted it to the floor—a device known in shipbuilding as a jig—to prevent the wobbling that made the holes on the cans fail to line up. A former Navy admiral, James Lisanby, who was brought up in August to assess the production process, concluded that, despite serious lapses in quality control, Wedtech was doing reasonably well on an extremely demanding job.

The Navy, unfortunately, did not agree. Even before the 1985 options were awarded, in March, Admiral T. J. Hughes of the Sealift Command was trying to persuade Wayne Arny to remove the program from the minority set-aside. "After careful review of Wedtech's progress to date," he wrote on February 20, "I now consider it imperative that we take what action we can to limit the exposure to their inability to perform." After seeing to the award of the 1985 options, Arny made his visit to Wedtech, was impressed by the company's progress, and decided to give it six weeks to sink or swim. By the end of this period, Wedtech had still not delivered a single acceptable pontoon.

The idea of awarding a second set of options to a company that had yet to prove it could even manufacture the product seemed insane. In early May, Admiral Hughes wrote to Arny in a tone of genuine alarm that Wedtech's repeated failures would be forcing the prepositioned ships to leave harbor without the causeways. Again he offered his "strong recommendation that we act now to cut our losses." Still the assistant secretary's office declined to act, though Arny assigned yet another independent study of Wedtech's abilities. Hughes sent yet another urgent note to Arny on August 26.

Wedtech's political campaign to win the 1985 options and oust Captain de Vicq scarcely slackened as it turned into a campaign to win the 1986 options and oust de Vicq. In late July, Mario and Bernie Ehrlich went down to see Biaggi, who in turn called Senator D'Amato and sent the two over. There they sat down with Shawn Smeallie, who had recently become D'Amato's staff aide in charge of his work on the Appropriations Committee. Mario and Ehrlich explained that the Navy was still hopelessly biased against the firm, and that only intervention from the top could carry the day. Smeallie telephoned Wayne Arny, and D'Amato called Navy Secretary John Lehman. The wheels were beginning to turn.

While the 1986 options, and with them Wedtech's future, hung in the balance, the company made the humiliating discovery that it could not win a competitive contract. It was crucial to prove to investors that Wedtech would thrive once it emerged from the 8(a) cocoon. The company sought contracts to build grenade launchers, M-113 fuel tanks, and emergency equipment lockers for jeeps. On virtually every occasion it would submit the low bid, and then fail the pre-award inspection. Wedtech had fallen behind on every one of its contracts, and the Army and DCAS had lost faith in the company's ability to turn out a high-quality product on time. It was a frightening portent for a company that claimed to be ready to compete on a global basis.

The sine qua non of Wedtech's lack of competitiveness was the company's endless and futile wrangle over a contract to build a frame for a repair vehicle the Army called the contact maintenance vehicle. In March Wedtech had submitted the low bid of $30 million but had flunked the subsequent pre-award survey. The Army hadn't awarded the contract to anyone else, but it was looking to the second-highest bidder. Everyone was thoroughly disgusted, and grumbled that it was all politics, just as always.

Political problems demanded political solutions. By now Mario and the General were using the shuttle like a commuter train. They were down in Washington stiffening Peter Neglia's spine, since Neglia was ready to leave the government but was still needed to keep Wedtech from being booted out of 8(a). They had been back and forth on the 1985 and 1986 pontoon options. Now, in August, they made the Biaggi-D'Amato-Addabbo circle route once more to marshal the troops against the Army. Biaggi, as always, sent them to D'Amato's office, where they again met with Shawn Smeallie. Smeallie heard them out, wrote down a list of middle-level Army officers to contact, and spoke to D'Amato, who agreed to call Army Secretary John Marsh. From D'Amato's office they went to Addabbo's, where they met with *his* military aide, Richard Seelmayer, who, along with Addabbo, made still more calls to the Army. In September, D'Amato sent a letter to Marsh, asking why the award had not yet been made.

By the time the Ambassadors' Ball rolled around on September 10, Wedtech seemed to wax and wane at the same time. Tony was stretching the rubber band farther and farther, but it hadn't yet snapped. Rusty London was heading off to Japan to convert the dreams surrounding the coating technology into big dollars. Frank Chinn was lining up institutional investors on the West Coast. The Navy had awarded the 1985 pontoon options, and Everett Pyatt's office seemed determined to give Wedtech the 1986 options. At a meeting in July the insiders had sat down with the company's consultants and in all seriousness divided up their global responsibilities. Who's got contacts in Egypt? they asked. Who's got France, Italy, Taiwan, Turkey? And yet Wedtech couldn't win a competitive contract. Its head was in the Fortune 500, but its feet were stuck in Minority Land.

The Ambassadors' Ball was an event such as only Bob Wallach could have staged, a mummery in black tie whose strange portents had meaning in only one realm: status. The Ambassadors' Ball was Wedtech's coming-out party, the public proof that it had attained the legitimacy for which Wallach had so passionately striven. It was a moment of blinding, if empty, success. All the Wedtech people had come down to Washington for the weekend, and had enjoyed an elegant dinner the night before with Wallach and his mother, whom he had imported from San Francisco for the event. Unlike the inaugural, there was no pell-mell rush, no limo gridlock, no sense of occupying the lowest rungs of the ladder.

At the ball itself, held in the Washington Hilton, it quickly became clear that Wallach had made good on his boasts to Larry Shorten. At the far end of the room was the table of Mr. and Mrs. Meese and the other guests of honor. A small dance floor separated this table from all the others. Immediately on the other side of the dance floor, and thus closest to the Meeses, were three tables. These were the tables purchased by Wedtech and Nofziger & Bragg. At the first table, along with Wallach and his mother and John and Jenny, was the Israeli ambassador, Meir Rosenne. At the next table, with Tony and Mario, was the Pakistani ambassador, Lieutenant General Ejaz Azim. At the Nofziger & Bragg table, along with a number of administration figures, was the ambassador from Egypt, Abdel Raouf El-Ridy. This was serious pull. It was also a commercial opportunity not to be missed, since Wedtech hoped to do business in each of these countries.

It was a lovely evening. The Wedtech boys could see the top people from the big military contractors, Republican pillars all, casting baffled glances at them from the edge of the outfield. Dignitaries and Cabinet officials on their way to the Meeses paused at Wallach's table for a chat. The dinner, the speeches, and the dancing went by in a fine haze. Toward the end of the evening Wallach rounded them all up for the supreme moment: they were finally, after these many years, going to meet their great benefactor, Ed Meese. (Mario had met Meese with Wallach back in January.)

As the flock of tuxedoed street characters and their wives, led by the beaming Bob Wallach, drew to within fifteen or twenty feet of the Meeses, Ursula looked up and said, "This must be the Wedtech clan." So they were that well known! But of course. Wallach had been speaking of them to Meese for years. Wallach introduced everyone to everyone, and Meese, the genial host, asked how they were, spoke knowledgeably of the pontoon contract, made some small talk, and thanked them for coming. And that was that. No promises had been made, no business transacted. Nothing had happened at all. But in the realm of the symbolic, the one realm in which Wedtech truly excelled, it had been a radiant moment.

TWENTY-EIGHT

A Special Invitation
to the Rooftop Garden

BY THE FALL of 1985, Wedtech was a large and complex organization with aspirations to grow very much larger and more complex. The
downward trajectory continued, of course, as the company struggled to
turn a profit and to win a competitive bid. But the struggles were almost
entirely invisible. What the world saw was a company bursting out of its
confining identity as a minority firm in the Bronx, seeking the sort of
global reach appropriate to a mid-sized military contractor. To its new
friend the ambassador from Israel, Wedtech could speak of its wholly
owned subsidiary in Tel Aviv, Carmo Incorporated, and of its hopes to
do business with the Israeli armed forces. And in the case of Egypt, Frank
Chinn had been working the contacts he had made through his wife to
bring military officers from that country to the South Bronx to discuss
potential contracts.

Wedtech had always been a heterogeneous, multinational place. It was
only appropriate that with its all-new identity, the Wedtech esteemed on
Wall Street and courted in Washington, the Wedtech with global ambi-

tions, everyone should have his own country to work up. Foreign travel shook a little bit of the stardust of sophistication on each of them. At the occasional meetings with Wallach and others in swanky hotel conference rooms, the insiders and the consultants tried to impress one another with their high-level contacts abroad.

Wallach, especially, was forever sending bulletins from exotic climes about new opportunities, and advising the foreign businessmen he knew of investment opportunities with Wedtech. He had had extensive discussions with an unimaginably rich Afghani living in Paris, Yunus Dil. He told Rusty London that he knew the Sultan of Brunei, the world's richest man, though he never got around to introducing the two. Wallach also discussed with a French firm the possibility that Wedtech might manufacture and market its tank treads in the United States. This initiative, like all of Wedtech's grandiose foreign schemes, dissolved in confusion or indifference.

Wedtech was now hiring executives based on their supposed foreign sales expertise. Over the summer the company had hired Jim Jenkins, the very man who three years earlier had taken the ball from Ed Meese and run it over the goal line. Jenkins had left Meese's staff in 1984 and embarked on an unsuccessful business career. He had been trying to put together deals with the Chinese government, but hadn't quite made it to the signing stage. Wedtech hired Jenkins, at $150,000 a year, primarily for his ability to talk man to man with the big uniforms in the Navy, but also in the hope of doing business with the Chinese. Wedtech's Israeli subsidiary was the patent holder for the Wankel rotary engine, a lightweight low-maintenance engine that had once raised high expectations. Jenkins was hoping to sign an agreement to have the Chinese manufacture the engine for sale in the Eastern European market.

Wedtech was also developing a multifuel version of the rotary engine in conjunction with the Wankel company itself, and considered the product a key element of its global marketing campaign. But the big-ticket item for the near future was going to be the M-113 armored personnel carrier. The M-113, as Larry Shorten told a group of Wall Street analysts in September, was the most common vehicle in the armies of the United States and its NATO allies. The NATO countries alone, Shorten reported, had 32,000 M-113s in need of the kind of retrofitting Wedtech was performing for the Pentagon. That represented about $350 million worth of work. The company had hired and promoted Howard Kegley, an Army man who had overseen M-113 production at the Red River Arsenal in Alabama, in order to develop overseas sales. Kegley, according to Tony, had solicited the letter from TACOM stating that the Army was prepared to order over $60 million worth of M-113 parts from Wedtech for the West German military. That contract was still hanging fire, but it was clear that the M-113 was going to be very, very big.

And then there was the pot of gold at the end of every rainbow, the coating process. At the end of August the New York representative of Sumitomo Electric had called the coating facility in Mount Vernon and spoken with Rusty London. The Japanese had shown interest in the process for a number of years, and London, as it happened, had done a good deal of business in Japan, had a Japanese wife, and said he spoke the language. After discussing the process, which he now probably understood about as well as anyone outside Dr. Pinkhasov's lab, London was invited to Japan with Pinkhasov to explain the process to the company's principal technical people.

London went to Tokyo to meet with Sumitomo executives on several occasions, the first time, at the beginning of September, accompanied by the cryptic Pinkhasov. Unfortunately, he was never able to offer much proof of the remarkable pudding. Since Pinkhasov had not bothered to install testing equipment to ensure quality control, the samples Wedtech sent out to potential customers tended to be grossly impure. London was afraid to show Sumitomo any samples from the coating lab, because the Japanese, with their passion for getting things just right, would have been appalled.

John had said, according to Mario, that if London could get a $50 million licensing payment from the Japanese, he could count on a $1 million commission for himself. But London found the Japanese more interested in signing an agreement to market jointly whatever coating products Wedtech developed, a deal that would involve no up-front payment at all.

While London was drinking sake with Japanese executives in darkened hotel bars, Mario and John were sitting beneath the stars on the terrace of La Fortaleza, the governor's mansion in Puerto Rico, and nibbling on fried bacalaitos, a local fish delicacy. Puerto Rico was another one of Wedtech's great new frontiers. Back in the spring of 1984, Mario and John had co-opted former Governor Luis Ferré by promising to share some of the pontoon work with subcontractors on the island. That hadn't quite happened, and in fact had left a bad taste in certain circles, but Wedtech, largely in the person of John Mariotta, was eager to work in Puerto Rico. John and Jenny flew down as often as they could to their palatial condo on the beach, and John dreamed of bringing to his new home something of the magic he had brought to the South Bronx. Through their association with Bobby Garcia, John and Mario had met any number of prominent figures on the island. Indeed, cutting a figure in Puerto Rico was a wish Wedtech shared with the congressman.

It wasn't an election year, but Garcia nevertheless had been putting the bite on his friends at Wedtech. In August he had called Mario in Mount Vernon with an air of urgency. He was about to embark on a trip to Spain and to the Middle East, and he needed money right away. Jane had gotten a chunk of money a few months earlier from business she had steered to her friend Ralph Vallone, but that had been quickly spent, and the couple's checking and savings accounts stood at minus $5600. The congressman must have been planning to travel like John Mariotta; he told Mario that he needed $20,000 for a four-week trip.

The request occasioned certain logistical problems. Mario's own checking account was also overdrawn, and the friendly bankers at New York National got upset when Mario's balance went beyond negative $10,000. So Mario had to get Tony to authorize Ceil to make out a check for him on the FHJ account to cover the $20,000 check to Garcia. But Garcia didn't want a check from a Wedtech executive to himself; that might be construed the wrong way. He had Mario make out the check to his sister Aimee Cortese, the occasional preacher in the Wedtech chapel and pastor of the Crossroads Tabernacle Church.

Cortese's church, curiously, was a crossroads in more than one sense. The previous November she had received $10,000 in cash from Richard Dortch, executive vice president of Jim Bakker's evangelical organization, PTL. Cortese, who sat on the board of PTL, was instructed to hand the money on to a former church secretary named Jessica Hahn. In exchange for the cash, Hahn signed a document promising to conceal that Bakker had, in her view, raped her. So many different thoroughfares intersected at the Crossroads Tabernacle Church!

Wedtech was in part responsible for the Garcias' misfortune. The company hadn't made a retainer payment since the beginning of the year. When Wedtech was strapped for cash, which was to say nearly all the time, payments to consultants, and such other nonessential items as employee expenses, tended to be pushed aside. Indispensable people, like Bob Wallach, got their money right away. The implacable, like Mark Bragg, got their money more or less on time. The rest had to wait until Wedtech needed them, or until it raised capital in the market.

But Wedtech needed Representative Garcia. It needed him to use his position on the banking subcommittee to call the lending banks and help raise the ceiling on the revolving credit line. It needed him to use his position on the Postal Services Committee to help win options on the contract, worth $60 million, to build the letter-carrying boxes. And it needed his help on an upcoming contract in Puerto Rico. When the congressman returned from his foreign junket, he suggested to Mario that they meet for lunch at the Post House, an Upper East Side restaurant somewhat more elegant and expensive than Lello's. Mario arrived with a check for $12,300, which represented payment for three of the eight months that Wedtech had fallen behind on the retainer.

The congressman said that he was already working on the bank problem. Jane, he suggested, could use her contacts to help in Puerto Rico. And then he reiterated that they needed money. Like Bob Wallach, Garcia was watching his style of living spiral way beyond his income. He found that he couldn't live on less than a quarter of a million dollars a year. Mario handed him the check and said that the remaining $20,000 would be forthcoming in a few weeks.

Two weeks after the lunch, on September 20, John and Jenny, along with Mario and Conchita, flew down to Puerto Rico. Since the spring, Wedtech had been pursuing a Puerto Rican government contract to build ferry boats for local transportation. The critical moment had come, for the government was about to release its request for proposals. Their Puerto Rican contact, Rafael Capo, had been pressing them to come down to the island to meet with top officials, including Governor Rafael Hernández-Colón. The timing was perfect, since Vice President Bush would also be down to speak to a meeting of the Hispanic Chamber of Commerce, which meant that the Garcias would be present as well.

Capo had been trying for weeks to arrange a meeting with Governor Hernández-Colón, and had gotten nowhere. Of course not, said Jane Garcia; Capo was a nobody. She told Mario and John that if they wanted to meet the governor, she could have it arranged in a day or two. That was on a Sunday or a Monday morning, as Mario recalled. Late Monday afternoon, when Mario and John returned to their hotel, Jane was waiting impatiently for them; the governor, she said, was ready to meet with her husband and them—now. And that was how John and Mario found themselves drinking wine and eating bacalaitos on the rooftop garden of La Fortaleza, surrounded by flowers, gazing at the darkening waters of Condado Bay, and expressing to the governor of Puerto Rico, as waiters passed lightly back and forth, Wedtech's great hopes of working with the commonwealth. It was the way power should be: private, gracious, filled with the courtesy of mutual understanding. It was a beautiful moment.

First John spoke of Wedtech's background, and Representative Garcia prompted him to recall his famous session with the President back in 1982. Then Mario laid out Wedtech's hopes for the ferry contract: coproduction with Puerto Rico, the construction of a new shipyard, and maybe, off in the future, Wedtech working with the commonwealth to bolster the commercial fishing industry. And that wasn't all. When the company started using its coating technology to manufacture silicon chips, why not open up a factory in Puerto Rico? Mario was weaving his dreams, deftly, plausibly. And the governor seemed entranced. After an hour and a half of this goodly conversation, when his visitors got up to leave, Hernández-Colón said, Mario testified, that "he was going to do whatever he could to help us get . . . the ferry boats."

Everyone was tremendously excited at dinner that evening. John simply could not believe that he had just spent a few hours sitting with the governor in his private garden, sipping wine and eating hors d'oeuvres, and he was overwhelmed with gratitude to the Garcias. The gratitude, Jane Garcia made it clear, was fully merited. Wedtech, she said, should fire Capo and use her and Ralph Vallone for their Puerto Rican business. Vallone himself was fascinated by the talk about silicon chips and electronics, and said that he would be eager to visit the company and work out some sort of consulting arrangement.

The following day the Wedtech party went off to St. Thomas in the Virgin Islands, where, apparently by coincidence, they met up with the Garcias and Ralph Vallone at a boutique that specialized in jewelry. All the men at Wedtech bought jewelry for their wives, companions, girlfriends, but no one, with the possible exception of Fred, could keep up with John, who spent tens of thousands of dollars buying trinkets for Jenny. Now, in one of his moods of unrestrained happiness and generosity, he asked Jane, according to Mario, whether there was anything she liked especially, and Jane said yes, that diamond-and-emerald necklace over there looked lovely. The next thing Mario knew, the clerk was telephoning American Express to make sure that John's card could cover the $1900 purchase price.

Later that day, Mario said, Jane came over to thank him for "the gift." He managed to bite his tongue before the words "What gift?" came out, and then asked John what was going on. John explained that he had bought the necklace, not as a personal gift but as a thank-you from the company.

Diamonds may very well be a girl's best friend, but cash is the companion you can't do without. A week after returning to New York Mario received a phone message from Ralph Vallone: "Have not received check." The tank was running practically on empty, but the Garcias' services had to be acknowledged. Mario had a check drawn up for $20,500 and gave it to Vallone when he arrived in New York in early October.

TWENTY-NINE

The Bell Tolls for John

GOLDEN MOMENTS like the weekend in Puerto Rico were becoming rare for John Mariotta. In the isolation of his Mount Vernon office he was sinking deeper and deeper into a funk. Perhaps it had started the previous June, when he was kicked upstairs. John was feeling ever more marginal in his own company. He had always been exceedingly sensitive to the sting of ridicule, of condescension; now he thought that he was being supplanted even by those closest to him. Mario, he had decided, was out to get him. For years Mario and John had been practically inseparable, the Sam and Eric of *The Lord of the Flies* that Jeff Rubin was reminded of. Mario had always stood by John, always been the soothing presence, always patiently endured John's raging fits. And now John turned on his old friend with terrifying fury. "Motherfucker," he would scream in his high-pitched, gasping voice, "you don't do any fucking thing in this company! You're fucking useless!" John would castigate Mario in front of dozens of employees or complete strangers, and Mario would stand before him, wide-eyed, and say nothing.

The fights, not only with Mario but with Fred, became an almost daily feature of life. John was so loud that he could be heard by people who had telephoned. As soon as the screaming began, somebody would call reception and tell them to shut down the phones so that no calls could come in. After a while the receptionist began shutting down the phones without waiting to be told. And the fights were often over the pettiest issues of authority. If a janitor got a raise and John hadn't been asked to sign the payroll form, he would spend hours walking up and down the hall at 595 Gerard, bitterly complaining that they were all trying to push him out. John felt a conspiracy forming around him. His paranoia had metastasized.

He was also becoming even more undependable. In early October, after he had been honored as minority man of the year by a small business organization inside the Commerce Department, John went out for a long lunch with Mario and Ralph Vallone. Vallone made wild talk about taking over as Wedtech's general counsel at $500,000 a year and a huge block of stock. But much more upsetting to Mario was the revelation that John had been talking to Vallone about raising enough capital to allow him to buy out the others, according to the terms of the stock purchase plan. The two-year waiting period would come to an end in January 1986. At that point John was supposed to renege. Now he said that he had changed his mind. Mario saw a desperate struggle looming, as did Tony. Only Fred serenely insisted that his old friend was too honorable a thief to welsh on a deal.

As the management situation became critical, the financial situation grew desperate. The company had reached the limit of its $30 million credit line. After a year and a half of practice, Wedtech was almost breaking even on the pontoons, but nonmanufacturing expenses were out of control. There were hundreds of new employees; there was a marketing staff journeying to the edges of the earth to advance the company's global strategy; there were more consultants than anyone could count; there were the millions being siphoned off through FHJ. The banks refused to extend the credit line unless Wedtech increased its equity capital by offering new shares to the public. On October 18, 1985, the board adopted a resolution to raise $20 million in the market.

One of the conditions of the offering, laid down by the company's banker and board member Paul Hallingby, was that Wedtech pay for an audit for the first three quarters of the year. Hallingby said that he didn't want another dispute to come out of the blue, as had happened with Main Hurdman. The new auditor was Touche Ross, where Tony had worked before joining Main Hurdman. Tony purposely chose the firm's

Long Island office, on the grounds that Wedtech would be a far more important client to a branch office than to the headquarters in Manhattan. He also offered the usual blandishment—a $200,000 contract to study the coating division.

The new auditors knew all about Tony's razzle-dazzle accounting techniques from having gone over Main Hurdman's work papers. Tony explained, however, that the reserve had been completely unnecessary, and apparently the Touche Ross team believed him. He also insisted, as a condition of engagement, that he be permitted to continue pooling unsigned contracts, and this, too, had been accepted. Tony then added into the pontoon revenues another $8.7 million from a contract the company had signed to build causeways for the Army, and $18 million more for options on that contract, which the company had not yet received and never would receive.

The audit, somewhat to Tony's amazement, was completely uneventful. Tony continued the process of underestimating projected costs so as to accelerate revenue recognition, as well as the receipt of progress payments. The books on the pontoon program now looked so good that Touche Ross did not cavil at Tony's projections and even allowed him to dissolve back into profits the $4.7 million reserve he had agreed to the previous spring. This generosity accounted in no small part for Wedtech's 1985 net income of $9.7 million, an increase of over 100 percent from the year before. Both numbers, of course, were completely specious.

As the fall drew on, and the auditors slogged through Wedtech's books, and the bankers and lawyers sat down with Tony and Larry Shorten to put together a registration statement, John seemed to become more unstable. He was turning into the crazy uncle you try to confine to the upstairs bedroom when visitors come by. Sometime in late November or early December, Frank Chinn's friend and former colleague David Meid came up to 595 Gerard with two potential investors for the equity offering, scheduled for January. Tony was giving the presentation when John suddenly burst into the conference room, puffing and blowing like a moose. "Gentlemen," said Tony, "I'd like you to meet John Mariotta, our chairman and CEO." But John wasn't listening. He was brandishing a magazine clutched in his fist. An article had apparently set him off. "I know the future of this company!" John shouted. "The future of Wedtech is garbage!"

"What do you mean?" said Tony, trying to preserve the remnants of corporate sobriety. "We have a very bright future, John."

"You don't understand," said John, glowering at them all. "I'm talking about a billion-dollar industry." And John embarked on a lecture on the garbage business—waste management, gas recovery, methane. Tony and the West Coast investors sat in silence while John rambled on and on about garbage. Finally David Meid gently interrupted, explained who he was, and said that he had wanted to ask John something: "When do you expect to earn your first dollar with the coating process?"

John was under increasing pressure to show some results from the millions of dollars he had poured into Dr. Pinkhasov's super-top-secret experiments. There had been more talk about bringing in outside partners, sharing the technology. John resisted fiercely, and the tension was making matters worse. Now he answered Meid's question by rattling on still more about waste management.

"Mr. Mariotta," Meid finally said, "I don't think you've answered my question. What about that first dollar?"

And John shouted about garbage. Meid tried again to steer him back to the coating process. Finally John stalked out of the room as abruptly as he had entered.

By December the stock purchase plan, which John had threatened to implement, was a serious issue. The problem was not that John was going to buy everyone's stock; by now nobody was taking him seriously, and it was expected that he would keep his end of the bargain. It was instead something that the tax department at Squadron Ellenoff had been worrying about for some while. If the agreement were understood to have constituted an option, then John's failure to make the first monthly payment would have been tantamount to declining to exercise the option, and the contract would have gone out of force. If, on the other hand, the contract were seen as a commitment, which is precisely what Wedtech had insisted to the SBA that it was, then the shares would have actually changed hands—as Wedtech told the SBA they had—and John's default would compel the others to repurchase them. In that case, however, the IRS would insist that the recipients pay capital gains tax on the profit they made from buying the shares at a lower price than they had initially sold them for—several million dollars, in Fred's case.

The Squadron Ellenoff tax lawyers hit on a simple solution to this dilemma: rescission. Withdraw the contract from existence. Of course this would constitute an admission to the SBA that the stock purchase had been a hoax all along, a legal fiction concocted to sustain the illusion that John Mariotta controlled Wedtech. Had John been permitted to default, it might have been claimed that he had proved unable to satisfy the obligations of a legitimate contract. Rescinding the agreement, declaring it "null, void and of no effect whatsoever," as the paragraph composed by the Squadron Ellenoff tax department put it, made it clear that the contract was never intended to be consummated. "It seemed odd to me at the time," says Seth Gelblum, then an associate at Squadron Ellenoff. "I remember thinking, 'Gee, is that what we planned all the time?' It certainly seemed convenient."

The agreement was signed, by the insiders as well as by Richard Biaggi and Bernard Ehrlich, on December 17, 1985. John said that he wanted to have the lawyers explain it to him. John no longer trusted Siskind or Rubin, but he trusted the others even less. The following day he met with the two attorneys. Siskind recalls that he explained the rescission and said, "If you're not going to buy the stock, it would be helpful to the others to sign this agreement." It's highly unlikely that Siskind would have bothered with the fiction that John might buy the shares. John submitted quietly to his fate, though he may have understood that the end game was beginning. When Rubin left John's office with the signed rescission, he walked over to Tony and said that John had announced, "Now they can get rid of me." (Rubin says that he does not recall the comment.)

The explosion came a few days later. Mario's secretary, Deborah Scott, had signed a memo as "administrative assistant" to Deputy Vice Chairman Mario Moreno. John, inexplicably, went crazy. He stormed into Mario's office, shouting, "She is no fucking administrator, she's a secretary! You make her change her title or she goes out of this company." This time Mario lost his composure. He stood up to John and said he would quit if Scotty, as she was called, was fired. "Go ahead," John screamed. "If you have any balls you'll resign right now!"

Mario, for once in high dudgeon, called a meeting in his office, down the hall from John. He told Fred, Larry Shorten, and Tony, who had been summoned from his work on the offering at Squadron Ellenoff, that either he or John would have to go. They pointed out that firing the chairman immediately before a public offering would not be a wise public relations move, but Mario was adamant. Fred agreed; he had had it with John, he said, pounding the table. "Let's go down there and fire that idiot right now," he demanded.

They strode down the hall like the Texas Rangers, marched into John's office, and sat down on one of the gigantic twin couches. Fred still had his dander up. "John," he said firmly, "we've got something to tell you." Then, at the thought of firing his friend and adversary of so many years, Fred, for once in his life, lost his nerve. "Tony," he said, "tell him." And so it was left to Tony, who had never been close to John, to explain that they all wanted him to leave the company. John said nothing; he seemed almost to be in a trance. At last he said, perfectly quietly, "Don't think I'm going to leave without a fight." And out they filed, to their Christmas vacation.

Down at his condo in San Juan, John bitterly nursed his grievances and plotted revenge. He told Rafael Capo that he had to find a way to win back his company. Out on the golf course Capo happened to meet a fellow lawyer, a partner in the corporate department of the giant New York firm Skadden, Arps, Slate, Meagher & Flom. Capo, who felt that John might win a proxy fight, asked the attorney whether he knew anything about proxy statements. One thing led to another, and when he returned from his vacation, John Mariotta found himself sitting in front of a roomful of corporate and litigation attorneys from Skadden Arps, throwing up his arms and choking on his words, and piteously, incoherently, unstoppably, and almost certainly falsely, relating the saga of his rise and fall.

Meanwhile, down in Tampa, where Fred, Mario, and Tony had adjoining condos, John's demise was being plotted. Fred had said on the average of two or three times a day for the last fifteen years that he would like to kill John, more or less the way Elmer Fudd threatened Bugs Bunny. Now, for once, he may have been contemplating the idea seriously. He had been over at Mario's pool bitching about what a lunatic John had become. Fred was getting himself worked up. Finally he swam over to Mario and said, "John is a complete idiot and is going to be causing a lot of problems. I think we should have him eliminated."

Coming from someone other than Fred that might have been an empty threat, but Mario knew that the former terrorist was capable of anything. Mario, on the other hand, was a singularly peaceable man. He told Fred that he would never do such a thing. Fred was completely disgusted by his friend's pacifism. "That's the problem with you people," he snorted. "You're Boy Scouts."

The public offering was looking frail even without any news about turmoil in management. Wedtech was no longer the freshest daisy in the entrepreneurial field. The coating technology, as David Meid had noticed, had yet to earn its first dollar. The 1986 pontoon options remained unsigned. Wedtech's future was thus scarcely assured. Late one night toward the end of December Tony was sitting in Mario's office with Frank Chinn. Earlier that day Tony had received a call from one of the Bear Stearns bankers, Bob Smith, who said that it was far from clear that the market would accept $20 million worth of new stock. Tony told Chinn about the call, and Chinn, who had wanted to replace Bear Stearns with friends of his own, and who held a low opinion of bankerly caution, said, "I told you that you should have let me handle it; I could put the stock away." And "half in jest," says Tony, he responded, "If you can put away two million shares, I'd give you a million dollars."

Jesting with Frank Chinn about moving stock was like jesting with Bob Feller about throwing a baseball through a wall. Chinn went off to get London, returned, and asked whether Tony was serious. Sure, said Tony, who believed that Chinn's efforts could be worth a good deal more than $1 million. Soon after, says Tony, Chinn and London returned the favor. Sitting in Tony's car outside the Plaza Athenée, London said that they had decided to kick back $200,000 of the payment to Tony, half of it in cash. Perhaps they thought Tony might need an inducement to live up to the terms of an expensive and unwritten contract. Another $200,000, they said, would go to Wallach.

By early January 1986, the insiders all knew that John was a goner. He could, if he wanted to, destroy the offering. But in the meantime they had to do what they could to sell stock. Tony and Larry Shorten went off to London to speak with potential foreign investors, and then returned to New York, planning to leave immediately for California. Back in his office for a day, Tony received a call from Frank Casalino, who had been growing nervous as John's termination approached. The month before, when he had met Tony to pick up his $10,000 wad, he had asked whether John was the kind of guy who might spill the beans once he was fired. Don't worry about John, Tony had said to him, with his usual bravado. Now Casalino said he had to talk to all of them. Tony explained that they had other things on their mind. It's urgent, said Casalino. They agreed to get together at the United Airlines lounge at Kennedy Airport immediately before Tony, Fred, and Larry Shorten flew to California.

Casalino arrived with a girlfriend, whom he sent off to the bar when the four Wedtech executives arrived. Fred, according to Mario's recollection, spoke first. "John," he said, "has become impossible. The man is completely irrational, and he's dangerous." Turning to Casalino, who he knew was not a Boy Scout, Fred said, "What are you going to do about it?"

Casalino was clearly appalled at the prospect of John Mariotta, whom he had always considered a nut case, at large in the world. But he was curiously circumspect, perhaps unsure of the loyalty of these men. He asked whether John could be trusted. "Maybe we should stop the payments," Fred suggested, putting in the needle. "No, no," Casalino said, horrified. "Let's not go that far." Maybe, said Casalino, they would have to "take care" of John. Meaning what? asked Tony. Meaning, said Casalino, "we should hit him."

Tony, who felt that his background equipped him to distinguish between real and spurious death threats, took it that Casalino was bluffing. Mario was appalled, and he and Tony said that murder was not in their playbook. Fred grumbled about Boy Scouts, and John's life, had it ever been in peril, was spared.

Mario returned to the Bronx; the others went on to California. It was a true Wedtech road show. While out on the Coast, Fred met one of his girlfriends and decided to make her a member of the team. While the Wedtech executives and the Bear Stearns bankers raced on and off planes and piled into limos, Fred's bimbette, with a miniskirt as her uniform, squeezed in alongside. Her job was to carry the slide projector and smile at the financial analysts.

Frank Chinn, meanwhile, was earning his million. Montgomery Securities, which Chinn had proposed to replace Bear Stearns, asked for 500,000 shares and had to settle for less. David Meid, even after the garbage debacle, signed up for 400,000. Florence Griswald of BA Investments said that she was in for 50,000. And back east, Chinn succeeded, according to Tony, in persuading the Harvard Pension Fund to purchase 180,000 shares. He was very good at what he did.

But everyone was still preoccupied by the problem of John. At a breakfast at the Century Plaza Hotel they told Howard Squadron and Arthur Siskind that John would have to go. It was obviously a dangerous idea, but it had to be done. Toward the end of the week they informed the board members that a special meeting was being called for the following Monday to discuss and vote on the firing of the chairman.

John received notice of the meeting on Friday. That left only the weekend to devise a way out of the dilemma he had gotten himself into. The Skadden Arps people were having a hard time taking him seriously, since they had never met a corporate official, not to mention the chairman of a $100 million company, as ignorant or crude as John Mariotta. They took him for a flake, which among corporate attorneys is a form of being much lower than, say, a snake. Richard Green, the young associate who had been assigned to deal with Mariotta, brandished a copy of the registration statement in his face and said, "Do you know what's in this?"

"No," said John.

"Well, look at it," Green instructed. John looked at the document for a few moments and said haltingly, "I think this is one of those things we did when the company went public." Green explained to John that once he signed a registration statement, he made himself legally responsible for its contents, which seemed to be news to him. He urged John to read the document. Green didn't understand that John could barely read.

Still, John Mariotta was very rich, and it was clear that he would spend all his money to get his company back. Skadden was happy to oblige. Over the weekend Tom Schwartz, a senior litigation partner, drew up a civil complaint based on Mariotta's story. The complaint alleged that the four insiders, along with Chinn, had "concocted" a "scheme" to oust Mariotta from the company "solely to enrich themselves at the expense of Wedtech and its shareholders." As part of the conspiracy, the complaint alleged, John had been hoodwinked into signing the rescission, and it alleged that the upcoming public offering was designed to dilute his ownership of the company.

A civil complaint does not have to be accurate to be effective, at least beyond the confines of the courtroom. Schwartz decided that he would accompany John to the board meeting, flourish the complaint, and, unless there was some satisfaction of his client's claims, telephone an associate standing on the courthouse steps at that very moment and instruct her to file the complaint. The law firm would then obtain an injunction preventing the offering from proceeding. Given Wedtech's extraordinarily unstable cash position, which was obvious from the financial documents they had obtained, the injunction would prove a most efficacious form of blackmail.

The meeting was called for five o'clock, and Schwartz talked to Siskind and Howard Squadron beforehand to let them know what he had in mind. Then the three walked down to the twenty-third-floor conference room, where they were joined by the board, along with Rusty London and John and Jenny Mariotta. Melodramatic threats proved unnecessary, the point having been made beforehand. "Mr. Mariotta," as the minutes put it, "introduced Mr. Siskind, who stated that the purpose of the meeting was to consider a proposal that the board enter into an employment agreement with Mr. Mariotta." The officers had agreed not even to attempt a vote to oust Mariotta. There would be no blood on the floor— not yet. Squadron says that he was pleased to offer John an employment contract, that he had argued against firing him in the first place, and that he personally was not fazed by Schwartz's threat, though some of the board, more excitable than he, may very well have been.

The equity offering was to take place on January 23. The afternoon before, after the market closed, Tony, along with Chinn and London, sat down with Paul Hallingby to price the offering. Hallingby was a large, handsome man often pictured in the society pages, in black tie, with his most recent wife, Mai. He was a managing partner of Bear Stearns, and the ease with which he moved in lofty social circles had helped him attract prominent clients to the firm. His name always seemed to be followed by the words "Donald Trump's banker." Hallingby was a throwback to the days when affability and social grace counted for more than drive and brains. Another investment banker refers to him as a member of the "dumb-old-boy network."

As both banker and board member Hallingby was in an ambiguous position, though one that was certainly common on corporate boards. As soon as the group sat down that afternoon, Tony concluded that Hallingby was putting Bear Stearns's interests in front of Wedtech's. Wedtech had closed at 10 7/8, but Hallingby said that he wanted the sale to go off at 10 1/8. Tony protested that Bear Stearns and Moseley Hallgarten, which occupied second position in the offering, would simply buy the shares at 10 1/8, sell them into the market at 3/4 of a point higher, and pocket the difference. On 1.75 million shares, that would amount to $1.3 million. The banks were already getting an underwriter's discount of sixty-five cents a share. Hallingby protested that he intended no such thing, and said that he needed the lower price to convince reluctant investors.

To prove his point, the banker dialed his head of sales, who in turn hooked Moseley's head of sales into the conversation. Both men argued that the market was too weak to risk a sale at 10 7/8, that only an "artificial pressure" had been keeping it at 10 7/8. Chinn, who had been silent, suddenly interrupted, as Tony recalls. "Artificial pressure?" he said incredulously. "You," he said turning to Hallingby, "have been shorting the stock for three weeks"; that is, selling options into the market. "The only reason you haven't been able to knock down the price of the stock is because I've been buying it all." Hallingby denied the accusation, which, if true, would have constituted a serious violation of his obligations as a director.

The stock sale went off successfully at 10 1/8, and on January 29, as agreed, Tony cut a check on Wedtech's Chemical Bank account for ONE MILLION DOLLARS AND 00/100. It was made out to IFCI, London's company. The money always went to London, who kicked back half to Chinn through various complex schemes, since Chinn sat on the board of directors, and any payments made by a company to one of its directors had to be publicly disclosed.

Chinn and London, in turn, made good on their promise to Tony. Chinn had boasted that he could always pick up a big block of cash at Caesars Palace; casinos provide such a service to high rollers. Some time later—Tony is not sure when—Chinn called Tony from the airport to say that he had the cash. Tony was working late, and asked Chinn to drop the money at his home on Long Island. When Tony arrived home that night he found sitting on his bar that iconic Wedtech article—a brown paper bag filled with money. It was shaped like a brick, and contained ten packs of hundred-dollar bills, with each $2500 interfaced. Tony recognized this as the form in which Caesars Palace wraps its money.

Wallach, too, seems to have gotten his piece of the take. Six days after London received the $1 million check from Wedtech, Wallach sent identical letters to London and Chinn, confirming a retainer agreement by which he would receive $75,000 in exchange for his counsel on "your financial and real estate partnership activities." As the prosecution pointed out at the trial of the three men, this was the same woolly-headed lawyer who had been asking for financial advice from "minds more expert than mine" only a few months earlier.

Wallach ultimately received $194,000 from the two men in 1986, though, given the superior value Wallach placed on his own services, he may have thought of the funds as fully earned, rather than as a kickback from the $1 million payment. At trial, London tried to establish that he had paid the lawyer for his advice on upcoming legislation; his advice, it turned out, had been wrong.

John had threatened, among other things, to withhold his signature from the final registration document, but his employment agreement was concluded the day before the document was published, and he grudgingly affixed his name. The lawyers from Skadden Arps had used their leverage well. Wedtech agreed to retain John as chief executive for one year and as chairman of the board and president of the coating division for three years; to pay him the same $360,000 he had received the year before; to buy him out of the contract in a lump sum should he be fired; and to fire him only for cause. All John had to do was control his temper and swallow his pride. Of course, this was impossible.

Possibly John decided to bring destruction on his own head rather than twiddle his thumbs while Tony and the others ran his company. What he did was to sign Dr. Pinkhasov, his secret sharer in lonely Mount Vernon, to a lavish new contract without informing anyone else in the company. When the others found out, in early February, they went crazy. Tony, Larry Shorten, and Frank Chinn drove up to Mount Vernon, where they met Mario, who now kept an office at the facility. They marched into John's office and told him point-blank that the company wasn't his to run anymore, and that the hundreds of thousands of dollars he had promised

Pinkhasov weren't his to promise. John began raining curses down on them, and told them to get the hell out of his office before he threw them out. It was the last shot John would fire.

At a board meeting on February 7, Tony demanded that the Pinkhasov agreement be nullified, which it was. The meeting was then postponed until the eleventh. At that time Fred presided. "Mr. Neuberger stated that the first order of business was a proposal that Mr. Mariotta be terminated as Chairman of the Board, Chief Executive Officer and President of the Coatings Division of the Corporation. After discussion, upon motion duly made, seconded and adopted by all of the directors present, with the exception of Mr. Mariotta, who opposed the motion," the termination was voted.

Mario, Tony, and Fred each made a little speech thanking John for having brought the company so far. Fred's speech, remarkably enough, was almost moving. "John," he said, "we've done everything we could. We've tried to cooperate, but it hasn't worked. I regret it has to come to this; it's the worst thing I could ever have to do." Richard Cavazos recalls feeling amazed. "I could never have believed anyone could have done it with such style and class," he says. "I thought, 'This can be a real gentleman. It was a shame he never exerted himself.'" As for John Mariotta, he said not another word.

It was the end of the world for John. He was a rich man, with $13 million worth of Wedtech stock and another $500,000 coming in from Wedtech to satisfy the terms of his contract. He tried to organize a factory in Puerto Rico to manufacture gallium arsenide chips in conjunction with Dr. Pinkhasov; he tried to invest his money in various ventures; but his heart wasn't in it, nor was he competent to do anything other than what he had done. After Wedtech, there was nothing. "Like I used to tell Freddy," Mariotta says, "you put yourself before the company. I put the company before myself."

John Mariotta *was* Wedtech, though Wedtech was no longer John Mariotta. He and Jenny had no children; Wedtech was flesh of his flesh. He had created it from nothing, nursed it when it was sick, toiled like a beast to ensure its health. He had failed, and then failed again, and then again, and finally, miraculously, he had made Wedtech an inspiration to the world. President Reagan had said so; the SBA had said so. Lawyers and bankers and accountants—all the people he thought of as "intellectuals" —had done his bidding. He had known power such as he could never have imagined. He had also lied and bribed and cheated and stolen. But in his heart of hearts, John Mariotta never believed that he had done anything wrong. He could never believe that about himself. He was a victim, a sufferer; it was never his fault.

Two years after he was fired, Mariotta could not speak of Wedtech without weeping—an agonized lament mingling rage, shame, confusion, and thwarted pride. "I was a failure," he said piteously. "I failed. I couldn't keep my company. I managed to give employment for twenty years. Like when I tell Jenny when I hear the song 'Argentina, don't cry for me.' I say, 'South Bronx, don't cry for me. Keep your distance. I didn't promise you anything. I'm only trying. I *can't* . . .' " And now Mariotta began to ricochet across the vivid landscape of his imagination. He was like Pancho Villa ousted from his own revolution; or Peter Sellers' Chauncy the gardener, a passive tool mistaken for a crafty genius; or like Walker, the crazed American missionary imperialist in Nicaragua, whom he had seen in a movie the night before; he was like sweet and sour —sweet, because he did his best, sour, because he failed; he was like Evita once again. His mind seemed to reel in a kaleidoscope. And then, his frenzy spent, choking with grief and gall, Mariotta heaved a huge, broken sigh and shuddered to a stop.

PART SIX

PART SIX

The Wheels Come Off

THIRTY

The Juggernaut
with Wheels of Clay

JOHN MARIOTTA vanished from Wedtech as if he had never existed. Mario took over his office at 595 Gerard, with the giant desk and mammoth twin couches, as well as his corner office in Mount Vernon, from which John had once imagined he could watch Richard Bluestine putt. Visitors to the company heard of John as a distant pioneer, a lovable and colorful figure from the founding era. He represented a past that the new Wedtech could not shuck quickly enough. The company had become embarrassed by the South Bronx accent it had once shamelessly exploited.

You could see the new Wedtech on display in the 1985 annual report. Wedtech's annual reports had sketched a history of the company's evolving self-image. In the 1983 edition an ocean of Hispanic faces beamed from the company gates. The 1984 version featured a bar graph piercing the upper border like a geyser. But by the 1985 annual report, which was issued in the spring of 1986, Wedtech was satisfied to present itself to the public in simple, somber navy blue. The only thing missing was a pinstripe. In a section entitled "Coming of Age," the company described itself as a "seasoned defense contractor . . . capable of holding its own in the competitive marketplace." Sailing into "the corporate mainstream," management was "now pursuing major contracts for complete military systems" as well as "configuration management and complete systems." And an unspecified "breakthrough" had finally brought the revolutionary coating technology, of which securities analysts had heard so much for so long, to "the threshold of commercial viability."

The report glossed over Wedtech's long-time minority status with a nonchalance bordering on snobbism. The set-aside program, it was stated, had provided "more a financial vehicle for the Company than a marketing one," a source of grants and loans to underwrite the company's astonishing early period of growth. "The awarding of actual contracts was based," of course, "on Wedtech's record of manufacturing excellence and success in competitive bidding." The set-aside program was a muddy channel far from the corporate mainstream, and at the new Wedtech it was mentioned as little as possible. In a presentation the previous fall to the New York Society of Securities Analysts, Tony had even described 8(a) as a program for "small companies," and had managed never once to mention the word "minority."

All this was, of course, the sheerest vanity and pretense. After ten years in the set-aside program, Wedtech had become, if anything, more dependent on noncompetitive contracts and options. The events of the previous year, when the Army had simply refused to award Wedtech contracts for which it had successfully bid, proved with humiliating clarity its continuing addiction to the opiates of Minority Land.

The truth of the matter was that Wedtech had turned into the sixteen-year-old eighth-grader of the set-aside program, and had finally been expelled when its violation of the membership criteria had become too gross even for the supremely lenient Small Business Administration. Nobody in the New York district office had been fooled by Frank Chinn's or Richard Cavazos' claims of disadvantage. Gus Romain, the local official then in charge of what the SBA calls "ownership control," says that it was perfectly obvious that the company was throwing anyone it could into the breach. But it didn't make any difference. Wedtech's membership was scheduled to expire in October 1986, and the expulsion process was so thoroughly encumbered with appeals and formal hearings that Wedtech could have postponed its ouster until then just by putting up a fight. Romain knew that the company didn't belong in the program, but his feeling, he says, was "Why spin our wheels?"

The acting regional administrator, Aubrey Rogers, could have moved along the process, but fortunately he had seen the wisdom of staying on Wedtech's good side. Rogers, according to Mario, was always available for briefings, and explained that the problem lay with a local official, who had caused a letter questioning Wedtech's continuing membership to be sent out in the middle of 1985. But Rogers also reassured him that the expulsion process could be strung out forever. Rogers was an ally, and Peter Neglia said that he was doing his best to get Rogers appointed as permanent administrator. Neglia was also trying to get a sympathetic hearing for the flimsy arguments being cooked up over at Biaggi & Ehrlich to justify Wedtech's membership in the program.

The SBA, incredibly, hadn't reacted at all either to the public disclosure of the rescission of the stock purchase agreement or to the stock offering, which diluted John's holdings to 27 percent of the company. But when *The Wall Street Journal* reported on February 13 that Mariotta had been fired, the district director finally issued a show-cause letter challenging Wedtech to explain why it should be permitted to remain in the program. Even after the show-cause letter, Wedtech was not exactly given the bum's rush. The company was permitted to withdraw from the program, and it waited until a March 27 board meeting to do so.

Peter Neglia had now done everything he could. Neglia had become sick and tired of playing the undercover agent in the halls of government. Every couple of weeks or so Mario or Bernie Ehrlich would buy the SBA chief of staff lunch or dinner at one of their haunts in New York or Washington, and Neglia would ask when he would be allowed to cash in his chips, as had been agreed a year earlier at the Reagan inaugural. Not yet, they said; Mario even tried to give Neglia an incentive to remain by offering him part ownership of his brother-in-law Reynaldo Berney's construction company, Adequate Power. Neglia, in exchange, would help see to it that Adequate Power, whose majority owners would be Berney and Mario's sister Martha, would be certified as an 8(a) firm.

But when the show-cause letter went out, Neglia finally got the all-clear. Eight days later he left the SBA. Soon after, the Brooklyn boy purchased a $317,000 house in northern Westchester, and his law office became a satellite of Biaggi & Ehrlich. Wedtech came through with the first $25,000 of his salary, but never paid $25,000 more, as had been originally agreed.

It wasn't only Neglia who was cashing in. The previous June, Chinn and London had reached their secret understanding with all four of the insiders to dispose of their shares at the highest possible price, and to pay themselves by taking the difference between $13 and the actual sale price on 10 percent of the stock. The previous fall, the stock had undergone a 3-for-2 split, so the trigger number was reduced to 8 2/3. SEC rules prohibited the insiders from selling their shares for sixty days after the January equity offering. As soon as the period ended, Chinn began unloading their shares in dozens of small transactions so as not to alarm the market.

Between late March and June 1986, the Wedtech insiders, by themselves and through Chinn, sold $8 million worth of stock. (John sold another $3.6 million.) Fred and Mario cashed in to the tune of $3.2 million each, Tony took home $800,000; and Larry Shorten, $700,000. The payment to Chinn and London, however, was in proportion to their overall holdings in Wedtech stock. At the end of April, Fred was presented with a bill for a staggering $553,283. Fred yelled about how he was being ripped off, but he was not a man to renege on a contract. He made out a check to one of London's corporate names, National Consulting Management, Incorporated. Mario forked over $90,000, and Tony and Larry Shorten, $20,000 each.

Everyone had so much money by now, between past stock sales and salary and theft, that the new cascade of cash scarcely made a difference. Fred invested in his myriad little companies and Mario bought a condo in Miami, where he and Conchita began spending all of their free time. In fact, Mario changed his legal residence to Florida. Tony put the proceeds into tax-free municipals—and watched happily as the dream palace at Matinicock rose out of the earth.

While Tony was blithely reassuring investors that the minority stage was well and truly jettisoned, Mario was struggling desperately to prevent the Navy from eliminating the company's only sizable source of income, the pontoon options. Wedtech's opponents in the Navy had exhausted themselves in their futile struggle to separate the company from the options. The battle over the 1986 options had been going on virtually since the 1985 options had been awarded in March of that year. Any further delay, as Wedtech and its congressional supporters were wont to point out, could only be harmful to the program. Admiral Hughes decided to split the 1986 procurement between Wedtech and another, presumably more competent, minority contractor. Captain de Vicq had located an 8(a) contractor in San Diego, Bay City Marine, which looked thoroughly professional to his eye.

Mario had gotten wind of this decision, probably from Robert Saldivar, and, rather than fighting it, had decided to attempt a reprise of the original pontoon award, when Wedtech had accepted the principal of sharing and then used its political power to eliminate the competition. It would be, as Mario testified, "a cat and mouse game." Jim Jenkins, an old San Diego hand, had heard that Bay City was a front for a white-owned company. Perhaps a timely investigation could be launched.

The Navy, however, saved Mario the trouble, or the pleasure. By January 1986, the Navy, throttling back its annual requests for big budget increases as the Reagan defense buildup crested, decided to reduce its pontoon procurements for 1986 and 1987. Splitting the procurement no longer made economic sense, and Admiral Hughes reluctantly accepted Wedtech as sole contractor once again.

The Navy also canned the company's great adversary. For years now, Wedtech and its allies, especially Senator D'Amato, had been calling on the Navy to do something about the recalcitrant Captain de Vicq. D'Amato had called Secretary John Lehman over the summer to complain about the project officer. Wayne Arny and a number of Wedtech allies inside the Navy had also set up an obbligato of grumbling. And in January, de Vicq was abruptly told that he was going to be transferred. It was clear to him that he had paid the price for his obstinacy, and that a long-hoped-for promotion would not be forthcoming. Rather than move along, he retired from the Navy, the only career he had ever had.

De Vicq's removal left only one adversary. Colonel Don Hein of the Defense Contract Administration Service had grown more disgusted as each year brought yet another Wedtech triumph. The company violated every rule, yet always got its way. Hein knew that Wedtech had fallen behind on half the contracts it was performing for the Pentagon, and his opposition had proved a significant factor in Wedtech's failure to win any of its competitive bids during the previous year. And now the Navy was preparing to offer the options once again, despite Wedtech's record of failure. Hein conceded that Wedtech had improved, but he didn't think the company had improved enough. When he learned, in March, that Wedtech had already depleted the $35 million line of credit it had arranged the previous fall, and was short on funds once again, Hein concluded that the Navy was about to make a big mistake, and he began calling for a reconsideration of the decision to grant the option.

It was the same battle Mario had been fighting since the initial assault on the Navy in the fall of 1983. It was a battle that Wedtech kept winning, because in the Navy, unlike the Army, Wedtech had friends in high places. Wayne Arny was a friend, and so was Everett Pyatt. Tony once called Mark Bragg to see how things were going with the pontoon options, and Bragg told him, "I can't talk to you right now. I've got two gin and tonics in one hand and I've got Pyatt standing next to me." Secretary Lehman himself seemed to be a friend.

They all listened very carefully when Senator D'Amato called. Perhaps D'Amato had gotten de Vicq out of the way. Mario had found that he could always call on D'Amato and count on a response, as long as Wedtech was generous when called on. The senator was up for re-election in November, and Fred, Mario, Tony, and the General had each given $2000 to the campaign; along with their wives and companions, other employees and consultants, and colleagues like Pat Simone, Wedtech, according to federal election records, ultimately gave at least $18,500 to D'Amato's re-election campaign. (In testimony Mario put the figure at $30,000.)

In the middle of March, with Hein suddenly kicking up a fuss, Mario and Ehrlich paid a visit to their favorite senator and closeted themselves with D'Amato's aide, Shawn Smeallie. Smeallie's notes from the meeting afford a wonderfully economical outline of Mario's campaign to crush the opposition: "not delinquent—Capt. Kelley will vouch for Wedtech." Captain Tim Kelley was David de Vicq's gratifyingly pliable replacement. "Col. Hein—continues to be critical of Wedtech on no basis." "(Debeck [sic] has been removed.)" "Bush made a call—not known to whom." Whom the Vice President called, or whether he made such a call at all, is still not known. "Les Aspin has written a letter and will make a call." Aspin was the powerful chairman of the House Armed Services Committee. Wedtech had already approached his brother Jim, who had gotten to know Vito Castellano. Jim Aspin persuaded his brother to write the letter, and was later hired by Wedtech.

If it was a war, it was an unequal one. Mario had marshaled influential legislators and leading Navy officials against one Pentagon civilian and his supporters in technical jobs in the Navy. Kelley seems to have appointed himself Wedtech's guardian. Hein recalls Kelley telling him point-blank, "I can't get to my new assignment until this contract is signed." Since Hein had by now come to assume that the entire Navy hierarchy, up to and including Secretary Lehman, had bent to Wedtech's will, he says that he was disgusted rather than surprised by the admission.

Kelley denies having held any such conversation, or being under pressure from his superiors to award Wedtech the contract. In fact, he says, he was looking into other contractors in case Wedtech was denied the options. But he didn't expect this to come to pass. By the spring of 1986, Kelley says, "they were producing acceptable units in accordance with the agreed-upon schedule." Hein, he says, was simply gnawing on the bones of old grievances.

On March 28, Kelley recommended that Wedtech receive the 1986 option, and that the option be awarded by letter contract—precisely the suggestion that had landed Arny in hot water the previous year. Two weeks later Hein checkmated Kelley with a risky move of his own, though the risk was entirely to himself. He wrote to the contracts officer for the pontoon program at NAVFAC, who would have been considering Kelley's proposal. Hein noted acidly that Wedtech had managed to get $87 million worth of pontoon contracts without ever submitting to a pre-award survey; this despite Wedtech's having incurred a loss on the base contract and on both options. Now, he wrote, with Wedtech suffering serious cash flow problems, and being cited for a range of contracting flaws, a pre-award survey was "strongly recommended." The NAVFAC official, who had not responded to Kelley's suggestion, agreed with Hein.

Kelley considered the survey superfluous, and in an April 25 memo to NAVFAC, the project officer predicted that the results "will be positive since they clearly have no basis for any other position." He also mentioned that General Charles St. Arnaud, Colonel Hein's superior and the commanding officer of DCAS, had called to "apologize" for having conducted the survey at all. Back in the middle of March, after his meeting with Mario and Ehrlich, Shawn Smeallie appears to have called St. Arnaud to air Wedtech's complaints.

The survey was completed on April 29. The pre-award monitor concluded that Wedtech had "a tremendous cash flow problem," and recommended against the award. DCAS pointed out that Wedtech could not survive without a new line of credit but that its bankers would not extend credit until Wedtech had received the option. Ten days later Wedtech submitted a new cash flow projection, which DCAS found riddled with misstatements. "They had changed the cash flow statement to make it look like a different company," Hein recalls. "They put down anything that we wanted to see"—just as the company had every time Hein or de Vicq had criticized it since 1984. Wedtech had a negative cash flow, the report concluded, of $4.6 million, not, as the company contended, a positive one of $6.2 million.

At this point Wedtech would have lost the option, and been forced swiftly into bankruptcy, had Kelley not insisted on yet a third survey. "We were getting conflicting information on what their financial picture was," Kelley recalls. DCAS, that is, was saying one thing, and Wedtech was saying another. Kelley wrote to NAVFAC that DCAS essentially could not be trusted: the first two surveys, he said, were "based on a pre-established position." His own view, he wrote, was that Wedtech could complete the options and maintain a positive cash flow even without the new line of credit—a claim that Hein, not to mention Mario and Tony, knew to be patently ridiculous.

Not only, in fact, was Wedtech's cash flow as choked and sluggish as ever, but Tony's cost-of-completion gimmickry had begun to exact a serious toll. By the spring the company had spent all the money allotted to it by the Navy on the 1985 options, though it hadn't yet started delivering the pontoons. Only by winning the 1986 options could the company get paid for the work it was doing now. In the first five months of the year, Wedtech asked for $23 million and received only $16 million. Even this represented every penny the Pentagon auditors could legally provide; the agency was doing everything in its power to cooperate. Hein says that he had been so thoroughly belabored by Ehrlich on the issue of progress payments that he had instructed his staff to pay Wedtech as much and as soon as was possible. Sometimes, in fact, a Wedtech official would telephone DCAS and ask it not to mail the check; someone would come and pick it up in person so that the company could make payroll.

Kelley and Hein were at loggerheads, so Wedtech, as it had so many times in the past, went over the head of its adversary, to General St. Arnaud. Senator D'Amato's office had already been speaking to St. Arnaud. Now Tony wrote an indignant letter. Don Hein claims that retired General James Rosenbloom, the Wedtech consultant, told St. Arnaud that Wedtech had decided to hit Hein with a $10 million suit for his role in obstructing the award of the option contract. Even Captain Kelley went to St. Arnaud to complain of Hein's intransigence—a brazen flouting, in Hein's view, of the military chain of command. Hein is also convinced that Kelley leaked to Wedtech some of the critical comments Hein had made about the company in his memos. No one but Kelley, says Hein, was in a position to know these opinions; Kelley denies that he relayed Hein's criticisms to anyone at Wedtech.

Summoned to his boss's office, Hein was instructed "to keep a low profile" while St. Arnaud himself supervised a third pre-award survey. At this point, as far as Hein was concerned, the fix was in. On May 15, St. Arnaud ordered yet another survey. The following day Wedtech submitted a new sheaf of financial data. This time Wedtech's fictional cash flow was accepted without comment; on May 20, DCAS recommended that Wedtech receive the option, whether or not the new line of credit was forthcoming. The following day the Navy awarded the option. And the day after that Citibank, Chemical Bank, and Irving Trust agreed to extend the new $63 million line of credit.

And now it was Don Hein's turn to pay the price for menacing the dream. Between his harshness toward Wedtech, and his misgivings about several other contractors, including Freedom Industries, Hein says, he had earned himself a reputation as a paranoid. In June, at the age of fifty-one, he took early retirement. "They never ask you to leave," says Hein. "It's more like they say they've lost confidence in you." His next promotion would have been to brigadier general, but, like Captain de Vicq, he knew that he was never going to get it. Hein left the military a bitter, defeated man.

Captain Kelley, on the other hand, did very nicely for himself. Soon after this episode, says Jim Jenkins, who saw Kelley occasionally at a society of former San Diegans, and spoke to him a number of times about Wedtech, Kelley had a job working directly for Secretary Lehman. Jenkins was surprised to see Wedtech's project officer spearheading the secretary's public relations effort to spread naval battalions to ports around the country. Jenkins, a former Navy captain himself, thought it was one helluva promotion.

On May 30 Senator Alfonse D'Amato presided over a press conference at 595 Gerard to announce Wedtech's receipt of the 1986 pontoon options, just as two years earlier he had lavished his hyperbole on the company when it won the original pontoon contract. D'Amato knew very well how much Wedtech's success owed to political pressure, especially his own, but the public and the press, of course, knew nothing of the sort. Nor would many in the audience be likely to have known that at $48 million the options were $20 million less than the figure Tony had booked a year before. No, from the outside the announcement looked like another token of Wedtech's maturity, another proof of its readiness to flourish in the big world.

Wedtech was putting up big numbers, as they say in the sports world. Touche Ross had finally insisted that Tony break his pooling habit, but the auditors hadn't blinked at the record year-end numbers Wedtech was reporting—$117 million in revenues, $9.7 million in profits, a backlog of $48.5 million. The first quarter of 1986 had been even better: revenues rose to a record $33.5 million, and net profits shot up 40 percent from the first quarter of 1985. The banks had fallen into line.

Wedtech's stock had dipped in the wake of John's firing, but portions of the investment community were eager to commit themselves to the future in the distance. In May, the securities firm of L. F. Rothschild, Unterberg, Towbin committed itself to selling $75 million worth of Wedtech subordinated debentures into the market. And on May 29, the Rothschild analyst Maeda Klein made a strong buy recommendation at 9 3/8 per share. Projecting startling profit margins of 30 to 40 percent over the coming two years, Klein praised the company's high-tech, low-cost manufacturing capability; noted that Wedtech's competitors had begun approaching the company for joint ventures; singled out the development work on rotary engines as a source of major potential sales, especially to the armies of China and Israel; and argued that the company's policy toward its coating technology had become more realistic. She discounted the risks of Wedtech's graduation from the 8(a) program, as well as of its rather perilously unbalanced books. "For a small company," she wrote, in what now reads like the understatement of the decade, "WDT appears to have rather strong political ties . . ."

But the wonderful thing was that, even now, with Tony running the finances as if he were aiming for the cover of *Fortune,* and John Mariotta and Minority Land receding into the dim distance, Wedtech still had the power to captivate. The company was never, even at this late date, a mere matrix of numbers. It was a collage of compelling images, a miracle of enterprise, a dream—and the dream continued to win new believers.

In April, Carlos Galvis, an émigré, like Mario, from Colombia, a witty and passionate talker with a résumé that testified to his restlessness—congressional staffer, State Department officer, founder of an investment advisory firm geared to the public interest—learned of Wedtech from his friend Jim Aspin. At a dinner with Mario, Jim Aspin, Bernie Ehrlich, and Vito Castellano at the Regent Hotel in Washington, Galvis was floored by the nonchalance with which the names of Wedtech's friends were being batted around. It was Lyn this, and Ed that, and all as if the group were hashing over yesterday's cocktail party. There was talk of taking the company private, of a leveraged buyout . . . Galvis was intrigued; he took The Tour.

The Tour, by now refined for potential investors, started off at the coating division. It was just a little ludicrous. Dr. Pinkhasov, apparently to accommodate previous tourists, had installed signs everywhere, which Galvis recalls identified things like "bunsen burner." But there were men in white coats, and samples everywhere, and an air of impending miracles. "My little guys in the South Bronx are doing this?" Galvis recalls thinking. "I mean, I see business all over the place. These guys just need a little guidance and we're going to make them AT&T."

Next, Moreno brought his wonder-struck guest to the factory to watch the engines and the M-113 kits being assembled. "I got there at lunchtime," Galvis recalls, "and the wives brought lunch to the workers. And it blew my mind, because I hadn't seen that since I left South America. I left there an absolute Wedtechie. I mean, these guys deserve medals. They deserve sainthood. I can't explain the feeling you have when you walk through a plant like that. I was blown away. You became a firm, solid, no-nonsense believer in these guys."

Galvis began to dream up possibilities for his new cause. He spoke to a friend at Manufacturers Hanover about the restructuring he foresaw for Wedtech. He talked to one of his clients, the FMC Corporation, which happened to be the Army's prime contractor on the M-113. Rather than spread its subcontracting work around, Galvis suggested, the company should designate Wedtech its sole subcontractor. He proposed to the New York City Financial Services Corporation the ingenious notion that Wedtech supply parts for the city's new Kawasaki subway cars.

The company that Galvis saw was, in fact, expanding in all directions simultaneously, like the universe. "Another component of our strategy for the future," as the annual report explained, "is diversification." Gone were the days when Wedtech lived or died on the nods of a few men in the SBA and the Pentagon. Rusty London was going back and forth to Japan in the hope of concluding an agreement for Wedtech and Sumitomo to license their respective coating processes to each other. The company was manufacturing electric generators through a subsidiary, Euclid Equipment, Incorporated, which it had purchased the previous December. It was scouting new markets for the Wankel rotary engine. There were talks, talks, talks for deals that were glimmering on the verge of realization.

On the home front, Wedtech had established an office in Washington, just like one of the big contractors, and installed its friend and former White House official Jim Jenkins as chief lobbyist, at $150,000 a year. Once a week Jenkins would meet with Mario and Larry Shorten and some of the middle management to talk about strategy. Jenkins was a believer, too; he had bought $10,000 worth of stock as soon as he began consulting for Wedtech the previous summer.

Like everyone else, Jenkins believed that the coating process was going to make him a millionaire, and he dreamed up military uses for it. He spoke to the Army about coating the barrel of the M1 tank, which had to be replaced after firing only eighty rounds, with tungsten. He talked about coating the uniforms of tank crews with a fireproof material. He talked to the Secret Service about coating currency with a conductive metal, thus making counterfeiting practically impossible. When Wedtech hired him, Jenkins had been trying, and failing, to put together deals with the Chinese government, and in March he signed an agreement with the Northern Industrial Company of China to manufacture the rotary engines for which Wedtech was patent holder and to sell them in the Eastern European market.

. . . .

Wedtech had always looked completely different to insiders than to outsiders. Now, however, the grandiosity of the public image had the effect of heightening the contrast. A new cadre of middle managers arrived in the Bronx in 1985 and 1986, expecting to find a humming little machine of defense contracting, and instead found themselves enmeshed in chaos. "It was the strangest operation in this world that I have ever seen," says Nick Weil, an Austrian immigrant who had come to Wedtech from Ingersoll-Rand in May 1986 to serve as vice president for engine technology. No one seemed to know just what Weil was supposed to do, or even where his office was to be. He soon realized that no one at Wedtech had ever held a position of responsibility in a large corporation or had any notion of how $100 million companies are run.

"One of my earliest questions," Weil recalls, "was 'Is there a short-term plan in existence?' And the answer was no. 'How about an operations plan for this year?' And again, the answer was no. These were questions I had never even thought to ask before. Wedtech was a seat-of-the-pants operation. Wherever you looked, it was catch-as-catch-can. The subjective impression you would have was one of bustle and activity and progress and motion"—all to no particular effect. The four principal executives seemed to be constantly traveling, or in any case unavailable. Weil had the sense that they shared a vanity of inaccessibility. In fact, Tom Mullan, whom John had hired to run engine production back in 1982, remembers receiving a memo from Tony to the effect that no one was welcome in his office without an appointment. On the bottom was a postscript from Larry Shorten: that went for him, too.

Another member of Wedtech's new class of managers, arriving in June, found that the company seemed to run by accident. "I think," he says, "it was one of these management cases where rather than the principal guys get together and work things out, it was like they were afraid to address them." He was amazed to discover that the people who ran the company sat down with one another, and with their top managers, only once a month or so, in the panoplied conference room next to Fred's office at 149th Street plant, and that even then scarcely anything was accomplished. When he tried to convene biweekly meetings of his own, he found that none of the top people from the company would come. On the other hand, he was free to do practically anything he pleased.

What he didn't know, of course, was that information could not be shared because so much of what really mattered had to be hidden from view. The numbers were lies, and the plans were dreams. Wedtech may inadvertently have furnished proof that no sizable company can thrive for long in a state of fraud, because a successful enterprise, unlike a successful dictatorship, depends on a free flow of information.

THIRTY-ONE
THIRTY-ONE

Comes the Hunter

MARY SHANNON was wondering what exactly she was going to be doing with her immediate future when two federal agents appeared in her office in early April 1986. The year before, when she was transferred to the public corruption unit of the U.S. Attorney's office in the Southern District of Manhattan, Shannon had had the unbelievable good fortune to be flung into the middle of the office's investigation of corruption in New York City government. It was the sort of gorgeously foul swamp that prosecutors live for. The party leaders in Brooklyn, Queens, and the Bronx were implicated in bribery and influence peddling, as were several of the principal agencies of the city. There was fraud stretching all the way to the horizon, and Shannon had been assigned to focus on Donald Manes, Queens borough and party leader and in many ways the heart of the investigation. A grand jury was hearing charges, and the newspapers were filled with lurid tales of secret meetings and cash drop-offs. Manes was steadfastly denying everything, though his behavior had grown increasingly bizarre. And then on March 13, while speaking to his psychiatrist on the telephone, Donald Manes stabbed himself in the heart. Suddenly Mary Shannon didn't have anything to do.

Shannon was a wiry thirty-two-year-old, dogged rather than brilliant, humorous in private though in public the very image of prosecutorial relentlessness. She was one of the hard-boiled Catholic working-class-type lawyers who lived on at the U.S. Attorney's office as if in memorial to an earlier time, before gentrification. She was a highly competent lawyer —and she was a great investigator. When Mike Raggi, of the Pentagon's Defense Criminal Investigative Service, and Steve Cossu, of the U.S. Labor Department, came to the U.S. Attorney's office with a fragmentary story to tell, it was to Mary Shannon, currently searching for something to dig her molars into, that they were directed.

What Shannon heard that first day was not likely to make her forget the Donald Manes era. The two men, independently of one another, had developed some circumstantial evidence of wrongdoing on the part of a company called Wedtech. All that Steve Cossu had to go on, in fact, were the educated suspicions of a career investigator. He had first heard the name Wedtech in January or February from an informant, who mentioned that the company was among the clients of Biaggi & Ehrlich, a firm that came within his purview in connection with the unions to which it provided prepaid legal services. Wedtech had settled into the lower reaches of Cossu's formidable memory banks until he read in *The Wall Street Journal* that the company had fired its chairman, John Mariotta. This made Cossu, a short, round-faced, soft-spoken man of formidable analytic skills, curious enough to look further. He went down to the SEC and started plowing through Wedtech's public filings. "The great thing about a prospectus," says Cossu, "is that before you go public everything has to be aired—all the dirt, whatever." It's instructive that Cossu did not "go to his sources" or skulk around with his fedora pulled down over his brow. He sat down and read public documents.

After fifteen years of working as a detective for New York's Waterfront Commission, Cossu had learned that you have to follow the paper trail if you want to get to the heart of the matter. He had also developed a preternatural sensitivity to the presence on the public record of dirt. Initially it was just the thickness of the pile of microfiche documents that gave him pause. Why so many filings for a small company that had gone public only two and a half years earlier?

The next thing that struck Cossu, alone, apparently, among the dozens or perhaps hundreds of investors, analysts, bankers, lawyers, and accountants who had had reason to scrutinize these documents, was a troubling pair of numbers. In papers filed for its June 1984 bond offering, Wedtech stated that it expected to spend up to $3.8 million to renovate its facility at 149th Street. But in the prospectus for the January 1986 stock offering, Cossu read that the plant had been made operational after an expenditure of $10 million. The sum struck Cossu as crazy, not to mention wildly at variance with the original projection.

But Cossu wasn't finished with his *analyse du texte.* The next thing he noticed was the nimble back somersault of the rescission of the stock purchase, after Wedtech's two years of claiming to be a minority-run company. "I didn't like the way it played," says Cossu, though in this case he was not alone. "I was reading this at a time when Mariotta had just left the company, and I said, 'Gee, this was a convenient transfer.' " Finally, he found that after three years of paying Biaggi & Ehrlich legal fees of $30,000 to $50,000 per annum, Wedtech had presented Bernard Ehrlich and Richard Biaggi with a staggering gift of $5 million worth of stock— this at a time when Squadron Ellenoff had become the corporate counsel. This sounded a lot more like Mario Biaggi's political influence than Bernie Ehrlich's professional acumen, which Cossu knew to be fairly dim. It was all vague and circumstantial, of course, but to Cossu there was something uncanny in the accumulation of telltale signs. "It was a little scary," he says. "I began to think, if nobody else has seen this, maybe I'm just crazy."

But when Cossu went to the Defense Department to offer his findings about one of its contractors, he found that he was not quite alone: a Pentagon investigator, Mike Raggi, had been looking into allegations that Wedtech had bribed a military official. Cossu met with Raggi, then went home and forgot about Wedtech. A few weeks later he got a call asking him to repeat what he had learned to Benito Romano, then head of the criminal division in Rudolph Giuliani's office. In early March, Cossu and Raggi spoke to Romano about Wedtech. Then Donald Manes killed himself, and the two agents were handed over to Mary Shannon.

It wasn't an especially promising set of facts from a prosecutor's point of view. Cossu had a gut instinct, and Raggi had heard a story. It looked like the kind of case where you wade through hundreds of cubic yards of documents and wind up with some technical-sounding violations. For the next several months Shannon chose not to alert the company to the government's suspicions by issuing subpoenas. Instead, Cossu began haunting the local office of the DCAS, where he quickly found "a certain amount of resentment about Ehrlich walking around in his uniform." Now DCAS officials, terrified that they would be implicated in Ehrlich's political bulldozing, began to volunteer information to Cossu.

But Mary Shannon was not the only prosecutor investigating Wedtech. Down in Baltimore the U.S. Attorney had gotten wind of the company's dalliance with the Mitchell brothers and, unbeknown to Shannon, had impaneled a grand jury and was preparing to send out subpoenas. And in the Bronx the District Attorney's office was looking into Wedtech as well. Phil Foglia, deputy chief of investigations and head of the public corruption unit for the Bronx DA, had happened on the company through an entirely different route. Like Shannon, Foglia had been wading hip-deep in tales of municipal corruption; as it turned out, 1986 would be the year that the shadow empire of theft beneath the surface of New York City politics finally collapsed.

Since early 1985 Foglia and others in his office had been investigating Stanley Friedman and the entire Bronx Democratic Party organization. When he subpoenaed the records of the borough president's office, the Bronx Democratic Party, and Stanley Simon's political club, the Riverdale Democratic Club, Foglia found, among other things, Wedtech's large contributions to Simon. Foglia was already working with Giuliani's office on a joint investigation, and when he mentioned to Mary Shannon that he was looking into this little company, she practically fell over backward.

It was clear that the two jurisdictions were working different ends of the same beast, though what was between the ends, neither knew. Foglia still assumed that Wedtech was a little insect on the behemoth of Bronx Democratic politics. The two offices agreed to divide up the investigation. Shannon and her agents took Biaggi and his firm and the defense-contracting fraud, including the progress payment fraud, of which they had learned. The Bronx DA focused on Stanley Simon, the leasing of 1 Loop Drive, John Tartaglia, and Pat Simone. As a former assistant DA, Tartaglia still had friends among the clerks and attorneys at the office, and rumors began to fly that Tartaglia was trying to arrange the theft of documents. Foglia removed the growing body of records from the safe in his office and placed them in a room that he had converted into a vault. The door had a series of locks, to which no one save the attorneys working on the case were given keys. The room, inevitably, was decorated with pictures of Stanley Friedman and Stanley Simon, used as dartboards.

It was the middle of June 1986, and Tony was sitting in the Squadron Ellenoff conference room with the lawyers and the bankers from Bear Stearns, preparing for a $75 million bond offering scheduled for the summer. Wedtech had initially agreed to have the firm of L. F. Rothschild underwrite the offering, and Rothschild had sent in bankers for the due diligence. When they were ready to start working on a prospectus, Tony had told Paul Hallingby about the arrangement, and Hallingby, says Tony, had hit the roof. Who was Wedtech's banker? Who had stood by the company through thick and thin? Tony was not too impressed by this line, and he pointed out that Rothschild was ready to go. So are we, Hallingby had said; Bear Stearns will furnish you with a commitment letter for $75 million immediately. It was wonderful to be fought over; Tony yielded, and it was Bear Stearns that, to its eternal regret, won the right to underwrite the bond offering.

A due diligence meeting was in progress that day in June when one of the bankers, Bob Smith, looked up from a set of documents and said, "What's this?" Smith had noticed a very large discrepancy. The figure for shareholders' equity, which represented the dollar value of stock sold, was greater by $1.14 million than the figure for additional paid-in capital, which represented the proceeds of the sale. Smith asked whether anyone could explain the difference. Tony said nothing, then quietly asked Jeffrey Rubin to follow him out of the room.

Tony now told Rubin for the first time of the payment to Rusty London, which, as an expense related to the offering, he had deducted from the paid-in capital. It wasn't an illegal payment, but it was one he scarcely wanted to explain to the board. First, it was a huge amount to have paid to someone other than the company banker; next, the check had been made out to London, though Tony knew very well that London had split the sum with Chinn. He had mentioned the payment to no one, and he had buried it as a debit to paid-in capital. The auditors had seen the debit and had passed on the numbers without comment. Tony simply took it for granted that nobody else would notice the discrepancy; he was wrong. He also did not know that the payment exceeded guidelines set by the National Association of Securities Dealers for the permissible ratio of expenses to actual proceeds in an offering. Chinn hadn't told him, because Chinn didn't know either. Tony called up Chinn and said, "I'm going to wring your neck, you stupid *schmuck.*" But it was too late for the wringing of necks or hands.

Rubin was flabbergasted, and ordered Tony to go back inside and tell the others. Tony went back and said that he had paid London $1 million, and had promised $140,000 in expenses, for work on the offering. Tony had concealed the payment, he had violated the NASD rules, and, above all, it sounded as if he was lying. It was Bear Stearns, after all, that had underwritten the offering; London wasn't even a broker. Now it was Bob Smith's turn to be flabbergasted.

It was a critical moment, since the initial offering documents were already at the printer. The London payment might be deemed to invalidate the January offering, which in theory could require the company to return the $20 million. Worse still, Mario had received a subpoena from the U.S. Attorney in Baltimore, asking for documents related to the company's former 8(a) status. Nobody took that as a serious threat, but it was clearly something to be hidden from the public, certainly until the offering was completed.

A board meeting had been scheduled by coincidence for June 20, two days after the fateful discovery; in the meanwhile Squadron Ellenoff decided to hold up the offering documents at the printer. Tony, who was trying to sustain the pretense that the money had gone only to London, called London in Honolulu and told him to send a letter confirming that that was the case. At the meeting Tony repeated to Hallingby, who was connected by phone—he, too, was in Hawaii—the story that the company had paid London for his work on the offering.

Practically everything that happened from this point is uncertain. Rubin says that he had instructed Tony to call Hallingby before the board meeting. From Hallingby's responses in the course of the meeting, Rubin says that it was clear to him that Tony had not made the call. It was, he says, the first time he felt that Tony had lied to him. Tony insists that it would have been pointless for him to call Hallingby, since Bob Smith had leaped for the phone the moment Tony had revealed the secret payment.

Hallingby flew in from Hawaii, and he and the lawyers from Shearman & Sterling and from Squadron Ellenoff began questioning Tony and the other Wedtech principals in an almost courtroomlike setting. Tony says that he maintained, as he had throughout, that the money had been paid to London alone for work on the equity offering. Both London's original invoice from January and his June 20 letter supported the assertion. Then, in the course of his interview, says Tony, he was asked whether he knew of any other monetary promises made to London. Actually, he said, he did recall a time when John Mariotta had said that he would give London $1 million if he could get a big contract from Sumitomo. "It was like I dropped the bomb," says Tony. " 'You promised London a million dollars?' " No, Tony recalls saying, it wasn't a promise, and the $1 million payment had nothing to do with the coatings. But the lawyers seized on this new story.

Not true, says Squadron; Tony had attributed the payment to John Mariotta from the beginning and never changed his story. And when the ad hoc committee called in the others, they, too, attributed the payment to a promise made by John about the coating technology. It had been late

1985, they said, when John was at the peak of his craziness. It was a promise, and now they had no choice but to honor it. Tony says they decided to tell this story because the lawyers and bankers clearly wanted to hear it.

Certainly it was an answer that was in everyone's interest. If the payment had not been made in connection with the offering, then there was nothing wrong with its nondisclosure, though it would have to be treated differently for tax purposes. And a promise made by John could not readily be verified or falsified. Jeff Rubin says he telephoned John's home in Scarsdale and spoke with Jenny, but John never called back. Neither Rubin nor anyone else made the forty-five-minute drive out to John's house. Given the effort that went into the interrogation process, Wedtech's lawyers do not seem to have made much of an effort to confirm the truth of the story with its alleged source.

At a July 1 meeting of the board, the ad hoc committee reported that, according to what it had been told, the $1 million payment arose from a commitment made by John Mariotta, and none of the money had been shared with any other officer of the company. London was asked to sign a new consulting agreement to replace the agreement he had signed in 1985, and to rewrite his June 20 letter to make clear that not only had he not shared the money with anyone else, but he would not do so in future. London complied. In a letter written that same day he added that no other employee or officer "will receive" the funds. The board asked him to ascribe the payment to his overall consulting relationship in 1986 and 1987, which he did. London reiterated that he had been paid for financial services; his letter did not mention the coating technology. But on the following day he sent an addendum, explaining that his work on the January offering had been limited to attendance at the road show and discussions with potential investors, and that his consulting agreement specifically stipulated work on the coating process.

The new consulting agreement was another polite fiction. During this entire period London had been asked whether he would make the payment seem slightly less outrageous by agreeing to return $240,000 or some other fraction of the total. He flatly refused. He had not, in fact, yet received the $140,000 in expense money, and he said that he would not sign any new agreement until he was paid. He would, on the other hand, allow Wedtech to treat retroactively the payment any way it wished. The new agreement that London signed thus described the $1.14 million as prepayment for a three-year agreement, running from 1986 through 1988, rather than as the two-year payment London had been asked to reference in his letter. It was, of course, neither.

Tony completed the process by admitting, if that was the word, that he had mistakenly classified the $1.14 million as a debit against additional paid-in capital rather than as an expense of doing business. Presumably he had thus committed accounting fraud, though nothing was disclosed to the SEC. On July 11 the board agreed to file an amended quarterly statement with the SEC in which $100,000 of the total was described as a cost related to the offering, and the rest as an expense. It was finally treated as a one-year payment instead of a two- or three-year payment.

The crucial question is not necessarily whether Wedtech's lawyers believed these claims to be true. "I took it all with a grain of salt," says Howard Squadron. He was not sure, he says, exactly why the payment had been made. London's insistence that he had not shared the money with Chinn, Squadron concedes, "strained credulity." It was assumed that the two shared everything. In early May, in fact, London had written out checks to Chinn worth $770,000, most of them formally ascribed to financial advice, research, or work on real estate deals. In fact, the figure represented slightly less than half the combined total of the $1 million payment and the checks from the secret deal over the sale of the principals' stock.

The law firm, says Squadron, made a good-faith effort to learn the truth. He had asked London to furnish his bank records to prove that he hadn't shared the proceeds, but London had refused. They had interviewed whatever principals in the transaction they could, and come up with a uniform answer. The one remaining participant who might have shed light on the situation refused to cooperate. Of course, says Squadron, he had his doubts, but "personal doubts are irrelevant." Besides which, he adds, the bank's lawyers, Shearman & Sterling, also signed off on it.

The question, perhaps, is whether Wedtech's highly professional retainers engaged in a diligent search for the truth or a diligent effort to refine the truth into a form that was both plausible and satisfactory, as they apparently had so many times before. Tony believes that they simply manufactured the truth from a casual comment of his. It was, as always, a cloudy situation. The facts were a muddle. It was just as hard to understand why John would have agreed to pay London $1 million for work that never produced a nickel as it was to fathom why Tony would have paid that sum for work on the offering. London and Chinn, or London himself, didn't seem to have done anything worth $1 million.

It was clear, however, that when the payment was first exposed, both Tony and Rusty London had ascribed it to the public offering. It was clear that that would be a ruinous story. It was clear that the peril would be lifted if the payment could be attributed to London's work on the coating technology. And that was what happened. The outcome was, to say the least, fortuitous.

On July 15, after a delay of only three weeks, Wedtech issued its initial prospectus. The document contained one tiny but glaring admission. Though quarterly revenues had leaped upward to $38,686,000, a 40 percent increase over the year before, backlog was down to $16.7 million. A company preparing to issue $75 million worth of bonds with a grand total of $17 million worth of assured work in front of it is a company with a huge shelf of debt cantilevered over a flimsy support of revenue. That, of course, is just what Wedtech was. In years past Tony had shored up the revenue support by pooling in his mystery contracts. Now, however, he had agreed with Touche Ross to stop pooling. Tony says that Bob Smith of Bear Stearns was pressuring him to come up with some kind of letter from the military approving a big contract award, as the company had in the past.

But now that Wedtech had been uncoupled from the great set-aside mother ship, there were no more contracts to be had. Tony says that his instinct was to string the bankers along with promises. And then, with Tony off on the road show, Larry Shorten said, in the great tradition of the Andy Hardy movies, "I got an idea." Shorten told Tony about what may or may not be a crafty old trick. "Do you know," he said, "that we can send a telex to ourselves?" All you have to do, Shorten explained, was keep the telex instead of sending it. Shorten went over to the DCAS office, found a copy of a telex from the Davisville office, copied the format and the codes, and fabricated a confirmation of a nonexistent $30 million supplementary contract for pontoons.

Tony returned to New York with Bob Smith and went immediately to a luncheon for potential investors. "It was before people started showing up. Smith and I were setting up the projector and things like that. Larry comes running in, saying, 'I got it! I got it!' waving the envelope. I couldn't believe it. And Smith at the lunch says, 'I've got a great announcement. The company's just been awarded *$30 million.*' I said, 'Oh, my God.' I was waiting for the Navy to jump on that one."

Tony says that the telex was designed solely to mollify the bankers, and was to be filed away and forgotten. But after Smith told the world, there could be no backing down. Tony included the $30 million in the backlog —at Smith's urging, he says—and the auditors permitted it. The telex purported only to be a statement of intent, so Tony had, in effect, gone back to pooling, but with his auditor's consent. The Navy never said anything; no one ever said anything. It was amazing what you could get away with.

Later in the month another subpoena arrived, this one from the U.S. Attorney in New York. That office seemed to want to know about the progress payments. This time Mario didn't ignore it. He called Wallach, who found Wedtech a top lawyer in Washington and another in New York. But nobody was concerned; the inquiries seemed niggling ones. Certainly the public knew nothing, and on August 22 Bear Stearns sold $75 million worth of 14 percent senior subordinated debentures into the market.

THIRTY-TWO

The Death Spiral

A PUBLIC OFFERING, for Wedtech, was somewhat like a triple bypass for a critical heart patient. Immediately before the operation the patient looks chalky and grim; a few weeks later, the ticker will be pumping like new. And then the blood flow may start thinning once again, and the patient will decline, and there's nothing for it but the knife.

September 1986 looked like a new morning at 595 Gerard. There were so many reasons to believe. Everything was just about to happen, to turn that corner which had been seen in the distance—the M-113 foreign sales, the Wankel engine, and above all the coating division. Mario, for one, had contracted a severe case of coating fever. He believed, mistakenly, that Pinkhasov had made the process consistent enough for commercial application, and he was excited by the interest of such big high-tech firms as Texas Instruments and Monsanto. Mario saw fifteen or twenty contracts, worth tens or even hundreds of millions of dollars, looming in the next few months. All through the spring the research department had toiled over a proposal for a $1 million grant from the

Department of Energy to coat portions of diesel and turbine engines in order to reduce stress fractures. Now Martin Marietta, which was operating the research facility for the government, paid a visit to Mount Vernon and left everyone in a state of nervous anticipation. In October the big aerospace contractor would announce that Wedtech had been chosen over forty-five applicants; it was the first time the magic coating technology would earn the company any money.

Like Tony and Larry Shorten, Mario had let Chinn sell all of his shares the previous spring, but he still had 300,000 unexercised options, and now he demonstrated his faith in the future by buying more. Through their secret understanding of the previous August, Chinn and London owned 60,000 of Mario's options. (With the 3-for-2 split their share had risen from its original 40,000.) At a lunch or dinner in early September at La Côte Basque, Mario had pulled Tony aside, along with London and Chinn, and said that he wanted to repurchase the options. London and Chinn detached themselves for their own huddle, and then Chinn announced that they would sell for $2.00 an option, which was a modest premium on the company's future.

There followed one of those scenes of mutual deceit and distrust which occasionally give the Wedtech story the flavor of an Aesop fable. At the board meeting the previous August, London had tried to induce Mario to sign a document formalizing the kickback, which Mario was understandably loath to do. At last, he had relented. Now, on September 8, when Mario handed London a check for $120,000, he asked to have the agreement back. Chinn reached into his briefcase and pulled out a copy of the document. No, said Mario, I want the original. Sorry, Chinn answered, we lost it. Tony, ever canny, had had the good sense neither to sign a contract nor to pay with a check. He simply returned to Chinn the $100,000 brick Chinn had dropped off in Jericho for Tony's kickback, and added an envelope with $20,000 in cash.

The critical problem, as always, was not the long term but the here-and-now. Pontoon production was smooth and efficient; all obstacles had been removed; millions of dollars' worth of pontoons remained to be made. But Tony had already grabbed the profit. Only $11 million worth of prospective pontoon revenue remained in the backlog. Wedtech was never going to coat anything with anything if Mario couldn't deal with the 1987 options. Unfortunately, when the Navy had decided in early 1986 to scale back, the 1987 options had been reduced to a miserable $32 million. This was a completely new problem for Mario: he had to make his way inside the legislative process and get the appropriation jacked up.

The previous November Mario had had the thrilling experience of accompanying General Ehrlich, Vito Castellano, and Representative Addabbo's chief aide, Richard Seelmayer, to the offices of the House Armed Services Committee. For Mario it was like penetrating to the inner sanctum. Here, he was told, is where the bills get drawn up; here is where the decisions get made in private before emerging onto the floor of Congress. Lobbyists who understood the system intervened at the committee level, and left no fingerprints.

Seelmayer introduced Mario to a professional staff member of the committee, Bruce Meredith. At lunch Mario explained that $32 million wouldn't be enough for Wedtech to keep its assembly line running. Meredith, says Mario, said that he would write language into the Navy's budget legislation increasing the figure. When the bill was reported out of committee, the Navy was directed to find an additional $48 million "to maintain the industrial base for production of" the pontoons—to keep Wedtech prosperous, that is. The chairman of the Armed Services Committee was Les Aspin, who had helped Wedtech with the 1986 options and whose brother Jim the company later hired.

The Senate, however, hadn't moved. By now Mario no longer had the time to do the gold digging himself, and he had a Washington office to do it for him. Jim Jenkins had hired a new consultant, John Campbell, and it was he and Campbell who worked their way through the Senate committee staffers. In early August they sat down with Shawn Smeallie, the aide to Wedtech's chief Capitol Hill subsidiary, Alfonse D'Amato, to get the process moving. The always obliging senator wrote a letter to Senator Ted Stevens of Alaska, chairman of the defense subcomittee of the appropriations committee, asking for the additional $48 million; draft language for the legislation was included. The act that emerged from a House-Senate conference in mid-October included the increased appropriation.

Tony, like Mario, was a believer, but he was scarcely swept away. It is the mark of a great liar, as opposed to a delusional figure like Bob Wallach or John Mariotta, that the one person he will not con is himself. Tony lived by the numbers, and he could read the downward trajectory plotted by those numbers with perfect clarity. "The balloon," he says in his metaphor, "was bursting." Or, to use John's metaphor, the rubber band was about to snap. Tony knew that he had to extricate the company from the consequences of three years of accounting fraud. His first instinct was to change the accounting format, much the way the government changes the way it counts unemployment when the figure gets too high. It was audacious; but, then, audacity was becoming one of Tony's major traits.

Tony proposed a shift from the cost-of-completion format to the more conventional shipped-and-billed format, whereby a firm books revenue only when an article goes out the door. In order to accomplish this switch, and thus bury years of deceit and misrepresentation, Wedtech would have to write off the entire discrepancy, of perhaps $100 million, between the profits the company had booked and the work it had actually accomplished. That would wreak havoc with the numbers, but it was a price worth paying. "I would have been slapped on the wrist by Wall Street," says Tony, "the stock would have tumbled, and then hopefully Mario was coming in with the Texas Instruments and Monsanto licensing agreements, the stock would have went back up, and we're all out of the woods." The auditors, who would have been extricated from their own mess, accepted the proposal in principal, says Tony, and even presented it to the board.

But the accounting switch was modest compared with Tony's really audacious inspirations. He and his financial people had been carrying on extensive talks with an Ohio engine manufacturer, White Engine, about a friendly takeover. While the bankers and financial consultants hoped that White could add to Wedtech's manufacturing capacity and expertise, Tony's secret hope was that he could blend together the books of the two firms in order to make Wedtech's loss vanish into White's $150 million revenue. Everyone liked the deal, and later in the fall a preliminary understanding would be signed.

But Tony's most extravagant device, as well as the most avant-garde, was a plan to raise a colossal sum of money and retire the debt in a single move. Soon after the bond offering, he and Larry Shorten left for London to compose the climax of Wedtech's ingenious financing. Wedtech would borrow $1 billion—or maybe $10 billion—from a consortium of European banks and use three quarters of the sum to purchase twenty-year prime bank notes. Since the notes carried a higher interest rate than the loan, Wedtech would, in effect, be engaging in interest-rate arbitrage. The bank paper would throw off enough interest to service the principal and interest payments on the debt. With the remaining $250 million Wedtech would annihilate the overhang left by the switch from cost-of-completion accounting. The loan would thus service both itself and the remainder of Wedtech's debt. It was a financial perpetual-motion machine, or, as Tony put it less poetically, "a self-liquidating loan." It was complex, ingenious, and completely abstract, a thing of beauty that produced nothing whatsoever.

Tony was very proud of himself, and he returned from London to present these glittering ephemera to the board at a meeting on September 17. It was a whole new world for Wedtech, a world beyond the ken of anyone save Tony and the other financial types. As Richard Cavazos sat through the meeting, he found himself wondering exactly what business Wedtech was in. "I kept waiting for someone to tell me how we could make the engines any cheaper. Steel and equipment so the pontoons could be made on schedule was the furthest thing from their mind. They had the greatest gold mine in the sky in the M-113, and that was just back in the backwash. The only thing Tony cared about was refinancing." Cavazos was an old-fashioned military man who didn't believe in what he couldn't touch, and he had the feeling that Wedtech was leaving the realm of the palpable.

While Mario and Tony chased their phantoms, the darkness began to close in around the squat brick battleship at 595 Gerard. In mid-September Nick Weil, who had been hired to promote the new engine products, went down from Mount Vernon to the Bronx to pick up a check he had been promised. In recent weeks the company had virtually stopped reimbursing employers for expenses or paying suppliers. It was a worrisome situation, and Weil was relieved to think that the $75 million infusion would finally permit Wedtech to behave like a proper corporation. He went in to see one of the company's chief bookkeepers, Joshua Purec, who had once, as a DCAA auditor, somehow overlooked the company's spurious progress payments.

"I found Joshua in a very pensive mood," Weil recalls. "That's when he told me he had decided to resign. I asked him why would he resign now. He said, 'You know we had this bond offering. And here it is two weeks later, and there's only $2 million left. And all of our creditors have not been paid off. Will that tell you enough why I am leaving?' " It was enough for Weil, in any case. In mid-October he called the research and development wing of John Deere, which had offered him a job several months earlier. He left Wedtech a few days before the bankruptcy, still owed $6000 in salary and $4500 in expenses.

By September, it had become clear to Mary Shannon and the agents that the initial subpoena had not unsettled anyone over at Wedtech. The company's new attorney, Stephen Kaufman—a former Southern District prosecutor and a leader of the white-collar bar, brought to Wedtech's attention by Bob Wallach—had gotten in touch, but there was no sign of cooperation with the grand jury investigation. And so a few weeks after the bond offering, Steve Cossu and Mike Raggi went up to 595 Gerard with Donna Merris, a third-year law student attending night school who had just been hired by the U.S. Attorney's office. Shannon had told Kaufman they would be coming, and asked to have the company put all the papers together in one room. When the three were brought to the file room, they found a mountain consisting of thirty or forty file boxes.

"We had no idea where to start," recalls Merris. "So we decided to begin looking at checks. We asked them to bring out the checkbooks, and we started going through them. And we saw all these payments to consultants in incredible amounts, and payments to Biaggi & Ehrlich, and checks to this person named E. Robert Wallach, and Squadron Ellenoff and Nofziger & Bragg. And we started wondering, Why does this little company need so many lawyers and consultants?" The group decided that they would have to bring the documents back to the U.S. Attorney's office. Raggi recalls that several trucks were conscripted from an Air National Guard base to haul the tonnage of paper to downtown Manhattan.

While the U.S. Attorney was starting to examine the tail of the Wedtech elephant, the Manhattan District Attorney was taking a close look at the trunk. The Manhattan DA, like the Bronx DA, had arrived at Wedtech obliquely. As part of the investigation into municipal corruption, the DA's office had been looking into the relationship of Citisource, a company partially owned by Bronx Democratic leader Stanley Friedman, with Portatech, a company in New Jersey controlled by Richard Biaggi and Bernard Ehrlich. An official from Citisource told the DA that Portatech had been set up to launder money to Ehrlich; the money was used, in turn, to pay bribes to a National Guard official, Vito Castellano. In early September the DA had subpoenaed the company's financial records and found checks that pointed to just this conclusion.

Assistant district attorney John Moscow then called in Stephen Kaufman, who represented Biaggi & Ehrlich and Portatech as well as Wedtech. Kaufman told Moscow that the federal authorities had already issued a subpoena to Biaggi & Ehrlich in connection with an investigation into Wedtech. This was news to Moscow, who foresaw the two investigations colliding with one another.

When the Bronx DA had faced the same problem the previous spring, the matter had been quickly solved when District Attorney Mario Merola agreed to sign on with U.S. Attorney Rudolph Giuliani, though in a clearly secondary position. Collegiality based on subordination was not, however, on the agenda in Manhattan. Nor, often enough, was cooperation. Probably in no other jurisdiction in the United States do the federal and state prosecutors' offices gouge, elbow, and traduce one another as they do in New York, or at least as they did during the five years when Rudolph Giuliani was U.S. Attorney.

It wasn't only Giuliani's flair for the melodramatic press conference, in contrast to DA Robert Morgenthau's characteristic propriety; it was also that both offices were extremely aggressive in an era when crime busting had taken on a shimmer of romance. With its superior investigative resources, its superior staff of attorneys, and, in any case, its superior jurisdiction, Giuliani's office tended to land the most glamorous cases and get the best press. To Morgenthau, himself a former U.S. Attorney, this was galling, and his staff collectively carried a chip on their shoulder.

The Citisource investigation was, in fact, one of the few morsels that Morgenthau had been able to pull from the plum pudding of the city government investigation. Back in March the two offices had been scrapping over Stanley Friedman, whom Morgenthau claimed not so much on jurisdictional grounds as on the grounds that the federal prosecutor was getting all the other goodies. Giuliani had won that one, indicting Friedman under the RICO statute governing racketeering enterprises, and convicting him and four co-defendants of bribing and corrupting the city's Parking Violations Bureau. Giuliani had agreed in exchange to allocate to the District Attorney several portions of the investigation, including Citisource.

And so when Moscow learned that even Citisource was jeopardized, he called up Mary Shannon and told her of Kaufman's comment. "No," Moscow recalls Shannon saying, "there's no investigation like that going on." Moscow says he took that to mean that the feds were not investigating Wedtech. Mary Shannon recalls the conversation very differently. "Moscow only asked if there was a Citisource-Portatech investigation going on. He said, 'Do you know about Portatech?' So I said, 'We're not doing that investigation.' I didn't even know that Portatech existed." Moscow concedes that he never so much as mentioned Wedtech, but insists that Shannon's failure to disclose the Wedtech investigation "shows a lack of faith on her part"—or worse. "Some weeks later when I spoke to Mary Shannon again," says Moscow, "she said that she had lied, that there *was* an investigation. She said that she felt that it wasn't her secret to give—those were her words."

This is a startling charge, but, then, John Moscow is a man given to making startling charges. (Given a chance, he said, his office could have lodged criminal charges against Ed Meese, though he's not sure what they might have been.) In recent years Moscow had become Morgenthau's star prosecutor, handling many of the office's most dramatic cases. Reporters loved him. A big man with a wrestler's stubby frame, close-cropped hair, and an incongruously quiet manner, Moscow was a provocative narrator who had mastered the skill of doling out confidences. He was a man who obviously loved secrets and conspiracy and intrigue, and had a genuine talent for fathoming labyrinthine schemes. Two years after going to school on the matter he could still retrace with perfect ease the twists and turns of Tony Guariglia's accounting maze. But his cockiness, his flair for publicity, and a certain air of sanctimony had made him a good many enemies in the U.S. Attorney's office and even among his colleagues. Wedtech was about to cement his reputation.

On September 25, Moscow received permission from a state judge to pool the federal and local investigations. Apparently he was trying to achieve by *force majeure* what he had failed to get by persuasion. "I sent the order back to him," says Shannon, who was growing disgusted with the confrontation but wasn't about to give way gracefully. "I told him I wasn't interested. I was already doing a state investigation." Moscow also called Foglia to suggest that they hook up and cut out the U.S. Attorney. "Our perspective," says Foglia, "was 'What's your connection to all this? We really don't need the Manhattan District Attorney's office to make all these cases.' "

The Wedtech insiders, along with Bob Wallach, were now aware that the company was under investigation in two separate jurisdictions. But the inquiries were only a nuisance, an occasional sputtering of sniper fire. And then the bomb dropped. On October 14, *The New York Post* reported that Richard Biaggi and Bernard Ehrlich owned stock in Wedtech, and that Mario Biaggi had "gone to bat" for the company. And then the following day, under the headline TAINTED PACTS TO BIAGGI KIN, *The Daily News* stated that the SBA had "improperly approved" Wedtech's 1983 stock purchase plan, because the agreement was ultimately rescinded without Mariotta's ever having taken possession of the shares. The SBA, the article reported, had initiated an investigation into the deal.

Reached for response, Mario Biaggi, always something of a hazard with the unrehearsed comment, dug the first shovelful of dirt for his own grave. The 225,000 shares of Wedtech stock given to his son and his former law partner represented, he said, "the gift of a very generous man," John Mariotta—and not, as he would later claim, payment for legal work.

With the *News* article, the conflict between Moscow and Shannon finally came to a head. Moscow had not known of the allegations on the stock purchase plan, and either the day the article appeared or the next day, he went to the New York regional office of the SBA to request that the agency turn over all of its files related to Wedtech. He did not tell Shannon and did not issue a subpoena. Moscow says that he thought the feds were looking only into potential stock fraud and had no interest in the SBA, which was, of course, a federal agency. The SBA agent to whom Moscow applied turned over all the files that same day. What Moscow did not know was that Shannon had been running an undercover investigation in collaboration with SBA headquarters in Washington. The *Daily News* article blew the cover off the inquiry, and she decided to close it down. She sent a federal agent over to the regional inspector general to explain the inquiry and pick up the files. Sorry, said the IG; she had given the files only the day before to the Manhattan District Attorney's office.

Mary Shannon is not an especially forbearing person. Her boiling point is very low, and she comes equipped with the full-blown prosecutorial sense of outrage. As soon as she learned that the SBA documents had been spirited away, as she recalls it, "I call Moscow and I issue forth with expletives. He says, 'Well, you weren't doing anything.' I say, 'You didn't call us. You didn't call the Bronx. Who the fuck do you think you are?' " At first several federal agents visited Moscow's office on the mistaken assumption that he would hand over the documents. Moscow took this as an act of war. His investigation was every bit as valid as Shannon's; he had gotten to the documents first; and the rule in the prosecutorial game as he understood it was "finders, keepers."

He had taken the precaution of stationing in his office an obviously armed New York City police detective so that, he says, when he refused to hand over the files, the agents would have a decent pretext for not insisting. "I am told," Moscow says impishly, "that I was almost locked up for obstructing justice." In any case, he adds, "I personally"—he emphasizes "personally"—"don't make a habit of keeping documents from other prosecutors. Mary Shannon didn't want those documents; she wanted us not to have them." Shannon wanted the documents so badly that she almost sent a federal marshal over to seize them. It took two weeks of skirmishing to pry them from Moscow's grasp. "It was," she concludes, "like negotiating over the release of hostages."

While the two great prosecutorial forces in Manhattan fought each other like rival drug lords, Wedtech began hunkering down. While in London Tony had opened up corporate accounts under the names Itad and Wydgeclyffe. He and Larry Shorten had first used these accounts to receive $200,000 they had stolen from the company. By now, FHJ was essentially defunct, and the money had been wired directly from the company to the foreign accounts. Then Tony made his last great killing. He had begun to catch on to Mario's secret deals with his brothers-in-law, and had questioned Mario about how so much money had disappeared. Mario said nothing, but a few days later he told Tony that Berney and Yaghoubi had agreed to a private deal with the two of them. The contractors then submitted almost $2 million in false invoices, and kicked back all but $185,000 of the total. Mario and Tony each received $800,000, and each put $300,000 into Itad and Wydgeclyffe. Mario placed the remainder in a Panamanian account, and Tony paid the construction firm working on his pleasure dome on the North Shore.

The bad news, meanwhile, kept raining down. On October 16 and again on Sunday the nineteenth, the *News* plunged into the Freedom Industries story, prominently featuring Henry Thomas' claim that Biaggi & Ehrlich had sought to extort stock from the company in exchange for the use of political influence. By Tuesday, October 21, the *News* was able to quantify the total winnings of "Biaggi kith & kin" at "1M." Though Mario Biaggi claimed to have severed his connection with Biaggi & Ehrlich, the *News* reported that he remained on the letterhead as "of counsel," and had reported receiving $34,000 in fees from the firm the previous year.

The official word at Wedtech was: Everything's fine. The *News* had a vendetta against Mario Biaggi; everyone knew that. It was all going to blow over. Wallach flew in and announced to anyone who would listen that from now he should be considered "coordinating counsel." Everyone was huddling over at Squadron Ellenoff. Filled with righteous indignation, Wallach was insisting that Wedtech sue for libel. Tony agreed, and so did Mario; no newspaper should be allowed to get away with smear tactics.

Squadron Ellenoff faced a delicate problem. The firm's biggest client was the media leviathan Rupert Murdoch, and on any number of occasions it had defended Murdoch's muckraking or sleazy publications, including *The New York Post,* from libel suits. It would look mighty hypocritical, even by the standards of a law firm, to turn around and make the opposite arguments. Everyone knew the virtuous litany: libel suits chilled freedom of the press; they were the wrong forum within which to seek redress; and so on. Squadron says that he was very reluctant to press action and did so only to mollify the madding crowd.

It was not, however, the first time that he had brandished the legal cudgel to defend Wedtech from the press. A year earlier, Squadron had managed to use the arts of persuasion to prevent two prescient young reporters from divulging the bad news on Wedtech in the pages of *The Village Voice,* a weekly that his client Rupert Murdoch had owned until recently. The two, Todd Jacobs and Richard Burns, were students at the Columbia School of Journalism who had learned from Wedtech's public filings that Richard Biaggi had received 112,500 shares of stock. Their interest piqued, they continued looking at public documents and later learned of the dubious stock purchase plan and its subsequent rescission, and several other details that gave off a telltale odor. They had found, by doing nothing more than keeping their eyes open, what any number of business journalists had missed.

Squadron had gotten hold of letters the two had written to federal agencies seeking documents under the Freedom of Information Act. Exactly how they came into his possession, he doesn't recall. Burns and Jacobs had been injudicious or inexperienced enough to say that they suspected criminal wrongdoing on Wedtech's part. Squadron quickly called his old friend Victor Kovner, a lawyer who represented the *Voice* on First Amendment matters, and in the course of an amiable conversation mentioned that journalists working on assignment for the *Voice* had published documents that might well prove to be libelous. It wasn't a threat, just a legal observation. Kovner, generally a stout defender of freedom of speech, knew that Squadron was right, since the letters counted as "published" material. Kovner advised the *Voice* that it would be putting itself in peril by publishing an article based on the inquiries. The authors, who protested that truth was a defense in libel suits, were "dumped like a ton of hot bricks," as Burns recalls.

So Howard Squadron was not altogether averse to genteel intimidation. What's more, he was outraged. The *News* had, by implication, called into question the integrity of his firm. Squadron fired off a "Dear Jim" letter to the *Daily News* publisher, James Hoge. Squadron asserted that the October 15 article about Biaggi "contains many inaccuracies," including "the suggestion that Wedtech is a failing company," and, of course, the story about the stock purchase plan. "Our client," Squadron concluded, "is pressing us to take legal action. On its behalf, please consider this a demand for a prompt retraction and the publishing of the correct facts in this matter."

The *News,* to its credit, let the Squadron bullet bounce off its hide, and kept charging. Indeed, other publications started picking up allegations from the *News.* When *Barron's,* a few days later, used the revelations as the basis for an editorial attack on the 8(a) program, Arthur Siskind fired off a letter of his own, calling the editorial "a flagrant abuse of a publication which is more commonly known for its high standards," and explicitly threatening libel.

No doubt Siskind was outraged; it was he, after all, who had devised the stock purchase plan. But he and Squadron were a trifle upset with their client. Tony, with whom they were in almost daily contact, had never said a word about the subpoenas. In fact, they had learned of them by accident, earlier in the month, when a Squadron Ellenoff attorney found that one of his clients, which was doing business with Wedtech, had itself received a federal subpoena. Only then did the attorneys discover that the client had been withholding critical information, including the fact that it had retained counsel in two jurisdictions. Squadron says that he threatened to quit unless Wedtech played straight with him. Tony and Mario came to the office and promised to play it straight from then on, and Squadron was placated.

Despite the deception, and despite their supposed misgivings about libel actions, Squadron Ellenoff prepared the legal papers. On October 21, when the *News* refused to apologize, Wedtech filed a libel suit. The suit repeated the allegations in Squadron's letter and asked for $100 million in compensatory damages and $300 million in punitive damages.

Meanwhile, life at Wedtech, as at some great empire in its final days, was entering a baroque phase. On Friday the seventeenth a Saudi prince had materialized in Manhattan. Prince Abdul Aziz al-Sudari had been brought to Wedtech's attention during the summer by Ray Kahng, a Korean friend of Ehrlich's. The Prince was looking for a contractor to take over a maintenance and training program for the Saudi Royal Navy that could be worth as much as $100 million over three years. The Saudis were a big part of the global program. Mario had paid $400,000 to a group of Saudi agents who claimed that they could deliver a major contract for their government's fleet of M-113s. It was definitely going to happen. In August, Kahng and Jim Aspin, Wedtech's one and only Wharton MBA, had flown to Paris to have lunch with al-Sudari and had flown back the same day.

Now al-Sudari suddenly called Aspin and said he had just stepped off the plane and was eager to see Wedtech. Nobody was around, but Aspin had the inspired idea of taking the Prince, a gambler of cosmic proportions, to Atlantic City for the weekend. The pair holed up in a large suite until the management at Caesars discovered that Mr. al-Sudari had "Prince" in front of his name, at which point they were installed in a suite the size of a basketball court.

Mario hustled over as soon as he heard about the royal appearance, and watched while the Prince went through a princely sum at the blackjack tables. After he had lost $150,000, al-Sudari asked Mario whether he would extend him some credit. Mario, who was nothing if not gracious, let his guest draw up to $40,000. The Prince went through that, and Mario added $20,000 more. When that evaporated, Mario handed over $12,000 in cash. Seventy-two thousand dollars vanished in the blink of an eye, but it was worth it. The two men worked out a joint agreement and signed it on the blackjack table, the sort of flourish that appealed to Mario's business style.

On the following Wednesday, the day after Wedtech had filed suit against the *News,* Jim Aspin's friend Carlos Galvis was sitting downstairs in the lobby of the Hilton in the suburb of Rye, waiting to take His Excellency on his first visit to the South Bronx. "So I'm waiting for him to meet me," says Galvis, "and I'm reading *The New York Times.* And the guy's taking some time. And I'm reading this thing cover to cover; I've read the obits twice. And in there is a little box—'Army General Cashiered.' Bernard Ehrlich, right? I look at this, I go, 'It couldn't be the same guy.' " So Galvis found a pay phone and called his *compadre,* Mario Moreno, who knew all about the article. "He goes, 'Don't worry about it, no big deal, we're taking care of it.' " Galvis, reassured, went back to wait for the Prince, who finally arrived and was whisked off to 595 Gerard.

Of course, it *was* a big deal. The article stated that Ehrlich had been fired for an unspecified breach of conduct. A few days later it would be reported that Ehrlich had been terminated when a grand jury heard allegations that he had accepted kickbacks after persuading the state National Guard to buy hand-held computers from Citisource, Stanley Friedman's company. When Galvis arrived at Mario's office, the Prince in tow, he found a scene of total panic. Mario was now occupying John's old office, with the aircraft-carrier desk and the monster couches.

"So," Galvis recalls, "they sit the Prince, who is supposed to be getting pitched by Mario, on this long couch. I'm sitting on the other side, with the Grand Canyon between us. Over in the middle of the room there's this guy Felter [Irwin Felter, a former military man hired only a few weeks before] and some sidekick of his, who are having this hushed discussion. On the other side, there's Bernie Ehrlich, pacing like his wife's about to have a baby. And to my left, at the other end of the couch, there's Richard Biaggi. Meanwhile, while all this is going on, Mario is furiously working the phones, saying, 'And we're going to sue the bastards for libel.' The whole place is going crazy, and the Prince doesn't know what to make of it either."

Someone told Galvis that Wedtech was suing *The Daily News.* This idea struck him as supremely stupid but somehow of a piece with the frantic scene unfolding before him. The fog began to lift from the brow of this passionate Wedtechie. "When I saw all this going on," says Galvis, "I said, not 'Something is rotten in the state of Denmark,' but 'Denmark is rotten.' "

THIRTY-THREE

THIRTY-THREE

Death

T HE DARKNESS was gathering slowly. Mario was still eagerly awaiting that big licensing deal, the *deus ex machina* they had all been expecting
for years. Tony was sure that he could transform an arbitrage or a lease
back or a defeasance of the company's debt into a big bundle of cash.
Saudi Arabia was going to come through, or Israel, or Egypt, or someone. Nick Weil may have left, but everyone else was staying on board.
The grand juries were still just a nuisance, nothing compared with the
potential effect of all that bad press. Mario and Tony and Larry Shorten
and Bob Wallach were scrambling to reassure nervous investors and
suppliers and consultants. Tony had even sent an interoffice memo to all
employees insisting that "it is the *News*, not Wedtech, that is guilty of
questionable conduct . . . *Wedtech has done nothing wrong,*" he wrote, in
case anyone missed the point.

And now it was time for Bob Wallach to rejoin Wedtech for one last
gallant effort in behalf of the cause that needs assistance. Wallach had
been not much in evidence recently. In late 1985 he had wangled a job

for himself as chief of the U.S. delegation to the U.N. Human Rights Commission. This was a prestigious position traditionally reserved for important Jewish supporters of the President. Howard Squadron, in fact, had hungered for the job as a sign of his standing in the Jewish community, and had gone to the uncharacteristic length of asking Wallach to intervene on his behalf with the administration. Wallach said he had asked around and found that the job could only go to a Republican. A few months later Wallach had gaily announced that he himself had been chosen. Out of the blue, he said, Leonard Garment had asked him whether he wanted the job. Squadron was incensed, and the friendship between the two men came to an immediate end. Wallach received his last $2500 monthly check from Squadron Ellenoff in early 1986.

Wallach had been in Geneva while the commission convened, from late January to mid-March, enjoying the international adventure that had been denied him when the pipeline deal ground to a halt a few months earlier. On his return, he continued to entertain his cynical friends at Wedtech with his pious memos and to contact his network of immensely wealthy businessmen. He spent much of his time in San Francisco and Washington, and only occasionally dropped by at 595 Gerard. But Bob Wallach loved nothing so much as the sensation of being needed, and when it became clear that Wedtech had serious problems, Wallach decided that he was needed.

In mid-October, just as the shells were beginning to drop, Wallach had arrived in town to buck up the troops and marshal the defenses. And now, on October 22, the day after the libel suit was filed, Wallach summoned Jack Kehoe, who handled Wedtech's investor relations, to a meeting at the Grand Hyatt. Wallach described his new role of "coordinating counsel" and alluded to charges Kehoe had scarcely even heard about: the Mitchell matter in Baltimore, the progress payments, the SBA inquiry. Of the substance of the allegations, Wallach said nothing; his sole concern was public relations. Don't say "investigation" when talking to the media, Wallach instructed Kehoe, who talked to the media virtually for a living; say "inquiry" so as to avoid even the suggestion that wrongdoing was involved. Wallach, who struck Kehoe as "an utter phony," roused Kehoe's worries about Wedtech for the first time.

Kehoe was now acting as Wedtech's liaison with the press. The libel suit had boomeranged, as libel suits usually do, goading the media, and especially the *News,* to substantiate the allegations. By the end of October a *News* reporter was calling Kehoe almost daily with new revelations. What about the progress payment fraud? What about a $5000 payment to Vito Castellano? Kehoe was dumbstruck; he had never even *heard* of

Vito Castellano. He asked the reporter to forbear until he could furnish some answers. It never occurred to him that there were no answers. But Wallach, the "coordinating counsel," wasn't speaking, and when Kehoe sat down with Tony and Mario, all he heard were diatribes against John Mariotta and the *News*.

It was only when Kehoe threatened to quit that he began to learn fragments of the truth. Tony knew that Kehoe's departure might be interpreted as a sign that Wedtech was the sort of place where an honorable man could not remain. Late one night in early November Kehoe received a call from Tony in London. "Please don't bail on me," Tony pleaded. "I want to be totally open with you." Tony offered Kehoe plausible and legitimate explanations for all the investigations and all the lawyers. "The guy is doing summary confessions," recalls Kehoe, whose susceptibility to confessions Tony may have been subtle enough to recognize. " 'I promise you, I swear to God' . . . Okay, you got me." Kehoe was back on the team.

But not, as it turned out, for long. Over the next several days Kehoe relayed the *News*'s questions to Tony. What about Castellano? How much did *he* get? And Tony, his unwavering cool, his air of omniscience, beginning to dissolve, said, "I don't know. We've got so goddamn many consultants around here, I don't know what we pay them." Kehoe, who didn't know about most of the consultants, was startled.

Kehoe was trapped. The press was clamoring for a response, and Wedtech had battened down the hatches. Kehoe had gone over with Siskind the discrepancy between Tony's assertions about the progress payments and the allegations being made by the reporter for the *News*, Jerry Capeci. From Siskind's notes emerged a draft of a letter to Capeci. On Friday, November 7, Kehoe and Tony sat in the Squadron Ellenoff office and discussed the letter over the phone with Siskind and Howard Squadron, who were away at a company retreat. Siskind says that Kehoe wrote the three-page final draft with Tony, but both Kehoe and Tony recall that it was the lawyers who were responsible for the document. Siskind, in any case, agreed to have the letter go out over his signature.

Kehoe had returned to his office to wait, along with a messenger from the *News*, for the final document. Finally, at eight or nine o'clock, the letter arrived. Several things struck Kehoe immediately. First, Siskind stated that what Tony Guariglia had discovered back in 1982 was not a mere "irregularity," but "a fabrication" of invoices from suppliers, and that the volume of fabrication had been very large indeed: "approximately $6 million." Siskind also stated, to buttress his point that Wedtech's books were beyond reproach, that the DCAA had insisted on auditing all of Wedtech's progress payment requests since that time. Finally, Siskind had said that he would include with his letter a copy of the original Biaggi & Ehrlich letter to the auditors stating that the fraud had been fully disclosed. But the Biaggi & Ehrlich letter was not there.

The Siskind letter, defensive and petulant though it was, contained too much truth to serve its purpose. The media were not impressed, and Jack Kehoe, who had glimpsed only the tiniest fingernail paring of Wedtech's deceit, who was under intense pressure to stay on board, who was owed $40,000—Jack Kehoe quit. He spent the weekend agonizing over the decision with his wife and children, and concluded that he simply had no choice. Two years of working with Wedtech had done nothing to blur the solid line between right and wrong that a solid Catholic upbringing had etched in Kehoe's mind. He now understood, as he says, "the fact that the people running this company resorted to fraud on the United States government to ease a cash flow problem, and that the people who did that had subsequently been promoted and were now in responsible positions in the company."

That the company had engaged in fraud, and then had waffled and even lied to him, in the course of admitting to it, was bad enough; but what was much more serious to Kehoe was that the fraud had never been disclosed in the registration statement. The omission was inexplicable and inexcusable. "Every investor," he says, "bought stock based on a presumption about their character. Every share ever bought or sold had been done so with inadequate information. And that was the singular basis for walking away."

The feeling at Squadron Ellenoff was that Kehoe had overreacted. Arthur Siskind says that the lawyers, too, were "upset" by the letter, which he insists was written by Tony, not by him. He too, he says, had been deceived. But Squadron Ellenoff was not upset enough to quit; Siskind had signed his name to the letter, no matter who wrote it, and had appended some belligerent comments that could only have been his own. Kehoe felt that the DCAA's heightened vigilance should have made it clear to anyone at the time that Wedtech had committed the kind of infraction that could not but be disclosed to investors. But Siskind took exactly the opposite point of view: the government's willingness to keep doing business with Wedtech implied that no grave infraction had been committed.

When he quit, Kehoe was well aware that a phalanx of bankers, accountants, and lawyers had acquiesced in the decision not to disclose the progress payment situation, whatever it was, to the SEC, and was standing by Wedtech even now. But it didn't make any difference. "There's a definition for things," he says. "And that's called fraud."

And now a very strange thing happened to Fred. Several years after the death of his second wife, Helen—he had previously been married and divorced—Fred had married once again. Wife number three, Eileen Vanora, was, like Helen, young, sexy, and vivacious. And, like Helen, she seemed to be a very unhappy woman. Fred had bought her a chain of beauty parlors to run, and then had taken the drastic step of adopting first one child, then a second. ("It's cheaper than those damn beauty parlors," he had told Tony.) The two children became the emotional core of Fred's life, a replacement for the family that had died in Europe. Eileen, however, was not made happy. She was a heavy drinker, and Fred's sexual free lancing may have driven her deeper into bitterness and despair.

On a number of occasions Eileen had walked out of the house and disappeared. It would be days before the police knew what to do with her, since often she wandered off carrying the ID of another woman, apparently an aunt. In 1984 or 1985 she had been fished out of the East River, near the Neubergers' Sutton Place town house, after a suicide attempt. She was obviously in grave distress. At a New Year's Eve party in 1985, drunk and uncaring, she had informed everyone that if Fred wouldn't fire John and take over the company, she would divorce him, take his share of the company in alimony, and run the place herself.

In early November Eileen walked away from home again. This time, however, she didn't return. She was the second of Fred's wives apparently to commit suicide, a coincidence that gave rise to suspicions. A few days earlier, it turned out, she had gone to the police to say that some of her jewelry was missing; she suspected the domestic help. A Wedtech employee would later be prepared to testify that she had overheard Fred saying that Eileen was growing too impossible and too expensive, and he was going to find a way to end his problems. A story also went around that Eileen had called several of the other Wedtech wives from the precinct house, threatening to blow the company wide open. But once again a police investigation found no further evidence pointing to Fred. And Eileen's prior history lent credence to the presumption of suicide.

Fred never had any use for appearances, so he made no pretense of grief. Several weeks later he flew in his girlfriend from London to spend the Thanksgiving holiday with himself and his adopted children.

. . . .

By early November the bad news was undermining every project. Tony's brilliant schemes hung in midair. Wedtech's consortium of banks was talking about calling in their credit line. Among the few bankers willing to throw caution to the winds were Wedtech's old allies Serafin Mariel and Ivan Irizarry of the New York National Bank, who agreed to lend the firm $1,735,000.

Now the insiders were starting to panic. Biaggi was calling Mario every morning at seven, asking what the hell was going on. Biaggi's stock, which he had refused to unload because Mario had told him that the coating technology was going to make Wedtech take off like a rocket, was turning into so much wallpaper. Biaggi didn't realize that Mario himself had already sold all of his own stock. Biaggi began working the *paisan* network to find someone willing to lend the company money. He told Mario that he had called Lee Iacocca and explained that Wedtech was in the capable Italo-American hands of one Anthony Guariglia. Maybe the Chrysler Credit Corporation could spare a few million. Apparently the congressman's appeal failed, because the loan was not made.

Biaggi also arranged to have Mario travel to Washington with Bernie Ehrlich and Carmine (the Baker) D'Angelo, head of the bakers' union and a reputed mob figure, to meet with Jackie Presser, the head of the Teamsters union. Presser had reportedly been placed in his job, as had his predecessors, by the Mafia, though unlike his predecessors he had been spared from indictment by the FBI, for whom he served as a key informant. Presser explained that he had no control over Teamster loans, presumably referring to the union's pension fund, but that he had friends with money "overseas" who might be able to help. This, too, came to naught.

Worse still, the auditors were waking up. Tony had paid a small fortune to purchase their somnolence. Earlier in the year he had handed Touche Ross a $500,000 contract to study management "decentralization." As a consequence of this charade, a battalion of recent college grads had spent several weeks swarming around the Wedtech facilities, asking receptionists how they apportioned their time and so on. The report was safely stowed away, and the auditors nodded as the overhang grew larger. But soon after the letter to the *News,* the heads of the audit team came to Tony to say that the company's losses were alarming. Far from earning $40 million or more in 1986, they said, it looked as if Wedtech was going to lose at least $65 million, since the company had just about run out of revenue. Only a few weeks before, Tony says, the auditors had accepted his suggestion that Wedtech switch from cost-of-completion to shipped-and-billed accounting.

By early November, with the SBA documents finally joining records from the Defense Department and from the company itself, the eighth-floor "war room" in the U.S. Attorney's office had almost disappeared beneath a jumble of boxes and files, and Merris and Cossu and Raggi and the others had to step over one another to get to their perches. But it is precisely this kind of tedious and exhausting labor that leads to most prosecutorial breakthroughs, at least in white-collar cases; and as the group turned over endless pages, the Wedtech scandal began to take shape, like a laboriously reassembled manuscript, before their eyes.

First there was the revelation that Wedtech had friends like Lyn Nofziger and E. Robert Wallach, men with connections far loftier than anything Mario Biaggi or Stanley Simon could dream of. Now the investigative team uncovered traces of active White House involvement. After hours of fruitless trudging through the endless wilderness of the SBA files, Donna Merris happened on a piece of yellowed onionskin that was a copy of a letter in which Nofziger's aide Pier Talenti had expressed to Secretary of the Army John O. Marsh, Jr., the White House's interest in Wedtech's bid for the engine contract. "That's when we started getting scared," says Merris—meaning, of course, thrilled. From the SBA files the group also learned of the tortuous path of the stock purchase plan and its rescission, as well as Peter Neglia's constant intervention on Wedtech's behalf.

Now began the hard work of assembling the formless information into a narrative with characters and causes, an exacting intellectual act that requires great reserves of patience and care. It was here that Steve Cossu, who was coordinating the investigation, proved to be a genius. Cossu is a practitioner of "link analysis," a system of visual mapping whereby degrees and varieties of relatedness are represented by symbols —solid and dotted lines, triangles, circles. It is as close as investigative work comes to pure logic. Throughout the fall, Cossu filled in these diagrams until they were schematic epics.

To take but one example, Cossu learned from Wedtech's initial prospectus that the company had received a loan from Bellinguer—something he found strange in itself, since entrepreneurs in the South Bronx don't often have recourse to capital from Netherlands Antilles shell companies. Public documents named John Tartaglia, whom Cossu had never heard of, as Bellinguer's nominee. From SEC documents he also found that Wedtech leased its 149th Street facility from one PDJ Simone Realty. Documents filed with the Bronx county clerk's office showed that PDJ Simone Realty's attorney was the very same John Tartaglia, and one of its officers was Joseph Simone.

Separately, Cossu had learned, from SBA documents, as best he can recall, that Wedtech maintained a bank account at the New York National Bank. The bank, he then found, had been started by Ivan Irizarry, who happened to be Peter Neglia's predecessor as SBA regional head in New York. One of *its* officers was Joseph Simone. "The loop," says Cossu, speaking in terms of link analysis, "was getting tighter and tighter." He now had more than enough reason to ask Shannon to subpoena the bank's records. These, in turn, disclosed that all of the Wedtech principals owned stock in the bank. So Cossu had joined Simone, Tartaglia, Irizarry, PDJ Realty, Bellinguer, and Wedtech.

But while the investigative team was bringing order out of chaos, the intramural fracas was turning into a riot. Before and during the time that Moscow and Shannon were mud wrestling over the SBA documents, they and others in their offices were trying to draw a line of demarcation between the two inquiries. As Shannon explains it, the agreement limited the DA to the Citisource-Portatech sequence of events, encompassing Castellano and, to some extent, Ehrlich and Richard Biaggi. But by the time of the discussions, Moscow had already learned of the 8(a) fraud from the SBA documents, and, from an interview with a Wedtech bookkeeper, of the phony progress payments.

Still smarting from the forced surrender of Stanley Friedman, and buoyed up by a sense of outrage at having been, he felt, lied to, Moscow was steaming full speed ahead. In late October he had called in a number of suspects, including Tony and Richard Biaggi. Tony was bland and evasive and self-assured and, Moscow concluded, the complete liar. He had also called John's lawyer, Jeffrey Glekel, and asked him to come in with John to discuss possible cooperation. After hearing John out, Moscow offered, and Glekel accepted, a preliminary understanding whereby John would agree to testify before a state grand jury in exchange for immunity from prosecution at the state level. On November 7, as Wedtech was fending off *The Daily News,* Moscow issued a letter formalizing the agreement and stating that the DA had not found Mariotta to be implicated in any of the alleged criminal activity it had examined.

Shannon learned of the letter from Glekel, not Moscow. She pleaded with Moscow not to conclude such a deal, and continued pleading even after the arrangement, unbeknown to her, was made final. Glekel, she insisted, would be able to claim at trial that evidence against Mariotta had been obtained from the state grand jury in violation of the immunity order, and was thus "tainted." (He did, but the motions were denied.) Moscow explained that he had anticipated this problem by including in the cooperation agreement a stipulation that Mariotta would waive his immunity. Federal law, Shannon pointed out, stipulates that an agreement not to prosecute effectively confers immunity.

Shannon felt that both the testimony and Moscow, who had heard the testimony, would be "infected." "I called," says Shannon, "and explained, 'You enter into an agreement, and I can't talk to you again. My witnesses can't talk to you. I'll just grab the documents.' " What was really infected at this point, though, was relations between the two prosecutors. The argument was lost before it started. Shannon now made good her threat. Thereafter, she says, she simply hung up when she picked up the phone and heard Moscow's voice on the other end.

"That's a crock of shit," says Moscow. The squabble sounds a lot like the other squabbles, but the acrid black smoke covers a genuinely grave difference of opinion. The state authorities were willing to promise John Mariotta that he would not go to jail if he would testify against his former colleagues; the feds were not. Moscow saw Mariotta, and continues to see him, as essentially a stooge. "John Mariotta," he says, "struck me as a nice guy." Moscow was impressed by Mariotta's struggle against poverty and illiteracy and by his total ignorance of the law. "He had given away 300 percent of the company," Moscow argues. "This guy did not have the foggiest fucking idea what he was doing." His crimes, in effect, were unconscious.

Shannon, and the prosecution team that eventually formed around her, did not feel much sympathy for Mariotta. They came to know a great deal more about Mariotta than Moscow ever did, and, perhaps more important, they came to see him through the eyes of his associates, who were to describe him as a kind of unhinged Mussolini. But even back in the fall of 1986, Shannon and her team did not doubt that Mariotta was a full-blooded member of the conspiracy. The only deal they were willing to offer was immunity in exchange for Mariotta's testimony on crimes to which he would have to admit. But John said then what he continued to say, without wavering, throughout the trial and later: he had seen nobody break the law, least of all himself.

By November the atmosphere at Foley Square had become intense. With the media now looking raptly over their shoulders and bringing to light the nuggets they had laboriously mined, the investigators began to feel ever more pressured. And the fear that the Manhattan DA might get to witnesses before they did, and offer them immunity in exchange for testimony, goaded the group to work even faster. Now they began putting some witnesses before a grand jury and interviewing others. Peter Neglia testified before the grand jury, pursuant to a subpoena, on October 24. He denied having had a corrupt relationship with Wedtech, and was later indicted for, and convicted of, perjury.

On Veterans Day, E. Robert Wallach agreed voluntarily to discuss his relationship with the company. Wallach came in his suit; the others were in their jeans. He spoke for four hours, smoothly, politely, even amiably. And he said nothing. He had mentioned Wedtech to Meese "in passing," recalls Shannon. He had never asked Meese to help the company. Wallach mentioned no other White House contacts. "It was very frustrating," says Shannon. "He wanted to appear like he was being very helpful and very cooperative in giving us the information that we needed. He just basically downplayed the whole thing." That, of course, was vintage Wallach.

He had not persuaded anyone: it was clear that the trail led directly to the Reagan White House. A few weeks later Shannon and a squad of investigators went down to the Old Executive Office Building, the magnificently pillared structure next to the White House where the records of top Executive Branch employees are kept. Here at last were Ed Meese's files—his correspondence, his telephone logs, his memos, his activity sheets. Among the carefully ordered material was a file—lo and behold!—marked "Wedtech," with memos from Wallach and notes to and from his staff and correspondence with the military. So much for Wallach's modest demurrals. Wedtech was expanding and billowing and all but blotting out the horizon. It seemed incredible that only a few months earlier the case had looked like a garden variety contracting scandal.

Carlos Galvis thought that if only he could get the attention of his friend Mario Moreno, disaster could be averted. Galvis simply could not imagine that Mario was a criminal, any more than Jack Kehoe could suppose that Tony was. On November 1, Galvis sent Mario a memo stating that the combination of investigations and bad publicity would almost certainly destroy the company unless it acted within five to ten days. Galvis suggested that Wedtech distance itself from both Biaggi and Ehrlich, fire its Washington consultants, retain outside counsel, and direct all strategy toward saving the company.

Several days later Galvis and Jim Aspin met with Mario at the Yale Club. To every impending disaster that Galvis or Aspin listed, Mario, friendly and mild and impassive as ever, said only, "We got that covered." Only once, when Galvis suggested that the Pentagon might use Wedtech as a scapegoat for its own scandals, did Mario say, "We hadn't thought of that." But it didn't matter; they had it covered. It was as if

Mario no longer needed to deceive them with his public face, and at long last felt free to expose the depth of his cynicism. Both men felt the harshness of the revelation: Mario had been conning them all along.

Nothing, of course, *was* covered. At first Stephen Kaufman thought that he would be able to work out an arrangement whereby the company would have to plead guilty to the progress payment fraud but the executives would be spared; the federal prosecutors, though, had made it clear that that wasn't enough, no matter what the DA's office decided. The insiders began to talk seriously about fleeing the country. Bernie Ehrlich, who was born in Bermuda, thought that he might do well to return. Mario thought about going back to Colombia. Tony still didn't feel personally imperiled by the investigation, but Pat Simone spoke to him of the virtues of Switzerland. Simone even gave him the name of a banker in Zurich, and promised to take care of his family.

By the end of November everything was moving at a terrible velocity. The money, for one thing, was running out as surely as the sand in an hourglass. The company had wangled a $6 million loan from the Yorkville Savings Bank through a friend of Ray Kahng's; within a week, to the man's horror, the money was gone. Expenses had gone unreimbursed for months, and managers had had to fund their own business trips. The White Engine deal was coming unglued; so was the contract with Martin Marietta. Every week Touche Ross told management of an even more staggering estimate of the company's losses—$90 million, $100 million, $120 million. And the auditors were insisting that the losses be booked, after years of shuffling them onto that cantilevered shelf.

On December 3, Squadron Ellenoff finally quit. Howard Squadron says that he was sick of all the lies and evasions, though he concedes that the law firm had been informed by federal prosecutors that, as a potential target of the investigation, it could no longer represent Wedtech. The last straw may have come when Tony and Mario stood by their "coordinating counsel," Bob Wallach, who, they earnestly believed, could deliver Ed Meese for them. Squadron now loathed the man to whom he had condescended for years.

On Friday, December 5, Wedtech announced that it was shutting down the 149th Street pontoon facility and laying off 266 workers. Its stock was down to ninety-three cents. Standard & Poor's had downgraded its bond rating to CC. Bob Wallach was on the scene to mitigate the concern. "The closing of the plant does not mean that the company is going out of business," he told *The New York Times*. The blow that sent the firm reeling came on December 8; a telegram from the Navy stated that by closing the plant, Wedtech had defaulted on the pontoon contract, which was, as of that moment, revoked. That was it; Wedtech was dead on its feet. And to add insult to injury, the auditors chose that same day to announce that they were quitting.

The darkness had closed in faster than anyone had imagined. Without a source either of capital or of work, Wedtech's bankruptcy became a foregone conclusion. The only thing left to avoid now was criminal prosecution. Within hours of the Navy telegram, Wallach had gotten a squad of lawyers from Dickstein Shapiro to fly up to New York. Tony agreed that Wedtech would pay the firm $500,000 and Wallach $95,000, bills equal in size to those Ed Meese ran up in the course of his year-long confirmation hearings and defense in the special prosecutor investigation.

On that evening and throughout the next two days, the Dickstein attorneys, a bankruptcy lawyer, and Martin Pollner, another lawyer brought in by Fred, went over Wedtech's legal and financial status. And yet by Sunday the tenth, the lawyers decided that the game was not worth the candle. According to the Dickstein attorney, James Kotelly, his firm believed that Wedtech was so strapped for cash, they themselves would be taking the last bite of cake, and the company's former employees would be decking their Christmas table with gruel. A slightly less charitable explanation is that the bankruptcy attorney they had brought up from Washington had gleaned from Wedtech's records and from several conversations the distinct impression that the company kept a second set of books. For this or some other reason, the attorneys may have felt that Wedtech was not on the level.

The Wedtech insiders, with their naïve faith in the corruptibility of the political system, still hoped that Bob Wallach would pull their chestnuts out of the fire. Wallach had been flying in and out of New York, and he had met twice with the insiders at La Guardia Airport to hear their desperate appeals for intervention. In his usual vague and circular way, Wallach kept implying that he was discussing the case with his friend and that everything was under control. And then at some point during the first week of December, Tony says, he decided to give Wallach some encouragement: I'll give you $100,000, he said, if you can get Ed Meese to call off the dogs. Mario said that he would do likewise. Wallach's answer, Tony recalls, was, "I'm very appreciative of the offer." He promised to do what he could.

Apparently Wallach meant what he said. On December 11, the day after his friends at Dickstein withdrew, leaving Wallach out in the cold, the coordinating counsel suddenly materialized in Meese's hotel room in New York. It was 10 A.M., and Meese was to spend the next half hour preparing for an interview with NBC. Instead, according to a story told to the special prosecutor by Terry Eastland, then Meese's spokesman, Wallach spent the next twenty-five minutes engaging Meese in what the special prosecutor called "a private and very intense conversation."

When the special prosecutor questioned him about the conversation, Meese at first said that it was "entirely possible" that Wallach had spoken of Wedtech, but he didn't recall. At a later deposition Meese amended "entirely possible" to "actually probable." With his memory prodded yet again, the Attorney General of the United States shifted to this final, definitively Meesian position: "It makes it even more correct then to say it is probable that he did discuss that with me even though I don't have any specific recollection."

But for Wallach, it was already too late. Dickstein's abrupt disengagement had suddenly left the principals without counsel. The Squadron people had tried to break the news to them that Wallach was not likely to "deliver" the Attorney General, no matter how good a friend he was. Martin Pollner had been intimating the same. Now, even as Wallach was frantically trying to arrange delivery, his friends abandoned him in favor of Pollner, who was a well-known member of the white-collar bar and a former assistant U.S. Attorney. On the morning of the eleventh, Fred, Mario, and Tony walked out of the Dickstein Shapiro office on Madison Avenue, hopped in a cab, and headed over to Marty Pollner's office on Lexington Avenue.

Wallach, panic-stricken at this loss of control, began to call Pollner to offer his advice, his legal wisdom, anything to put him back in the center of the process. Pollner ignored him, and Wallach floated out to sea. From this moment forward, Wallach lost all connection to the Wedtech boys he had loved so much.

At 11 A.M. on Friday, December 12, the board of Wedtech voted to file for bankruptcy. The following afternoon, at two o'clock, the managers of the principal divisions were summoned to the conference room at 595 Gerard and told that, effective immediately, the company was closing its doors. They were to go back and tell the employees to pack up and go home. The managers, by and large, had known that the company was collapsing, but many of the shop-floor and clerical workers had had absolutely no idea. They were looking forward to receiving their annual Christmas bonuses. When the news shot from floor to floor and hall to hall of 595 Gerard, it produced not an uproar, but a vast silence. As hundreds of employees filed out of 595 Gerard, many of them for the last time, they were simply too shocked to speak.

THIRTY-FOUR

Semi-Unconditional Surrender

WITHIN DAYS of the bankruptcy, Mary Shannon called Wedtech's new attorney, Marty Pollner, with the news that the government was about to issue a racketeering indictment against the company and would use the provisions in RICO, the racketeering law, which allow for seizure of the company's assets. Pollner pleaded with her not to destroy the company, to give him time to reorganize Wedtech. Shannon agreed to desist. Pollner believed that he could seek the protection of the bankruptcy court, purge the company of alleged wrongdoers, and emerge with new management. He was spending dozens of hours, whole days, with management, primarily with Tony, to untangle the affairs of the company in order to reorganize under Chapter XI.

Pollner was acutely aware of the delicacy of his own position. The executives had no criminal counsel, so Pollner's firm was almost forced into the position of representing them as individuals. But he represented the company, not the principals, and the interests of the two were swiftly and permanently separating. Pollner's priority as corporate counsel was to persuade all of the current board members to quit, and to assemble a new board as fast as he could. He knew that if any of the executives was indicted while he was still sitting as a director, Wedtech would be given over to a court-appointed trustee, who might feel no qualms about liquidating the firm. But time was running out. On December 22, Shannon called again, this time to report that she was ready to indict both the company and the individuals. Pollner said that he was close to persuading the principals to leave the company and the board.

Pollner was now working virtually around the clock. It was a heady time for him, with Wedtech hanging in the balance and no one except himself—or so he saw it—standing between the company and its ruin. There is a feverishness to Pollner's weary, late-night, too-many-cigarettes manner when he talks about the frantic attempt to find a board that would satisfy creditors and contracting agencies. Tony's authoritative manner and detailed knowledge of the company's affairs had deeply impressed Pollner, as it had so many others before him. Tony had cited General Cavazos as the cleanest of the board members, and Pollner concluded that a man who had been the highest-ranking Hispanic in the military, and who had sat on the Wedtech board for over a year without apparent wrongdoing, would be hard to beat as the new chairman of the board.

On January 2, 1987, a Friday, Pollner had dinner with Tony to talk further about the new board, and then met with Fred, Mario, and Tony to drive home the injunction that they quit. On January 5, Pollner met with Mary Shannon and Benito Romano, pleading yet again for a little more time. Romano repeated that indictments of the principals were imminent. Pollner then went over to the office of the U.S. Trustee, where, still arguing for the company's life, he asked that the company not be committed to the hands of a trustee, as would be the usual procedure in a case of bankruptcy clouded by fraud. Under the control of a new board, Pollner insisted, Wedtech could rise from the ashes.

By early January, Pollner had resolved his ambiguous situation by placing all four principals with criminal lawyers. The government still knew about only the tiniest number of their crimes, and it looked as if they had a reasonable chance to fight and win in court. Tony told his new lawyer, the late Norman Ostrow, that the government had nothing on them but the progress payment fraud. Ostrow loved the swordplay of a trial far too much to relish the prospect of pleading, and both he and Tony were prepared to fight. Fred, according to his new lawyer, Kalman Gallop, hadn't made up his mind one way or the other, and was waiting to see what the government knew.

Mario, on the other hand, seemed already to have undergone a change of heart. "He told me he had been stupid and greedy," recalls Arthur Christy, Mario's new lawyer. "Mario said that he had permitted greed to overcome his scruples. It was obvious to him that he couldn't avoid jail, and he was ready to work out some kind of cooperation agreement with the government." At that first meeting, Mario, unlike Tony and Fred, spent three hours patiently detailing to an astonished Christy the crimes he had committed over the preceding six years. He was prepared to cooperate, even if it meant testifying against Fred and Tony and Larry Shorten.

And then Mary Shannon, acting on nothing more than a hunch, said to Marty Pollner's colleague John Lang, "We know about the FHJ account." (This was not the same John Lang who was once a partner of Biaggi and Ehrlich.) What she knew, she didn't say. All she knew, in fact, was that Wedtech had kept a hidden bank account in the early 1980s. "It looked like a slush fund, it sounded like a slush fund, it smelled like a slush fund." She told Lang that she had subpoenaed the FHJ documents. Lang had no idea what FHJ was, so he asked Tony. "And I turn white," Tony recalls. "And Marty Pollner sees me turn white. And I say, 'I don't want to discuss this.' And Marty comes over to me that afternoon and he says, 'Look, I saw the fear in your face. I want to talk. Let's go for dinner tonight.'" Tony had ordered Ceil Lewis to destroy Wedtech's FHJ records, but the FHJ Associates bank account, he knew, would destroy them all.

That evening Pollner took Tony to Domenico, the old-fashioned Italian restaurant on the ground floor of the building. Domenico had already become an annex of the lawyer's office. A few nights earlier he had dined there with Bernie Ehrlich, who had panicked at the news that the others had sought criminal counsel. Ehrlich had lost the ability to think rationally. When he was stripped of his rank, it was as if a hole had been torn in his skin and all the life had rushed out. His air of bravura, never more than a millimeter thick, had vanished. He was inconsolable, and he had begun drinking heavily. He was, in fact, suicidal. Pollner made a point of inviting Ehrlich's wife too, and he says that he forced Ehrlich to confront his suicidal impulses in front of his wife. Later, Pollner says, he found Ehrlich a therapist.

Now Pollner knew that he had to move delicately. He was Wedtech's lawyer, not Tony Guariglia's. "Did anyone ever explain to you what it means to cooperate with the government?" he asked. It wasn't a question Tony had ever before needed to ponder, but in the last few hours it had taken on a pressing relevance. Pollner explained that the government takes cooperation into account in recommending a sentence, that cooperators can effectively choose the judge before whom to plead. Tony's eternal confidence suddenly deserted him, and after listening to Pollner he decided to throw in the towel. The following night Pollner invited Mario to the Domenico bargaining table, and then Fred. The end game was beginning.

Pollner was also nearing his goal of keeping the company afloat. On January 8, around the time that Tony was seeing the virtues of cooperation, Pollner met General Cavazos for the first time, and satisfied himself as best he could about the man's character. He found other board members, a new accounting firm, new executives for the post-bankruptcy company. On January 13, Cavazos and the new board were installed, and the old board members, with the exception of Frank Chinn, resigned. Chinn refused to quit. Pollner says that he finally brought Chinn around by explaining that "I would have to bring an action to force him out, and I pointed out that that might not look good when his trial came around."

Tony, Mario, and Larry Shorten, having given up the fight, went off to Europe to explore one last option. Shorten had made arrangements with a Greek businessman for the three of them to buy phony Swedish passports. The fact was that they had all been contemplating flight for several months, but none of them had been able to bring himself to leave his home for a new life in a strange country, even a life of wealth and ease. Tony had never lived more than thirty miles from his birthplace in Brooklyn. Fred and Mario knew something of the world, but they too found themselves unable to flee in the face of peril. Still, each shelled out $10,000 for the passport. Even if it was only insurance, it was worth paying for.

Back in Manhattan, it was time for that great subsidiary art form of criminal defense practice, the plea bargain, to commence. Plea bargaining is a form of treaty negotiation in which the loser, suing for peace, seeks to bribe the conqueror into a state of amiability by offering up the dazzling treasures of incriminating information. It was obvious to the lawyers that in this case the treasures were practically incalculable. If you're going to pursue a life of crime, you can't do better than conscript into it public figures who can later be offered up for sacrifice. But it was also obvious that the government was about to drop the bomb. If the four were indicted before working out a plea, they would be arraigned, and the judge who arraigned them would ultimately sentence them. Under a practice then common in New York, defendants who agreed to cooperate could choose the judge before whom they would be sentenced. So you had to do your judge shopping before the indictment came down.

Each of the four lawyers now paid a visit to the U.S. Attorney's office in Foley Square to enact the opening scenes of the plea-bargaining ritual. As Arthur Christy recalls, the initial meeting, with Mary Shannon and Ted Planzos, an assistant district attorney who had been "cross-designated" to the federal office from the Bronx, was a languid affair of broad hints and cautious circumlocution, a highly formalized theater of nondisclosure. The conversation, as Christy reconstructs it from his notes, went something like this:

CHRISTY: Where do you have interests?
SHANNON: The bribery of federal officials.
CHRISTY: Who do you have in mind?
SHANNON: I can't say.
CHRISTY: I understand from my conversations with Mr. Moreno that there are two individuals you could indict directly.
SHANNON: We already have some evidence, but not enough to indict, on several higher officials.

Christy asked what other interests Shannon had, and she mentioned the falsification of figures in public filings, the abuse of cost-of-completion accounting principles, and the progress payment fraud. The conversation concluded with a last series of parries and thrusts:

CHRISTY: What charge are you thinking of?
SHANNON: RICO.
CHRISTY: Mario Moreno might be willing to cooperate; it would depend on your attitude. If you would drop the RICO, he would probably cooperate.
SHANNON: We'll be getting serious in two to three weeks, and you'll be hearing from us. We can guarantee that we can work out a plea in the Bronx, but not necessarily in Manhattan.
CHRISTY: Are Giuliani and Morgenthau at war?
SHANNON: No, but there is strain.

It was clear that a deal could be cut, though it was just as clear that the Manhattan DA could knock the whole thing into a cocked hat. Over the next week Mario, who had returned from Europe, disgorged whatever remained of the Wedtech story, with places and dates and acts and, above all, names—twenty-seven politicians, government officials, businessmen, union officials, and low-level sleazes. "I was staggered," says Christy. On January 21, defense counsel for the four met to coordinate their tactics.

Christy was delegated to meet with the prosecutors again to advance to the next level of specificity in the artful game of "What do we get if we give you this?"

Moscow, meanwhile, was refusing to fold what he considered a strong hand. He told Lawrence Bader, one of the lawyers representing Tony, that his client was looking at an indictment for racketeering and for at least two bribery counts that the feds didn't even know about. When Christy made his pilgrimage to Moscow's office on January 22, he was told that Mario was looking at counts of forgery, grand larceny, and a few other crimes beyond the ken of the U.S. Attorney. When Moscow was ready to bring the indictment to a grand jury, he would give Mario forty-eight hours to make up his mind.

It was a desperate situation, but there was nothing to do but cooperate with federal prosecutors and then pray that Giuliani could bring Morgenthau in line. On January 23, Christy met once again with the defense lawyers, then went down to Foley Square to dicker with Shannon and Planzos, who were now joined by Howard Wilson, head of the criminal division. "I went in there and said, 'All four are prepared to cooperate, and they could tell you a lot.' " Christy then offered what is known in the trade as a "generalized proffer."

"We can give you," he promised, "three congressmen, one that we can lay out and you can finish off, another that's not finished, and a third where you'd still have to gather hard evidence; five federal officers who got money and a sixth who got favors; and two New York State officials." In exchange, Christy said, there would be no RICO count, and none of the four would have to plead to more than one count of bribery and two counts of conspiracy. As a former federal prosecutor and even, briefly, U.S. Attorney, Christy knew whereof he spoke. It was time to invite the lawyers in for a massive proffering and deal-making session.

On January 25, Super Bowl Sunday, Tony got a call in London from Norman Ostrow, saying that a deal had been worked out. Take the next plane home, said Ostrow. It was an agonizing moment for Tony, who had been in a daze since deciding two weeks earlier to cooperate. "I remember standing in Heathrow Airport with my U.S. passport and my ticket home in one pocket, and I had the Swedish passport in the other pocket. And I was looking at the next flight under the Concorde to New York, which was a flight to Madrid." It was to Spain that Tony had contemplated fleeing. "And I said, 'Which one do I get on?' " Tony's one loyalty, good Italian boy that he was, was to family. He couldn't abandon his wife and child. He got on the Concorde.

On the morning of January 26, Fred Neuberger, Mario Moreno, Tony

Guariglia, and Larry Shorten, accompanied by their lawyers, went up to the eighth floor of the U.S. Attorney's office to plead guilty. They were separated from one another, and in four separate rooms told the stories that their lawyers had promised they would tell. The confessions went on for several hours, though they barely scraped the surface. There was Biaggi and Garcia and Simon and Meese and Wallach and Nofziger and Ramirez and on and on and on. "At the beginning," says Lawrence Bader, "there was a sense of 'Holy shit, look what we've got!' It was a sense of absolute amazement. But after hours and hours, you begin to get desensitized. After a while it became almost laughable—'Now, let me tell you about the next guy we bribed.'"

Finally the four ex-colleagues and their lawyers were put in the same room and told the charges they would have to accept, in the Southern District as well as in the Bronx. All four would plead guilty to conspiracy to bribe federal, state, and local officials; all but Shorten would plead guilty to conspiracy to defraud the Defense Department, the SBA, and Wedtech's stockholders; and Mario and Fred would plead guilty to mail fraud. Mario had agreed to accept the mail fraud count in exchange for a promise that the authorities would not seek to indict his sisters. He offered to take another count to protect his brothers-in-law, but the offer was refused. All but Shorten agreed to plead guilty to grand larceny in Bronx County.

It was impossible to include potential New York County charges, too, since the Manhattan DA's office was still operating on its own. The lawyers had asked for reassurances about Morgenthau's office before agreeing to the plea. It was the weekend, though, and no one in authority at the District Attorney's office could be reached. Howard Wilson insisted that Morgenthau had agreed not to indict, though in fact he had not agreed to drop his investigation. The four had signed their preliminary plea agreements with this understanding.

And that, in the normal course of things, would have been that. But Wedtech had never been the normal course. By the following day it was clear that the understanding with Morgenthau, which Wilson had so blithely promised, did not exist. The defense attorneys were outraged. Giuliani, meanwhile, was furious at Morgenthau. "Rudy's response," says a prosecutor, "was 'Fuck 'em, we're not going to deal with these people.'" Giuliani called in the defense lawyers and proposed a deal that, if nothing else, was breathtaking in its brazen combativeness. Should no agreement be reached, Giuliani said, the cooperators could appear before a Bronx grand jury, receive immunity from state prosecution on anything they testified about, and tell the grand jury absolutely everything. Morgenthau's office would have nothing left to prosecute on.

It was a grotesque moment. The showdown at gunpoint over the SBA documents was bad, but this was truly the low point. Mario Merola had been trying to call his old pal Bob Morgenthau, but had found that he couldn't get through. "We were very concerned about how the case was going to come down at this point," says Phil Foglia, "and we felt that it was in real jeopardy." The Giuliani plan was put into effect the very next day, January 28. "We went up to the Bronx," says Bader, "and we prepared the assistant DAs on what areas to cover, and we had a big conference room up in the courthouse there. We've got the four cooperators, the lawyers, the assistant DAs, and we're waiting for the telephone call telling whether there is to be peace or war between the U.S. Attorney and the Manhattan DA. We waited a few hours, and we finally got a call: 'Everything seems to be all right.'" The call seems to have come not from the contending parties but from Foglia, who recalls that Merola decided "it was a little disingenuous to use the grand jury only to confer immunity." Instead, the four had a more limited immunity written into their plea agreements with Bronx County.

In late January and early February, Giuliani and his aides met several times with Morgenthau and his aides. Morgenthau finally agreed that he would shut down that part of his investigation which involved the four cooperators, and that he would indict them for crimes no more serious than what they had already pled to, so that, in all likelihood, the sentences could run concurrently. On February 10, Mario and Tony admitted in New York State Superior Court to having arranged to bribe Vito Castellano, and Fred accepted guilt for bribing Bluestine to suppress knowledge of the progress payment fraud.

And that, in effect, was the last word in a five-month-long farce set in motion by John Moscow's famous egotism, though surely sustained by a spirit of acute competitiveness between perhaps the two most prominent prosecutorial jurisdictions in the country. As conflicts go, this one was both grim and ludicrous. Indeed, the only thing the two sides agree on now is how embarrassing the entire spectacle turned out to be. "The whole thing was appalling," says Moscow, his leg twitching with agitation. "They had their own agenda, and I assume what they did was pursuant to their own agenda. If they thought that getting Mario Biaggi was worth giving these guys a walk, it was pursuant to their agenda. It was a hell of an agenda." Science fiction writers use the locution TANJ, says Moscow—There Ain't No Justice. That's how he thinks of the Wedtech prosecution today.

Mary Shannon takes a significantly less cosmic view of events. Had John Mariotta agreed to cooperate, and Fred, Mario, Tony, and Larry Shorten refused, she would have happily run the case the other way around, she says. But it didn't work out that way. What upsets Shannon is the impression that the good guys didn't show much more purity of heart than the bad guys. "It's terrible," she says. "It's really terrible. There is so much crime in Manhattan, the police department is totally inundated, there aren't enough deterrents in the system, and then you add an assistant DA concerned about making a case based on headlines. To me it was the most egregious example of John Moscow overreaching."

And beyond all those admirable sentiments, it was a supremely fitting last act to the dark comedy of deception and intrigue that was Wedtech.

THIRTY-FIVE

Trials and Tribulations

TONY RECOGNIZED the magnitude of what he had done, he says, only when he emerged from pleading in federal court to face a battalion of shouting, shoving reporters and cameramen, as if he were Lee Harvey Oswald. To the press—to the world—Wedtech was a mammoth conspiracy, an epic of fraud. To Tony and the others, Wedtech was their life, in all its buzzing confusion. Had there been a conspiracy? It never seemed that way. There was no master plan, no long-range program. Things just happened. It had all been a muddle, a chain of compulsions, one lie forcing another, everything improvised on the moment. Everything had seemed natural at the time. There had never been any time to reflect. Wedtech had been like a car careening downhill without any brakes.

And now that the car had smashed into a hillside, there was plenty of time to reflect. Fred and Mario and Tony and Larry Shorten had a new career: they talked about themselves for a living. For the next several months they would talk, without drawing a breath, to federal agents and prosecutors. They would talk about everything they had done since they had joined the company, three or four or seven or sixteen years before. It was as if their inner substance were endless, a ball of thread that never unwound. "It took weeks," says Mary Shannon, "to get the bulk of the information. In a whole day of debriefing, you couldn't even begin to comprehend what they had done." The agents started out with the public officials. They put together a list of seventeen names—Biaggi, Garcia, Simon, Neglia, and so on—and went down the list. What did you give him? What did he do for you? The permutations seemed endless. Half the U.S. Attorney's office seemed to be sitting in a room somewhere debriefing Wedtech executives.

The personalities of the men, unknown to the investigators at first, began to emerge in the weave of their narration. At first they all came in jackets and ties, and said "Miss Shannon." Then they started to loosen up. Shannon had a soft spot for Fred, whose toughness, candor, and total lack of sentimentality she admired. Fred would speak for only a few hours at a time, and then lose interest. He had never been able to sit still, a fact that John attributed to a lurking childhood fear of the jackboot on the staircase. Fred tried neither to minimize his misdeeds nor to embellish them. He said what he recalled, and that was that. Tony was a matrix of facts and numbers. He had total recall of anything that could be quantified, and he was proud of his memory and his intellectual grasp. Mario was like the Ancient Mariner. He could talk for hours, an endless, seamless narrative. He knew everything, and he seemed compelled to confess. Waiting for a debriefing to begin, he would sit and listen to his tapes of Shakespeare or his French lessons.

From the very beginning it was clear that the prosecutors would have to surrender jurisdiction over the White House officials who had been involved with Wedtech. The Ethics in Government Act provided for the appointment of a special prosecutor, or independent counsel, in case of allegations against high-ranking federal officials. Even before the cooperation agreements had been reached, the Southern District office had effectively sealed off the potential investigation of Lyn Nofziger and referred the matter to the Justice Department's Public Integrity Section. On February 2 an independent counsel was appointed by the Appeals Court in Washington. In early April the same process was repeated with Ed Meese. On May 11 the Meese inquiry was also referred to Independent Counsel James McKay.

Meese's behavior in the spring of 1987 offered a vivid demonstration of his moral unconsciousness. In January, says Mary Shannon, Meese had orally recused himself from the Wedtech investigation when he was informed that his friend Bob Wallach was a potential target. At the end of

March, James Baker, who had just taken over as White House chief of staff after the firing of Donald Regan, asked Meese's chief aide, Ken Cribb, to join his staff. Meese needed to find a replacement and spoke to Bob Wallach about finally taking the job he had always wanted.

It is so inconceivable for the Attorney General of the United States to offer the job of chief aide to a friend facing possible indictment, no less indictment in a scheme involving attempts to influence the Attorney General himself, that Meese tried to convince himself that he didn't do it. In mid-April he told a federal agent that he hadn't talked to Wallach about a job since 1985. Three days later he called back to say that, in fact, he had offered Wallach the chief of staff job a few weeks earlier. Several months later he had forgotten about the offer once again. And now he says that he had "considered" the idea but concluded that "it was not a viable option." Ken Cribb, a diehard Meese loyalist, says that Wallach was one of only two candidates.

But Meese's flair for the unthinkable seems to have taken him even deeper into folly. Meese has said that he withdrew whatever offer he may or may not have made to Wallach on April 8, when he was officially notified that Wallach was a target, and formally recused himself from matters involving his friend. But Deputy Attorney General Arnold Burns informed the independent counsel that Meese had told him *after* April 8 that the offer to Wallach remained open. Burns says that he was "astonished," but "felt that this was something that Mr. Meese wanted to tell him." Meese says that the Burns story is "totally untrue." Later both Burns and another ranking Justice Department official, William Weld, would quit in protest over Meese's behavior.

On June 3, the U.S. Attorney's office filed an indictment against Stanley Simon, which was almost immediately superseded by an indictment adding John Mariotta, Mario Biaggi, Bernard Ehrlich, Peter Neglia, Richard Biaggi, and Ronald Betso. They were charged with operating a racketeering enterprise involving extortion, bribery, defrauding the federal government, obstruction of justice, and mail fraud, to name only a few of the infractions. An omnibus indictment of all the Wedtech perpetrators would have led to an impossibly cumbersome trial, so the others were separated out, and the investigations were taken over by other prosecutors.

In Washington, Lyn Nofziger and Mark Bragg were charged with violating the Ethics in Government Act, though Nofziger was also charged with violations of the act in two incidents unrelated to Wedtech. And in Baltimore the Mitchell brothers were charged with conspiring not to bribe their cousin Parren Mitchell, since there was no evidence that they had tried to do so, but to impede his committee's investigation.

Wedtech and the former Wedtechies were now in the process of collapsing. All the principals had agreed to make restitution to the company, and the concealment of assets was strictly forbidden by the prosecutors. If defense lawyers found any asset they had conveniently ignored, they could be charged with perjury, and their cooperation agreement could be torn up. Fred, Mario, Tony, and Larry Shorten continued to live well, continued, in Tony's case, to gamble, continued, in Mario's case, to receive money secretly from foreign accounts. But they had all spent or invested what they had, and as the investments were slowly liquidated, the money was set aside for Wedtech or for the IRS.

Wedtech itself was going down for the ten count. The company had tried to resurrect itself by selling off certain assets, such as the coating division and some of the real estate, and by presenting a new and honest face to the military. The Army and Navy, though, had had quite enough of Wedtech, in no matter what incarnation, and it proved impossible for the company to get new business. In July the board, most of whose new members had already resigned, decided to bow before the inevitable, sell everything, and "pursue the recovery of [the company's] assets through litigation." Later in the year an auction was held, a doleful scene in which one machinist, a big and intimidating man, hugged his machine and wept.

The Biaggi trial, as it came to be known after its most notorious defendant, began in the middle of March 1988. The auguries were good. In Baltimore, the Mitchell brothers had already been convicted. In Washington, Lyn Nofziger had been convicted, though Mark Bragg had been found not guilty after the handwriting on a critical piece of evidence had proved impossible to verify. (Nofziger's conviction would be overturned on appeal in 1989.) The government had had a year to prepare its principal witnesses, who were, of course, the four cooperators. Through its subpoena power the government had also gathered thousands of documents—bank records for FHJ Associates, letters to and from the SBA, notes taken by Mario Biaggi's accountants, board minutes, internal company records, expense forms, photographs. The tactics and logistics of large racketeering trials tend to bear a strong resemblance to those of conventional warfare.

Mario was chosen to lead off the trial, and he remained on the stand, bewildering stenographers with his thick accent, for three long weeks.

Mario was the Wedtech archivist. He had been present at the inception of every crime save the misrepresentation of ownership, and he had the gift for narration of his fellow Colombian, Gabriel García Márquez. One of the defense lawyers objected that "the witness constantly makes a narrative out of a simple question," and it was true. Mario could not answer a question without some reference to the weather, the menu, the furniture, or the personal quirks of his former colleagues. He had the ability to portray the unusual, the so-crazy-it-must-be-true. When, for example, Mario was asked about the initial efforts to obtain the engine contract, he gave a long, rambling answer that ended with John and Fred hurling chairs and pictures at each other, and Mario himself standing between them as both bled from the arm.

If on direct examination Mario had an almost scholarly grasp of detail and causality, on cross-examination he had something of the stoicism of a Latin peasant weathering a hurricane. "Moreno was almost a perfect prosecution witness," says Ed Little, the prosecutor who worked with him for months and conducted the direct examination, "because he would only rarely let his ego get in the way. When he was getting hammered on cross, but there was a basis for it, he would accept it. Sometimes you have gray areas with a witness where the cross exaggerates what they've done, and the witness starts to fight it. Moreno would accept it."

But Mario would not accept everything. There was at the base of his testimony an insistence on distinctions that seemed to spring from a sense of principle. What little he held on to could not be pried from his grip. There was the following exchange with his fiercest adversary, Dominic Amorosa, attorney for Richard Biaggi.

AMOROSA: Would it be correct to say, Mr. Moreno, that from 1981 to 1986 you were, in essence, a fraud?

MARIO: Yes.

AMOROSA: . . . Would it be fair to say, sir, in those years lying and stealing came very easy to you?

MARIO: Not easy, but I did it.

AMOROSA: . . . You were very sorry about what was happening at the time you were doing it, correct?

MARIO: I thought about it many times.

AMOROSA: . . . But you went ahead and did it anyway?

MARIO: Yes.

Tony, at two weeks, logged the second longest period on the stand. His testimony often seemed directed at convicting people who were not on trial, like Arthur Siskind and Pat Simone, but he provided critical support for Mario's testimony. Where Mario was anecdotal, Tony was brutally factual, unambiguous. He too could not be broken on the wheel of cross-examination. The same could not be said of Fred or Larry Shorten. Shorten was willing to admit to practically anything on cross, driving the prosecution team to despair. And Fred did fine until he was asked about an account at Barclays Bank that he had not disclosed to the government. Fred wasn't about to give up his money, so he tried to lie. Still, he knew when he was caught. Afterward Mary Shannon said, "Fred, what's this about the account? You lied." "Yes, I did," said the unembarrassed Mr. Neuberger. Shannon had Fred admit to his lie on the stand.

The case ultimately turned on John Mariotta's testimony. It was a mesmerizing performance, and it evoked in his listeners a combination of laughter, horror, and pity more appropriate to bear baiting than to a trial. John was playing dumb, because his sole defense was that he had been too illiterate and too ignorant to recognize the web of crime being woven all around him. But John was struck dumb, as well, paralyzed by the torrent of his feelings, his anger and terror and despair. He was ungovernable. He spoke in a high-pitched shout, his voice growing higher and higher and louder and louder until it broke, and he heaved to a stop, taking in big gulps of air as if he were afraid of drowning. His attorney, Jeffrey Glekel, growing visibly desperate, reduced his questions to a level of simplicity suitable to an idiot, and John would begin to answer, and then shoot off into a wholly unexpected direction, mixing wisdom with madness like Lear's fool.

Sometimes John would stop talking altogether, and look down at his shoes through his tinted glasses, and Glekel would have to prod him back into the world. Sometimes he would break down and weep. Sometimes he would turn away from his lawyer and address the jury directly, appealing to them from the depths of his heart. His answers were preposterous. FHJ, he said, stood for "Fred, Helen, Jewelry," since Fred had once worked as a diamond cutter, a little piece of Fred's résumé he simply invented. It was the way John had always been, only more so. He was taking the crusade to a new audience. Once the garbled confusion had hidden a message; now the confusion *was* the message. And it worked. John was at least as believable as Mario. He didn't seem to be acting; quite the contrary, he seemed unable to quell his own impulses. His incoherence was too frightening to be feigned.

"We were devastated," says Ed Little. The prosecutors didn't know John Mariotta; they knew only what the cooperators had conveyed to them: the image of a petty tyrant, a brute, a thief. Perhaps they had not understood the depth of his belief in himself or his self-delusion. "There were jurors smiling at him," says Little, "who wanted to believe the sob story. He had some of them eating out of his hand." It seemed all too possible that John Mariotta, the only Wedtech principal who had refused to cooperate, would walk. The cooperators, says Mary Shannon, "would have been psychologically destroyed." Worse still, the jury might have found it impossible to convict the others, who had been depicted as parasites, if the Wedtech conspirator himself had been acquitted.

The trial seemed to hang on Shannon's cross-examination. "I am a very hotheaded person," Shannon concedes, "and I have this terrible temper. Everyone was terrified that I would make John Mariotta seem sympathetic. And I had in my own mind spent weeks developing the notion that I was just going to be very calm and cool and methodical. And that's what I tried to do." The cross-examination began on July 15, four months to the day after Mario had first taken the stand. It opened as follows:

SHANNON: Good afternoon, Mr. Mariotta.

JOHN: Good afternoon, Ms. Mary Shannon.

SHANNON: Mr. Mariotta, what does *tateleh* mean?

JOHN: Well, Freddy used to call me *tateleh*.

SHANNON: What did you understand it to mean?

JOHN: A little kid.

SHANNON: Mr. Mariotta, is it correct that you actually received over $9 million, approximately $9.6 million from your sale of Wedtech stock?

JOHN: . . . I don't keep—how you say?—figures in my mind, but if you say that's what I received, then I will leave it to your better judgment.

And that, in a nutshell, was the prosecution's strategy—to show that, childish though he may have been, John Mariotta had used Wedtech to make himself fantastically rich, and had engaged in crimes to protect and advance that source of wealth. And John, dependably, led with his chin. "He was not manipulative or deceptive enough to survive the cross," as Ed Little puts it. John's anger and frustration got the better of him, and under Mary Shannon's relentless attack he began to seem truculent— and thus, ironically, lucid—rather than bewildered. He claimed that he couldn't make out the names or numbers on evidence that Shannon offered him; he couldn't identify dates because he didn't know that numbers were used to indicate months. He brought the cross-examination to a halt for minutes at a time while he fumed and fumbled and played a great deal dumber than he was. And Mary Shannon swallowed and looked up at the high coffered ceiling and waited for John Mariotta to speak.

The prosecutors already knew, through subpoenaed bank records, that John and Jenny had removed $3.35 million from their money market account at Chase and transferred it to an account in Jenny's maiden name on the very day the guilty pleas were announced, February 4, 1987, presumably to hide the assets in the event of an indictment. And a few days before the cross-examination was to begin they obtained the last of John's bank records, and found that $500,000 in gold bars had been purchased in Jenny's name in April 1987, and literally carried out of Merrill Lynch. From the records they had received from the defense, they could see that John had not told his attorney about the account.

When John was presented with his financial records, he foundered. Minutes dragged by as he refused to admit that he recognized his wife's handwriting. When Shannon was finally able to ask him about the transfer of over $3 million, he said, "I have no recollection regarding to that." Shannon had felt sure that John would have a story ready, that he would say he was protecting Jenny. She knew that she had him now. What about the half million dollars in gold? she asked. John seemed dumbfounded. He claimed to know nothing about the gold. Shannon feigned disbelief. Nothing? And John feigned ignorance. Finally, after going around and around, Shannon said, "Sir, your wife had never told you that she purchased sixty pounds of gold?" "No," said John, "but I'm going to find out." The audience roared. Mary Shannon looked away. John looked cornered, and he was.

There were flaws in the government's case. Larry Shorten was a wasted witness. Fred lied on the stand and also insisted that Stanley Simon had demanded his $50,000 in June 1984, at an event that, in fact, took place in November. But the documentary evidence was overwhelming, and the principal witnesses—Mario and, to a slightly lesser extent, Tony—withstood the carpet bombing of the cross-examination. The principal argument raised by the defense, that the defendants were too unimportant to be bribed when Wedtech had the Meeses and the Nofzigers, was feeble, even desperate. All of the defendants except Ronald Betso were found guilty on almost all of the major counts.

It would be a year before the other great Wedtech courtroom spectacle, the trial of Bob Wallach, Rusty London, and Frank Chinn, began. Between the trials, in the fall of 1988, Richard Stolfi and Frank Casalino dutifully took their licks. They were the sort of characters who would sooner have their limbs hacked off than cooperate with the government, and in fact might have had their limbs hacked off had they done so. Their lawyers put up only token resistance, and the two joined a long and illustrious line of Teamsters as they were found guilty of racketeering.

The Wallach trial began in late April 1989. Once again Mario opened the festivities, offering the jury an extensive guided tour of the Wedtech house of fraud. And once again all but a very few of the defense's blows rattled off his supple but sturdy exterior. Tony was an even more important witness this time, because he had worked with Chinn and London much more closely than Mario had. He testified with a supreme, almost disdainful, self-assurance about such complex matters as the $1.14 million payment in January 1986 and the subsequent cover-up. His grasp of detail was almost intimidating.

Tony had discovered that his precision and literal-mindedness could be a valuable weapon under cross-examination. He would ponder the simplest question with pedantic gravity. A full twenty seconds lapsed as Tony peered up at the ceiling through his square glasses before he could say how many times he had spoken to Wallach about the Ontonagon shipyard. "Three," he finally decided. Tony found a way of refusing to accept the premise of practically any question that could put one of the defendants in a good light. "Incorrect," he would say with a schoolmarm inflection, or "Not exactly." Tony drove Bob Wallach's attorney, Gary Naftalis, around the bend with his unwillingness to say yes to anything. "That's extraordinary," Naftalis finally murmured in full earshot of the jury, and the prosecutors rose as one to protest.

The really electrifying moments of the trial involved Wallach's extensive defense case. Rumors had eddied around the courthouse on the subject of Ed Meese's testimony. The special prosecutor had concluded, as had his predecessor in 1984, that the evidence of a quid pro quo was inadequate to warrant indictment. Meese, however, had been forced to resign in disgrace, and he was not likely to be a sympathetic figure before a New York jury. One morning, however, Meese suddenly materialized in court. In his direct testimony Meese was calm and genial, a huge pink pillar of judicial rectitude. Wallach, he explained, had never really sought his active assistance and had only vaguely discussed the possibility of a White House job.

Under cross-examination, though, the former Attorney General grew testy, and his pink face purpled as the prosecutor, Baruch Weiss, led him through his wiggles and waffles on the question of the job offer. Weiss then raked Meese over whatever other coals came to hand—the pipeline, the relationship with Chinn, the failure to file his taxes. Meese grew ever more belligerent, but the presiding judge, Richard Owen, was obviously enjoying himself and permitted everything. At the end of the day Weiss made the unkindest cut of all by reading from a report by the Justice Department's Office of Professional Responsibility. "Were he still serving as Attorney General," the report concluded, "we would recommend to the Acting Attorney General that the President take disciplinary action." Meese sat in the witness chair with a fixed smirk that was intended to convey indifference but failed.

Wallach attempted to call innumerable character witnesses, especially famous ones, but Judge Owen limited him to ten. One of them, Avital Sharansky, wife of the famed Soviet dissident Natan Sharansky, flew in from Israel, where her mother lay deathly ill. The prosecution objected to her planned testimony as prejudicial, however, and Judge Owen said he needed a day to think it over. The defense pleaded that Mrs. Sharansky had to return to Israel to be with her mother. No matter, said the judge. The following morning Judge Owen said that he had decided to accept limited testimony. But Mrs. Sharansky had already flown back to Israel.

Defendants do not have to testify in their own behalf, and very often don't, in part because judges take their testimony to have been perjurious if the jury decides against them. But E. Robert Wallach, like John Mariotta, was a man who believed, from the very bottom of his heart, in his innocence—indeed, in his goodness. Wallach, like John Mariotta, insisted on testifying. His testimony was only slightly less bizarre than John's had been, but possibly every bit as convincing.

Wallach appears to have seen himself in the role of Sir Thomas More, humble but steadfast, facing his persecutors. He walked up to the stand holding a Bible and placed his hand upon it as he swore to be truthful. During the first break he ostentatiously browsed through its pages until the prosecutors objected. Wallach's steadfastness deserted him almost immediately in favor of a funereal gloom that spoke of a martyrdom foreordained by the surrounding forces of evil. He spoke slowly, haltingly, of a lifetime of doing great good and asking little in return. He was very nearly inaudible. Wallach's eyes seemed to shrink into dark half moons under the shaggy eyebrows, and at times he looked as if he wanted to weep. Even his own attorney seemed to cause him pain. At times Wallach would interrupt Naftalis or contradict him or explain to him a fine point of law. He acted as if he wanted to conduct his own direct examination.

Baruch Weiss began his cross-examination as Mary Shannon had begun hers, by confronting the witness with something essentially irrelevant but telling. In 1985 Wallach had filed an affidavit with the Federal

Appeals Court asking to be reimbursed, according to the guidelines of the Ethics in Government Act, for his representation of Meese the previous year. In 1984, the affidavit had stated in support of a $200,000 request, Wallach had earned no income. "Isn't it a fact," asked Weiss, an unyielding and humorless figure whom Wallach clearly hated, "that you earned over $200,000 of income during that time period?"

And Bob Wallach, like John Mariotta, began to waffle. "Yes, semantically you are correct, but I think in terms of import and in terms of my oath, I am accurate in what I have said." The knight of the woeful countenance stood revealed as a canny, equivocating lawyer, defending himself with "semantics." Weiss pursued the flimsy logic of this assertion, and Wallach pursued Weiss, spitting out two-word answers. His anger showed through, and his plaintiveness turned to sarcasm. Weiss raced Wallach up and down until he had him pinned in a corner. "Is it your testimony," he asked, for the *n*th time, "that at the end of 1984 you were not aware, sir, that intentionally submitting a false affidavit to a federal court is a federal crime? Is that your testimony, sir?"

"That is my testimony, Mr. Weiss."

"When you come to a good stopping place," said Judge Owen, "we'll stop."

"I think," said Weiss, with splendid understatement, "this is a good point, Your Honor."

There was a very great deal more, but it may be that Wallach's pose of virtue had already been hopelessly compromised. London, too, had taken the stand—Chinn had not—and though he had kept his sangfroid, the other prosecutor, Elliott Jacobson, had riddled his story of innocent financial transactions with so many holes that it sank by the end of his cross-exam. The jury found all three guilty, though Wallach was found not guilty of receiving, through London, the $150,000 he had supposedly been promised after Mario and John met with Bragg in 1985. Jury members later said that they were convinced by the documents rather than by the testimony, but both the prosecutors and the defense lawyers agreed that the documents without the story would not have been enough.

"Arrogant is no part of Mario Biaggi and never has been"—or so said Mario Biaggi himself as he faced Judge Constance Baker Motley, who held his fate in her notably unsympathetic hands. It was November 18, 1988, and the congressman, along with the six others found guilty with him, were being sentenced. The Wedtech sentencing record had been mixed so far. The Mitchell brothers had received thirty months each; Lyn

Nofziger had been hit with only ninety days. It was obvious that some new records were going to be set.

A sentencing is a spectacle that seems to bear vestiges of an older, ecclesiastical authority. Sentencing guidelines have begun to replace personal judgment, but a sentencing remains the one moment in a courtroom where the legal formulations, the rules and the precedents and the haggling in fine degrees, drop away, and a man stands naked before judicial power. He stands, literally, below the robed figure of the judge and pleads for mercy. And the judge, invested for this moment with a supreme moral power, weighs the man's sins against his contrition or his good works or the state of his health; or, often enough, the judge doesn't weigh the other things at all. The sentencing, after the intricate protocol and artifice of the trial, is all too real, and even the most aggressive prosecutors do not exult when the grim machinery of judgment is unveiled.

But a sentencing is also, like everything else connected with a courtroom, a ritual. It is a moment of solemn imposture, in which certain phrases, certain emotions and sentiments, are expected. The guilty party must deeply regret his poor judgment, the pain he has caused others; but he must not admit to his guilt, since his case remains on appeal. He must be sorrowful rather than bitter. He must plead for mercy without wallowing in self-pity.

Mario Biaggi was wallowing. It was a performance reminiscent of that day in 1973 when he had raged against the press for exposing his lies. He denounced the witnesses who had testified against him. He asked the judge to recognize the pain it had cost him to resign his congressional seat. He spoke of his philosophy of government service, of "human rights." His eyes seemed to water. There was something operatic in his display of emotion. Judge Motley listened to Biaggi and then to his lawyer, James La Rossa, and the moment La Rossa sat down the judge sentenced Mario Biaggi to eight years in prison.

Next came Stanley Simon, with his heavy shuffle and stooping gait and his half glasses, which gave him an almost professorial air. Simon was brief and piercing. "As borough president," he said in his soft, sleepy voice, "I was on top of the world." And it was true. Ed Meese probably never took half as much pleasure in practically running the United States government as Stanley Simon did in lording it over his unhappy little fiefdom in the Bronx, in taking the senior citizens to Atlantic City, in receiving suppliants at the coffee shop in Riverdale. From this position of eminence, he told Judge Motley, he had been consigned "to suffer each day and be at the bottom, when people ignore me, nobody calls me anymore. I walk in the street, they whisper." Judge Motley looked up when he was finished, and gave Simon five years.

After Simon came Peter Neglia, whom Judge Motley sentenced to three years in prison. And then came John Mariotta, looking as lost and desperate as he must have looked that morning in the White House in 1982. John's skin seemed unable to contain the turbulence of his emotions. He spoke on and on, his voice rearing and plunging, choking on his misery and his gall. He blamed the school system for his ignorance and illiteracy, he blamed the others for deceiving and exploiting him. Nobody interrupted him, so he staggered onward, until the other defendants and even his own lawyer looked bored. "Next time," John whimpered, "I just stay a simple tinsmith and stay at my bench." And with that, he had said his last. And Judge Motley looked at John Mariotta and said, "With respect to Count One . . ." John, like Mario Biaggi, got eight years.

Richard Biaggi was sentenced to two years. Bernie Ehrlich was then under psychiatric care, and sentencing was postponed. Later he would be given a six-year term, and still later he would agree to cooperate with the government.

Bob Wallach, Frank Chinn, and Rusty London were sentenced on October 16, 1989. Judge Richard Owen was known to be harsh, both as a trial judge and as a sentencer. He had already borne out the former part of his reputation; now he was going to prove the latter. Owen began the sentencing by arguing with Wallach's lawyer, Gary Naftalis. After Naftalis made a lengthy plea for community service rather than incarceration, which Owen heard out with evident impatience, Wallach spoke on his own behalf. Even now, at this final moment, there was something self-absorbed and vain about his presentation to the judge. He spoke of how everyone, white and black, had grown "afraid of what is now apparently the increasingly apparent unraveling of American society," as if his trial had been a symptom of the breakdown of law. "I have engaged," he said, "in what Your Honor will concede to be, if not an unparalleled, at least a highly laudable history of activities on behalf of others less fortunate than myself and my children . . . Of course," he said in passing, "I feel remorse."

Judge Owen was not content to read Wallach his sentence. The judge was disgusted, and he wanted the convict to know exactly why. And so for fifteen or twenty minutes, though it seemed like an eternity, Judge Owen denounced E. Robert Wallach as a snake. He enumerated not only the crimes but the other misdeeds raised in the course of the trial, and quoted unnamed lawyers who had criticized Wallach in a newspaper article. "The litany of these things," said Judge Owen, "I sicken to talk about them." But revulsion did not get in the way. He spoke of "these two faces that you can put on," the humble man of virtue and the browbeater. He referred to his "apparent pro bono work." He tallied Wallach's winnings, and totaled up his lies. Wallach tried to interrupt in order to save the remnants of his ego, but the judge flattened him. Wallach's new wife was sobbing, and the rest of the audience gaped in awe.

The sentence of six years was almost mild in comparison to the rhetoric. Judge Owen sentenced Frank Chinn to three years, and Rusty London to five. London had made the mistake of testifying in his own behalf; Owen considered perjury a crime no less grave than the ones of which he was accused.

Back in the spring, on April 13, Mario Moreno had become the first of the principal cooperators to be sentenced. Six months earlier he had done something that, as far as anyone could remember, no cooperating witness in the Southern District had ever done: he asked to have himself remanded to prison before sentencing. Mario had many strategic reasons for doing so. Since he was spending all of his time in the U.S. Attorney's office in any case, he realized that he might as well go home to the prison next door rather than to the Bronx. Conchita had left him, and the sentencing judge might be impressed by his display of contrition.

Other men in the same situation, however, do not make the same choice. Liberty is too dear, the prospect of confinement too painful. What if the judge had decided not to sentence him to jail time? Mario insists that he wanted to obviate that outcome. "I would not have felt good getting a walk without going to jail," he says. "I felt that if the judge was not going to punish me, I was going to punish myself." Alone among the Wedtech principals, Mario was a reflective and self-conscious man. In the weeks and months of confession that followed his cooperation agreement, he had finally seen himself clearly, and understood the harm that he had done. All of the prosecutors, and above all Ed Little, had been struck by Mario's remorse. And it was precisely this self-understanding, or acceptance, that had made Mario such an extraordinary witness— probably the most successful government witness that the Southern District had seen in years.

At the sentencing, Ed Little spoke so forcefully of Mario's cooperation and remorse that Mario's attorney, Arthur Christy, truthfully said there was almost nothing for him to add. Then Mario stood, a figure in gray— gray hair, gray suit. He spoke without notes, and the emotions he expressed seemed to be fresh ones—both pain and puzzlement. He tried to explain how the company, and he with it, had gone wrong. At first, he said, he had left a good job on Wall Street for the dream of rebuilding the South Bronx. "There was no greed then," he said. But the dream had been threatened, and he had sanctioned the progress payment fraud to protect the company. Then, he said, they broke other laws, and crime became "the *modus vivendi*," and they no longer thought about it.

"I don't know why I did it," Mario said, slowly and almost wonderingly. "I have examined my mind very deeply in the last two years, and I think that I don't have the answer yet. There is some internal desire in me to succeed. I had never failed before when I was doing things with good conduct in an ethical way, and I still don't understand why I didn't stop at one of the points that I had the opportunity to stop." Mario went on to speak of his shame and remorse, and of the "economic and moral liability that I will carry throughout my life." He said the things everyone says, and it was all, in a manner, calculated; yet his words seemed artless —and incontestable.

Judge Charles Stewart, a famously sympathetic sentencer whom the cooperators had been permitted to choose, was visibly moved by the end of Mario's recitation. He asked for a recess, and when he emerged he announced that he would sentence Mario to eighteen months in prison. Mario says that his probation officer told him that Judge Stewart had planned a stiffer sentence until he heard Mario's speech.

By early 1990 the mills of justice were still grinding. Robert and Jane Lee Garcia had been tried on bribery and extortion charges and convicted. Garcia resigned his seat in Congress, and then he and his wife were sentenced to three years in prison. Fred was sentenced to eighteen months, probably because of his feeble health rather than his remorse, plus another six months for perjury. Larry Shorten was sentenced to probation rather than jail time. Gordon Osgood was indicted for receiving bribes as part of a racketeering conspiracy with the Wedtech principals. Civil suits were pending against almost all of the lawyers, bankers, and accountants who had worked with Wedtech, as well as all of the principals and many of the consultants.

And, as a dismal grace note to the entire affair, Tony Guariglia turned out to have been lying to the government and to his lawyers and to the ladies and gentlemen of the jury, as he had been to the shareholders of Wedtech. In the first days of the new year, when Tony had come in to the U.S. Attorney's office to talk about Wedtech's involvement with Pat Simone, the prosecutors confronted him with evidence that he had violated an order of the bankruptcy court by gambling in Puerto Rico in November 1988. At the Wallach trial, Tony had insisted during cross-examination that he had not gambled after agreeing to cooperate with the government, so he had perjured himself. The person who told the government of Tony's gambling also alleged that Tony had approached him to invest in his little office products' company, and in the course of doing so had said that he was skimming money off the company's books —FHJ in miniature.

At first Tony angrily denied the allegations, both to the government and to his lawyers. Then he began backing down. Then he confessed to the gambling, though he continued to deny the other charge. "What can I do?" he said. "I screwed up. I'm sorry." Sorry, however, was not good enough. The government at first threatened to tear up Tony's cooperation agreement. Tony was sentenced on the original counts in mid-February, and, with the help of an impassioned presentation by his lawyer, Michael Rips, received an extraordinarily lenient sentence of five months' jail time. It was understood that he would be charged separately with perjury, and perhaps indicted for tax fraud as well. Lawyers for Wallach, Chinn, and London were petitioning the court for a retrial. Tony had made himself almost useless as a government witness, thus compromising, if not derailing altogether, the Simone investigation and perhaps others.

There was no end. There was no end to the lying and to the delusions of impunity.

THIRTY-SIX

THIRTY-SIX

A Creature of the Times

THE STREET-LEVEL WINDOWS that once let thin shafts of morning sunlight into the shop floor at 595 Gerard are all shattered now. The brick façade above them is plastered with signs from real estate agents, for the new owner is hoping to rent the place. Only a single watchman roams the corridors, though at night a friend sometimes comes to help him ward off the thieves and the street people who try to break in. There's not much to take these days. Some of the offices still have stacks of papers that seem to have settled haphazardly into boxes, or that remain in the files they were placed in four or five or six years ago. Here's a copy of a memo about a "termination contract" from a DCAS official. Here, in the corner room that faced south and west, the room where the Russian engineering staff worked, is a computer supply catalogue, and a travel brochure, "Israel's Leisure Time Is Money." An organization chart of the engineering department lists the names Dima Guner, Felix Chervony, J. Dragutin, L. Zolotarev, B. Novoselsky . . .

Along the northern side of the building, which looks out over the parking lot, the state prison, and the magnificent white hulk of Yankee Stadium, weeds pry up the titles of a courtyard. Around to the east again, the Gerard Avenue side, the conference room is oddly intact, the long table, the leather chairs, the carpet. The huge oblong desk still dominates John's office, and the tall armchair is parked behind it. The dimmers work, the door to the bathroom opens smoothly on good hinges, and the Xerox machine stands in the corner, ready to spit out copies of another article on coatings or on garbage. Double doors open from the office onto the central courtyard a few steps above, but the courtyard was flooded, and the water seeped down and through the doors to leave John's carpet a squelchy, mildewed mess. The giant twin couches of yore are gone.

Downstairs, in the vast semidarkness of the shop floor, big cages are filled with parts that were never assembled, gleaming cylinders and sleeves and heavy plates. Farther down, on the lower floor, are tables full of dies, strange and beautiful metal sculptures, each designed to turn out one particular object and no other. The sculptures have tags, perhaps because they are the unwanted orphans of the last auction. "Discharge Body L & R," says one, "P/N/E 13-12-51-52." Yours for any price. The assemblage looks like a Dali painting.

They serve as a reminder, these artifacts of a lost civilization, that Wedtech was not an artifice or a shell game or a Potemkin village. The ledger books were a fiction, and so was the commanding prose in the annual report, but the work was real. With all the force of his maniacal personality, John Mariotta had willed his little company into existence. He had made a living thing out of the dead matter of the South Bronx. More than that: he had designed his creature to achieve great things. And the gleaming remains on the shop floor prove that he did not altogether fail.

But the inventor had infused his creation not only with his energy and passion but with his egotism and his blindness. A man-made thing can't be better than the men who make it, and Wedtech reflected all the virtues, and all the follies and the appetites, of the men who fashioned and guided it. It was a strange and wonderful creature, even noble, yet something corrupt destroyed its greatest possibilities.

Was it nature or nurture? Did Wedtech become a criminal because of its parentage, or because of the world in which it was reared? Forensic genetics offers no clear answers to questions like these. John's bitterness and rage, Fred's contempt, Mario's blind determination, Tony's arrogance—all portended a future of recklessness for their offspring. Mario likes to say that if only the company could have been pried from the grip of Fred and John, much could have been achieved. But perhaps it was from Mario and Tony that Wedtech needed to be rescued. Each man was, in his way, the begetter of the company's successes and of its ruin. Wedtech was born bad, as they used to say. The company would not have survived its early years if the men who ran it had not been willing to break the law.

So much for nature. A nurture theorist, on the other hand, would point out that Wedtech grew up in a tough neighborhood. Where were the free-enterprise role models in the South Bronx? Where was the pathway, even hard and rocky, to success? In the South Bronx you either survived or succumbed. You bribed the unions, you paid off the politicians, you used muscle, and you used guile—whatever it took. John and Fred, especially, learned about business from the street, not at school. They did the same things everyone else did, only they did them better, so they flourished.

And so doing, they catapulted themselves out of the environment of the Bronx and into the world of Washington and New York. Perhaps that was their problem: they tried to apply South Bronx rules to Capitol Hill and Wall Street. But in fact they were keen learners, especially Mario and Tony, and what they did was to dope out the rules, or perhaps the atmosphere surrounding the rules, of their new milieu.

From the point of view of raising a law-abiding company, the 1980s may simply have been a dangerous time to grow up, a time when many energetic youths came to no good. Perhaps it was only a provocative coincidence, but all sorts of wrongdoing came to light at almost the exact moment that Wedtech's did, leaving the inference that the forces shaping Wedtech shaped others. In September 1986, a month before the first Wedtech articles appeared in the press, the arbitrageur Ivan Boesky pleaded guilty to filing false documents with the SEC, and implicated all the bankers and lawyers who had helped him make hundreds of millions of dollars through traffic in inside information. "Insider trading" became a shorthand term for the naked ambition of the moment. And then in early November an Arabic newspaper printed a story about top American officials going to Iran to propitiate the Ayatollah Khomeini with a Bible and a key-shaped cake—the first intimation of what came to be known as Iran-contra. It was, it seemed, a season for the revelation of avarice, self-dealing, and the creative re-interpretation of the rules.

And it went on and on. In the late 1980s greed and corruption achieved the status of spectator sports. There was the New York City payoff scandal, which eliminated almost the entire Democratic Party political leadership; there was the Reverend Jim Bakker, accused of raping a church secretary and then indicted and convicted of stealing millions from the faithful; finally there was the nonstop fireworks display of the final year of the Reagan administration. The Reagans' closest friend in government, former Deputy Chief of Staff Michael Deaver, was convicted of lying to Congress and to a grand jury about the millions of dollars he had made peddling his influence after leaving the White House in 1985. The Virginia federal prosecutor revealed that he had undertaken a massive investigation of fraud in the Pentagon procurement system—Operation Ill Wind—and consultants and corporate executives and defense contractors began to plead guilty to what amounted to a gigantic insider-trading scheme.

And last of all came the HUD scandal. Nearly all of the millions of dollars in discretionary funds available to HUD Secretary Samuel Pierce, it turned out, had been awarded to developers represented by prominent Republicans. Among their ranks was former Interior Secretary James Watt, a passionate conservative, one of the leaders of the Reagan revolution. Watt explained to a congressional committee that he had received $300,000 in exchange for making eight phone calls to high-ranking HUD officials and holding one brief meeting. His client had received millions of dollars in housing subsidies. Taxed by hostile congressmen for engaging in such blatant influence peddling, Watt angrily defended himself before memorably conceding, "The system is flawed."

Was it the system or the men? After Michael Deaver was convicted, Special Prosecutor Whitney North Seymour offered his own blunt analysis. Denouncing the Reagan administration for condoning behavior like Deaver's, he said, "There's too much loose money and too little concern in Washington about ethics."

Little remains of Wedtech save tedious litigation. Still, the small bathroom between John's and Fred's offices looks ready to adapt itself to a new tenant. The white tiles still gleam like perfect teeth, the gold-plated faucets and spigot still sparkle, and the shower stall remains in working order, except for the lack of water. It must have been a great little bathroom in its day. But it wasn't just a bathroom; it was an impromptu stage on which the Wedtech melodrama was enacted.

On one side, in the big office littered with cigar boxes and girlie magazines, Fred sat chewing a cigar and barking into the phone. On the other side, in the bigger office with the twin couches and vast desk, John sat dreaming about coatings and about garbage. And in the middle, in that cramped passageway of white tile, scenes from Wedtech's strange history took place. It was here that John and Fred stood toe to toe yelling about how much stock they were going to give Mario Biaggi. It was here, too, that Tony told an astonished Fred that John was about to agree to give Bob Wallach $300,000, payable immediately. Perhaps the bathroom should be preserved as a monument.

They don't make bathrooms like that anymore. John and Fred, the one in the Allenwood federal prison facility, the other in Danbury, already have the outsized character of historical figures, as the Rumania and the Bronx in which they grew up have become historical places. And the story of Wedtech itself, noble and ignoble, dreamy and ruthless, seems stitched into a faded tapestry. Was it only a few years ago that Mario and Fred babbled in French as they drove across Manhattan with a suitcase full of cash?

ACKNOWLEDGMENTS

THIS BOOK began with an inexplicable act of faith in a first-time book author. My former agent had pronounced it, or me, untenable. Her successor, Joy Harris, helped give life to the proposition, and then passionately expounded it. And Nan A. Talese, my editor, found it, or me, plausible enough to take a flyer.

Michael Rips first planted the Wedtech bug in my ear, and later went to great lengths to persuade his client, Tony Guariglia, to talk to me. His contribution was extraordinary.

Much of my understanding of the day-to-day life of Wedtech, and of the texture of some of the more dramatic events, comes from those key actors who chose to speak with me. These include not only Tony Guariglia but John Mariotta, Mario Moreno, Bernard Ehrlich, E. Robert Wallach, Stephen Denlinger and Richard Ramirez.

When you write a book about crime the only people really eager to talk to you, at least if all goes according to their plan, are the prosecutors and investigators. Some were especially generous with their time and guidance, and none more so than Donna Merris of the U.S. Attorney's office in the Southern District of New York. A good deal of the information in this book came from evidence and transcripts of the Wedtech trials, especially the Biaggi trial, and Donna Merris logged a good many hours first finding the documents, and then explaining them.

Also in the ranks of the extremely helpful were federal prosecutors Ed Little, Mary Shannon, Elliott Jacobson and Baruch Weiss, Labor Department investigator Steve Cossu and assistant district attorneys John Moscow and Phil Foglia. Peter Levine and Jack Mitchell of the Senate Committee on Governmental Affairs conducted the committee's investigation of Wedtech's procurement practices, and authored its exhaustive and incisive report, upon which I also depended heavily, especially in my account of the pontoon contract. My narrative of the SBA's attenuated investigation of Wedtech would not have been possible without the help of congressional investigator Tom Trimboli, as well as former SBA staff member Janine Perrignan. Several individuals on the staff of the special prosecutor who must, perforce, remain nameless, also gave freely of their time and understanding.

A number of attorneys either for Wedtech defendants or cooperating witnesses went to great lengths to keep me on the straight and narrow, and to persuade their clients to speak to me. These include Lawrence Bader, Leslie Lepow, Arthur Christy, Martin Pollner, Jeffrey Glekel and Richard Green.

A number of people who may have questioned the wisdom of talking to me chose to do so anyway—in general because, rightly or wrongly, they believed in their own innocence. Ed Meese was certainly one such person, as was former Small Business Administration head Jim Sanders. Attorneys at the law firm of Squadron Ellenoff spent several thousand dollars' worth of billable hours explaining their position to me.

Officials still with the government were, in general, reluctant to speak to me, at least for attribution. Several former officials agreed to speak about their role, despite the fact that Wedtech remained a sore, or even agonizing, subject for them. These included Bob Webber, Robert Lhulier and Henry Wilfong of the SBA, Carlos Campbell of the Economic Development Administration, David de Vicq of the Navy, Don Hein of the Defense Contract Administration Service and Jim Jenkins, Ed Meese's former chief of staff.

Many perfectly innocent people associated with Wedtech also shrank from talking to me, but some did so anyway, and at length, including Jack Kehoe and Tom Mullan. Carlos Galvis not only spoke with me willingly, but urged others to do so as well.

Buddy Stein, publisher of the Riverdale Press, served as my Virgil in the underworld of the Bronx. Winky and Robby Smith served as my foster parents in Washington.

Various portions of various versions of the manuscript were read, with a mixture of compassion and trenchancy, by Phil Weiss and Lynn Ashby. Kathy Trager probed its depths for all its legal complexities. Javier Ergueta read an entire draft, and even asked for more. Title consultancy was offered by Lisa Ruddick, Yasmine Ergas and Leonard Groopman.

In my postpartum phase I was treated with the greatest care at Doubleday by Gail Buchicchio, who worried about whatever needed worrying about, and by Sergei Boissier. I was also fortunate to have fallen into the stern hands of a truly gifted copy editor, Pixie Apt. She has become a fixed portion of my superego.

My parents, Marvin and Lee Traub, tolerated, and even encouraged, my wayward, rolling-stone career for at least as long as is consistent with parental responsibility.

Writing a book can be a very tedious business. If life itself was never tedious, all the credit goes to the charms, the whims, the inspirations, of my wife, Elizabeth Easton.

INDEX

INDEX

ABOUT THE AUTHOR

James Traub has written about crime, business, and politics for *The New York Times, The New Republic, Harper's,* and *Spy.* Mr. Traub lives in New York City.